The Explosion of Deferred Dreams
Musical Renaissance and Social Revolution in San Francisco, 1965–1975

Mat Callahan

The Explosion of Deferred Dreams: Musical Renaissance and Social Revolution in San Francisco, 1965–1975
Mat Callahan
© 2017 PM Press.

ISBN: 978-1-62963-231-5
Library of Congress Control Number: 2016948149

Cover by John Yates / www.stealworks.com
Interior design by briandesign

10 9 8 7 6 5 4 3 2 1

PM Press
PO Box 23912
Oakland, CA 94623
www.pmpress.org

Printed in the USA by the Employee Owners of Thomson-Shore in Dexter, Michigan.
www.thomsonshore.com

For my children, Entelechy and Shannon,
born amidst great turbulence

and

For their mother, Sandy,
with whom I shared these years

What happens to a dream deferred?

Does it dry up
like a raisin in the sun?
Or fester like a sore—
And then run?
Does it stink like rotten meat?
Or crust and sugar over—
like a syrupy sweet?

Maybe it just sags
like a heavy load.

Or does it explode?
—Langston Hughes

Contents

ACKNOWLEDGMENTS   xi

PERSONAL INTRODUCTION   xv

FOREWORD   xix

CHAPTER 1   Portals of the Past, or "Why San Francisco?"   1

CHAPTER 2   Children of the Future   25

CHAPTER 3   Making Music to Change the World: Diversity, Unity, and Liberation   42

CHAPTER 4   Making Music to Change the World: Authority and Authenticity   58

CHAPTER 5   If You're Going to San Francisco: What One Song Tried to Usurp   78

CHAPTER 6   Songs of Innocence and Experience: Music's Rivalry with the State   104

CHAPTER 7   The Underground Is on the Air: Radio, Recording, Innovation, and Co-optation   119

CHAPTER 8   1968 and Beyond: Culture, Counterculture, and Revolution   170

CHAPTER 9   Power to the People: Nations, Classes, and Listening to the People   190

CHAPTER 10   Humanhood Is the Ultimate: Women, Music,
              and Liberation   209

CHAPTER 11   The Future Foreclosed: Counterrevolution and
              Defeat   224

              APPENDICES   243

              BIBLIOGRAPHY   267

              NOTES   274

              ABOUT THE AUTHOR   293

              INDEX   294

Acknowledgments

Writing this book was a collaborative effort in more ways than one. Aid and encouragement came from friends and colleagues, some of whom I've known since we worked and played together in the Sixties. But far more than good will was involved. Excavating decades-old memories, rescuing important data from oblivion, and revisiting bitter controversies some might prefer forgotten, could only be achieved with the assistance and corroboration of active participants. The many books, essays, films, and recordings I consulted could not replace the testimony, often absent from the historical record, contained in the interviews conducted for this book. The interviews are, in fact, a crucial component of this project, precisely because, taken together, they confirm a basic premise, namely that the history of the Sixties has been woefully misrepresented. While the many individuals I spoke with hold diverse views on substantive issues, they nonetheless share an unrepentant spirit regarding the struggle to change the world. In this sense, the interviews are really parts of a large conversation, crossing generations and continuing unabated to this day. I am indebted to each and all who participated, but must thank Barry Flast, in particular, for making available to me interviews he'd conducted for his Artists Archives project. Sadly, Barry passed away in 2013, before this book was completed, so he never saw the fruits of his dedicated labor, above all, his ability to ask the right questions.

While my gratitude extends to dozens who helped along the way, there are three people whose contributions were especially noteworthy, in that they were largely responsible for me deciding to write this book in the first place: David Rubinson, who offered advice from the outset, as well as little known but vital information regarding the music of the period, the evolution of the recording process, and the role of the music industry; Joel Selvin, who provided access to archival material, especially from the *San Francisco Chronicle*, as well as insights based on years interacting with some of the key figures in this story; finally, Lincoln Cushing, who, as curator of the Michael Rossman poster collection, offered invaluable assistance compiling the visual images appearing in this book. The Rossman collection is made up of over twenty-five thousand posters Rossman himself collected over the span of four decades. Lincoln produced a book, *All of Us or None*, presenting not only representative posters from the collection but an analysis of their artistic and historical significance. This, in turn, provided crucial evidence and inspiration for my own effort.

The Interviews

Over the course of two years, 2009 and 2010, I conducted more than one hundred hours of interviews with a wide range of artists, journalists, technicians, and political activists. All were participants in the events described in this book. Their contribution is incalculable, not only in providing eyewitness accounts or anecdotal curiosities but also for the thoughtfulness and reflection they bring to the subject of the Sixties. While the arguments advanced in this book are my own, I have endeavored to faithfully convey what each person who so graciously gave their time and insights intended.

Peter Albin (interview conducted by Barry Flast)
Donna James Amador
Marty Balin (interview conducted by Barry Flast)
Frank Bardacke
Bruce Barthol
Bill Belmont
Fred Catero
Bill Champlin
Ron Davis
Joe Ellin
Fat Dog
Barry Finnerty
Jon Fromer

Pete Gallegos
Steve Ginsberg
Paul Harris
Joan Holden
Billy X Jennings
Ken Kessie
Mark Kitchell
Saul Landau
Taj Mahal
Claude Marks
Joe McDonald
Dennis McNally
Barry Melton
Doug Norberg
Tom Powell
Julia Rosenblatt
David Rubinson
Joel Selvin
Nina Serrano
Jerry Slick (interview conducted by Barry Flast)
Roger Strobel
Paul Stubblebine
Greg Tate
Pat Thomas
Richie Unterberger
Ricky Vincent

Finally, I need to thank the people who undertook the reading of this book from its first to its final drafts. Thomas Powell made the first attempt and helped immeasurably in corroborating particular experiences he and I shared, as well as focusing the questions that needed to be answered for the general reader. Aaron Leonard, whose own project of excavation was underway at the same time I was researching this book helped me distinguish what were necessary data from the myriad of interesting, but less important, minutiae in which any researcher can become buried. My editor Romy Ruukel's patient and thorough reading of the manuscript brought to light many important questions of fact and interpretation. Clarification of these points greatly improved this book. Last but not least, the unflagging support and insightful questions of Yvonne Moore, my life partner, kept me going through all the trials and travails encountered along the way.

Thank you all.

Personal Introduction

I was hanging around with my buddies in the schoolyard. Herbert Hoover Junior High in San Francisco, to be exact. It was Monday morning, February 10, 1964. What we were wearing said as much about us as anything: Ben Davis or Levi jeans, Pendletons or work shirts, Keds or Converse sneakers, the basic look of kids into sports, cars, and girls. For a couple of us, this meant surfing. Though we lived in San Francisco and the Pacific Ocean is cold, we had graduated from baseball, football, and basketball to surfing, because it was cool. We were killing time before the bell rang for homeroom and up rushed some of the girls we hung out with. "Did you guys see them last night?" they said all at once. "Who?" I asked. "The Beatles!" the girls exclaimed in unison.

I'd heard a song on the radio. I knew the name. But I'd missed the show. (I certainly didn't miss the next broadcast on February 16!) Still, I'd heard music around me all my life. My mom played Bill Haley, Ray Charles, Billie Holiday, Gene Vincent, and Elvis Presley. I had heard folk music from Pete Seeger and Woody Guthrie to Joan Baez, Odetta, and Bob Dylan. In fact, *The Times They Are a-Changin'* had just come out and was in heavy rotation at my house. But something was going on here that didn't quite fit the picture. Instead of more music, another song in an endless stream of songs, we had a disruption, a break in the continuity. Of course, in hindsight, it is easy to see how we were being manipulated by the mass media, how the Beatles were just another in a tedious parade of teen heartthrobs, and that their appearance on *Ed Sullivan* was contrived by a cabal of executives in the entertainment business. But this does not diminish the fact that for us it was different. Very different.

With remarkable speed, a transformation began. I was bounced from one trajectory to another, from heading down a path common to most kids of that time to becoming a musician. Or, maybe it would be truer to say I went from having no path at all to finding one I wanted to follow. While there were other contributing factors, the moment I declared my intention to play the guitar is indissolubly bound up with the Beatles and the subsequent "British Invasion." In fact, it came within weeks of first seeing the group on television. Moreover, the controversy unleashed in my house by my wanting to play *guitar* is indicative of what was at stake. (I'd been taking piano lessons since I was nine, so it was not music per se that was the issue.) My father strictly opposed it. He predicted I'd start playing "that racket" (as he called rock 'n' roll), start taking drugs, and become a bum. My mother prevailed upon him to reconsider. He did, but only on the condition that I get a *classical* guitar. Nylon strings. No electricity. Lessons.

Of course, that didn't stop me from almost immediately taking that guitar (classical, nylon strings) and the few chords I'd learned to begin playing rock 'n' roll with a couple of my friends who, like me, had caught the bug. Now, it's hard to separate what I think I knew from what I actually knew then. It's difficult to be certain I'm not imposing what my sixty-four year old memory tells me happened onto what my thirteen-year-old mind actually thought at that time. But there are a couple of important thoughts I'm quite certain came to my brain at that time and are not invented memory. One is that in a flash, sports and cars were out and music was in. The hero was no longer the athlete, the emblem was no longer the hot rod or the surfboard. And the girls? . . . Well, the cutest girls idolized musicians (musicians who played instruments, not teen heartthrobs like Fabian).

Within a few months, another eruption took place that would yet again shake me from my predetermined path onto another, one not chosen for me. I mean, I might have become a longshoreman or a dancer. That's what my father and mother were, and in 1964 most people still did something similar to what their parents did. Upward mobility? The truth was that you emulated and accepted your "station in life." That was the horizon of possibility. Anyway, my father awoke my sister and me at 4 AM to drag us over to Berkeley, California, where the students had taken over Sproul Hall. It was December 3, and the government was finally cracking down, eventually hauling eight hundred students off to jail. The same man who didn't want me playing rock 'n' roll wanted me to "see history being made" and, most importantly, to take sides with the students. On the one hand, my experience with the Beatles is one I share with millions. On the other, my experience with the Free Speech Movement is uncommon. How many fathers shook their children awake at 4 AM to carry them to the site of chaotic turmoil?

Yet there I was, and I vividly remember the scene of my sister and I marching along in support of the students, as the police dragged them out of the building they had been occupying since October 1, throwing them violently into paddy wagons. Such things leave an impression on young minds; it certainly did on mine.

A bit more background is in order. My father and mother were communists. My father worked on the waterfront and was a member of the International Longshoremen's and Warehousemen's Union (ILWU). He was a militant in a militant union with a history (often retold) in which he played a part. He'd been there in the 1934 General Strike (although as a member of another union), which more than any other event had made San Francisco a "union town." He'd participated actively in every other major battle that created and nourished the labor movement in Northern California. This continued throughout the McCarthy era into the blossoming of the civil rights movement, including the sit-ins and demonstrations that took place in the Bay Area in the early Sixties. My sister participated in the famous demonstration at the HUAC hearings in San Francisco on May 3, 1960, where demonstrators were hosed down City Hall steps by the police. This marked the end of McCarthyism, because a new generation was no longer afraid.

What took place in a few months of one year, 1964, heralded all that was to come in the decade ahead and the themes with which this book is concerned: 1965–1975 in San Francisco and its environs. The two formative experiences of my own youth are the seeds of music and revolution that, in the eyes of the world, made San Francisco the center of both for a brief moment in time. But some moments are forever. These are moments that disrupt the continuum, disorder the "natural" or accepted norm, and create entirely new, unpredicted conditions for social thinking and being. They are moments in which people cease being objects and become subjects, determining the course of events instead of only being determined by them.

Three years later, the final rupture between sports and music took place in my life. I had made the high school football team, so my mother had bought me new cleats (shoes worn for football). But I was simultaneously in a band. We played a "battle of the bands" at our high school (Lick-Wilmerding). There were only two bands in the competition— ours and another composed of close friends. We set up on the auditorium floor. On the stage above us was a band that will play an important role in this story: The Sons of Champlin. We were sixteen-year-olds. They were twenty-year-olds. Men. How that four-year difference matters. And how we idolized these guys who were already on "the road," as it appeared to us. Besides, they were a great band, and that is not just my memory playing tricks on me. Their first LP *Loosen Up Naturally* still sounds fresh and exciting today. There'll be more about that later on in this narrative; for now, suffice it to say that after that event, I left my uniform and my new cleats in the locker room and never looked back. From that point on, I was a musician.

Foreword

When I began researching a book about San Francisco in the Sixties, it became immediately apparent that I had before me not one task but two: there are the events in question which need to be accounted for and then there is all that has been written about them in the half century since they occurred. The latter amounts to a voluminous literature that fills libraries and continues to be added to with each successive decade. In 2007, for example, a host of books was published examining or reexamining the historical record as it had been previously assembled in 1997 and even 1987 (when history, as opposed to journalism, began to be written, notable examples here being Todd Gitlin's *Sixties* and Ronald Fraser's *1968*). Generally speaking, these books (and essays, documentaries, etc.) fall into three categories: histories written mainly about social movements and political organizations; sociological or cultural studies of music and related popular arts; and pop music journalism, which has continued to dominate public discourse since its founding in San Francisco. (*Rolling Stone* magazine is the prime example of this, originating in San Francisco in 1967.) Thus, *There's a Riot Going On*, a study of rock stars and revolutionary politics was published in 2007, quickly followed by not one but two books entitled *1968*. The list is virtually endless and I cite these examples not because they're extraordinary in a qualitative sense of good or bad, but because they exemplify the most recent layer of silt accumulating on the riverbed of what transpired as a sequence of events at a particular time in a particular place.

It so happens that by 2008 capitalism was entering another of its periodic Great Depressions to be followed three years hence by the "Arab Spring," the Indignado movements of western Europe, and the first stirrings of mass resistance in the United States. I admit to both a sense of exhilaration and vindication at this cluster of eruptions that demonstrated beyond any doubt the return of history. Not that history is so great, but its loudly trumpeted "end" following the collapse of the Soviet Union was a sham and a delusion pawned off on a public in the wealthy countries, guilt-ridden in their bloated consumption of toxic foods, gadgets, debts, and ideas.

Yet, even if history was back, I nonetheless began to question the worthiness of my own project. Does the world need another book on the Sixties? Now that a new generation is rising to challenge ruling dogma and overthrow despotism, isn't it time to simply join this wonderful current and be carried along?

Reflecting on this dilemma led me back to my original questions, questions that had arisen in 2007 when the clouds of financial crisis and civil unrest were barely discernible on the horizon. These questions boiled down to three: Why music? Why revolution? and Why San Francisco? They had formed in response to the hype and hoopla surrounding the fortieth anniversary of the "Summer of Love" and the pressing need I felt to correct the false impressions being foisted upon new generations who were not even born yet are nonetheless affected by the music of the Sixties and a vague mythology attached to youth and rebellion. The need I felt to address these questions was only partly a result of my having been a participant in those events. More, it was the stark realization that the entire edifice of Sixties discourse was built on falsehoods constructed in many cases at the very moment the actual events were unfolding. Terms such as "hippie," "flower power," and "the Summer of Love" were manufactured by corporate media and propagated to undermine forces that threatened their dominance, yet all these and more have become not only legend and lore but established as historical fact. More significantly, the terms that *were* common parlance are blithely ignored. Terms such as "the system," "the movement," "consciousness," and "liberation" circulated widely, expressing what participants considered important, yet are either absent altogether or referred to as if they were only the jargon of marginal sects. Were only such trivial names or the omission of keywords at stake, however, I might still have considered the effort of writing a book to be unnecessary. But another problem erupted in the present, crying for a reexamination of the past.

Fifty years have passed since 1965 and nothing has been resolved. This is not to say that following the storms of the Sixties, everything returned to normal and everybody resumed the positions they occupied in 1959. Quite the contrary, the net effect of the past fifty years has been the ruin of the founding premise which guided the world, capitalist and communist alike, for most of the twentieth century, namely *progress*. Fundamentally, it mattered little whether one was an American, a Soviet, or a Chinese citizen, the future existed as a predetermined and desirable goal toward which every sacrifice, every tragedy must be submitted for judgment. If the means were ugly, the ends were beautiful; every step, however torturous, was a step forward.

No one believes that anymore. Now, it's common sense that the future is bleak: "Smile, the worst is yet to come." Every morning delivers another lecture on what ails humanity. From every pulpit, a litany of woes. From every lab or observatory, a doomsday scenario. From every politician, handwringing, finger-pointing, and excuses. Every institution, scientific or religious, warns of the End Time. We are in a war of all against all and it's every man (*sic*) for himself. Amen.

Consider then that for the youth of 1968, be they in Paris, Shanghai, Prague, Mexico City, or San Francisco, there was only one unquestioned assumption: the future belonged to them and it would be glorious. Such overwhelming confidence made any risk worth taking, not only because the old was so rotten but because the new was so promising.

What went wrong?

To answer this question is to address the urgent demands of young people today. If the Sixties deserve any attention at all, it is to provide perspective and insight for the struggles unfolding now. But this task is greater than simply setting the record straight or unearthing previously undiscovered data, as worthwhile as such endeavors might be. What is required is a thorough critique of fundamental premises that have dominated historical, sociological, and journalistic accounts for five decades.

The treatment of music, revolution, and San Francisco have been to a great extent conditioned by defeat. While some historians and theorists—notably Immanuel Wallerstein—have taken defeat into account and written accordingly, the preponderance of the writing to which the youth of today are subjected, reflects the verdict handed down by the victorious counterrevolution. Without ripping away the mask of authority that was carefully reattached in subsequent decades, we will learn little that might be useful in our current predicament.

What I propose, therefore, is to define the problem, devise a method for interrogating it, and draw conclusions. This necessitates a survey of the existing literature. In doing so, however, attention must be paid to the uses of key words. Clear and distinct ideas cannot be developed when words like "revolution," "politics," or "music" are not defined. This likewise applies to categories, political and artistic, that have been used to organize discussion and debate. For example, class, nation, and religion were superseded by youth, race, and war as designations of the fault lines of political and cultural conflict. Added to these was the role of gender as women mounted the parapets to declare war on male supremacy. With clearer definitions and categories, I will attempt to reassemble the historical data in accordance with these definitions and categories in the hopes of making a more accurate assessment of what actually transpired. Finally, I hope to both draw conclusions that might benefit further inquiry and help people today make use of the positive and negative lessons of the past.

The Problem

The problem can be stated: during a ten-year period beginning in 1965 and ending in 1975, San Francisco became a focal point of the world's attention due to an explosion of art—above all music—and revolutionary politics, notably the Black Panther Party. While the dating can be debated and will be discussed in detail further on, there is a broad consensus among historians that events in 1965 mark a beginning of this era, while the conclusion of the Vietnam War marks a definite end. Since beginnings and endings are always problematic, the point here is to designate the period that is commonly referred to as "San Francisco in the Sixties" and to explain the use of the spelling of a number, 60, in place of the usual referents, 1960s, 1970s, and so on. This is because the Sixties are more of a symbol than a date. The Sixties represents a constellation of social and artistic movements that were neither confined by temporal coordinates nor limited by conventional political cycles as defined by state, church, or calendar. Indeed, the Sixties retain interest due to the challenge they posed to all convention. But while San Francisco in the Sixties is definitely "remembered," it is remembered in a peculiar way. No doubt music and politics (along with drugs, youth, sex, and Eastern religion) are included in this "memory." But systematically excluded are components that were nonetheless decisive in putting music and San Francisco in the forefront of a worldwide revolution. These components can be separately identified, but it should be always kept in mind that in practice, at the time, they were largely overlapping, interpenetrating and mutually reinforcing. Fundamental to my argument is that what made "San Francisco in the Sixties" what it was cannot be separated into neat, discrete compartments, except in the specific practices of any craft or skill, such as art-making, political organizing, and so on. Indeed, as all convention was challenged, so were conventional views of what exactly music and politics were. But when all conventions are challenged, chaos ensues. In response, much of the literature has sidestepped the interaction and concentrated on either music or politics, merely acknowledging their simultaneous appearance on the historical stage.

Survey of the Literature

My inquiry begins with a survey of the literature, broken down chronologically and categorically in the following manner:

Chronologically indicates the different periods in which the writing was done:

- contemporary accounts, i.e., what was written between 1965 and 1980;
- the first "histories," which began to appear in 1987 and continued until the end of the 20th century;
- new writing from 2000 until the present. I am speaking here of primary sources (contemporary accounts), data that was either missed by earlier accounts or not considered important, and some new material that assesses outcomes forty to fifty years after the fact.

Categorically indicates both different themes and diverse approaches, i.e., historical, sociological, journalistic, etc.:

- the Sixties generally, including the New Left and the counterculture, largely focused on white youth;
- liberation movements, including black, Third World, women's, and gay liberation;
- GI and veterans' movements;
- civil rights, antiwar, farmworker, and environmental movements;
- music, theater, posters, comic books, and other arts.

(It should be noted here that by "the literature" I mean books, articles, interviews, and documentary films. It should further be noted that by "survey," I am referring to a cross-section of influential writing, not a comprehensive account of all that has been written—an impossible task.)

Lastly, there is a category of critical theory/philosophy that spans centuries. It begins with Plato and continues uninterrupted to the present day. This category is important since it is part of history. Writers who profoundly influenced a broad range of social and artistic movements must be included in any account of the period. More importantly, the method I am using has more in common with these thinkers than with historians, cultural theorists, or journalists. I do not mean to dismiss the valuable contributions writers in those fields can make. In fact, I am to a great extent relying on them for the factual data that is always necessary to an accurate assessment. But I am not attempting another history. I am attempting to organize what exists into a framework suitable for radical reappraisal. This will inevitably prove controversial because what I have deduced from poring over the literature is in direct conflict with what I will show is the "standard narrative" or the "official story." The latter is not simply what "everyone knows," as in legend and lore, urban myth, or popular culture as they proliferate spontaneously. It is instead the result of a deliberate filtering of the existing historical record to weed out what challenges the legitimacy of the state and its corporate masters. The state is not only the government. The state includes religious, educational, and other institutional authorities. In the case of the United States, it also includes the music industry, albeit in the guise of "free enterprise." An illusion of independence has been successfully maintained, and it is only in recent years that scholars have begun to expose this as a fallacy to a wider readership. Three exemplary books are among a much larger number that have broken new ground: *The Cultural Front*, *Selling Sounds*, and *American Folk Music and Left-Wing Politics*. One of these, *The Cultural Front*, was, it must be admitted, written in the late 1990s, and therefore appears to be in the "wrong" category, given what I said above. But this book was, in a sense, ahead of its time and sparked the kind of inquiry that has become more common since.

The reason to call attention to this specific point at this early stage of my inquiry is that it is necessary from the outset to establish first principles and the factual and theoretical bases on which they were formed.

For example: any discussion of music, especially popular music in the twentieth century, must confront the relationship between the state, the music industry, and the populace (from which most music and musicians derive). It can be safely assumed that most people in North America and western Europe know that the single most important element in what has come to be known as American music (and the only one indigenous to America) is the music of enslaved Africans and their descendants. Black music. The implications of this obvious fact are not drawn because interested parties cannot allow it. While the state (meaning the federal and state governments) was responsible for enforcing slavery, Jim Crow, apartheid, etc., the music industry was responsible for propagating racism as an ideology. In return for state sanction, especially copyright law and the licensing of manufacturers, broadcasters, publishers, and distributors, the music industry systematically erected a structure that would reinforce the oppression of black people, divide them from white working people, while hiding this structure behind a cloak of "entertainment." Entertainment, however, not only propagated racism but did so while claiming to be "giving the people what they want." The "people" (ostensibly sovereign in a democracy) was, in this case, a fake; a distorted image of the actual populace, which could nonetheless be used to legitimize the music industry's claim to represent them. Though this sordid tale has been written about extensively, the key link has usually been overlooked, namely that the music industry is an arm of the state.

In and of itself, this linkage might not seem very significant, nor would it arouse much controversy were it not for another factor central to my thesis: music is a *rival* of the state. This rivalry was recognized as far back as Plato but was brought forcefully into current affairs by Kenyan author Ngugi wa Thiong'o, in 1998. Ngugi draws the necessary conclusions, and I am indebted to him for a crucial tool in my own effort.[1] This insight enables a more effective analysis of the role of music in society than the outmoded, yet prevailing, notions which use lyrical content and musicians' intent to determine social effect.

There is one more aspect to the theme of music and politics that is important factually and methodologically. As society was thrown into turmoil old distinctions between art as political statement and art as entertainment were thrown into turmoil as well. Instead of, or alongside, clear lines between political and apolitical, left and right or proletarian and bourgeois, questions of authenticity, authorship, and authority became paramount. While the folk music revival played an important role, the driving force in this development was the vast expansion of the appeal of urban black music, specifically rhythm and blues and soul. This posed for musicians and audiences alike the contrast between the real and the phony, the genuine and the fake, and in a very important sense, the true and the false. Why? Because a comparison between the black original and the white cover was made inevitable by radio, the pale imitation losing, hands down, every time. To many participants, this was viewed aesthetically, not politically. Yet, due to the history of the United States and the increasing militancy of black people, its political aspect could never, at least in America, be completely ignored. There are many recent books providing valuable data on this, including *Voices of Latin Rock, Listen, Whitey!*, and the aforementioned *There's a Riot Going On*. This will be explored in greater detail but here it serves to illustrate how I plan to proceed.

With this method in mind, let's return to my original three questions: Why music? Why revolution? And why San Francisco? Here, in outline form, are the definitions of the terms and a brief summary of issues what I will consider in detail in subsequent chapters.

Music: I will look at music as such, not as separate genres or styles. I will consider music's rise to preeminence among the arts, as well as its rivalry with the state. And I will address questions of authenticity and of music as an instrument of political change.

Revolution: revolutionary politics emerged out of three movements that were determinedly reformist, namely the civil rights, farmworkers and antiwar movements. The word "revolution" was part of common parlance, its political meaning rooted in the American, French, and Haitian revolutions and subsequent attempts throughout the world to overthrow governments. This use of the word was front and center in the Bay Area. It was in the hearts and minds of large numbers of people, with an even larger section of the population passively supporting it. In this context, causes and effects need to be accounted for. Why did revolution present itself as the only way forward, and what effect did that have on the political configurations that arose and their subsequent defeat?

San Francisco: Here we find what are perhaps the most glaring and obvious historical omissions. Fortunately, the data is clear and accessible. The task, therefore, is to situate music and revolutionary politics in the context of a local situation.

Finally, to return to an issue touched upon above, the general categories of youth, race, and war have to be compared and contrasted to class, ✓
nation. and religion. which were, prior to the Sixties, the main lines along
which art and politics were organized. To this would forcefully be added
the category of gender, which hitherto had run parallel but subordinate
to the other categories, often designated as "the Woman Question."

The categories I'm referring to are, in a certain sense, obvious. Even
the most hackneyed accounts of frolicking hippies and student dropouts
call attention to the "generation gap." Everyone knows that America is a
racist country and that black people rose to claim their humanity. Who
can forget the eruption of women's liberation? And though it is now a
distant memory, no one denies that millions of Americans opposed the
Vietnam War or that the U.S. suffered humiliating defeat at the hands of
a small, Asian country. But, once again, the implications of a generation
breaking with doctrines based on class analysis, the nation-state, and the
scientific anti-clericalism of the previous six decades of the twentieth
century have not been adequately explored.

For example, the lines separating the New Left from the counterculture are not only fuzzier than most accounts have made them out
to be, but the very terminology obscures the reality of those who were
actually involved. Simple facts are overlooked; the most basic of these is
that this was a mass movement in a qualitative sense and not merely a
matter of numbers involved. Many commentators have tacitly, perhaps
unwittingly, accepted Ronald Reagan's portrayal: a bunch of spoiled
brats and their permissive parents were responsible for the breakdown
of public order. Since even the designations "New Left" and "counterculture" say less than they appear to at first glance, it is necessary to
examine once again what those who coined them, namely C. Wright
Mills and Theodore Roszak, actually said. Furthermore, the Old Left,
especially the Communist Party, did not end as if it were simply swept
aside by a younger generation. Nor did the reformist leaders of the civil
rights, antiwar, and farmworkers movements cease to be effective. If
anything, the Old Left and the reformist movements saw their influence
grow during the Sixties, recovering much of what they had lost during
the McCarthy era. Above all, the Sixties were not a rejection of Marxism
or of class analysis; rather, they were a recognition of the fact that in
the U.S., at least, the working class was not revolutionary. Youth, black
people, and women were. The key questions were: Who would fight the

battle that needed to be fought? Who would actually take to the streets and combat U.S. imperialism? And who would usher in a new world? If the "proletariat" had to be redefined, so be it.

In this regard, few have made sufficient use of certain prescient texts such as W.E.B. Du Bois's *The Souls of Black Folk* (1903) to understand either music or politics as they manifested themselves in the Sixties. It was Du Bois who first declared, "The problem of the twentieth century is the problem of the color-line—the relation of the darker to the lighter races of men in Asia and Africa, in America and the islands of the sea."[2] Furthermore, Du Bois's brilliant evocation of black music wedded this deep river of feeling to the struggle for emancipation, making them one. To this must be added Simone de Beauvoir's *The Second Sex*, which similarly added an indispensable analytical tool to the struggle for human emancipation. These are but two of many vital texts that illuminate both the course history took and the errors made by failing to grasp their full import.

On the other hand, defeat notwithstanding, conflict has never ceased. Long after Reagan and Thatcher managed the "restoration of imperial command," and throughout their efforts to do so, resistance in one form or another continued unabated. There has been little enough time to reflect. It is understandable therefore that people committed to a world free of war, poverty, and oppression would proudly defend the trajectories that led them to maintaining their principled stands. It is not surprising that this dedicated service to a complete transformation of society would bring with it a healthy skepticism about any attempt to question the premises upon which such dedicated service was based. But this has made reappraisal, even a revolutionary one, more difficult, since allegiance always fears "throwing the baby out with the bathwater." In other words, once, you dump class and nation as units of analysis, you dump the analytical tools used in all the successful revolutions of the twentieth century. But this only begs the question: What is success? What is the world Marx said the workers must win, and how are we going to win it?

If the word "revolution" is to have any usefulness as a description of historical events, let alone future prospects, its definition cannot be the act of revolving in circles but must instead indicate overturning and transforming. If "change the world" meant anything to the generation that made this a guiding axiom, it cannot be construed as mere motion, which in any case happens whether we want it to or not. Above all, change meant (and continues to mean) freedom as liberation and a radically different social organization than the one capitalism provides. But applying these simple definitions as tools of analysis is often undermined by assumptions that betray a crucial lack marking the Sixties not only as a break with the past but also as the culmination of a much longer historical sequence.

As Marx famously wrote, "Philosophers have only *interpreted* the world in various ways; the point, however, is to *change* it." Alas, the particular context in which this was written is forgotten along with much else Marx wrote that contradicts the conclusion erroneously drawn from it, namely that philosophy was dead. Along with Freud and Nietzsche, Marx's name was associated with what effectively became the burial of philosophy in the twentieth century. Marx, Freud, and Nietzsche became household names associated with politics, psychoanalysis, and the poetic imagination, symbols of what was commonly viewed as accomplished fact: philosophy's purpose had been taken over by science, art, or politics and there was no longer any role for the method of thinking and the pursuit of truth that were philosophy's self-appointed tasks. Perhaps there was some role for ethics, as a sort of religion for atheists. But, outside of university philosophy departments, which were devoted mainly to the history of philosophy and not to active philosophizing, the twentieth century, especially the Sixties, was largely content to quarrel over positions whose coordinates were drawn either by political, scientific, or artistic means. It is no accident that Martin Heidegger published *The End of Philosophy* in 1964, or that Alain Badiou's pioneering work *Manifesto for Philosophy* appeared in 1989, initiating what has by now become a global effort not only to defend philosophy against its enemies but also to apply it to current conditions—not only for philosophy's ethical or methodological value but for its capacity to apprehend injustice and articulate emancipation. Badiou's subsequent works, including *The Communist Hypothesis*, have further elaborated on these basic premises and have been especially useful in my work of excavation.

What does this use of philosophy entail? It is certainly not an attempt to reestablish hierarchies of thought, much less to convene a monastic order of "thinkers" to sit in contemplation of the riff-raff. It is, however, to directly confront *opinion* on the one hand and a certain *relativism* on the other. The relativism to which I refer is not to be confused with Einstein's relativity, Heisenberg's uncertainty principle, or

Gödel's incompleteness theorem, all of which have been proven beyond reasonable doubt, and all of which have been used in a popular context to suggest that "everything is relative," the opposite of what their authors had in mind. The relativism in question has features that commonly appear in connection with music and politics: "It's all a matter of taste" in the case of music and "I have a right to my opinion" when it comes to politics. This is in fact the *rule* of opinion, which by definition is an assertion that can neither be proved nor disproved. Truth does not exist, and even if it does, we cannot know it, and even if we know it, we cannot share it with others. Therefore, we just have to muddle along and tolerate each other (an assertion that is paradoxically said to be true). As philosophers since Pythagoras have pointed out, this leads inevitably to the conclusion: might makes right. Out of the muddle always emerges a coercive force that declares itself the sole arbiter of right and wrong. If nothing else, philosophy's articulation of the good, the beautiful, and the true remain diametrically opposed to that single principle which, in the end, has served the oppressor for millennia. In raising the questions, however, philosophy makes no claim to ultimate Truth—certainly not Truth as a static object of contemplation or obeisance. Instead, philosophy recognizes that there are truths, mathematics being a prime example, and that these truths are universal. On this basis, philosophy agitates for a ceaseless process of interrogation, the boundless exploration of questions arising from phenomena, including, and above all, the phenomenon of human consciousness.

From the remove of half a century, we can see that art, science, and politics have not produced the glorious results each of their proponents claimed they would. But neither has capitalism, which makes money God and the market its place of worship. While the Sixties as a historical period are over, so too is the subsequent period of counterrevolution coming to an end. What we can clearly see from this perspective is that we are entering a new historical sequence. Perhaps we can gain from the experience of the last great revolutionary upsurge. Perhaps our new situation provides a vantage point from which to calmly evaluate what were errors that could have been avoided and what were the consequences of our enemy's superior strength. We must never lose sight, however, of the courage and commitment exhibited by millions of ordinary people determined to change the world.

CHAPTER 1

Portals of the Past, or "Why San Francisco?"

While it is always desirable to separate the fabulous from the factual, it is indispensable to do so in the case of San Francisco and the worldwide notoriety it acquired during the tumultuous Sixties. It is certainly not the case that good weather, low rents, and tolerant authorities were what attracted youthful adventurers to Haight Street. For one thing, as we shall see, the authorities were never so tolerant as they have often been portrayed. For another, there were other cities on the West Coast that offered good weather and low rent (Los Angeles being a prime example). Key to San Francisco's reputation was that local residents coalesced there around artistic and political movements that were both disproportionately large in comparison to their counterparts in other cities and were often more radical. Running battles waged in the courts, workplaces, schools, and streets all attest to the size and influence of an aroused populace. An underlying continuity connected people and movements over the span of three generations and included as many people born or raised in the region as those coming to it from other places.

Prevailing notions of white middle-class dropouts from elsewhere suddenly appearing en masse to create a utopia in Golden Gate Park are misleading on several counts. First and most significantly, they ignore the powerful civil rights movement in the Bay Area, which mobilized a large number of people of all ethnicities in the battle to end discrimination in employment and housing. This movement quickly linked with the farmworkers organizing in the Central Valley of California and established bases of popular opposition in the Fillmore, Hunters Point, and Mission districts of San Francisco. This connection led to the April 1965 launch of *The Movement* newspaper in San Francisco by "Friends of

SNCC" (Student Nonviolent Coordinating Committee), a forerunner of what came to be known as the underground press. Second, the corresponding artistic movements, especially music, theater, and graphic art (posters and murals), were never confined to any single constituency or neighborhood. One has only to recall Santana, Teatro Campesino, and the murals that still grace the walls of the Mission District to realize that any account of the period that fails to acknowledge these developments is at best incomplete. Finally, it is important to distinguish between the image of tolerant liberality cultivated by San Francisco's elites from the city's inception and the creative expression and radical resistance that formed the real basis of San Francisco's attraction for poets, artists, intellectuals, and revolutionaries. The City Fathers were never enlightened champions of social progress. Indeed, the rulers of the Golden West were robber barons and purveyors of "yellow journalism," bent on Empire. William Randolph Hearst, who started his newspaper chain in San Francisco, was an arch-reactionary, a champion of U.S. imperialism, and a determined enemy of labor.

What we will explore, therefore, are key figures, organizations, and struggles that were responsible for the attention paid to San Francisco long before the Sixties. None of this had been forgotten in San Francisco; in some cases, it directly influenced the course events took after 1964.

The Port

The heart of San Francisco was its port. From the Gold Rush of 1849 to the 1960s, everything revolved around one of the world's great natural harbors. Though, by 1965, a slow, almost imperceptible decline had begun, the waterfront and maritime trade remained the foundation of social life. This included more than the immediate area around the docks. Extending inland to occupy almost a quarter of the area within the city's boundaries were warehouses, coffee roasters, breweries, slaughterhouses, and tanneries. An industrial zone occupied by American Can, Best Foods, Planters Peanuts, Armour Meats, and the Lucky, Hamm's, and Burgermeister breweries, as well as the Hunters Point shipyards and Schlage Lock, stretched from the Embarcadero south to Daly City. Closer to the waterfront itself were the Hills Brothers and MJB coffee roasters, as well as innumerable ice houses (cold storage facilities for fish and other perishable goods), ship chandlers, and stevedoring companies. North Beach, well known as the center of the city's nightlife and home to its bohemian subculture, was surrounded by and dotted with warehouses and small factories. The residents of North Beach included a large number of longshoremen, warehousemen, sailors, and teamsters. Until very recently, the area had numerous hotels that provided single rooms on a weekly, monthly, or ongoing basis, catering mainly to single men. Just across Broadway, Chinatown was far from the quaint tourist attraction it is today. Hidden in its narrow alleys, in basements and back rooms, were the sweatshops where hundreds of Chinese women worked in illegal or semilegal conditions. Companies like Esprit were founded in San Francisco largely on the basis of this labor. Other parts of the city, from South of Market and Potrero Hill to Dogpatch and the Mission District, were populated by people employed in the city's various industries, all of which directly or indirectly depended on the port.

This was not simply the bequest of nature but rested on the Treaty of Guadalupe Hidalgo and the discovery of gold nine days before its signing on February 2, 1848. The annexation of half of Mexico by the United States and the Gold Rush of 1849 transformed a small agricultural, Catholic, and Spanish-speaking community into a roaring port based on the export of gold and the import of manufactured goods. Within less than a decade, the city's population had expanded from two thousand to thirty-four thousand; its name had been changed from Yerba Buena to San Francisco; and it had already delivered an extraordinary percentage of the world's gold reserves into the vaults of U.S. and British banks.[1]

Corresponding to this sudden economic clout of global importance were attempts by San Francisco's elites to extend their reach to political and cultural affairs as well. The robber barons whose names still grace Nob Hill hotels and Stanford University therefore invested in great promotional efforts that included financing the arts and sciences while reaping unprecedented profits from logging, railroads, and the control of trade. By the turn of the century, a pattern had been established that continues to the present day. Its most prominent feature was fostering an image of a quasi-European, liberal sophistication capable of competing with New York or Los Angeles while committing grand larceny and brutally suppressing dissent.

Though San Francisco itself was never a major manufacturing center like Chicago or Detroit, its population was overwhelmingly engaged in fishing, transportation, light manufacturing, and construction as well as office and clerical work. Notwithstanding its bohemian reputation and the early establishment (1868) of the University of California in Berkeley, the fact remains that until the deindustrialization that occurred *after* the Sixties, a significant percentage of the population of the Bay Area was working class. Indeed, contrary to the common notion of affluent college dropouts composing the armies of the counterculture or that these kids were an invasion from somewhere else, the social forces unleashed in the Sixties reflected the composition and legacy of the city's origins and early development. While certainly multifaceted and contradictory, this would always remain connected to the waterfront, North Beach, Chinatown, the Mission District, and the Fillmore as much if not more than the Haight-Ashbury. When one considers the euphoric hype that surrounded the "Summer of Love," one hears echoes of past "Eurekas!," of "California, Here I Come," and, of course, the fate that awaited the vast majority who came seeking riches from the goldfields.

Modern Dance and the Labor Movement

San Francisco's reputation as a haven for lunacy and a hotbed of radicalism was established in the early years of the twentieth century. Literary figures such as the native San Franciscan and socialist Jack London, master satirist Ambrose Bierce, and the irreverent anti-imperialist, Mark Twain, enjoyed popularity writing about a West they intimately knew. *The Call of the Wild* was more than the title of a book set in the Klondike Gold Rush, it was a metaphoric appeal to the adventurous, youthful spirit abroad at the dawn of a new century. London in particular was active in the Socialist Labor Party and later the Socialist Party of America delivering agitational speeches in Oakland (for which he was arrested) and writing and lecturing on socialism the better part of his life. Such enduring works as *The Iron Heel* and Bierce's *Devil's Dictionary* provide a sense of the social milieu in which they were written, including the first sparks of working-class militancy and opposition to imperialism, not to mention heavy doses of mocking anti-clericalism. As influential as these writers undoubtedly were, they never constituted a literary movement or constellation of writers greater than the sum of its parts or one so closely identified with San Francisco as the Beats would be decades later.

What ultimately made the greatest impression on the cultural life of the Bay Area itself and fostered its enduring image in the eyes of the world was the life and work of Isadora Duncan. In a speech entitled "The Dance of the Future" delivered in Berlin in 1903, Duncan said:

The dancer of the future will be one whose body and soul have grown so harmoniously together that the natural language of that soul will have become the movement of the body. The dancer will not belong to a nation but to all humanity. She will dance not in the form of nymph, nor fairy, nor coquette but in the form of woman in its greatest and purest expression. She will realize the mission of woman's body and the holiness of all its parts. She will dance the changing life of nature, showing how each part is transformed into the other. From all parts of her body shall shine radiant intelligence, bringing to the world the message of the thoughts and aspirations of thousands of women. She shall dance the freedom of woman. . . . This is the mission of the dancer of the future. . . . She is coming the dancer of the future: the free spirit, who will inhabit the body of new women; more glorious than any woman that has yet been; more beautiful than . . . all woman in past centuries: The highest intelligence in the freest body![2]

Though her training, creative work, and subsequent reputation were made far away from San Francisco, Duncan always insisted on the intimate connection between her innovations and her birthplace; for that, she will forever be associated with San Francisco. More importantly, the movement she inspired took root and gained widespread influence in the Bay Area from its very inception. This was evident by the time the Panama-Pacific International Exposition celebrating the opening of the Panama Canal was held at the San Francisco Palace of Fine Arts in 1915. The new form, called at the time "classic dance," was already being performed by local dance companies. Joining Ruth St. Denis and Ted Shawn (from Los Angeles) and Loie Fuller and Anna Pavlova (from Europe), the California Dancing Girls led by San Francisco native Anita Peters Wright began performing "classically free" dancing modeled after Duncan's work as early as 1912.[3]

It is noteworthy that in its early stages what became modern dance was called "classic." This turn toward a remote past is characteristic of many artistic and social movements that are in fact directed toward the future. Certainly, ever since Rousseau, and influenced by his writing, virtually every movement, be it literary, musical, theatrical, or otherwise, has sought authority and authenticity from a more or less utopian past.[4] Revolt against established hierarchies of dominance demands justification and the support of a precedent that supersedes the claims to legitimacy of current regimes. This was certainly the case with Isadora Duncan in particular and modern dance in general, for it was the challenge that the new dance deliberately posed to ballet, artistically and institutionally, that gave it both onus and impetus.

In the first place it was not just a matter of bare feet and scanty costumes versus toe shoes and tutus, though such "undignified" attire worn by "ladies" did scandalize the bourgeois art patron around the turn of the century. As articulated by its earliest practitioners, modern dance sought dignity and recognition as true art, not mere theatrical entertainment. This necessitated a double-edged critique directed at the rigid limits placed on bodily expression, whether it be *Swan Lake* at the Opera House or the can-can at the dance hall. The refined and dainty as well as the sexually prurient were its targets. Isadora Duncan's performances were the literal embodiment of this critique. One San Francisco dancer recalled her performance there in 1917: "And Isadora in *The Marseillaise!* [one of Duncan's most famous pieces]. No slender flower but an aroused Valkyrie . . . in her passionate fervor she rent her garments, revealing her bare breasts to public view. In a day when her appearance in bare feet and filmy chiffon was something of a shock, this was a daring feat. As I watched spellbound, I felt that I was seeing the human spirit released from bondage, never having seen anything like it before."[5]

This explains a special characteristic distinguishing modern dance from other art forms. Its foundation rests on the liberation of the body, most importantly the female body. Both institutionally and aesthetically, women were its leading creative force, and modern dance was, by its very nature, a challenge to patriarchy, male chauvinism, and the like. In other words, the actual dance companies were founded and led by women who consistently rejected the view of women promulgated by ballet and other accepted forms of dance. While this certainly did not exclude or limit the participation of men, it can truly be said that men were never numerically or creatively dominant.

Duncan explicitly fused this contentious artistic and aesthetic dimension with social revolution from the outset. In *Isadora Speaks*, editor Franklin Rosemont notes: "In *My Life* [Isadora's autobiography] she asserts she was 'already a dancer and a revolutionist' at the age of five!"[6] Furthermore, she acted upon her widely expressed convictions by directly supporting the Russian Revolution of 1917. Though her views were not shared by all her colleagues, and certainly much of modern dance was never overtly political, the fact that it was initiated by women and to a large extent practiced and developed by them made modern dance a singular expression of something profoundly novel in the world.[7] As she vividly expressed it, Duncan's "dancer of the future" had two interdependent significations. The obvious one is that dancers *in* the future will be of a different type than today. The second is of the dancer bringing the future into being: "she is coming the dancer of the future: the free spirit." This was, in fact, how many artists in the first decades of the twentieth century viewed what they were doing, but for modern dance it was its *raison d'être*. The human body, after all, is both the corporeal being of every individual and a universal form shared by all. Exposing it to free it, particularly by a woman, was a radical rupture with the past.

A second spectacular event took place at the same time, which, combined with Isadora Duncan's exploits, focused the world's attention on San Francisco. This was the Preparedness Day bombing and the case of Tom Mooney and Warren Billings. Mooney was a socialist labor leader who, along with Billings, was convicted and sentenced to death for planting a bomb that exploded killing ten people at San Francisco's Preparedness Day Parade, on July 22, 1916.[8] This notorious frame-up inspired an international campaign for the two men's release. Millions of people from many parts of the world marched in countless demonstrations under the banner of "Free Tom Mooney." By the time Mooney was released and pardoned in 1938 (Billings was pardoned a year later), a generation of San Franciscans had come to view him as a hero and symbol of labor's struggle against capital.

Almost immediately upon his release, Mooney led a triumphant march up Market Street from the Embarcadero, stopping at Third and Market to thumb his nose at the Hearst Building, headquarters of the hated Hearst newspaper empire, which had not only led the chorus calling for Mooney's execution but was also a champion of U.S. imperialism and dedicated to crushing the labor movement. Both the public outcry and the enduring memory of this case would continue to identify San Francisco with radical politics for generations.

Had modern dance and the Mooney/Billings frame-up been isolated cases, anomalous and uncharacteristic, they would not be worth mentioning in the context of a discussion of San Francisco in the Sixties. But these two streams would cascade together into a powerful current that

7

would flow through the Bay Area and out into the wider world. Inspired by Duncan's perspective not only on dance but on revolution and the emancipation of women, schools such as Peters-Wright Creative Dance and organizations such as the San Francisco Dance Council flourished in close connection with the growing influence of socialism and the women's movement. Carol Beals and Bonnie Bird exemplified such connections through artistic and organizational forms including schools for dance, large-scale dance recitals and collaborations with musicians and composers such as Lou Harrison and John Cage.[9]

Meanwhile, the long struggle to organize maritime workers reached a climax with the General Strike of 1934. The battle to organize longshoremen and seamen had been raging for decades. When ship owners unleashed the police and National Guard in a violent attempt to break the most recent efforts to establish a union, it led to the killing of two workers by police on what came to be known as Bloody Thursday, an event commemorated by Bay Area labor for decades thereafter. The killing of Howard Sperry and Nicholas Bordoise enraged the populace, spurring a general strike that lasted for four days, compelling the surrender of the ship owners and their acceptance of the workers' demands. This became not only the stuff of legend but the cornerstone upon which was built both the International Longshoremen's and Warehousemen's Union (ILWU) and the reputation of Harry Bridges as a fearless and incorruptible leader. The struggle raged on through numerous subsequent strikes and attempts to get Bridges deported (he was an Australian citizen) on various grounds, including membership in the Communist Party.

The strength of the labor movement in general and the ILWU in particular lay not only in its membership but in the broad popular support it enjoyed. Part of the reason it did so was because it did not confine itself to the struggle for better wages, hours, and working conditions as did most unions in the United States. Instead, the ILWU confronted racism head-on by inviting black and other minority workers into its ranks on an equal footing, including into its leadership, awarding honorary membership to Paul Robeson among other radical champions of labor. Furthermore, it supported campaigns for peace with the Soviet Union and opening trade with Communist China. This in turn produced far-reaching social consequences for the Bay Area. In many long-running battles, involving several generations, a close connection developed between the arts and labor. This meant personal ties between artists and labor organizers, collaboration on the creation of artistic works and the interwoven institutional frameworks of unions, schools, performances and arts organizations.

Diverse efforts such as the California Labor School, the San Francisco Dance League, and the San Francisco Actor's Workshop were all sheltered by the umbrella of the labor movement. As far back as 1934, a group of muralists supported by the Public Works of Art Project (PWAP) had painted the interior of Coit Tower in a style inspired by Diego Rivera and containing controversial images depicting the lives and struggles of working people in California. (So controversial were these images, in fact, that they were covered over for many years.)[10] Rivera himself came to San Francisco several times in the 1930s and '40s to paint frescoes, including one at the San Francisco Stock Exchange and another at City College. The port and the struggles of those working in and around it shaped the social life of the Bay Area far beyond what one usually associates with trade unionism or work-related issues—and to a far greater extent than in most American cities.

This raises another significant fact: the cultural life of San Francisco was locally based. The Bay Area was not, as some have portrayed it, merely a stopover for touring performers or literary figures. It was not simply a provincial backwater importing its cultural nourishment from New York or Europe. Indeed, for the better part of the twentieth century, San Francisco had cultivated a local arts community full of unique characters and characteristics. Kenneth Rexroth and Lawrence Ferlinghetti were only two of the many artists drawn to San Francisco by its radical traditions, who would in turn contribute to those traditions in notable ways. In particular, Ferlinghetti would, in 1953, co-found City Lights Books, a base of operations for the literary movement that gained international notoriety as the Beats. The subsequent publication of Allen Ginsberg's *Howl* (1956) and Jack Kerouac's *On the Road* (1957) were so closely associated with San Francisco that they cemented the city's reputation as a center of radical creativity.

This community was thriving when the generation born during and shortly after World War II came of age. The groups that formed the core of what blossomed into the world-renowned music of the era were inheritors of an existing structure, including coffeehouses, nightclubs, and, above all, a supportive audience. It is not an accident that Harry Smith's highly influential *Anthology of American Folk Music* was assembled in

San Francisco, where Smith was simultaneously working in film, light projection, and painting. Nor is it an accident that a San Francisco newspaper would make Ralph Gleason the first full-time jazz critic in the United States.[11] In a complicated exchange, San Francisco's geographic distance from New York and Los Angeles to a certain extent shielded artists from the art business, while simultaneously linking them with the world, as port cities often do. Certainly the works of Bennie Bufano, Emmy Lou Packard, Bernard Zackheim, and Victor Arnotauff were informed by world events, while nonetheless drawing inspiration from their regional environment. Indeed, artist colonies dotted the Northern California coast from Mendocino to Big Sur, in part due to the beauty of the surroundings but also to the encouragement of kindred spirits.

Poet and storyteller Nina Serrano recounts what brought her to San Francisco in the early 1960s: "I came for two basic reasons: first, the Actor's Workshop, which had a growing reputation for new approaches to theater, and I wanted to be in theater. Second, because of Jerry Stoll's book *I Am a Lover* which was a collection of photographs depicting the area around Telegraph Hill in North Beach with its cafes, poets, and jazz. In particular it showed an intriguing ethnic mix, unusual for those days. It suggested new ideas, new forms, *revolution*."[12] Most importantly, the interweaving of disparate threads—different art scenes, political perspectives and social conflicts—had already come to signify San Francisco, distinguishing it from New York, in particular. As Ron Davis, founder of the San Francisco Mime Troupe put it: "What was exciting was not one thing, but the crossovers, the creative mix, skilled people but from different disciplines exchanging points of view. There wasn't the rigidity or hierarchy you found in New York."[13] Serrano's and Davis's experience was shared by many artists who came to San Francisco in the 1950s and early '60s. In fact, it is this broader context that explains the attraction San Francisco held for Jack Kerouac, Allen Ginsberg, and others associated with the Beats. The notoriety the Beats attracted tends to overshadow their diverse and well-established forerunners. But an even more fundamental shift in population had earlier laid the basis. Given the widely accepted notion that San Francisco attracted a mass influx of white middle-class dropouts somehow out of the blue in 1967, it must be recalled that a much larger and more significant migration occurred many years before. What brought the greatest numbers of people to San Francisco since the Gold Rush was World War II.

World War II and the Great Migration

The Great Migration followed the Great Depression. Everyone is familiar with Steinbeck's *Grapes of Wrath* and the plight of the Okies and their odyssey to California. But this was only one aspect, albeit an important one, of a much larger pattern that made up the largest internal migration in American history. To put it simply, millions of poor southerners, white and black, migrated to the manufacturing centers in the Northeast, the Midwest, and on the West Coast. The process had begun even before the Depression, but it became a transformative phenomenon, demographically and culturally, in the buildup to World War II.[14] The San Francisco Bay Area was one such destination. While the largest numbers moved to Chicago, Detroit, New York, and Los Angeles, a significant number of people found employment in the Bay Area's industries, especially its shipbuilding and the maritime trade. In the 1940s alone, this brought about a 600 percent increase in the black population in the Bay Area.[15] The composition of the population thus changed quantitatively, but it would produce an even greater qualitative effect culturally and politically. As part of what historian Michael Denning has called "the southernization of American culture," the move northward of people from the South meant they brought with them the music that was their most important cultural expression. By the late 1940s, this was already manifest in the growing popularity of "hillbilly" and "race" music and, the proliferation of juke joints and nightclubs throughout the working-class neighborhoods of cities far away from the Mississippi Delta, New Orleans, or Nashville. San Francisco was no exception. But in another sense it was.

As the struggle for civil rights gathered momentum in the South, it took on a special focus in San Francisco. In a 1994 paper, Larry Salomon argued that the national civil rights movement concentrated on the abolition of Jim Crow, desegregation of public facilities from transportation to education, and the securing of voting rights. But in San Francisco, the focus was on discriminatory hiring and housing practices. What Salomon points out is that black people in the Bay Area had enjoyed the benefits not only of plentiful work but also of the influence of the ILWU as a bulwark against racism in a key industry during the war. The black community had gained organizing experience and political sophistication and could not be easily marginalized or appeased with empty promises. Indeed, there were advocates, such as Dr. Carlton Goodlett, publisher of *The Sun Reporter*, whose influence could mobilize public

opinion both within and beyond the black community. These circumstances fueled outspoken opposition to the "last hired, first fired" policy,
which threw a vastly disproportionate number of black people out of
work when the war was over. Contrary to San Francisco's image of liberal
sophistication, it had become abundantly clear by the 1950s that the
city's black population was being locked out of jobs and locked out of
decent places to live. Salomon quotes James Baldwin, who said in a 1964
interview: "All right, they talk about the South. The South is not half as
bad as San Francisco. The white man, he's not taking advantage of you
in public like they're doing down in Birmingham, but he's killing you
with that pencil and paper, brother. This city is a somewhat better place
to lie about is really all it comes to."[16]

Protest against these conditions certainly drew its inspiration from
the burgeoning movement in the South, as well as the increasing politi-
cization of students at Bay Area colleges. But San Francisco's civil rights
movement concentrated less on moral suasion and more on economic
force in mobilizing its constituency. Local branches of CORE, the NAACP,
and the W.E.B. Du Bois Clubs confronted the "white power structure" (a
term first used at that time) with grassroots organizing and large-scale
demonstrations. A rally of twenty thousand in solidarity with the struggle in Birmingham, Alabama against Bull Connor and his racist assaults
took place in front of City Hall in 1963.[17] Following this show of strength,
a campaign was launched to force the city's hotels, restaurants, supermarkets, and auto dealerships to sign agreements disavowing discrimination and guaranteeing the hiring of black and other minority people. By
1964, this struggle was changing the political landscape of San Francisco.

As Salomon's paper points out, most accounts of San Francisco in
the Sixties fail to acknowledge the significance of this aspect of the civil
rights movement, not only in relation to black people but in spurring
the development of the New Left and the counterculture as well. This
is confirmed by concert promoter and band manager, Chet Helms, who
described the founding of the Family Dog, the first dance concerts, and
the birth of a new San Francisco music scene in precisely such terms:
"Luria Castell, myself, Terence Hallinan . . . all of us, had been political activists."[18] Helms had been active in the civil rights movement in
Texas before moving to San Francisco, Luria Castell had been active in
the W.E.B. Du Bois Club in San Francisco, and Terence Hallinan, also
active in the Du Bois Club, was the son of Vincent Hallinan, the lawyer

who'd successfully defended Harry Bridges. Such ties went broader still, connecting virtually all the people originally involved in launching San Francisco's musical renaissance. In spite of Helms's notoriety and the ready availability of his recollections, this crucial data remains largely ignored. Scholarship has focused on everything *but* the pivotal role black militancy played in unleashing what would soon simply be called, "the movement." And these are not just minute details. What their omission conceals is that these struggles for civil rights were *successful*. In fact, by the time the Free Speech Movement had begun, there had been a succession of local victories that inspired confidence in direct political action, a point we will return to shortly.

Invasion! A Generation Discovers America

Three weeks after the Beatles' performance on the *Ed Sullivan Show* announced the British Invasion, another invasion took place on the other side of the continent. On the morning of March 8, 1964, a boatload of Indians landed on Alcatraz Island in San Francisco Bay claiming the recently abandoned prison under the terms of the Sioux Treaty of 1868. While apparently unrelated, the coincidence of these events opened an aperture through which would pass a blinding light leading to a generation's discovery of America.

The Beatles, in a highly orchestrated media offensive, took the country by storm, with unintended consequences. The Bay Area Sioux, on the other hand, attracted mainly local attention, as they aimed to test the validity of a treaty that promised the Sioux lands that were not in use or had been abandoned by the federal government. This, in turn would call attention to the more than six hundred broken treaties, and the innumerable other injustices suffered by Native Americans at the hands of that same government. The occupation lasted for four hours, whereupon the acting warden of the now inactive federal prison arrived on the island to tell the Indians to leave or face arrest. As Adam Fortunate Eagle would recall years later, "Of course it was a stunt. History is full of stunts that were pulled primarily to publicize a cause. Dumping tea into Boston Harbor was a stunt, and those guys didn't even have the courage to own up to their real identity. They dressed up as Indians instead, but that subterfuge didn't stop the history books from making heroes out of them. Our men were Indians, real-life Dakota Sioux, and they wanted the world to know it."[19]

The world might not have known it that day, but it was going to be rudely awakened five years hence by the second invasion of Alcatraz. At the time, however, the *San Francisco Examiner* put the story on the front page under the headline "Sioux on the Warpath."[20] Fortunate Eagle explained:

> The landing party totaled about 40 people, including the five who were going to stake the actual homestead claims, their lawyer Elliot Leighton, a bunch of us from the Bay Area Council of American Indians, and reporters and photographers we had invited to ensure the widest possible publicity for the Indian cause. There was a lot of street theater in the Bay Area in those days, and this was another kind, one which was intended to put its message on a bigger stage via the media.[21]

The street theater to which Fortunate Eagle referred was pioneered by the San Francisco Mime Troupe, which had performed its first Commedia del Arte piece, "The Dowry," in city parks in 1962. By 1964, they had performed numerous other plays and captured the imagination of the public. Soon thereafter, their radical politics and inflammatory performances led to confrontations with the authorities that bore a striking resemblance to those of the Indians on Alcatraz. It is difficult to overstate the impact and innovation of the Mime Troupe's street theater; they played a pivotal role in subsequent events. Indeed, street theater was, in its own right, a hallmark of the Sixties that greatly affected music and politics. It should be noted that a question raised by both the Mime Troupe and the Indian occupation of Alcatraz was the difference between theater that was political and "political theater," or the "stunt," as Fortunate Eagle aptly described it. On the one side is the act as the performance by an actor, musician, or dancer. On the other is the act as an action taken to bring about political change. In subsequent years, the difference between the two became increasingly difficult to discern. While both could be effective, blurring the distinction between them could be problematic, and this proved to be a source of controversy among artists and political activists throughout the Sixties.[22] At this stage, however, direct political action combined with the Mime Troupe's innovations to produce inspiring results.

The same front page that on March 8, 1964, carried the story about the Alcatraz invasion had as its leading headline: "Pact Ends Siege at Palace."[23] This headline announced the victorious culmination of a

35 Hotels OK No-Bias Hiring

Pact Ends Siege at Palace

Shop in S.F.
Stores Open
Monday 'Til 9

San Francisco Examiner

AMERICA FIRST

MONARCH OF THE DAILIES

WEATHER

SUTTER 1-2424   EAST BAY 834-7240   SUNDAY, MARCH 3, 1964   234 PAGES   5CH Daily, 10c   Sunday, 25c

Shelley Gets No-Bias Pact On Hotel Jobs

By PETER TRIMBLE

An agreement ending the civil rights struggle at the Sheraton-Palace Hotel and establishing a policy of minority race employment at all major San Francisco hostelries was reached yesterday.

The settlement was signed by integration leaders and representatives of the San Francisco Hotel Employers Association after an angry Mayor John F. Shelley summoned principals of both sides to an extraordinary session in his office.

Shelley was obviously upset by the 20-hour demonstration at the Sheraton-Palace during which youthful pickets invaded the lobby and dared police to arrest them.

80 JAILED

One hundred and sixty-seven demonstrators were jailed in a tumultuous scene in the hotel lobby and another 700, less than five per cent of them Negroes, stretched out on the floor for a marathon sit-in early yesterday morning.

The negotiations were conducted in an air of bitterness.

More stories and photos of the hotel siege on Pages A, B, 2, 3 and 5. Names of those arrested on Page 27.

A Frenzy In Palace Lobby

By DAN NORTH

The jubilant frenzy that greeted the announcement of the civil rights settlement yesterday in the lobby of the Sheraton-Palace Hotel nearly matched in its fury a far-earlier morning breakdown in the Big Cabin.

The announcement was made without a word being spoken.

It was brought by Ad Hoc Committee co-chairman Tracy Sims, Mike Meyerson — racing simply through the crowded lobby cheering and waving mimeographed copies of the agreement over their heads.

Ballard leaned high in the air over and over again. She was hoisted on her feet yelling hoarsely.

For a moment all was still.

400 HOARS

Then the tired crowd, which had been seated on the floor in the south end of the lobby singing furiously, caught on.

The 400 demonstrators jumped to their feet with a groan. Girls hugged boys. Boys hugged girls. Demonstrators, many of whom had been at the hotel for 20 hours, whistled, stamped, clapped and shouted.

"We came in here dealing with the Sheraton-Palace and we walk away with an agreement involving 35 hotels. We got everything we asked for," shouted Miss Sims, who looked quiet was restored.

Comedian Dick Gregory climbed to the rostrum, a lobby table, and announced that he plans to appear Tuesday at the Cow Palace to a benefit show for the Ad Hoc Committee. He said he is trying to get pianist Count Basie and gospel singer Mahalia Jackson to appear also.

Gregory asked for 15 volunteers

(Continued on Page B, Col. 4)

A Gloomy Bay Area

The Bay Area will be gloomy with clouds today and there is a 40 per cent chance will fall from the overcast.

The Weather Bureau also announced that temperatures will remain in the chilly low 50s to mid 50s. In the Sierras, there will be snow flurries with slightly warmer temperatures.

THE VICTORS — TRACY SIMS WEPT on ROY BALLARD'S SHOULDER
"We got everything we asked for," she told the cheering, weary crowd

A Boom For Lodge Shapes Up

Mark Sullivan, association attorney, pointed out that DuBois before his death joined the Communist Party and renounced his American citizenship. Michael Myerson, Ad Hoc Committee member, admitted that he represents the DuBois Clubs but insisted that they are "Socialist Action youth groups."

Under the two-year agreement, binding on 35 local hotels including three downtown, the employers agreed to make an attempt to have 15 to 20 per cent of all hotel workers come from minority groups.

The association also agreed that within 90 days and every 30 days thereafter it will inform civil rights leaders of the number of minority group employees working in hotels and list their job categories.

BY JULY 20

The objective, as spelled out by the pact, will be to accomplish this by July 20.

Editor's Report

Isle of Discord —Soviet Steps In

By WILLIAM RANDOLPH HEARST JR.
Editor-in-Chief, The Hearst Newspapers

MANCHESTER (N.H.) (UPI) — Ambassador Henry Cabot Lodge was declared a candidate for the Republican presidential nomination today in a proxy announcement from spokesmen for the Draft-Lodge campaign organization.

They based their announcement on information that Lodge, who is now ambassador to South Vietnam, would not withdraw his name from the May 16 presidential primary in Oregon.

Robert R. Mullen of Washington, national co-ordinator of the draft-Lodge committee, said he had been advised that Lodge would not withdraw and hence "is a candidate for the Republican nomination for President of the United States."

A well-organized campaign is under way to a win-write

(Continued on Page 3, Col. 1)

The unanimous final vote in the United Nations Security Council authorizing a peace force and mediator for Cyprus seemed on the surface just the story we've been hoping to read for a long time—the Soviet Union finally co-operating to put out a war fire.

That is, it would seem so except for the difficulty of believing that the leopard can change its spots—or the Communists their red dis-amie suits.

So, not convinced of the arrival of the millennium, I phoned our Hearst Newspapers' bureau chief at the U. N., the canny Pierre J. Huss. Pete, who has been watching the Soviet toss monkey wrenches into the U. N. machinery for lot these many years, had a

(Continued on Page 19, Col. 5)

Sioux on the Warpath

By SAM BLUMENFELD

An American Indian "rights" movement to invade and take possession of Alcatraz Island is planned here by members of the Sioux tribe, The Examiner learned yesterday.

Tribe leaders say they have

the right to claim the island under provisions of old treaties and they plan to parcel the land into homesites.

A boatload of claimants and their supporters will land on the bleak Island and stake claim to it "possibly" today, a spokesman said last night.

The leader of the group is

Richard Delaware Dino McKenzie, a huge genial Sioux who left the Rosebud reservation of South Dakota as a child to settle in Oakland.

The group will land on the island equipped with a tent and provisions for several days, he explained, with the expectation that supporters

will remedy their particular ally.

He brandished a feathered staff which he will use to stake his claim, which will then be recorded with the Federal Land Office.

"We're trying to avoid any

(Continued on Page 8, Col. 5)

'Brown Tried To Bury Me'

Engle's Charge

Ailing Sen. Clair Engle claimed yesterday that Gov. Edmund G. Brown has been trying to "bury him since last October to make room for his own Senate candidate.

The charge was promptly denied by Brown, who said the time "is the most disappointing I have faced in all my years of political life."

The exchange of statements appeared to mark a complete break between the state's two top Democrats.

Engle, in his statement issued in Washington, said he was regaining his health and useful friends.

He added: "When I didn't oblige him (Brown) by dying, he tried to persuade me to resign from office to have him could appoint his own candidate."

Engle recalled that when Brown first ran for governor and was challenged by his highway chief Nixon in his bid for re-election "and when he made his decision on the Cousteau case ... I came to his defense. When he needed a friend I was there to be counted."

But now that the situation is reversed, "Governor Brown seems to have forgotten me past.

"It is obvious that he has aligned himself with those who would reject my long

(Continued on Page 8, Col. 5)

Johnson-- More Trade With Soviets

By MARIANNE MEANS
Examiner Staff Correspondent

WASHINGTON — President Johnson opened the door yesterday for more large trade agreements with Russia in the wheat sale by promising that he will be "happy to explore the possibility."

President Johnson told his seventh press conference broadcast live by TV and radio, that he is willing to discuss expanded, long-range trade agreements with the Soviet Union "if they need additional wheat or anything else we have."

Johnson gave those reporters:

• A Vietnam — It will be up to the at-the-hour findings of Defense Secretary Robert S. McNamara whether U. S. personnel in the Red Sector

(Continued on Page 8, Col. 1)

Life Terms for Two

Three Guilty in Sinatra Kidnap

LOS ANGELES—(UPI)—A federal jury, rejecting defense claims of a hoax, yesterday convicted three men of kidnaping Frank Sinatra Jr. Two defendants immediately were sentenced to life imprisonment.

Barry Worthington Keenan, 23, asserted mastermind of the plot to kidnap the crooner's son and Joseph Clyde Amsler, 23, both were found guilty of the actual abduction and faced a maximum prison term of life.

The jury deliberated 6 hours, 38 minutes after receiving the case Friday night.

The trial came to an end on the 34th day. All defense attorneys indicated they would appeal.

HOAX ISSUE

Neither young Sinatra nor whether the jury agreed Frank Jr. was kidnapped in a deliberate — though bungled — crime, or if he was involved in a hoax for international publicity.

APPEAL PLANNER

The third defendant, John William Irwin, 42, was convicted on five counts but found innocent of a sixth—aiding and abetting Amsler and Keenan in the Dec. 8 kidnap at Lake Tahoe. His sentencing was delayed.

McNamara Pledge: We Will Stay in Vietnam

SAIGON — (AP) — Secretary of Defense Robert S. McNamara pledged today the United States will stay in Vietnam as long as necessary and provide whatever aid is needed to beat the Communist guerrillas.

He told a cheering crowd as he arrived for an on-the-spot survey "there is no question of the United States abandoning Vietnam.

"We shall stay for as long as it takes. We shall provide

(Continued on Page 11, Col. 1)

INSIDE THIS EDITION

	Sec. Page			Sec. Page
Auction Ads ...IV		Opinions...II	
Aviation News ...II		Comments ...II	7
Books ...BW		Pets ...II	7
Bridge ...II		Photography ...I*	
Business ...II	11-13	Radio ...TV	2-4
Crossword ...II	7	Real Estate ...WA	
Deaths ...II		Shipping ...II	14
Editorials ...III	2	Still-Word ...III	7
Film Clock ...III		Social Security ...III	10
Horoscope ...III	4	Sports ...IV	1-8
Inquiring		Stanley ...II	5
Photographer ...III	3	Suburban	
Little People's		Theaters ...SF	8
Puzzle ...III	7	TV Logs ...TV	4-15
Newton ...TV	1	Travel ...T	
Soothsayer ...SF	8	Vital Statistics ...II	13
Film Guide ...II		Want Ads ...WA	
Obituaries ...II	13	Weather ...II	13
		Woods ...V	2

BOOK WEEK (BW); HOME AND HOBBY (H); PEOPLE (P); SHOW TIME (ST); TELEVISION (TV); TRAVEL (T); WOMEN (W); WANT ADS (WA).

struggle to end discriminatory hiring practices at San Francisco's Sheraton Palace Hotel. Large-scale demonstrations and sit-ins had been taking place since the previous November, first at Mel's drive-in, then at Lucky's Supermarket chain, then at the Palace, and shortly thereafter on Auto Row, the long line of car dealerships on Van Ness Avenue in San Francisco. These protests were not political theater or a stunt. They brought the force of the rapidly growing civil rights movement to bear on the local Establishment, compelling it to give in. In fact, along with the boycott and the strike, the picket line, the demonstration, the sit-in, and the occupation were the main forms popular struggle took in America and had been for most of the twentieth century. They were often met with violence, even deadly violence, but their efficacy lay in their ability to exert the popular will against a militarily superior foe.

The local victories in the civil rights struggle lent encouragement to another outburst of popular protest that had sprung up in San Francisco in recent years. This came to be known as the Freeway Revolt and it galvanized a mass movement.[24] Sue and Arthur Bierman, themselves veterans of the civil rights struggles, organized the Haight Ashbury Neighborhood Association to prevent the construction of a freeway that would destroy the Panhandle section of Golden Gate Park and a good deal of housing along with it. On May 17, 1964, this organization held a rally in the Polo Fields in Golden Gate Park, where Kenneth Rexroth spoke and Malvina Reynolds sang. Rexroth was one of San Francisco's leading poets and a literary figure of international renown. Reynolds was a San Francisco native who'd recently had a hit record with "Little Boxes," the song she'd penned to mock the construction of tract homes, that were all "made out of ticky tacky" and "all look just the same."

Not only was this movement successful in preventing the construction of the freeway, it led to the widespread growth of neighborhood groups determined to resist corporate and government incursions bent on "redevelopment," a code word for destroying communities. In the course of the coming decade, there were running battles in the Fillmore, Mission, Hunters Point, and other districts that drew tens of thousands of ordinary people into political activity, many for the first time. This is another overlooked component of the Sixties that contributed to San Francisco's world repute.

What would have become of the Haight-Ashbury had that freeway been built?

The Red Menace
What followed these forgotten episodes was Freedom Summer in the South and the Free Speech Movement at UC Berkeley in the fall. Since these are far more famous incidents, they need less elaboration here. But

all this ferment resulted in more than the sum of the issues or numbers of people at demonstrations. They formed the immediate basis for an opposition that was growing in confidence and militancy. The atmosphere was charged with a sense of purpose and possibility. Since the 1960s began with the first sit-ins in Greensboro, North Carolina, on February 1, 1960, and the demonstration at the House Un-American Activities hearings held in San Francisco's City Hall on May 13 of the same year, a fault line appeared that would shake society's foundations for the next twenty years. The Greensboro sit-ins launched the Sixties, as such, riveting the eyes of the world on the southern United States and the American Negroes' struggle for freedom. The anti-HUAC demonstration signaled the end of the 1950s and the defeat of McCarthyism in the one city in America that had refused to succumb to the witch-hunt. By 1964, there was little doubt in the minds of many people, particularly those in their late teens and early twenties, that they were part of an advancing wave that would force America to live up to its promises or be torn apart by its failure to do so.

It was also at this point, and not coincidentally, that music began to emerge as preeminent of all the arts. This subject will be more deeply explored in subsequent chapters. But here, it is important to highlight its development in connection to the struggle for civil rights, the most important social issue of the era prior to the Vietnam War.

For many years, folk and jazz had provided sanctuary for creative imagination, political subversion, and the exploration of the forbidden territory of race, sex, and intoxication. The music and the venues that provided it were meeting points for anyone seeking shelter from guardians of public morals and nourishment for adventurous dreams. Music provided the meeting ground where black and white people could socialize without fear and address each other with some measure of respect. It was also where they could recognize a common enemy. The magnet that drew a young Robert Zimmerman to New York and to the bedside of the ailing Woody Guthrie was the music that was untainted by commercial exploitation, purified in the cleansing waters of ordinary life and popular resistance. It was, furthermore, the music that had come directly under attack by the same forces that were charging through Hollywood tarring anyone Red who'd had the slightest sympathies with unions, the Soviet Union, peace, or civil rights. The 1961 trial and conviction (later overturned) of Pete Seeger was one recent and infamous case.

While folk and jazz were obviously different musical forms, they shared an audience distinguished as much by urban sophistication and left-wing sympathies as by musical taste. The hungry i, a nightclub in San Francisco's North Beach, is the definitive example: a venue featuring jazz, folk, and comedy, whose success was based on cultivating just such an audience. The hungry i also cultivated the talents of comedian Lenny Bruce, later arrested for obscenity at the Jazz Workshop (two blocks from the hungry i). Bruce's notorious case, which along with obscenity trial of Allen Ginsberg's *Howl* a few years before, focused attention simultaneously on San Francisco and on the question of freedom of speech. Cases such as these, venues like the hungry i, and the socio-musical context created by folk, jazz, and civil rights forged links of solidarity in opposition to government repression that would broaden exponentially in just a few short years.

While these were national, even international, phenomena, their unfolding in San Francisco was uniquely affected by one factor largely written out of the historical record: the enduring influence of the Communist Party. As longtime activist and author Frank Bardacke summarized:

> The CP in the Bay Area was not as isolated as it was in the East. It was a more open organization with deeper roots in the left-liberal community. *The People's World* was read by a lot of people, unlike the commie newspapers in the East. There was also the ILWU, which was communist influenced, which provided jobs for lots of people. Not only a newspaper that was looked to, but it was rooted in the working class who controlled the port and the jobs. That was not true in the East at all. So the relationship between the new and old generation of leftists was smoother in the Bay Area than it was in the East. That's point 1. (And it's no accident that the ending of HUAC with that demo in San Francisco, happened in San Francisco. And that's possible because you have a student movement that comes to the support of communists, because communists were not as discredited as they were in New York.)
>
> Point 2: the beatniks—San Francisco is a cultural center for folks who had dropped out before there was any notion of drop-ping out! And that's tremendously important. Ginsberg was at the demos and at the Fillmore in 1965.

So there's a relationship to the Old Left, which stayed alive much longer in the Bay Area than in the East, and there's a relationship to old cultural folks, which in this case is poets and theater people—the Actor's Workshop, the San Francisco Mime Troupe—so there was already a cultural resistance, a cultural dissent, some kind of anti-bourgeois response to the '50s, much more than in New York or Chicago. So you got the combination of the communists not being as discredited as elsewhere, a port city, which makes it more sophisticated, and an anti-bourgeois cultural strength that sets up the Sixties.[25]

It is no coincidence, therefore, that the Family Dog (pioneering organizers of the dance concert/festival characteristic of the era) and the first experiments in poster art included those who had been involved in organizations and movements led by the Communist Party. This is not to exaggerate the numerical strength of the CP, much less to suggest that the direction taken by a new generation met with the CP's approval. On the contrary, the CP, to a large extent, frowned on much of what was to follow, failing to grasp its potential and criticizing its development. Nonetheless, it cannot be overlooked that a substantial number of the earliest participants in both artistic and political movements that would subsequently be associated with the counterculture were at one time or another involved in CP activities. Furthermore, this connection did not end in some neat "before and after" scenario.

The influence of the CP continued throughout the Sixties, perhaps most famously in the case of Angela Davis, herself a party member defended by another party member, her lawyer Doris Walker. Davis's 1970 arrest and trial for conspiracy, kidnapping, and murder, became an international *cause célèbre*, rallying support from famous artists and musicians along with the broadest ranks of the international left. Furthermore, Davis's case was the outgrowth of the struggle to free the Soledad Brothers, which had itself gained world renown. Indeed, the Angela Davis and Soledad Brothers cases concentrated all the issues and many of the key personalities central to the Sixties as a historical period. Certainly, George Jackson, the Black Panther Party, and Jean Genet (who famously wrote the introduction to Jackson's 1970 bestseller *Soledad Brother*) were the in the "eye of the storm," which, not coincidentally, was centered in the Bay Area.[26]

Perhaps due to the lingering fears of McCarthyist red-baiting, the role of the CP has been largely absent from musical and political accounts of San Francisco in the Sixties. The price paid by thousands of people for their dedication to what they considered to be the liberation of humanity is reason enough to be wary of being labeled a communist—to this day. But this is all the more reason to emphasize it here. San Francisco was not only a haven for lunacy; it was a haven for refugees from the blacklist and imprisonment.

China Books

Another crucial influence that has subsequently disappeared from the historical record is the opening of China Books and Periodicals on 24th Street in the Mission District in 1964. Compared to City Lights Bookstore, made world famous by the *Howl* obscenity trial, China Books might appear to be only an obscure historical footnote. But China Books illustrates both the particular attraction of San Francisco (in comparison to New York or Chicago) and was a key ingredient shaping the City's reputation. As its founder, Henry Noyes, explained: "From 1964, San Francisco was the right place for us to be." Not only did San Francisco face west, its port favoring trade with China, but it was also "a germinal period in American culture and we found ourselves in the centre of new movements fertilized by a confluence of intellectual and political cross-currents." Noyes was born and raised in China but had returned to the United States to enlighten the public to China's revolutionary transformation. Shortly after opening, China Books attracted the attention of Herb Caen, columnist for the *San Francisco Chronicle,* and quickly became a crucial hub that linked radicals throughout the Bay Area.

As an agent for a foreign power, authorized to operate by the United States Department of the Treasury, China Books was at first the only source of literature published under Chinese government auspices. Soon everyone from Black Panthers to Diggers, from activists in Chinatown to actors from the Mime Troupe, could be found pouring through the wide range of publications from *Peking Review* to *Red Star over China.* Noyes specifically mentions the Diggers' frequent visits. Since they had no money to buy anything, they would sit on the floor devouring "books on the Chinese revolution, guerilla warfare and communism."[27]

In the spring of 1967, the first shipment of Mao's *Little Red Book* was received and immediately sold out. By the end of 1968, more than

250,000 copies had been sold.[28] The Black Panthers famously used the book for fundraising, buying up large quantities and selling them on the streets of San Francisco, Oakland, and Berkeley. Indeed, the impact of Mao's writings and the Great Proletarian Cultural Revolution, launched in 1966, was immediate and far-reaching. The quest for theory validated by successful revolutionary practice would lead many to take up the study of Mao's thought, albeit in the form of pithy sayings extracted from longer works and compiled in the *Little Red Book*. The debates that erupted within the Mime Troupe leading to the departure of those who formed the Diggers, in part reflected this influence. Furthermore, events in China had a special dimension in San Francisco, due to the size of the city's Chinese community, which was as old as San Francisco itself. The battle between supporters of the Kuomintang and the supporters of Red China was intensifying in Chinatown and would continue to do so throughout the Sixties, one example of how the local and global were bound by many practical links, not only by concepts like "change the world."

The success of China Books confirmed the heightened interest in revolutionary ideas. Moreover, it shows how China Books contributed to San Francisco's growing reputation as a "centre of new movements," indeed, *the* center, in comparison to other American cities, of the most radical challenges to the Old Left posed by the New Left. One such challenge would be particularly acute in the Bay Area and would, furthermore, serve to separate the Sixties from preceding decades: the Sino-Soviet split.

The conflict between the USSR and China burst into flames in the early 1960s. It had profound implications, affecting revolutionary movements and communist parties everywhere. Fundamentally, it was a dispute over peaceful coexistence versus revolution, between the maintenance of a post–World War II status quo by the U.S. and the USSR or support for revolution, especially those revolutions that were already breaking out in Asia, Africa, and Latin America. This polarization went further still, highlighting major differences between the Chinese and Soviet approaches to building socialism. In the U.S., the Sino-Soviet split was expressed in sharply divergent views within organizations and popular movements, be they for peace, civil rights, labor organizing, or free speech. This is a subject too big to explore here, but suffice it to say that the Sino-Soviet split ended the Soviet Union's previous monopoly over Marxism, socialism, and the path to human emancipation. The emergence of a revolutionary alternative, in this case China, played a key role in the development of the New Left and the liberation struggles characteristic of the Sixties, in general.

This took particular form in San Francisco, due, on the one hand, to the continued influence of the old Communist Party (oriented toward Moscow) and, on the other, to the rapid growth in influence of China's position—partly the result of China Books. Mired in a dogmatic adherence to Soviet policy, the CP could not comprehend the revolutionary aspirations taking hold of youth. Indeed, the CP appeared conservative and unimaginative. The New Left was "new," not only as a response to the crisis of Marxism revealed by the Sino-Soviet split but to a reinvigorated, youthful opposition growing on college campuses and in the South. Already, sociologist C. Wright Mills's *Letter to the New Left* (1960) and Students for a Democratic Society's *Port Huron Statement* (1962) had raised a banner for a new politics. Soon, Martin Luther King's I Have a Dream speech (1963), Herbert Marcuse's *One-Dimensional Man* (1964), and *The Autobiography of Malcolm X* (1965), made changes in what *radicalism* consisted of, rejuvenating its appeal. Marcuse, perhaps the most widely influential Marxist philosopher in the U.S., provided a stunning reappraisal of classes and consciousness in postwar America, leading some to call him "The Father of the New Left."[29]

In this context, the introduction of Mao's thought played an important role in shaping the way a new generation identified its enemy: the system, inclusive of both the U.S. and the USSR. Unwilling to accept doctrinaire Marxism or unquestioning allegiance to the Soviet Union, the overwhelming sentiment among insurgent young people was to challenge any authority that suppressed dissent. The complexities of geopolitics could not justify Soviet tanks in Budapest (or, later, in Prague). And as Mao famously said, "Marxism comprises many principles, but in the final analysis they can all be brought back to a single sentence: It is right to rebel against the reactionaries."

The presence of China Books therefore explains what might otherwise appear to be weird anomalies or chance occurrences. The turn struggles took in the wake of the world revolution of 1968 bore the indelible imprint of Mao's thinking. In particular, the Black Panthers and others inspired by their example, adopted the terminology and method of analysis used by Mao. Indeed, the rise of the New Communist

Movement, centered in the Bay Area, is directly linked to the opening of China Books. Only in recent years have scholarly attempts been made to account for this phenomenon, in spite (or because?) of its significant impact at the time.[30]

High Schools

A final point needs to be made in answering the question "Why San Francisco?" This is also to address two issues raised earlier regarding the composition of oppositional movements and the duration of the Sixties beyond 1969. A crucial reason San Francisco became the site of renaissance and revolution was its high schools. Earlier than many cities in the United States, and largely due to the struggles of black people discussed above, San Francisco had begun desegregating its school system. The first of the Sixties generation entered high schools that were no longer completely segregated. Segregation in housing placed limits on how extensive such integration could be, but the largest public high schools (Washington, Galileo, Balboa, Wilson, Polytechnic, and Mission) were mixed with different proportions of different nationalities. (Two others, Lowell and Lincoln, were predominantly white, with some Chinese students.) These schools concentrated all of the social conflicts of the day, especially those of race and the draft. They would be spawning grounds, continuously replenishing the ranks of young militants. While it is certainly true that the Sixties were launched and led by people born as early as the late 1930s, the draft alone ensured that a much larger number would eventually be drawn from young people born in the late 1940s and early '50s.

This is pertinent on two counts: the changes wrought in music and in the revolutionary thrust of political struggle from 1968 onward, on the one hand, and the class and ethnic composition of the most important artistic and political developments of the "second half" of the Sixties, on the other. The Mission District contributed as much, if not more, to the artistic and political ferment as did the Haight. Musical groups and graphic art provide compelling evidence today of the historic significance of, for example, the Alcatraz occupation, the case of Los Siete de la Raza, and the San Francisco State strike (to be explored in subsequent chapters). These examples cannot by any means be solely attributed to high school age students or the schools they attended. Yet the sequence of events stretching from the civil rights era through the

Free Speech Movement to the farmworkers struggle and onward to those that followed is also marked by the coming of age of the younger sisters and brothers of the original participants. That explains both the political sophistication and the growing militancy of this younger cohort. The same trajectory is mirrored in musical developments as well. If the Grateful Dead and Jefferson Airplane epitomized the earlier period, Santana, Sly and the Family Stone, and Tower of Power would characterize the subsequent period.

A great deal of attention has been paid to the influence of Eastern religion, psychedelic drugs, and self-absorbed hedonism to describe and account for what transpired in San Francisco in the Sixties. Books like *Acid Dreams*, *The Summer of Love*, and *The Haight Ashbury* provide useful information about those influences. Furthermore, the formative impact of the Beats is explored in an enormous quantity of highly informative literature. Lawrence Ferlinghetti's *Poetry as Insurgent Art* and Allen Ginsberg's *The Fall of America* being two good examples by actual participants.[31] But, as the forgoing has shown, these influences (and others, as well) were by no means hegemonic. They were part of an array of *contending* ideas that combined to make popular consciousness combustible. Yet none of them could account for, let alone predict, that music would have the greatest influence, providing the spark that would ignite a powder keg of deferred dreams. The ensuing explosion produced a break in the passage of time, and music became the oracle of truth for millions.

CHAPTER 2

Children of the Future

God gave Noah the rainbow sign
No more water, the fire next time
Pharaoh's army got drownded
Oh, Mary, don't you weep
                                    —old slave song

L angston Hughes first published "Dream Deferred" in 1951. Before his death in 1967, Hughes not only saw the poem republished in his last testament, *The Panther and the Lash*, but he knew the answer to the question his poem had posed: deferred dreams explode. The intervening sixteen years witnessed an acute crisis, driven as much by demographics as by the long saga of black emancipation. On both sides of the racial divide, exploding birth rates led to a postwar generation so much larger than its predecessors that its sheer numbers altered the calculus of political and economic power. Children born in 1945 and thereafter had no experience with the Great Depression, the struggles of workers, and the fight against fascism that culminated in World War II. The affluent society promised jobs, education, and advancement in a land of plenty; it was even possible to imagine ending segregation and second-class citizenship for blacks. Indeed, the desegregation of the armed forces and the Supreme Court's *Brown v. The Board of Education* decision gave every indication that the U.S. government was finally acting to right the historic wrongs of slavery and Jim Crow. But as the new generation approached adolescence, it was already becoming clear that these moves were largely symbolic, made to improve America's image in the Cold

War world, rather than to make substantive changes in the conditions faced by black people. As Langston Hughes duly noted in his dedication in *The Panther and the Lash*:

> To Rosa Parks of Montgomery who started it all when, on upon being ordered to get up and stand at the back of the bus where there were no seats left, she said simply, "My feet are tired," and did not move, thus setting off in 1955 the boycotts, the sit-ins, the Freedom Rides, the petitions, the marches, the voter registration drives, and *I Shall Not Be Moved*.[1]

The steady advance of the civil rights movement between the years 1955 and 1963 was made in the face of a reactionary onslaught spearheaded by white racists in the South but aided and abetted by agents of government and business in the North, as well. When James Baldwin published *The Fire Next Time* in 1963, he gave a prophetic warning: "The Negroes of this country may never be able to rise to power, but they are very well placed indeed to precipitate chaos and ring down the curtain on the American Dream."[2]

Within one year, and in Harlem, where Baldwin had issued his warning, *The Fire Next Time* became "Burn, Baby, Burn." The Sixties, as a rupture with the past, a break in the continuity of time, had well and truly begun. This break was initiated first and foremost by the massive urban unrest that shook America from 1964 until well into the 1970s. No institution was unaffected, no social relationship unscathed, and "Dancing in the Streets" took on ominous implications.

The connection of these events with rock 'n' roll and the subsequent evolution of music in general has to be explored since not only did they coincide historically, but each infused the other with a social content that made them insurrectionary. This is not only a question of "meaning" in the sense that signification is assigned to acts or forms of expression to explain their occurrence or their effects. It is more importantly to establish the ways and means young people chose—or were compelled—to resist oppression and to fight for liberation and how, within particular, perhaps unique, historical conditions, this led to a powerful interaction between, on the one hand, youth, race, and war, and on the other, music and revolution. In any case, repeated uprisings, year upon year, in cities throughout the U.S. produced the cracks and fissures that unleashed the Sixties as a whole. Only the Vietnamese and their heroic struggle against

U.S. imperialism would be of equal importance, producing equivalent effects in American society and the world.

Ghettos on Fire

As every schoolchild in every classroom in America arose each day to pledge allegiance to the flag, they repeated the words, "liberty and justice for all!" The descendants of slaves, making the same pledge, said, "Yes, but when?"

The Kerner Report, formally entitled the *Report of the National Advisory Commission on Civil Disorders*, was published in February 1968. It was commissioned to examine the causes of more than 300 "disorders" in more than a hundred American cities. In one year alone, 1967, there were 164 "urban riots" (or, as participants called them, *rebellions*) in 128 cities.[3] Harlem, Newark, Watts, and Detroit were not just cities, they were blazing headlines throughout the world, their names associated with oppression and resistance. The Long Hot Summer, so named by the press and in popular usage, became an international symbol of America in crisis. By the time Martin Luther King was assassinated, unleashing an even larger outburst, the Long Hot Summer had become an annual event.

Of course, the Kerner Report typically missed the point, fatuously stating: "Our nation is moving toward two societies, one black, one white—separate and unequal," when everyone knew America had always been two separate and unequal societies. What the report could not overlook, however, was that participants were in the main young black people, and in many cases they were armed. The mere fact that the National Guard had to be called in repeatedly, thereby placing the American military in the streets of American cities, confirms the size and ferocity of the phenomenon. (One example: the Detroit rebellion of 1967 resulted in 43 dead, 1,189 injured, over 7,200 arrests, and more than 2,000 buildings destroyed.)[4]

The report failed to acknowledge (indeed was institutionally incapable of acknowledging) the thinking behind what it could only view as frustration and rage. While no one would deny that these uprisings were spontaneous, unplanned, and certainly not the work of any organization, what could account for their frequency and continued recurrence if not certain ideas that had been diffused among black people throughout America? Had the Harlem riot of 1964 been a one-time occurrence, it might be attributable to the frustration and rage of an unruly mob, but years of outbursts throughout the length and breadth of America, in the main occurring *after* the Voting Rights Act of 1965, can only be explained by the thoughts and feelings of those involved. While by no means confined to political or economic factors (and we will explore other factors shortly), there can be little doubt that the unceasing agitation of revolutionaries contributed to the popular mood among black youth.

Frantz Fanon, Robert F. Williams, Stokely Carmichael, H. Rap Brown, and, above all, Malcolm X, had brought an internationalist revolutionary critique to the impasse confronting the civil rights movement. Faced with violent attacks by the Ku Klux Klan, aided and abetted by sheriffs, police, and other law enforcement agencies, the determination to arm and defend themselves had arisen among many involved with an avowedly nonviolent movement. By the time of the Watts rebellion (1965), many young black people had read Williams's *Negroes with Guns*, had heard Stokely Carmichael lauding the efforts of the Deacons for Defense and Justice,[5] and had fully embraced the stance and attitude of Malcolm X. Indeed, at the time of his assassination, Dr. King had been eclipsed by Malcolm as a spokesperson for the aspirations of young black people.

For a new generation, it was not only that the pace of change was too slow, it was that the change required went far beyond inclusion—even nominally equal inclusion—in a thoroughly corrupt and, racist society. The white power structure was incapable of "integration," since it depended on black subordination to maintain rule over all members of society, including poor whites. It was only in 1967 that the Supreme Court heard the marvelously named *Loving v. Virginia* case and struck down the laws against interracial marriage still enforced by sixteen states at that time. As recently as 1948, thirty states, including "liberal" California, had laws against miscegenation that included not only marriage but sexual intercourse of any kind.[6] Besides, black people didn't need the beneficence of American culture. They'd seen their every creative expression ripped off and pathetically imitated by commercial and governmental agents of that culture, while they in turn were made the butt of ridicule in coon songs, servile caricatures in theater and film, and happy niggers selling syrup and rice.[7]

Inevitably, Black Power combined with urban unrest to produce a terror-stricken reaction on the part of the government and corporate media. The liberals who'd looked to Johnson's Great Society programs, and specifically the Voting Rights Act of 1965, to finally, at long last, "heal a nation," were deeply shocked to learn that they were increas-ingly viewed with contempt by the very people whom they'd so sincerely believed they were helping. What confronted the liberal was an enigma born of delusion. They took it "personally" when it was the liberal vision of a just order that was being rejected as a sham. This rejection, moreover, was not a wild, emotional outburst, but sprung from a nuanced analysis of the situation facing black people in America, bringing to it the anti-colonial perspective of the national liberation struggles that were making headway in Africa, Asia, and Latin America. Viewing black people as an internal colony of the United States, allied more closely with its counter-parts in the Third World than with white America, cast freedom and its achievement in a new light. It also, and perhaps for the first time since the Civil War, raised the prospect of revolution in its classic form: the violent overthrow of the government. As many documents available only years later prove, this was exactly how the U.S. government viewed it.

This sequence was concentrated with greatest intensity in the San Francisco Bay Area for many reasons explored throughout this book. Two events in 1966 would define the moment: On September 27, police shot and killed Matthew Johnson, a young black resident of the Hunters Point district in San Francisco. This shooting sparked a four-day riot that spread from Hunters Point to another largely black neighborhood, the Fillmore (site, coincidentally, of the Fillmore Auditorium). The National Guard was called in, and a curfew was enforced until the street fighting died down.[8] On October 15, across the bay in Oakland, Huey Newton and Bobby Seale announced the formation of the Black Panther Party for Self-Defense. The Panther platform and program clearly articulated demands that were in fact widely shared by black people. The document concluded by recapitulating the United States' own Declaration of Independence, reminding everyone of America's broken promises and placing them in the context of a revolution to come.[9] The Panthers would chart the course from disjointed, spontaneous urban uprising to sustained, organ-ized militancy, from "Burn, Baby, Burn" to "All Power to the People!"

Ironically, the fact that young people in America viewed themselves as a "generation" was initially a result of mass marketing by corporate merchandizers.[10] In one of history's best examples of "the law of unin-tended consequences," the tumult and disorder of the Sixties were partly the result of the invention of the teenager and rock 'n' roll. The demo-graphics are a simple matter of fact. But that youth and music *transformed themselves* into major factors in the worldwide revolution of 1968 was clearly not on Madison Avenue's agenda. It is therefore doubly necessary to understand corporate and government strategy, since it explains both the coincidence of Rosa Parks's momentous act in 1955 with the birth of rock 'n' roll and it follows the evolution of popular consciousness as it headed in a revolutionary direction over the subsequent ten years.

Teenagers and Rock 'n' Roll

"In the years just prior to World War II, there were no teenagers, no teenage magazines, teenage music, or teenage culture. The word itself had not even been invented."[11] Sociologists called attention to this fact because every aspect of private and public life, from tampons to television, had, since the mid-1950s, undergone a reappraisal based on a newly constituted social category: the teenager. Using techniques pioneered in the '20s and '30s by the Father of Public Relations, Edward Bernays,[12] Madison Avenue unfolded a strategy whereby teenagers could be separated from children and adults by, on the one hand their exaltation, and on the other, their demonization. This was extrapolated by means of scientistic proclamations from psychologists, sociologists, educators and criminologists and, contrarily, by the deliberate mystification of cravings, sensations, manias, and hysteria as if this "creature," the teenager, was both subhuman and superhuman at the same time.

Necessarily, this was tightly interwoven with the *parent*. In this case, parents who had survived the Depression and World War II and were bound and determined to provide for their offspring the benefits and rewards attained through hard work and sacrifice. This was the American Dream of ever-increasing abundance in a wonderland known as leisure. Leisure was the coveted prize toward which all one's efforts were directed. It was also what teenagers seemed to already possess, without having to do anything to get it. So, while they had to be protected and nourished, pampered and soothed, teenagers also had to be monitored and disciplined, making the preponderant image of the late 1950s and early '60s that of the juvenile delinquent. Films like *Blackboard Jungle, The Wild Ones*, and *Rebel Without a Cause* (portraying raucous music, motorcycle gangs, drugs, orgies, and pointless mayhem) focused on teenagers, presenting an intoxicating cocktail of nihilism, hedonism, and acne.

Fear and loathing of these disobedient, hormone-deranged, young people was put on a par with anticommunism and by similar means. In every media outlet, a somber, rational tone alternated with shrill alarums, enveloping public life in a climate of suspicion and foreboding. As Joseph McCarthy and J. Edgar Hoover were driving reds out of government, education, Hollywood and, above all, the trade unions (eleven unions representing more than a million workers were purged from the CIO in 1949–50, only two of which, the ILWU and the UE, survive today), a hue and cry was simultaneously orchestrated warning of the grave threat to the morality of America's youth.[13] The finger was pointed at everything from *MAD* magazine to Maynard G. Krebs,[14] but music, especially black music, was identified as the key danger.

The name "rock 'n' roll" was given to a musical form already named "rhythm and blues," which itself had replaced the earlier name, "race music" used to distinguish its intended audience, black people, from their white counterparts (the audience designated by "hillbilly," later changed to "country and western"). While this naming process is a story in itself that will be explored later in this book, the point here is to establish the conjuncture of the creation of the teenager and the creation of rock 'n' roll—that is, as a name suited to selling black music, performed by black musicians, to white youth. But what was rhythm and blues? Historian Eric Hobsbawm summarizes:

> Rhythm-and-blues, as it developed after the Second World War, was the folk music of urban Blacks in the 1940s, when one and a quarter million Blacks left the South for the Northern and Western ghettos. They constituted a new market, which was then supplied by independent record labels like Chess Records, founded in Chicago in 1949 by two Polish immigrants connected with the club circuit, and specializing in the so-called "Chicago Blues" style (Muddy Waters, Howlin' Wolf, Sonny Boy Williamson) and recording, among others, Chuck Berry, who was probably—with Elvis Presley—the major influence on 1950s rock-and-roll. White adolescents began to buy Black r&b records in the early 1950s, having discovered this music on local specialized radio stations which multiplied during those years, as the mass of adults transferred its attentions to television.... As soon as the music industry became aware of this potential white youth market, it became evident that rock was the opposite of a minority taste. It was music of an entire age-group.[15]

Charlie Gillette elaborates upon this in *The Sound of the City*:

Throughout the late forties and early fifties, increasing numbers of white adolescents became interested in black "rhythm and blues" music. By 1956, this group had grown so large that its taste was reflected in the hit parades. The change in attitudes forced a change in institutions. The large radio stations, which at first had resisted the broadcasting of records by black singers by suggesting that the words of the songs were corrupting America's youth, were obliged to play the records or give up their audience to the smaller stations that did play the records. The major record companies which had recorded black singers with white styles, or white singers with black songs, yielded to smaller independent companies that recorded black singers with their own songs and styles.[16]

To disc jockeys like Alan Freed, it was readily apparent that a growing section of white youth wanted the "real thing" and were willing to pay for it. Coining a term "rock 'n' roll," was simply a way to identify this "new" teenage phenomenon.[17] This led "the vanguard of white youth," as Eldridge Cleaver would describe them, to not only reject "Bing Crosbyism, Perry Comoism, and Dinah Shoreism," but to embrace rhythm and blues/rock 'n' roll with a fervor antithetical to their *Father Knows Best* upbringing.[18] Cleaver summarized this succinctly: "They [the young] couldn't care less about the old, stiffassed honkies who don't like their new dances; Frug, Monkey, Jerk, Swim, Watusi. All they know is that it feels good to swing to way-out body rhythms instead of dragassing across the dance floor like zombies to the dead beat of mind-smothered Mickey Mouse music."[19]

Cleaver's remarks are not as hyperbolic as they might first appear. Indeed, they accurately express the spirit with which young white people took to this music. As musician Steve Van Zandt would describe it decades later, "An art form born to serve the needs of a new species of humanity called the Teenager. Chuck Berry and Bob Dylan would add the eloquence and the specifics, but we didn't need anything more than Little Richard. He opened his mouth and out came liberation."[20] Little Richard, himself, adds important details: "People called rock & roll 'African music.' They called it 'voodoo music.' They said that it would drive the kids insane."[21] No matter what its commercial purveyors intended, their products' essential characteristic was undeniable: rock 'n' roll was dance music.

And dancing, in this case, led to wild abandon. As Little Richard explained, "We played places where they told us not to come back, because the kids got so wild. They were tearing up the streets and throwing bottles and jumping off the theater balconies at shows. At that time, the white kids had to be up in the balcony—they were 'white spectators.' But then they'd leap over the balcony to get downstairs where the black kids were."[22]

While rock 'n' roll generated enormous profits for the music industry as a whole (publishers, record companies, retailers, and broadcasters), it generated enormous controversy, as well.[23] This was not confined to the liberal Establishment worried about the music's corrosive moral influence or to bigots like the Ku Klux Klan who organized the banning and burning of records of "nigger music."[24] Among the large numbers of people for whom folk music and jazz represented genuine alternatives to Tin Pan Alley trivia, rock 'n' roll appeared to be commercial pabulum at its worst. When the Weavers reunited in 1955, the folk music revival, simultaneously with rock 'n' roll, began its rapid rise in popularity. Not only did this event mark the return of a commercially successful group that had been blacklisted by McCarthyism, it was immediately followed by the chart-topping successes of the Kingston Trio, Harry Belafonte, and Peter, Paul and Mary—to name only a few.[25]

Even more significant was the use of folk music by the civil rights movement. Drawing on the rich legacy of slave songs, spirituals, gospel music, and blues, the black struggle for emancipation was inspired by and identified with its singing. From this perspective, rock 'n' roll was not only crassly commercial; it was adolescent lyrically and furthermore seemed to be perpetuating the old music industry game of ripping off black musicians to enrich whites. (Big Mama Thornton's version of "Hound Dog" being commercially overshadowed by Elvis Presley's version is a notorious example. The fact that the song was written by two Los Angelenos, Lieber and Stoller, only complicated the nefarious practice.)[26]

When the new generation brought forth artists like Joan Baez, Buffy Sainte-Marie, Phil Ochs, and Bob Dylan, it not only offered an alternative to rock 'n' roll—and a highly successful one, at that—it more importantly symbolized the resurgence of popular protest and the healthiest linkage between music and the betterment of society. The infamous clash at the 1965 Newport Folk Festival was about something far more significant than Dylan playing with an electric band.[27] That event, and

1965 as a year, represents a generation reaching adulthood, and simultaneously rejecting designations—folk, rock, jazz, etc.—and embracing the music in such designations, that is, the physical, emotional, and social content of a wide range of musical forms. What the young had learned from experience was what theorists and salesmen had failed to grasp (or failed to conceal!). The pigeonholes of purists and the labeling of marketers were obstacles to partaking in music's diversity and its multifaceted gifts.

At the same time, it was dawning on many young people that the Old Left—inclusive of the Communist Party, elders in the civil rights movement, as well as liberal politicians and intelligentsia—was more concerned with maintaining respectability than maintaining principles. The legitimacy of "progressive" politics depended on their being conveyed by normal, hard-working Americans. The open hostility many in the Old Left displayed toward rock 'n' roll simply confirmed their incomprehension of the struggles being waged by youth. These struggles were not, in the main, between bosses and workers, but between authority, as such, and an increasingly alienated generation. When *On the Road* was published in 1957, it announced a dissenting current beholden neither to the Old Left nor to rock 'n' roll. Indeed, the attraction of the Beats was to a large extent based on their critique of the quality of life to which the Old Left *aspired*. Home ownership, household appliances, and television were *not* what life was all about. Furthermore, the Beats drew on the mystique of jazz and the subterranean world whose topography was charted by the "hip."

Getting Hip: From White Negroes to Freaks

Before there was anything to be called a *counter*culture, there was a thriving *sub*culture, organized around black music, language, and aspiration, but populated by all ethnicities—anyone, that is, who was hip. In a widely read 1957 essay entitled "The White Negro," Norman Mailer identified the features of this subculture:

> In such places as Greenwich Village, a ménage-à-trois was completed—the bohemian and the juvenile delinquent came face-to-face with the Negro, and the hipster was a fact in American life. If marijuana was the wedding ring, the child was the language of Hip for its argot gave expression to abstract states of feeling which

all could share, at least all who were Hip. And in this wedding of the white and the black it was the Negro who brought the cultural dowry.[28]

Hip was a compass guiding the initiate through the snares and delusions obstructing their path, the path that was itself the destination. The traps were laid by the squares whose heavy hand held the reins of power, but whose arthritic grip could be eluded by those lithe and supple enough to slip through it. Rituals and elixirs were provided that both illuminated and reinforced the social bond between the enlightened. Music, particularly jazz, was fundamental. Improvisational, existential, difficult to master, and obedient only to the Muse, it was the sonic expression of a worldview that incorporated diverse elements from urban sophistication to unfettered expression.

Celebrating sexuality as both an end and a means of escape from the neurotic and repressed personality constructed by the "White Anglo-Saxon Protestant" introduced not only the sexual but the interracial. The combination of music and race-mixing, particularly in its sexual dimension, made being hip dangerous. Imbibing or at the very least experimenting with marijuana and other drugs did, too. The drugs involved in the first decades of hip also included alcohol, but did not include psychotropics. The significance of other inebriating substances (e.g., marijuana, heroin) was as much a matter of their illegality as of their chemical effect. Indeed, the outstanding characteristic of hip was its moral superiority to an illegitimate authority. Disdain for the law, the cops, the courts, and any other symbols of an unjust and hypocritical social order were the common currency.

While there was an inevitable connection with sin and vice—the gambler, the pimp, the dealer, the petty criminal—the quintessentially hip was the black jazz musician. The fact that musicians from Louis Armstrong to Duke Ellington were as undeniably accomplished as any classical musician did not do much to change either the milieu in which they spent much of their professional lives or their music being ranked below European classical music. Even at the height of its respectability, jazz retained enough of its brothel and barroom origins to be looked down upon—hence hipsters' reverence for it.

It should not be forgotten, however, that the wellsprings of hip were far more substantial than vague bohemianism or dilettantism, and in two important ways. First, there was the intellectual connection between New York—Harlem in particular—and Europe, especially France. It was a connection that went both ways, with Sartre, Beauvoir, and existentialism crossing paths with Langston Hughes, James Baldwin, Richard Wright, and many others, producing a vital discourse that found expression in literature, music, and philosophy. Harlem was the capital of black America, and its Renaissance in the 1920s and '30s profoundly affected every aspect of American life.

Second, the overtly political aspects, including links between communists and other radicals, contributed much to what is often viewed today as being no more than a protest against racial discrimination. One song, "Strange Fruit," exemplifies a much broader field of relationships. Composed by Abel Meeropol under the pen name Lewis Allen, it became Billie Holiday's signature tune and the defining statement against lynching and an entire social order built on racism and oppression. Meeropol was a communist who later adopted the children of Julius and Ethel Rosenberg, whose case was, along with those of Sacco and Vanzetti and the Scottsboro Boys, among the most celebrated of the twentieth century. The linkages go further still when one considers that a widely read book, *The Jazz Scene*, was written by Marxist historian Eric Hobsbawm under the pen-name Francis Newton. He chose this name because of Frankie Newton, who was a trumpeter in Billie Holiday's band, including on the "Strange Fruit" sessions, and a known communist. In the decade and a half following World War II, jazz enjoyed its second and greatest "golden age," thus broadening the influence of "hip," but it did so with the support of people such as John Hammond Jr., who was described by Hobsbawm as remaining "an unreconstructed and militant 1930s leftwinger to the end, even though the FBI could never tie him down as a card-carrying communist."[29]

Hammond, of course, signed Billie Holiday, Aretha Franklin, Bob Dylan, and Bruce Springsteen to Columbia Records and was viewed, along with a select few, as being undeniably hip, although he displayed none of the outward trappings, such as clothing or hairstyle. Other hip notables include Harry "the Hipster" Gibson, Mezz Mezzrow, and Lenny Bruce. But perhaps the classic and emblematic figure was "his royal hipness," Lord Buckley. The literary and philosophical content of Buckley's wild verbal flights puts the lie to any inference that being hip was only a matter of style or appearance. Above all, musicians like

Charles Mingus and Max Roach let no one forget what was at stake, both musically and politically, if you wanted to cross the threshold into their "world." Mingus's "Fables for Faubus" and Roach's *We Insist! Freedom Now Suite* forever marked the territory, drawing a line in the sand that no hipster could ignore for the next two decades.

Out of the Nightclub and into the Street

Not only was none of this lost on the young, it was a magnet attracting them in increasing numbers. By the time the Sixties began, there was an influential minority of hipsters scattered throughout the urban centers of America. As sociologist George Lewis pointed out, "As these youths grew older, they were neither accepted nor absorbed in adult society— rather they became the outlaws of America, allying themselves more with the bohemian culture of the beats."[30]

They were still a small number in absolute terms, but there was a change underway marked by two distinguishing features. Whereas hip had formerly been an exclusively adult affair, never to be confused with teenage musical taste, now young college and even high-school-age kids were beginning to demand entry into the inner sanctum. They'd read *Howl* and *On the Road*, they'd listened to Mose Allison and Ray Charles, they'd smoked dope and broken curfews. They'd begun to follow the course taken by Gnossos in Richard Farina's *Been Down So Long It Looks Like Up to Me*, through the Cuban revolution, campus rioting, race mixing, and risk taking. Undeterred by a bit of derision from their elders, they felt themselves to be an irresistible force. The demographic shift in the population as a whole included a corresponding increase in attendance at college or university at the very moment when the civil rights movement was reaching a crescendo and campus unrest was breaking out. This meant there was a large enough presence of hipsters in virtually every social situation to attract new enthusiasts, leading inexorably to hip's exponential growth by the middle of the decade. What finally exploded in San Francisco was so much larger in scope, however, that it could no longer be seen through the visage of a jazz musician in a suit and tie (even if he was wearing dark glasses to hide bloodshot eyes).

The second feature was that of confrontation. The freaks were coming out and were in full regalia within a few short years. They were still using the vocabulary of the jazz musician, and of black people, in general, but they were emboldened to challenge rather than to elude the condemnation of society at large. As one early participant put it, "The Beats were dark, intellectual, individualistic. We wanted color, dancing, the body, the collective."[31] While never denouncing their forbears, young white people began to tread a different course, inventing and experimenting with what hipness was mutating into. This explains why "hippie" was such a pejorative term, both in its creation and its prevalent usage at the time. Journalists created it to denigrate young white people rebelling against societal norms (see Appendix 1). It was then used widely by straights as an epithet, usually accompanied by "take a bath" or "get a haircut." "The Haight was a combat zone between '66 and '69," recalls one such freak, "Long hair made you a target. It was dangerous and not 'cool' in high school or on the street. The vibe was originally one of confrontation, not acceptance."[32]

Such attitudes were reinforced by changes at their source. *Say It Loud, I'm Black and I'm Proud* (1969), a pathbreaking record by James Brown, announced that "Negro" was out, and with it the quest for acceptance by "White Amerika." Freedom Now led inexorably to Black Power, nonviolence to armed self-defense and the rise of the Black Panther Party. Getting hip could no longer be defined as "never losing your cool"; getting hip had to mean being aware of the changes unfolding among the people who originated the term in the first place. In other words, "no more of this integration shit, it's time for justice and by any means necessary."

The Future Ain't What It Used to Be

Meanwhile, the United States was rapidly expanding its involvement in Vietnam. We'll explore this aspect of the Sixties in greater detail elsewhere. But by 1965, there were already the first antiwar protests, the first signs of opposition to the draft and the merging of the black liberation struggle with the antiwar movement that would define the next ten years. Teenagers and rock 'n' roll were fictions created to sell not only material goods but an ideology of narcissistic self-aggrandizement. The problem capitalist ideologues encountered was the origin of the music and the destination of the American teenager, i.e., black people and Vietnam.

By 1965 40 percent of the population was under twenty-one and the oldest of this cohort were now in open rebellion.[33] The "old white man"— God, father, headmaster, banker, general, pope, or president—was feeble and frail, his manifold injustices no longer propping him up but weighing him down. The judicial robe, the prelate's vestments, the white lab coat, the military uniform and the grey flannel suit no longer exuded authority and command, instead they projected exhaustion and senility. The young in all their vitality and naiveté announced, "It stops here, with this generation. Your crimes and your neuroses, your hypocrisy and your betrayals, are not ours. We will not pass them on." As their protests were met with lordly disdain and brutal repression, this only convinced young people further that they were right. Instead of silencing opposition, the authorities only emboldened it, driving ever-larger numbers into the embrace of an entirely different kind of resistance than Authority was prepared to meet. Because this generation posed the profound question: "How are we to *live* and not merely exist?" Authority's only answer was, "Obey." So, a generation found its own: "Change the world!"

Only a few months after Kennedy's assassination, these momentous shifts were famously announced by none other than Bob Dylan and the Beatles. Dylan's "Times They Are a-Changin'," released January 13, 1964, summed it up in the famous words, "Your sons and your daughters are beyond your command." Actually written before Kennedy's assassination, they expressed poetically what was a matter of fact. As powerful and emblematic as this was it was quickly reinforced by a second blast that would startle and arouse even those making it. When the Beatles performed twice in February 1964 on the *Ed Sullivan Show*, no one expected it to be anything more than another diversion, albeit an exciting and profitable one. But the times that were changing were being changed by a generation for whom time itself had become a question. It was no longer the clock, the calendar, or the orderly procession from birth to death that would dictate the terms of debate. Suddenly, it was music that became both their voice and their argument. This produced remarkable effects due, in part, to the nature of music itself. For one thing, music makes its own time, which does not correspond to past or future existing only in the present. Secondly, it is not necessary for it to mean anything the way language does. Music is immediate and its impact is felt physically, not only intellectually. These qualities obviously appealed to impatient youth. For some people this indicated a step away from politics and, in the case of the Beatles, merely a ruse by which a generation could be "brought back into the fold" of tranquilized consumerism. But it became evident very quickly that not only was the future being impacted by the young but time itself would be reconfigured by making music its expression as opposed to word or number. In other words, now was the only time that mattered, and music was the proof.

Time Has Come Today

One song by one group illustrates this entire historical process. Though the song was a huge hit, and the group became a top concert draw as a result, the episode is virtually absent in accounts of the period. "Time Has Come Today" is the song, the Chambers Brothers are the group, and the story of its making illustrates how the rejection of the old in music and politics actually transpired and what was at stake. First, their own trajectory linked the past and the future in musical and political terms. Musically because, like many other Sixties groups, they emerged out of the folk music revival of the early 1960s, playing acoustically at clubs and festivals featuring old time, blues, and gospel music. Politically, because the group and the folk music revival were closely aligned with the civil rights movement, which was then experiencing its radical shift into the Black Power/black liberation struggle. Secondly, they were swept up in the musical ferment that would lead decisively away from folk music and into the new kind of rock music being pioneered in San Francisco. This was especially important as regards the role music played in race and the role race played in music. When a black singing group took up the sound and attitude of rock no one could object since this was "their" music to begin with. But when they incorporated what some described as "white" influences, their record company rejected it, specifically suggesting that their song "Time" be given to a white group to record. But this led to a third point: the musical and lyrical content of the song pointed to what can best be described as the world outlook of a generation, black *and* white. The decisive moment had arrived, "can't put it off another day," "I don't care what others say," "the rules have changed," and one had to act. None could miss the stark contrast with "We Shall Overcome" and its wistful conclusion "someday." Not only had "We Shall Overcome" characterized an earlier period, but the phrase had been co-opted by none other than Lyndon Johnson in a nationally televised speech to Congress on March 15, 1965.[34] It could no longer speak to the urgency of new demands.

The Chambers Brothers' story bears closer scrutiny. Briefly stated, the band had appeared at the Newport Folk Festival in 1965—the one made notorious by Dylan's electrification—at the invitation of Pete Seeger. They were an overwhelming success with an electrified band.

"That was rock 'n' roll!" said the MC following their performance. The Chambers Brothers were immediately brought to Columbia Records and to David Rubinson for production. Originally, "Time" was recorded in 1966 but it died. At some personal risk due to Columbia's refusing to record what they viewed as a "white" song by a black group, Rubinson rerecorded the song in the expanded version the Chambers Brothers had developed in their live show. It was recorded in one take. Rubinson called Clive Davis, head of Columbia Records, and told him he had to get down to the studio immediately to hear this. Davis was impressed but skeptical. Still following the record business dictum: "no hit single, no album," an attempt was made to release a shortened version of this new take of the song (the album version was eleven minutes long). Radio station KYA broke the record in San Francisco and it went to No. 1 in two weeks. This led to its becoming a nationwide hit soon afterward. (Not, however, without an enormous promotional effort including extensive touring.)

Rubinson recalls, "The Chambers Brothers and their one great song certainly broke down all the barriers between folk, rock, black, white, political and apolitical before anyone else really realized what was happening. Later, of course, Sly Stone would take this to extraordinary heights and groups like Tower of Power and Cold Blood were doing similar things. But it is now almost forgotten that the Chambers Brothers and that song really broke it open."[35]

The implications of a now-integrated group (The Chambers Brothers were in fact brothers but they had a white drummer, Brian Keenan) playing "integrated" music were far-reaching. Jimi Hendrix (another black musician who, incidentally, braved criticism to "integrate" his music) asked, "Are you experienced? Have you ever been experienced? Not necessarily stoned, but beautiful?" This posed a question to all young people regardless of race and it did so by establishing its own universal criteria. Criteria, furthermore, that measured hipness, not in stylistic terms but as a bold leap out of "your measly little world" into one of infinite possibility. Followed soon after by Sly Stone's *Stand!*, a territory was defined and everyone found themselves confronting these imperatives: youth, race, war, and music. Where one stood might be a matter of one's choosing, but that a stand had to be taken was impossible to avoid.

CHAPTER 3

Making Music to Change the World: Diversity, Unity, and Liberation

There have long been revolutionary songs and from every corner of the world. The "Marseillaise" and the "Internationale" are two notable examples from a countless number. But the revolutionary Sixties are associated with music in general, with songs, musicians, and festivals too numerous to count, all commonly viewed as heralds of a world transformed. The difference is not only quantitative. Rather, there is a change of roles affecting the status of the word, of the state and of the body. Music suddenly challenged the authority of the word, be it poetic or doctrinal, as well as the state as legislator or representative of the popular will, and it posed this challenge through the participatory act of the dancing multitude. Perhaps nowhere was this more in evidence than in the San Francisco Bay Area between 1965 and 1975. Beyond the protest songs by which both the civil rights movement and the folk music revival had been characterized, music of unprecedented diversity galvanized a generation as no literary or artistic movement had done before. In so doing, music came to be viewed as not only the *herald* but the *instrument* of change.

Subsequent study of the subject has often been confined to rock music, ignoring the more significant fact that rupture with stylistic limitation and the intermingling of elements from disparate sources characterized music of the era. Furthermore, most commentators have focused on lyrical content to determine political intent or effect, failing to account for the fact that music in itself became politically subversive. Finally, musicians were not alone or even mainly responsible for such challenges to convention. Rather, it was the audience that gathered to demand it.

Conditions

Two factors are particularly relevant to music and need to be mentioned before going into historical details. First, it should be recalled that prior to the breakthroughs of 1965, the music industry maintained a tight grip on music production in the United States. While some musicians strained mightily against this control, such resistance was marginalized and largely contained. Certainly, musicians like Woody Guthrie, Paul Robeson, Pete Seeger, and Max Roach could eloquently express popular opposition, enjoy large audiences, and exert broad influence. But until the civil rights movement raised a *political* challenge to segregation and racist law, music industry dominance maintained itself precisely by the divisions it sowed with the sale of its products—black and white charts, black and white radio stations, black and white nightclubs, and so on. Though diverse forms persisted, diversity itself was inimical to the formulas most successful in securing markets for particular styles. For example, we have already seen how rock 'n' roll began as a marketing ploy designed to sell rhythm and blues to white youth.[1]

Breakthroughs in San Francisco, however, were made in direct opposition to these strategies. Young people began listening to and participating in a vast array of musical expression, from Indian ragas to African polyrhythms, from salsa to soul, from free jazz to experimental electronic. On any given night, concerts featuring Charles Lloyd, the Young Rascals and Count Basie, Bola Sete with Country Joe and the Fish, or Lenny Bruce and the Mothers were attended by large and growing numbers.[2] No doubt rock music predominated in the scene, but what constituted rock music was more diverse than is usually acknowledged. So many influences converged under the umbrella of rock that listening today to representative samples well known at the time defies categorization (except, perhaps, that it was widely popular). Indeed, the rock that emerged then bore little resemblance to its forebears in two outstanding ways. First, the song format, especially the three-minute limit established by radio programming, was stretched beyond recognition to the point where much of the music people listened to could not even be called "song." Second, more and more musicians began incorporating into their work elements foreign to American popular music as it was previously conceived. These included musical components borrowed from other cultures as well as technological components developed by avant-garde experimentalists, making the sonic character of music as important as its melodic, harmonic, or rhythmic qualities. Ultimately, the era can be characterized by a wholesale assault on the formulas and structures established by the music industry

The second point is that these new possibilities were first pioneered not primarily by musicians, but by artists in other disciplines. Experiments in theater, dance, and the visual and graphic arts were the immediate predecessors and initial inspirations for the direction music would subsequently take. The San Francisco Mime Troupe, the Committee, and Teatro Campesino, to name only a few, explored innovative approaches to the dramatic arts. Not only did these groups develop new techniques that would later influence theater worldwide but they profoundly affected cultural life in the Bay Area, specifically in regards to politics and public performance. The Mime Troupe is crucial here because their performances in public parks opened a space that would later be filled by musicians and the dancing multitude. Indeed, one such Mime Troupe performance was the direct inspiration for an event decisive in unleashing San Francisco's musical renaissance, and we'll return to this shortly.

Developments in poster art were closer to music, since posters were used to announce shows. But new approaches, such as virtually unreadable lettering and intricate design, were visible even before the music had taken its most innovative steps; poster art in fact *announced* the new ground being broken in the Bay Area, and it would soon come to have global influence in its own right. (This was, furthermore, accompanied by the unprecedented invention of the light show, as we'll see further on.) Not surprisingly, such creative ferment was mutually reinforcing, and necessarily so, given that it arose among artists who intermingled creatively in a hub of social conflict. But what cannot be missed is that people coming from *outside* the usual channels of music production and performance were the ones who saw possibilities that few operating *within* those channels had before. This is partly explained by who these people were. Among the first longhairs and freaks were a disproportionate number of red diaper babies, children of liberal professors and bohemian artists, not to mention those directly participating in the civil rights and Free Speech Movements. Many were drawn from the three major schools in the Bay Area: University of California, Berkeley; San Francisco State College and Stanford University. Contrary to their assigned role of preparing the next generation of bureaucrats and managers, these institutions had become cauldrons of creativity and radicalism.

Sparks

Within these broader social and artistic conditions, musicians found themselves struggling against the limits placed on public performance. Age restrictions, noise ordinances, and customs associated with different musical styles were now viewed as obstacles awaiting only the audacity and inventiveness required to remove them. Such conflict was a direct outgrowth of changes in music-making practices, specifically, the incorporation of electric instruments, drum sets and the expanded role of amplification. The explosive growth of bands, replacing solo, duo, or trio acoustic performance, strained the limits of rehearsal space and of stages at venues. The musical fuel was gathering needing only a spark to set it ablaze. Two such sparks were struck in the few short months between the summer and the end of 1965.

The first was the opening of Mother's in North Beach, then the center of San Francisco's nightlife. The venture was, from the outset, burdened by the past. It was a bar with a liquor license, meaning it was for adults only. Mother's was launched by Tom Donahue and Bobby Mitchell in a club previously called Sugar Hill. Sugar Hill had been founded by folksinger Barbara Dane and had featured the likes of Mama Yancey, T-Bone Walker, and Mance Lipscomb. Both the music and the atmosphere at Mother's were different from its predecessor and from other North Beach nightclubs (including the world famous hungry i, nearby). Local artists painted the entire venue, including the toilets, in deep colors and fabulous shapes, likened by one observer to a painting by Hieronymus Bosch. Mother's was also the first club in San Francisco to present a light show, projected by Del Close of the Committee, a political-satirical theater company. The Lovin' Spoonful, riding the national charts with a hit called "Do You Believe in Magic," played the opening night. The Great! Society also rehearsed and performed an extended run at Mother's.[3] The greater significance of Mother's, however, was that it was the first *psychedelic* nightclub in the Bay Area, perhaps in the world.[4] While Mother's failed as a business venture, closing its doors within the year, it nonetheless brought together the crucial musical and visual elements that soon mutated into the San Francisco musical renaissance.

The second such spark was the brainchild of Marty Balin who was determined to bring together electric guitars and drums with folk songs to create something simultaneously as exciting as rock 'n' roll and as intelligent or adult as folk music or jazz. As Balin would tell it, the problem was that "we couldn't get any work because of the drums and electric pickups on our guitars." The sound limitations of coffeehouses and the age limitations of the nightclubs were the problem. When given an opportunity by acquaintances to open his own club to present such music, Balin quickly seized it and converted an old pizzeria into a music venue. Because of its collaborative atmosphere, the Matrix immediately became the center of the San Francisco music scene.

Though it has long been overshadowed in legend and lore by the Fillmore and the Avalon, the Matrix was perhaps the single decisive "do it yourself" effort needed to nourish the quantity and diversity of musicians that marked the era.[5] For one thing, Balin insisted on booking "the blues guys" like Lightnin' Hopkins, Furry Lewis, and John Lee Hooker, clearly establishing that the club was not only for young, white folkies. For another, the Matrix was no flash in the pan but a sustained effort to bring a new sensibility to musicians and audiences alike. Many important artists (such as the Wailers, and Steel Mill, featuring Bruce Springsteen) made their first Bay Area appearances there, reflecting the reputation the Matrix enjoyed outside San Francisco—and the reasons it enjoyed that reputation.

The Matrix opened on August 13, 1965. A line circled the block for what a simple black and white poster had announced as the launching of "San Francisco's First Folk Night Club." It was not only the debut of a new club, it was the debut of a new band: Jefferson Airplane. While it would be easy to attribute the notoriety of this band to the attention they immediately received in the *San Francisco Chronicle* (several feature stories in a few days), this would be to overlook the musical and historical significance of Jefferson Airplane's arrival. Musically, the Airplane did announce a change. While the new genre they heralded did not emerge fully formed in one fell swoop, their combination of musical elements marked a significant difference from what had come before. This was neither folk nor rock, as those categories were known. Of course, it bore the stamp of its immediate influences, the folk rock of the Lovin' Spoonful and the Byrds. But its distinct features are what caused it to ultimately become known as "acid rock," "psychedelic rock," or, more pejoratively, "hippie rock." Not the least of these were the playing of lead guitarist Jorma Kaukonen and bassist Jack Casady, neither of whom sounded anything like their predecessors in "folk rock." It didn't hurt that, unlike some of their cohort in the early days (1965–67), the Airplane was good. They sang and played well. While their sound reached maturity with their groundbreaking second album, *Surrealistic Pillow*, there was enough evidence on their first, *Jefferson Airplane Takes Off*, to suggest great potential from the start.

Historically, however, the Matrix and the Airplane played perhaps an even bigger role. For the first two years of the San Francisco musical renaissance, the club and the band were in the forefront of events, raising the banner and rallying the troops. The Airplane performed at virtually every major gathering, from the Family Dog's first show to the Mime Troupe Appeals. In those first heady years, the band seemed to be everywhere—in the parks, in the ballrooms, at political demonstrations, and at benefits. They were also the first to spread the gospel to the rest of the world.

The Walls Come Down

In 1969, noted music and social critic Ralph J. Gleason published *The Jefferson Airplane and the San Francisco Sound*.[6] The book's opening chapter is entitled "The History of the San Francisco Rock Scene." Gleason was without peer or precedent in the annals of American music journalism, having as much impact on the scene about which he was writing as any of its participants. This was partly due to his position at the *San Francisco Chronicle* as the first full-time jazz critic on a daily newspaper in the United States. It was also due to his dedication and commitment to music and to social justice, as he championed causes from the civil rights movement to the defense of comedian Lenny Bruce. He enjoyed the peculiar status of being read by young and old alike, indeed, by anyone with any interest in popular culture. That what was happening in San Francisco was already worthy of a "history" only four years after it had first captured public attention is one measure of how important these developments appeared to be at the time. Now, a half century later, Gleason's work is indispensable for his insights and integrity as well as his proximity to the matters at hand.

Gleason's narrative begins with a visit he received from a group calling itself "The Family Dog." They had asked to meet him to discuss their plans for a "dance concert" and enlist his support. But this was a far cry from the conventional sales pitch Gleason regularly received from publicists and promoters. What poured forth from the three founders of the Family Dog was instead a grand vision for how San Francisco could become the new Liverpool (a reference to the Beatles' hometown and its thriving music scene) and what separated San Francisco from New York ("too big and confused") or Los Angeles ("super uptight plastic America"). Furthermore, they articulated in a few brief words what was at stake. "Music is the most beautiful way to communicate, it's the way we're going to change things," said Luria Castell. "Half the population is teenaged now. . . . Dancing is the thing."[7]

This conversation would have consequences beyond the wildest imagination of its youthful prophets. What were they thinking? Music is the way to change things. Youth are the majority now. Dancing is key. Taking the last point first, they were not talking about ballet, and they weren't talking about social dancing, such as waltzes or fox trots. They drew some inspiration from the various dance crazes that had followed one upon the other over the previous five years, from the Twist to the Frug to the Jerk and so on. Gleason recalled that they explicitly referred to Martha and the Vandellas' recent hit "Dancing in the Streets," with its stirring opening lyric: "Calling out around the world, are you ready for a brand new beat? / 'Cause summer's here and the time is right for dancing in the street." (This caused the song to be banned in some cities where authorities feared it was an incitement to riot.) But these were only reference points. The substantial question raised by Castell was not dancing in the abstract, but actual celebratory, public, physical movement inspired by loud, rhythmic music. The "enveloping sound," as she described it. This in fact characterizes a festival. Not in the narrow sense of a jazz or folk festival organized to present a form of music to a listening audience, but an ancient, communal festival as it might be found in Carnival or the Feast of Fools or any seasonal rite where people come together to publicly celebrate. Gleason commented that what was being proposed was "like a feast day or a saint's birthday and I thought at the time that a new religion was in the process of evolving."[8] The Family Dog initially called them "dance concerts," which was something of a novel concept at the time, but they were quickly identified explicitly as festivals, tribal stomps, be-ins, happenings, and an assortment of other names. The reference was consciously made and immediately understood by all concerned. People were not coming to observe, much less to be entertained; they were gathering to participate.

"Half the population is teenaged now" was a dual reference. First, there had been widespread media coverage of the demographic bulge that had occurred following World War II and the problems and promise this held for society. Second, and more relevant to Castell's case, was that this youthful cohort was restless, questing, and increasingly disobedient, as had recently been manifested by a number of political confrontations, including the civil rights and the Free Speech Movements. It was also expressed by the unruly crowds that gathered at many rock 'n' roll shows, creating public disturbances and sometimes having violent confrontations with the police. Liquor laws, curfews, dress codes, and, in the case of San Francisco, prohibition era statutes empowering police to arrest people and fine venue owners if dancing took place without the requisite permit, meant that minors were narrowly confined and strictly regulated in their enjoyment of rock 'n' roll. The main venues for young people to experience the songs they heard on the radio and see the people singing them were sock hops, high school dances, state fairs, and big package shows, presenting a dozen or so acts performing for twenty or thirty minutes each at the Cow Palace or the Civic Auditorium.

Nightclubs prohibited minors and generally featured jazz. Coffeehouses, and in some cases churches or union halls, had presented folk, jazz, or ethnic music, but these were mainly gathering places for adults. Symphony halls and other highbrow civic venues certainly offered access to all ages, but none of them would host a rock 'n' roll show, let alone allow dancing. What the Family Dog envisioned was innovative because it offered a means by which the elements of music, dance, and festival could be brought together, while evading existing laws. They correctly assumed that there were a sufficient number of people who shared this vision to make their events successful. (This did not prevent the police from enforcing San Francisco's peculiar law, including the notorious arrest of Bill Graham at the Fillmore for allowing a minor to dance without having a dance hall permit.)[9]

Castell's first point, however, is the most compelling: "Music is the way we're going to change things." This, above all, foretold the distinguishing feature of music in the Sixties, particularly as it developed in San Francisco. What otherwise might have been a lively but routine exercise in a predictable evolution of musical style, determined largely by the music business, became something radically different. This difference is evident in both the music and its social effect. The change Castell referred to was obviously vague, but it was nonetheless widely understood to be necessary and large in scale. Change the world. Coming from Castell, this statement was also more profound and explicit than it would have been coming, for example, from someone in the music business (the likes of whom would be repeating it, *ad nauseam*, a few years later!). Castell's insight derived from her political activism, which included involvement in the W.E.B. Du Bois Club and, in 1963, joining a group of students violating a U.S. State Department ban on travel to Cuba.[10] Though she inferred in her conversation with Gleason that politics was behind her, her ideals were clearly intact, experience had taught her how to organize and that the world needed changing was the consensus of her generation.

By the time the Family Dog had its brainstorm, activism on both the UC Berkeley and San Francisco State College campuses had blossomed into major social movements, mobilizing thousands, and soon tens of thousands, of young people. In fact, it was from San Francisco State in particular that many of the first freaks emerged. Though overshadowed by UC Berkeley (due to that school's greater size and the world-renowned Free Speech Movement of 1964), San Francisco State was a vital center for everything from experimental art to radical politics. Many of the musicians, light show operators, poster artists, poets, and participants in the early San Francisco scene were either enrolled there or hung out on the campus. Luria Castell, for example, attended State. Its milieu gave nourishment to the ideas and, creativity of a significant number of the people who would launch the "San Francisco Rock Scene" about which Gleason was writing his history. One example is the light show. San Francisco State art instructor Seymour Lock had pioneered the exploration of light projection in the 1950s. Among those inspired by his work were Bill Ham, Elias Romero, Tony Martin, Glenn McKay, and Jerry Abrams, who formed the vanguard in the development of one of the key artistic expressions characterizing the era.[11]

The Audience Was the Show

Bill Ham brought his primitive light show to the Family Dog's first dance concert and the stage was set. What happened next made history.
Gleason's description is worth quoting at length:

> A hippie happening which signified the linkage of the political and the social hip movements. SNCC buttons and peace buttons abounded, stuck into costumes straight out of the Museum of

Natural History.... The crowd danced all night long...and I mean they danced! After the dance, on the long bridge ride over the San Francisco Bay, [Gleason lived in Berkeley] the little Volkswagens with Freedom Now stickers and SNCC and FSM signs in the windows driving back to Berkeley would pass me, packed with the long-haired young people, a giant convoy of escapees en route back to real life.[12]

Meanwhile, the San Francisco Mime Troupe had been performing its inflammatory and innovative theater for a number of years. Their notoriety was increased by performing in city parks. One such performance, on August 7, 1965, prompted the arrest of the Troupe's founder and director Ron Davis. This led to a highly publicized court case and the necessary fundraising to pay for the Troupe's defense. They decided to throw a benefit concert at their 924 Howard St. facility. Their business manager, Bill Graham, organized the benefit, which took place on November 6, 1965, and like the Family Dog show at the Longshoremen's Hall a month earlier, attracted at least a thousand people. In the combination of music, dancing, light show, and support for a radical theater group, something new emerged. From the outset it was not a purely musical scene. It was a "happening," with people joining together to create a collective performance for themselves and each other, rather than for an audience as such.

Into this stew was poured the psychotropic drug LSD, a subject I'll return to in more detail later. I only mention it here to establish LSD's place in a historical sequence of events. Owsley Stanley and a couple of his friends began supplying their homemade, high quality, and *completely legal* LSD to friends and associates in May 1965, and to the Merry Pranksters and the Grateful Dead in September 1965. This substance was soon being widely disseminated, particularly in the Bay Area, and it both literally and figuratively captured the imagination of adventurous youth. Certain conditions surrounding the introduction of LSD should be recalled when speaking of the role it played socially. First, a lot of young white kids were already smoking pot in 1964. Second, alcohol was out. It was not hip to drink, although people still did. Wine, beer, and liquor were associated with the older generation against whom youth were rebelling. Third, the name of Owsley attached to a tab guaranteed its quality. Furthermore, it carried with it the unspoken message: "Take this, brothers and sisters, and everything will be different. You'll see."

Many years later, Owsley would say that he had been performing a community service, but for a particular community.[13]

Things happened fast. Pleasant surprise at the outset became eager anticipation within weeks. When more than a thousand people turned out for the Family Dog's first event, it delighted and amazed those in attendance to discover that so many like-minded people existed. Within a year, the numbers had swollen tenfold. By the time of the January 1967 Human Be-In, at least twenty thousand people were directly participating (some estimates run as high as fifty thousand). This encouraged the widely held notion that a new day was indeed at hand. Whether this was the dawning of the Age of Aquarius or the launching of a revolution, the certainty that something of earthshaking importance was underway permeated the atmosphere. No matter how illusory that might appear in hindsight, an all-encompassing movement composed of farmworkers and mutinous GIs, Diggers and Black Panthers was afoot; it unfolded in dramatic demonstrations and the occupation of public buildings, in benefit concerts and in the lyrics of songs. Music was regularly performed outdoors for free, musicians flooding into the new arena the San Francisco Mime Troupe had pioneered with its guerrilla theater, transforming public space into a "liberated zone" of vibrant social interaction and filling it with a dancing multitude.

In all the excitement, enhanced by increasingly sophisticated light shows and psychedelic drugs, you didn't have to watch the band; in some cases, you couldn't even see them. As producer David Rubinson commented, "It wasn't the headliners that drew people to the Fillmore, it was the experience."[14] This led to unfettered experimentation on the part of the musicians, with the active encouragement of the audience. Virtually all of the participants in this exuberant unfolding have said, as Rubinson did: "The defining characteristic was the audience. Failure was not judged. You could be free. A bad set one night and a good one the next, and the mixing together of such a mélange of musicians, it was the audience that nurtured this." Or, as sound engineer Paul Stubblebine put it: "The audience not only let the bands stretch, but showed appreciation when they did. You'd have three bands, and then the jam. The last two hours was this experimentation, and the audience stayed."[15]

The "mélange of musicians" was greater than the sum of its parts. Diversity was more than simply many different things. Diversity seemed limitless; it was definitely not limited by customs or norms, and breaking boundaries quickly became a principle and a goal. As programs grew bolder, the expectations and explorations of the audience grew with them. This combined with another element that was, in fact, unprecedented. Encouraging unity in diversity, lending social purpose to celebration, were the large number of benefit concerts held at the Fillmore, the Avalon, and other venues. Virtually every major struggle or movement from Vietnam War resistance to black liberation and from the farmworkers to the Chicano Moratorium held concerts to raise funds, rally support, and, above all, to raise consciousness. The posters of the era tell the story eloquently.[16] Even a cursory glance at posters from 1965 to 1969 indicates both the diversity of performance and the sheer quantity and regularity of benefits.

The fact that an audience gathered to hear music they had never heard before and to support political struggle in which they may or may not have been directly participating points to an astonishing conclusion: the audience was decisive in making the changes by which the music of the era was defined. Not only were they the show as their own focus of attention but they created the possibility and inspiration for the adventurous exploration of music. This is not to take away from the immeasurable talents of the musicians themselves; musicians are, after all, the ones who make music, including innovations in it. But the audience was consistent enough and discerning enough to propel musicians through the barriers erected by the music industry and the status quo. The public participated in the music-making process in a manner different from conventional concertgoers who simply applaud louder or softer to register their degree of satisfaction. Not only did they dance, but they encouraged the imaginative and discouraged the banal and did so on a regular basis. The changes thus produced were qualitative and can be heard in the music itself even before it took the world by storm or became the banner at festivals like Woodstock. If anything, the quantitative increase—which was in fact exponential—was a product of this qualitative shift and not the other way round. In other words, the audience grew as its effect on music was felt. More people came because more people heard what was happening to music because they came to hear it. For a brief period, this reinforcing process was powerful enough to wrest control from the authorities. That it did not last almost goes without saying. But undeniably, for a moment in time, music and musician were set free.

The People's Republic of Music

The pace of events was itself a factor in creating the sense of an insurrectionary, liberating moment. Simultaneously, the speed with which change occurred confirmed music's decisive role. This did not, however, mark a return to the time-honored practices by which "political" or "protest" songs were made, rather it produced a different, unanticipated result: music itself suddenly challenged the status of the word. Hitherto, conventional wisdom had it that the lyrics to songs, the titles of instrumental music, or the stated convictions of musicians were what determined music's sociopolitical content. From Joe Hill to Woody Guthrie, from Pete Seeger to Bob Dylan, it was understood, especially by the Left—Old *and* New—that music's message was actually conveyed by words and/or the commitments of the musicians. This logic was now upended and superseded by the astonishing presence of an unclassifiable, multidimensional *sound* that was furthermore the clarion call and basis of unity for the broad ranks of youth flocking in ever-increasing numbers to concert sites. The perplexity with which this was greeted by right-wing politicians and pundits such as Ronald Reagan or William F. Buckley was not surprising. But, as Ralph Gleason would pointedly remark, it threw liberals and radicals into confusion, as well.[17] This noisy, blaring cacophony was a threat to reasonable discourse and rational judgment. How could it possibly aid in building a social movement necessary to change the world?

Yet the fact that society's "reason" had produced the madness of nuclear war and the phobias of racism unleashed music as society's conscience, its most unimpeachable and uncompromising judge. It's not that "everything is political," as the saying went at the time, but rather that the good, the beautiful, and the true were unattainable by rational argument. A generation appealed to music precisely because music moved the body and the soul in a manner no words or authority could. Indeed, music manifested the good, the beautiful, and the true, and it did so on a regular basis.

The point remains obscure due in part to the orthodoxy adhered to by historians, journalists, and political or cultural theorists. As mentioned earlier, many books about music in the Sixties rely almost entirely on the titles and lyrics to songs or the public statements of famous musicians to determine the social effects of music.[18] Such reasoning is supported by the fact that there *were* many songs and musicians in the

Sixties explicitly stating their political convictions. Furthermore, these can be compared to other songs and musicians that did not, which seems to validate the argument. Yet this line of thinking rests on two fallacious premises. First, words are needed to tell us what music means. Second, music's main function is *accompaniment* for other arts and social practices. While few would deny that musical movements have deliberately sought to make music (without words) serve revolutionary ends,[19] it is nonetheless assumed that verbal explanation is required for them to take effect.

Political convictions expressed in words were not unique to the Sixties. And most songs and musicians in the Sixties were not political in any conventional sense of the word. So, what made music politically subversive at the time?

At this historic juncture Plato's famous maxim, "The musical modes are never changed without changes in the most important of a city's laws" became urgently relevant. Indeed, it was invoked, perhaps first by Ralph Gleason, but in any case by many commentators at the time. We'll explore this in depth in Chapter 6. But that music's ancient rivalry with the state burst into open confrontation cannot be overlooked. As Ngugi wa Thiong'o put it:

> The struggle between the artist and the state can best be seen in performance in general and in the battle over performance space in particular. . . . With the emergence of the state, the artist and the state became not only rivals in articulating the laws, moral or formal, that regulate life in society, but also rivals in determining the manner and circumstances of their delivery.[20]

The state (referred to at the time as the system) included the government, of course, but also the music industry that colluded with the government to redirect rebellion into harmless but profitable avenues. If anything defines the Sixties, however, it is the radicalization of millions of young people as they were propelled into active opposition to the war in Vietnam and support for the black liberation struggle. In this social context music—especially music deriving from the descendants of African slaves—became the banner around which a generation rallied. While the songs of the civil rights movement and the folk music revival blazed a trail that established music's unrivaled importance, that era was above all defined by participatory singing. The next generation made dancing—albeit dancing of a special type—the defining characteristic. Physical movement, unleashed by rhythm, but uninhibited by any formal steps or patterns, demonstrated the power of music to transform a mass of differentiated individuals into a communal gathering. Moreover, such bacchanalian revels were self-aware. Participants knew what they were doing and why. In combination with performance sites and methods of delivery, the festival directly challenged laws and social customs, at the same time as it violated norms established by the music business. Within a short time, music was quite literally legislating on a wide range of social behavior from authority and authenticity to sexual and social mores, from dress codes and intoxicants to consciousness and liberation. The more the state (or system) tried to reassert its dominance, the more it delegitimized itself and legitimated its rival.

Coda

"Making music to change the world," therefore, has three distinct points of reference. First, the phrase was used by active participants, including those who shaped events, to describe what they were doing and what they hoped to achieve.[21] Second, "making music to change the world" refers more generally to music's role in the service of social and revolutionary movements. Examples of such music are abundant, and from the world over. Some of this music was well known in the Sixties, appearing in the repertoires of musicians dear to the hearts of a generation coming of age.[22] Finally, the phrase encapsulates a broader, more universal aspiration that neither began nor ended in San Francisco or in the Sixties.

Making music to change the world remains a salient feature of music-making as a human capacity and activity. Its very existence poses a challenge to claims made by the authorities—be they state or industry representatives—that music's true calling is to entertain or to provide solemnity to official functions. This, furthermore, explains what would seem to be a paradoxical phenomenon: the extraordinary attention paid to music ever since the Reagan/Thatcher counterrevolution that immediately followed the 1960s and '70s. That subject is beyond the scope of this chapter, but it is important to note that the general strategy of the state after the Sixties was to avoid the errors of the post–World War II period, especially the failed attempts to marginalize and suppress folk music and rock 'n' roll. Indeed, the exact opposite strategy has been employed, celebrating music's unique properties and embracing music as a sign of liberal democracy's tolerance for diversity and defense of individual liberty. To a large extent this has amounted to nothing more than a vast proliferation, an attempt to drown oppositional views in a sea of such plenitude that none may hear anything but a din. Nevertheless, music to change the world continues to be made. There may never again be a convergence of historical, musical, and political factors enabling music to play the extraordinary role it did in the Sixties, but whatever circumstances prevail, music will always be called upon to serve the struggle for human emancipation.

CHAPTER 4

Making Music to Change the World: Authority and Authenticity

"Authenticity remains essential:
once you can fake it, you've got it made."
—Samuel Goldwyn (movie mogul)

"Hey, you know something people?
I'm not black
But there's a whole lots a times
I wish I could say I'm not white"
—The Mothers of Invention,
"Trouble Every Day," 1965

By the late 1950s, authenticity had become an issue of passionate concern to growing numbers of young people. Brought to prominence in American thought by folklore studies and existential philosophy, authenticity was more popularly represented by the folk music revival, on the one hand, and by literature, exemplified by Jack Kerouac's *On the Road*, on the other. Cold War America was so steeped in hucksterism and fakery, not to mention hypocrisy, that authenticity became a lodestar and a practical matter, especially for young musicians.[1] This was not political in any conventional sense; it was an aesthetic or spiritual quest. As Norman Mailer put it, "We are a Faustian Age determined to meet the Lord or the Devil before we are done, and the ineluctable ore of the authentic is our only key to the lock."[2] Yet the problems authenticity had to confront were complicated by the twin incubi of race and commerce that forever menaced even its most sincere pursuit. The oppression of black people and the commercial exploitation of black music were indissolubly linked, and no one even vaguely interested in popular culture could ignore that. What erupted in the wake of the civil rights movement and the folk music revival was conditioned by these concerns, but it also represented an escalation and a *break* with the terms previously set for the conflict. When Black Power was first enunciated, coinciding with massive urban unrest throughout the United States, the question of authenticity took on a decidedly more confrontational tone. Since this was accompanied by the vast expansion in the popularity of urban black music, especially rhythm and blues and soul, there could be no escaping the fact that in both music and politics, to paraphrase Sam Cooke, a change was gonna come. In fact, it already had.

This process has to be recounted in some detail, not only to appreciate how it transpired but to explain why music gained unparalleled social importance. In doing so, we encounter specific distortions that have been fostered by interested parties, especially those in the music industry and their mouthpieces among rock critics and historians who are guided more by fame than by underlying causes and effects. Fame, in many cases, is a manufactured product corresponding little or not at all to what actually makes history or changes social relations. According to this logic, many of the most important social actors of the Sixties, including important musicians, simply did not exist. Perhaps more to the point, fame is often a ruse by which self-appointed authority arrogates to itself the power to determine what is authentic. Makers of a phony substitute have therefore the authority to say it is not a phony substitute but a genuine fake! This twisted reasoning and warping of history obscures the more pertinent fact that the authenticity project collapsed because it had to "face the music." Facing the music meant acknowledging music-making practices (such as collaboration between musicians and combinations of form that violated industrial norms) as well as rapidly unfolding political events.

What in fact transpired, and the quest for authenticity had to confront, was that the black liberation struggle and resistance to the Vietnam War ripped the mask off American identity. White supremacy and imperialism were laid bare. For young white people (especially white musicians), it became imperative to *stop being white* and *start being human*. This could not mean a return to the image of the White Negro, to Harry the Hipster, Mezz Mezzrow, Lenny Bruce, or even His Royal Hipness,

Lord Buckley, as brilliant as Buckley was. Rather, the situation demanded the forging of a new identity, purged of blissful ignorance and infused with genuine hipness, that is, hip to the fact that the system caused suffering and injustice and had to be overcome by any means necessary.

One example illustrates the foregoing. On his album *Honkey Blues*, Doug Sahm sang: "Are inlaws really outlaws? Civil war is comin' on. Vibrations all across the nation, ten million people can't be wrong." To be an outlaw, or a freak, was to subtract oneself from the "national consensus" and to declare one's independence from the white identity constructed by a racist order. Titling an album using a term employed by blacks to ridicule whites, Sahm (a young Texan transplanted to San Francisco) went beyond self-deprecation, boldly declaring that more was demanded than covering over "whiteness" with costumes and hip lingo. To stop being white meant rejecting "whiteness" as a source of privilege and superiority, because in the domain of music, the masters were not white and superior ability was not determined by white skin privilege. On the contrary, the standards by which musical quality was judged were set by Ray Charles not Mitch Miller, Aretha Franklin not Patti Page. Proof of this assertion lay not in the lyrics but in the music: how it was made and what it sounded like. From the compositions to the performance, *Honkey Blues* is definitively rhythm and blues, as groovy and soulful as anything made in Memphis or Detroit.[3]

Don't Call Me Nigger, Whitey

These developments did not, indeed *could not*, involve only young white people. On the contrary, all young people were swept up in the ferment, no longer willing to accept the roles society had assigned them. "Popular music and Black power merged in *Ebony* magazine when a summer 1967 issue declared it the year of 'Retha, Rap and Revolt'. For a mainstream publication like *Ebony* to link the Queen of Soul, militant SNCC leader H. Rap Brown and the wave of ghetto riots that were sweeping across the nation in one succinct headline signaled a major paradigm shift in Black America," writes Pat Thomas in *Listen, Whitey!*[4] Rap Brown's speech "Die, Nigger, Die!" and Nina Simone's song "To Be Young, Gifted and Black" marked the line between before and after. The happy Negro and the benevolent white were dead. Even the hipster, the "White Negro" of the Beat era, was behind the times. Though a profound, decades-long interchange between artists, intellectuals, and political radicals had once given hipness a greater substance than its mass media image might suggest, new conditions had produced new demands, and young people were not content with being a *subculture*. As Eldridge Cleaver wrote at the time, "The characteristics of the white rebels which most alarm their elders—the long hair, the new dances, their love of Negro music, their use of marijuana, their mystical attitude toward sex—are all tools of their rebellion. They have turned these tools against the totalitarian fabric of American society—and they mean to change it."[5]

As black insurgency asserted the dignity and humanity of black people it necessarily confronted *mental* slavery, the poisoned chalice of assimilation. As Last Poet member Abiodun Oyewole put it, "The truth was, many of us still saw ourselves as 'niggers' and slaves. This was a mindset that had to change if there was ever to be Black Power."[6] "Wake Up, Niggers," "Black Is Beautiful," and "Black and Proud," all evinced the rejection of an ethos, which had in fact been imposed, especially by the music business. "From the time popular music had been recorded, there had never been complete exclusion of Negro music," Charlie Gillette explains, "but there had been two kinds of assimilation. One of these was to accept Black singers who adopted styles that were specially developed for the white audience (and so had little relation to styles popular with the Black audience). The other was to take a song or style from the Black culture and reproduce it using a white singer."[7] In this sense, to stop being white applied to everybody, albeit in distinct ways. For people of color, it meant rejecting the hierarchical structure whereby the lighter your skin the higher your status, the more "white" you sounded—that is, the more like Bing Crosby—the better you were. Put another way: the closer you resembled the white supremacist *ideal*, the greater your chance of "success."

What young people suddenly confronted in the Sixties was the unraveling of a royal scam. Everything, even rock 'n' roll, had hitherto been a fraud perpetrated to maintain American apartheid. Now music demanded that its sources of inspiration and the purposes it served be seen in the light of day. This meant more than the frank acknowledgement of black music's crucial role, it meant acknowledging the rich musical legacies of many peoples that had been obscured and suppressed under the regime of racism. This of course required that the genuine be distinguished from the fake. But music could now be used to make that distinction rather than to hide it. Authenticity was defined *against* the music industry, *against* racism, and *against* the plastic, uptight, straight society responsible for an intolerable situation.

As discussed in the previous chapter, new performance sites were crucial to this development. These venues presented on a continuous and regular basis music of such variety and incongruity that it was possible to imagine a future, made present by music, toward which all could strive. The bringing together of all ethnicities, all styles, even all ages of musicians enabled the envisioning of a society transformed. Overcoming the violent, destructive conflicts by which society was beset was self-evidently possible since it was happening on this stage, tonight!

This encouraged experimentation and collaboration among musicians who would have previously been segregated, socially and musically. Outstanding examples are the bands led by Miles Davis, Ornette Coleman, and Sly Stone. In Sly's case, an interracial band was a deliberate statement.[8] Such exploration became a defining characteristic of the period, producing musical hybrids that challenged prevailing notions of authenticity. Indeed, a gauntlet was thrown down by music, musicians, and audiences alike—authentic *liberation* not a phony substitute.

Music and the Construction of Whiteness

The struggles of black people challenged a model constructed by the music industry that had not only ripped off black music and musicians but had made the white imitator a "star." From blackface minstrelsy to Pat Boone, the pattern was established. In 1930, in his study of what he called "The American Music Racket," Isaac Goldberg observed: "From the first, the white has been under some psychologic compulsion to mimic the Negro, at first in ridicule and superiority, then in understanding and sympathy."[9] In 1967, Ralph Gleason would say much the same thing: "The drive behind all American popular music performers, to a greater or lesser extent . . . has been to sound like a Negro."[10] What Goldberg and Gleason failed to acknowledge, however, is that this "psychologic compulsion" or "drive" was an industrial product, not a "natural" occurrence, and it had two purposes: the propagation of white supremacy and the replacement of music spontaneously arising from the populace with a manufactured substitute.

From the outset a case of mistaken identity must be fully exposed— music is one thing, the music industry is another. Furthermore, music and business are not joined in happy communion but are locked in a life and death struggle to determine each other's fate. On the one hand, the music industry claims not only to be the best means of providing society's musical needs but also the best judge of musical quality. On the other hand, its monopoly of production and distribution is constantly threatened by music's origins among the people and the basic fact that music is an activity, not only a product. People do not need an industry to make music and never did. There is a vast repertoire of music, passed down through the centuries, that originates among common people of different backgrounds. Before there was a "white race," diverse populations arrived in America bringing with them living musical traditions. English, Irish, Scottish, Italian, German, and many other European peoples brought with them rich legacies that circulated in churches, workplaces, union halls, and at community gatherings. These diverse streams converged under new circumstances, both maintaining tradition and cross-pollinating in a way that is always and everywhere the result of music being shared. This took place all over North America, but it was in the American South that it would develop the distinct musical features that remain recognizable to this day.

At an even more fundamental level, slaves and their descendants created a musical legacy that defined America. As Du Bois wrote in *The Souls of Black Folk*, "there is no true American music but the wild sweet melodies of the Negro slave; the American fairy tales and folk-lore are Indian and African; and, all in all, we Black men seem the sole oasis of simple faith and reverence in a dusty desert of dollars and smartness. Will America be poorer if she replace . . . her vulgar music with the soul of the Sorrow Songs?"[11] This stunning observation. was confirmed by all the evidence. By the mid-nineteenth century, the systematic gathering of folklore, especially slave songs and spirituals, was well underway. And it was not only slaves and their descendants who were aware of the powerful effect this music had. Its influence was indelibly stamped on the American musical landscape. Everywhere, from rustic shack to urban concert hall, black musicians brought the soul-stirring virtuosity born of their experience. Indeed, in 1903, when Du Bois was writing *The Souls of Black Folk*, James Weldon Johnson and his brother John were composing Lift Every Voice and Sing, the "Negro National Anthem."

On the one hand, music was being composed and performed by the common people long before there was anyone buying or selling it. On the other, the establishment of music publishing, especially after the

Civil War, based itself, not only on the expropriation of this music but on its replacement. This strategy had two components, comprising the twin pillars upon which the music industry was built.

First and foremost was the minstrel show, or minstrelsy, involving blackface performers imitating in speech, music, and dance, the behavior of black people. The song, "Jump Jim Crow," by blackface performer T.D. "Daddy" Rice, provided not only the model for a type of song and its performance but the name given to the laws that were imposed to re-enslave black people in the South after the Civil War. This song is more than symbolic however. Published in 1832, it was widely popularized, establishing, even before the Civil War, the method by which black music could at once be expropriated and turned against its makers.

Extensions of minstrelsy and blackface were the coon song, the cakewalk and various musical or dance "fads" based on the same racist premise. Music publishing thrived on this traffic, even in some cases employing black composers and performers to mock their own people— for example, "All Coons Look Alike to Me" was written by a black man.[12] It is important to recall that blackface and minstrelsy continued well into the twentieth century. The first successful, feature-length talking picture, *The Jazz Singer*, released in 1927, featured Al Jolson in blackface.

The second component was a formula for the manufacture and sale of songs that could be copyrighted and monopolized by publishers. This led to what is known as Tin Pan Alley, at one time an actual district in New York City where music publishers and songwriters were concentrated. The Copyright Act of 1909 and its supplement in a Supreme Court decision of 1917 laid the legal foundation necessary for the music industry to flourish. In sum, the two pillars of the American music business are the expropriation of black music with its concomitant promotion of white supremacy and the substitution of copyrightable songs for the music made by the common people themselves.

Meanwhile, black people not only waged a struggle for emancipation but developed out of the rich soil of their own music new forms that would ultimately take the world by storm. By the time the music industry had established its current structure, ragtime was all the rage—and so was the model of the pale-faced imitation. In 1911, "Alexander's Ragtime Band," a song composed by Irving Berlin, became a big hit in the United States. There is some evidence that Berlin borrowed (to use the polite term) the music from a song that Scott Joplin had written and submitted to Berlin's publisher.[13] In any case, the song made explicit lyrical reference to a widely popular musical style that had been created by black people and was associated with them in public consciousness. These two, interrelated phenomena exemplify the fact that while co-optation was and remains a favored technique, its objective is not only to economically exploit a product but also to suppress a threat. Music poses this threat in a number of ways, but the music of oppressed people is always intimately bound up with their struggle for freedom. This is not some vague or ephemeral substance rendered nostalgic by the success the music industry undoubtedly achieved. Rather, there are concrete musical expressions, particular songs, and entire genres that are living proof of this ongoing conflict. Recall, for example, that 1911 was also the year that Joe Hill's "The Preacher and the Slave" was written and disseminated widely by the Industrial Workers of the World. Indeed, popular music in America always contained songs of rebellion, albeit in different forms corresponding to different social groups. Opposing minstrelsy and Tin Pan Alley, music was used in the struggle to abolish slavery, to build the labor movement, and to unite all people in the struggle for freedom.

Each successive generation since the Civil War has rediscovered what the music industry sought to erase. The period between World Wars I and II can in musical terms be characterized by the collection and publication of great quantities of people's music deemed unfit for commercial exploitation. The work of John and Alan Lomax is perhaps the best-known example of this, but there were numerous others. The song collecting of Lawrence Gellert is one case in point. The album he produced, *Negro Songs of Protest*, is an outstanding instance, both in terms of the character of the songs collected (represented by the title), but also its fate—until very recently it has been consigned to the shadows.[14]

Shortly after World Wart II this pattern resumed, most notably with Harry Smith's *Anthology of American Folk Music*, published by Folkways Records in 1952.[15] This collection became the "bible" of the folk scene in New York, San Francisco, and elsewhere, its eighty-four songs carefully selected by Smith from over ten thousand 78's he'd found disused in record stores, secondhand stories, and in private collections. For those "in the know," Harry Smith's *Anthology* posed the question of authenticity in another way. Smith deliberately chose recordings that were made for commercial release implying that this made them *more* authentic than the songs collected by folklorists such as the Lomaxes. That is, more authentic because they were what people had chosen to buy. While this is a questionable distinction in musicological terms, it nonetheless highlights the fact that these recordings represented a period of transition in American life, including the technological development of recording itself. What sharpens the authenticity question, however, is not how Smith defined it, but what was has been largely overlooked in all except Gellert's work. There is a large body of music composed and performed by class-conscious workers such as Joe Hill, Sarah Ogan Gunning, Florence Reece, Paul Robeson, and of course Woody Guthrie, all of which is authentic by any definition of the term but somehow doesn't meet either the folklorists' or Smith's peculiar criteria. One book, published in 1967, proves this beyond any doubt. *Hard Hitting Songs for Hard-Hit People* by Alan Lomax, Woody Guthrie, and Pete Seeger compiles many songs that belie the notion that the music made by the common people was confined to lamentation and resignation.[16]

The interwar period can also be characterized by the Great Migration of poor southern whites and blacks, who brought their music with them.[17] The twin influences of preservation and migration had effects that are only superficially contradictory. While some, like Pete Seeger, would find a great source of inspiration in the old, rural traditions, others would explore the new possibilities available in the northern cities. The former would lead to the folk music revival, the latter to jazz and rhythm and blues. What was not lost on any of these musicians, however, was the tortured relationship between authority and authenticity.

The reason conflict was often posed in these terms was the result of musical practices, not arcane academic debates. The enduring presence of old music, passed down through the generations, meant that musicians and audiences had reference points that made comparison with the novelties produced by the music industry inevitable. That old songs retained a power and vitality untainted by commerce was self-evident. (One example of this enduring phenomenon is the soundtrack to the Coen brothers film *O Brother, Where Art Thou?*, in which old songs sound as alive and fresh as if they'd been written today.)

At the same time, incessant pressure from the music industry to submit to its norms clashed mightily with musicians' sensibilities and creative inclinations. Composers and musicians were told what was acceptable, that success required obedience, and that listening to their "inner voice," or their conscience, led to failure. The resulting conflict with authority, therefore, was most often not over political rights; it was against the phony or artificial. This had political ramifications, of course. The phony and the artificial were closely intertwined with racist stereotypes and the construction of whiteness: the jigaboo and the peckerwood, "race" and "hillbilly" music charts, and so forth.

In the context of music-making practices, policing by authority made authenticity a means of self-defense. In the broader context of a society in turmoil, music became the motive and the means for young people seeking to discover or invent a new identity. Music thus became not only the voice to which young people most attentively listened but also the voice with which they spoke. What follows will illustrate this process by looking at the experiences of a cross-section of the young musicians who were active in the Bay Area in the Sixties.

Be for Real: The Quest for Authenticity

Peter Albin and his brother Rodney grew up in the South Bay, listening to the rock 'n' roll of the 1950s on AM radio, seeing Elvis on *Ed Sullivan* and following the various dance crazes that came and went as regularly as the seasons.[18] But when they took up playing music themselves, they began with folk. At first, this was by way of the Bay Area–based Kingston Trio. Through devoted research, the brothers quickly discovered, however, that there was much more to this music than the squeaky clean, college prep variety. Inspired by the New Lost City Ramblers, they formed a band called the Liberty Hill Aristocrats that included Pigpen (later of the Grateful Dead), whose father hosted a blues-oriented radio program. The search for kindred spirits and opportunities to perform led the Albins to the Boar's Head, an unused loft in a bookstore in Palo Alto where they began hosting hootenannies in 1961. They had a coffee machine, a tip jar, and lots of dedication. The whole operation was volunteer-run. Peter found Jerry Garcia playing at Kepler's Bookstore nearby, and invited him to the Boar's Head to play, which he subsequently did along with Robert Hunter and others who would later call themselves the Wildwood Boys. Also joining in this small but thriving circle were Jorma (at the time, "Jerry") Kaukonen and Paul Kantner, who would soon join San Francisco folk musician Marty Balin in Balin's new electric band. Also frequenting the Boar's Head was David Freiberg who would go on to cofound another electric band vital to the era. That this trajectory was followed by the founders of Big Brother and the Holding Company, the Grateful Dead,

Jefferson Airplane, and Quicksilver Messenger Service is obviously significant. Even more significantly, this charts the musical and social trajectory for a large segment of what became the San Francisco rock scene.

All these young musicians were listening to KPFA, specifically Gertrude Chiarito's *Midnight Special*, where authenticity was the cardinal virtue being proselytized on a weekly basis by way of recordings that rarely if ever got anywhere near the "Hit Parade." These were supplemented by live, on-air performances by local and visiting folk or acoustic blues musicians. At the same time, there was a loose network of coffeehouses throughout the Bay Area where these musicians could perform: the Cabale and the Jabberwock in Berkeley; the Fox and Hound, the Coffee Gallery, and the Drinking Gourd in San Francisco; St. Michael's Alley and the Boar's Head in Palo Alto; the Offstage in San Jose and numerous others.

Significantly, the Albins went from organizing the Boar's Head hoots to putting on a folk festival at San Mateo City College in 1962. When they moved up to the city to attend San Francisco State College, Rodney organized a folk festival there, featuring Sam Hinton, Mike Seeger, and Jean Ritchie.[19] A young folk singer from Texas whom Peter had met at KPFA was also on the bill but failed to show up. Her name was Janis Joplin. Between 1963 and 1965 the folk festivals at San Francisco State would host artists that included Barbara Dane, the Chambers Brothers, the Blues Project, and Richard and Mimi Farina.[20]

These formative experiences taught musicians to love and seek music that was intimate and altruistic, rather than commercial. In fact, an anticommercial attitude became a principle that these musicians would carry with them into their electrified future.

Meanwhile, in the largely black suburb of Vallejo, a young Sylvester Stewart was honing his musical skills. Though his ambition would lead him to unabashedly pursue commercial success, he was already fully aware of the criteria that black culture applied to determine the authentic by virtue of being steeped in gospel and rhythm and blues. By the middle 1960s, the term "soul" was in widespread use, both as a name for a genre of black music and as a way to define a quality of that music. Soul expressed emotional and spiritual integrity born of lived experience: to have paid your dues and to spread the news. "Be for Real." "Tell It Like It Is." "Tell the Truth." These song titles express the attributes sought in the music accompanying their lyrics and, for that matter, any music worthy of one's attention. Sly Stone had to have known that, just as he had to have known that was what the public he wanted to reach demanded. As former Black Panther and historian Billy X Jennings put it:

> Sly Stone was influenced by the Bay Area. We're at a special time in our history, and knowledge is being passed down to us from people we don't know. So people are having leaps of consciousness every day. You had this mecca in Northern California between SF State, Stanford, and UC Berkeley. We had this trove of information swirling. Everybody was into reading at that time. You could find anybody on the AC Transit reading a *Red Book*, anybody. Because people was looking for that knowledge, for something different. They were looking to raise their consciousness, to come out of that darkness of the '50s and early '60s.[21]

We'll trace Sly's path in greater detail later on, since his music played an indispensable role from the beginning to the end of the San Francisco musical renaissance; indeed it *marked* both the beginning and the end. But before doing so, it's important to look at other crucial examples of how similar lines were being drawn in comparable ways by people from dissimilar backgrounds.

In Marin County, a different group of young people found itself drawn to rhythm and blues. The teenagers who would become the Sons of Champlin were, like many of their suburban counterparts, listening to Top 40 radio and following all of the latest musical and dance fads, but ultimately finding their inspiration in James Brown, Ray Charles, Lou Rawls, and other urban black music. Along with any musician's appreciation of "chops"—the craft of writing, arranging, and performing well—the Sons and other young "soul disciples" shared a finely tuned sense of what was jive and what was genuine. In fact, as aficionados, they prided themselves on this ability. At another time and place, they might have followed what was a normal route into the music business, working the college and high school dance circuit and the various clubs and bars in the Bay Area, but their visits to the Fillmore Auditorium sent them in another direction. As Bill Champlin tells it:

> We had a manager who was this artist/photographer named Fred Roth, who, in order to be closer to the scene, was slinging burgers at the Fillmore. And we were always going to the Fillmore and

ended up talking to this guy with radical long hair, and he was seriously connected with Gary Snyder, along with Allen Ginsberg, Allan Watts, even Tim Leary. He's the guy that turned us onto all the shit you needed to be turned onto. With the different businesses in the U.S., the corporate versus the . . . It wasn't really political but it was about the ecology and stuff none of us had ever thought about. He was the guy who hipped us to all of that, and he was the guy who turned us on to LSD.[22]

There are several reasons to call attention to this particular group, the first being that much of their story is so typical. Many young musicians in the Bay Area were inspired by the same things as the Sons, consciously orienting themselves around urban black music, rather than folk or rock 'n' roll. While the Sons never achieved the fame of Sly or the Grateful Dead, they were considered one of the best and most important bands in the Bay Area, because they raised the musical bar and broadened its range, defying media stereotypes like "acid rock," "folk rock," or any of the other dubious labels that obscure the actual sound and diversity of the music that was being made. They also put the lie to music industry and the mass media claims that the best music of the era was made by the "stars" who produced the "hits." Along with the Sons, groups such as Mother Earth, Mad River, the Loading Zone, and Cold Blood were not only making good, sometimes great, music; they were representative of what would become a wholesale assault on AM radio formatting, the three-minute song, and rigid adherence to formulas determined by music business hacks. As the Sons sound engineer Paul Stubblebine put it: "The Sons were part of a collective of bands called West Pole run by Ron Polte; all were thinking collectively. We honestly thought we were changing the world. That it wasn't just about getting high, but that this was the dawning of a new age, and we were gonna do things differently."[23]

Yet another example: in Oakland and San Francisco's Mission District, music originating in the Spanish-speaking Americas—Puerto Rico, Cuba, and Mexico, in particular—was deeply rooted in the community. Musicians like the Escovedo family were personally and musically connected to established local composers and performers, including Cal Tjader, Vince Guaraldi, and Ed Kelly, all of whom were enjoying widespread popularity in the early 1960s, during what some called the "second golden age of jazz." Brothers Pete, Coke, and Phil Escovedo performed together and lent their skills to bands playing in a network of clubs that was the Latin music equivalent of the folk scene. Residents of the Mission District, the Santana family, were steeped in the Mariachi and Norteño musical traditions of northern Mexico, with the elder Santana teaching his children to play at a young age. In fact, one vital but often overlooked component of San Francisco in the Sixties was the profound influence of Latin music, particularly Afro-Cuban, and the groups that would introduce its influence into rock. Santana and Azteca are famous examples of many such groups vital to the era. Without this component, one cannot fully appreciate other causes and effects. It's doubtful, for example, that limited to a handful of bands emerging from the folk scene, San Francisco would have become the mecca for music that it did, not to mention the international breadth of its influence, extending even to Africa and Latin America. On the other hand, Latin rock to a large extent came about because of San Francisco and what transpired there in the Sixties thereby providing a stunning example of how music and music-making were transformed.[24]

It is important to note, however, that the largest influence in Oakland and the Mission District was American black music, specifically rhythm and blues. Most of the young bands forming in the high schools and Boys Clubs were, like Sly Stone in Vallejo, playing music they heard on black radio, specifically KSOL. This included music, such as that of Mongo Santamaria, which broke through jazz, Afro-Cuban, and popular music barriers to reach young working-class kids who otherwise might not have heard it. But still, most young bands were playing soul and rhythm and blues inspired by Motown in Detroit, Stax in Memphis, and the ubiquitous and incomparable James Brown.

Age restrictions meant most performances took place at schools, churches, and social functions. But there had long been a circuit of bars and nightclubs that featured dance music (some salsa, even some country and western, but mainly rhythm and blues) that musicians could "graduate" into as they got older and better. This street level, multiethnic, working-class stew is as responsible for the San Francisco musical renaissance as any other. Contrary to the impression created by the disproportionate attention paid to the Haight-Ashbury and the "hippies," the musical and social links forged between the Mission and the East Bay were decisive in two particular ways. First, they immediately infused the "rock scene" with the skills and stylistic approach born of this culture. Second, rock 'n' roll was already beginning to move away from the classic format pioneered by Chuck Berry, Little Richard and others. By the Sixties, bands ranging from Trini Lopez playing an electrified version of Pete Seeger's "If I Had a Hammer (the Hammer Song)" to Booker T. and the MGs playing the instrumental "Green Onions" were all loosely associated (labeled rock 'n' roll, rhythm and blues, or soul) and could be heard in cover versions by teenaged bands in the Bay Area.

Equally important and similarly overlooked is how other parts of the city were harvesting the seeds sown a decade earlier and whose shoots first bloomed under the influence of the Beatles. North Beach is usually associated with the Beats, City Lights, and what at the time was the center of San Francisco's night life: the Broadway clubs featuring popular music and jazz. What is forgotten is that at the time many working-class families lived in the area and sent their kids to Galileo High School or alternatively to one of the two large Catholic high schools, Sacred Heart and Saint Ignatius. This is where Sal Valentino formed one of San Francisco's most important pre-psychedelic era bands, the Beau Brummels, a band that was a crucial link between Sly Stone, who produced them, and Tom Donahue, founder of Autumn Records. Along with the Beau Brummels, Autumn signed other local bands including the Mojo Men, the Vejtables, and the Great! Society. Donahue also hired Sly Stone to produce them. It's no stretch to say that prior to the eruption of 1965, this constellation characterized the San Francisco music scene at least as far as rock 'n' roll was concerned. But this was not limited to the groups actually recorded by Autumn Records.

A whole host of bands came out of this part of the city, most notably, the Hedds.[25] Their name suggests something in itself, as it soon became the term (alternating with "freak") by which participants in the emerging scene would identify themselves. Most importantly, the Hedds and their manager Joy Johnson organized their own dances at venues such as the California Hall for reasons strikingly similar to those of the Family Dog. People between the ages of seventeen and twenty-one were in a social limbo, since laws governing alcohol, public gatherings, and dancing could only be circumvented if you organized your own event. The Hedds were popular enough and savvy enough to know they could pull it off.

While substantial attention has been paid to what unfolded at the Fillmore and Avalon ballrooms, it must not be forgotten that many young musicians from different cultural backgrounds were simultaneously organizing their own shows and drawing together like-minded people outside the confines of venues sanctioned and surveilled by the authorities. None of what transpired in San Francisco in the Sixties was confined to one neighborhood, let alone the Haight-Ashbury. In fact, it was not even limited to San Francisco. It was also taking place in high schools all over the Bay Area. The widespread participation was a key outcome of the Beatles/British Invasion, which encouraged a vast number of young people to play music, and that in itself signaled a cultural shift.

Prior to this period, other activities, from sports to vocational training, were the predominant outlets for youthful creativity. Not only had music been successfully turned into a product for consumption, separating it from its sources among the people themselves, making music was frequently frowned upon by concerned parents, teachers, and society at large. "You have to think of your future, son. Music won't pay your bills." This was, of course, truer for white working-class youth than for their black or Latin counterparts, for whom music (along with sports) could be a way out of the ghetto. But, generally speaking, the fact that it suddenly became possible, even fashionable, to be in a band had serious implications *and* consequences. Before anything like a counterculture existed, thousands of Bay Area teenagers joined groups and played music publicly—not as a hobby, but as a way of life.

Trying to Make It Real, Compared to What?

It was precisely these practices that led to authenticity itself being called into question. The concept had been adopted uncritically from folklore studies and existentialism, which had been particularly influential during the 1940s and '50s. But as musical exploration proceeded at a breakneck pace, musical results challenged the premises on which both folklore and existentialism based their claims. In the case of folklore studies, the question of "who are the folk and what is their music?" is fundamental. As a mass movement rose to challenge the *state*, this question would be cast in a new light. Instead of an idealized figure of undiluted purity, the "folk" reveals itself to be, above all, a political category. Who is a member or citizen of a given community? Who will decide? "We the people" are the folk, are we not? Yet, shrouded in the mists of legend, cloaked in the idylls of romance, the folk are also nonexistent—more like hobbits than any actual people.

The stubborn persistence of such idealization is a product of the foundation of folklore studies itself.[26] The Brothers Grimm and subsequent folklorists chose to define authenticity in a certain way. In an attempt to construct national identities (German, in the Grimm's case), they sought to differentiate the creative expressions of the uneducated or uncivilized masses from those that have "suffered" acculturation by bourgeois norms. *Das Volk*, in the words of Johann Gottfried von Herder, was the organic nation, arising out of a primordial past, bound together by language and certainly not artificially constructed to serve any class or state, king or peasant. It's no accident that this interest in folklore arose during and after the French Revolution, when the figure of the *citizen* became paramount. The sovereign was not the king but the people. In fact, folklore's true inspiration was Jean-Jacques Rousseau, whose influence is difficult to overestimate. Crucial to Rousseau's argument was that "man was born free, and he is everywhere in chains," free because nature is virtuous and in chains because civilization is corrupt. This is also the core attraction of folk music: a longing to return to the bosom of nature, harmonious with the land and with one's fellows unsullied by the mystique of money and servitude to industrial production.

That we are still within Rousseau's horizon cannot be in doubt. Neither can the fact that the rural idyll of which he waxed so eloquent did not exist. For Rousseau, it was utopia, and he knew it. The revolution he was calling for imagined a time before the aristocrat or financier dictated to the artisan or peasant, before masses were huddled in squalid cities full of pestilence, crime, and unrewarded toil. Little wonder that in the wake of the revolutions he inspired, many educated men would go in search of the "noble savage," who was, in fact, all around them. This quest overlooked the fact that an inexorable migration had already begun, first from the country to the city, then from Europe and Africa to America. This process radically transformed the "folk," even though traces of ancient customs remained, in some cases thriving to this day. Consequently, there never was a folk nor could there be, since the great mass of humanity could only be one of two things, either slaves or free citizens. If the former, then they were certainly not noble, even if savage. If the latter, then they had to be included in deciding how society is governed. In historical fact, the *nations* espousing such ideals (in particular the United States and France) mobilized their *citizens* for *imperial* conquest. Their "civilizing mission" rendered the "folk" inhabitants of the realm of fairy tale and myth. As far as music was concerned, there were people making ancient songs on crude instruments alongside people making highly sophisticated music on the latest innovation. This corresponded to a large extent to whether they lived in town or country and who their audiences were. In any case, the origin of the category of the "folk" was political struggle. The quest for the pristine purity of preindustrial life, which was one product of that struggle, could not escape this fact.

As for existentialism, its roots could similarly be traced to Rousseau and the radical critique of Enlightenment rationalism. Through many twists and turns, including contradictory positions taken by its seminal figures, existentialism arrived in San Francisco with the Beats. For the Beats, authenticity was a cry of anguish raised against the hallucinations of Cold War America. The age of mechanical reproduction brought with it a mechanical man, emptied of spirit and filled with programmed responses. Authenticity was the name given to the irreducible essence to which one could seek to attain. The authentic self, as in "to thine own self be true," was the Holy Grail. The absence of God, the destitution of the sacred, and the power of illusion made one's life, death, and meaning one's own self-appointed task. Or, as Adorno would put it, "There was a time when the subject thought itself a small divinity, as well as a law-giving authority, sovereign in the consciousness of its own freedom."[27] Confronting existence, raw and unadorned, meant facing these conditions without remorse. Making a withering critique of the affected mannerisms and herd-like conformity of bourgeois society, authenticity exalted experience, defiance of authority, and the poetic imagination. It's no wonder the Beats were the standard bearers of authenticity or that works like *Howl* and *On the Road* identified the authentic with the Negro and jazz and the inauthentic with Moloch and Madison Avenue. Indeed, some Marxists, like Marshall Berman, sought to link authenticity to its radical roots in Rousseau, "to make modern liberal society keep the promises it has made, to reform it—or revolutionize it—in order to realize the ideals of modern liberalism itself."[28]

This conception was undeniably attractive, but it would come to ruin in the Sixties. A rose by any other name is still a rose, and oppression by any other name is still oppression. Authenticity would prove to be a linguistic sleight of hand, an attempt to create through language a means of excavating a pre-political nature from a prehistoric past to expose the fraud by which technological progress had perverted humanity. It claimed the possibility of a return to where it all began, before there was a lawgiver, before there was even the concept of justice, a return to the Garden before the Fall. While this could be and was construed in a radically antiauthoritarian manner, it was also appropriated by Nazism. Indeed, authority authenticates itself through what it certifies. The authentic is always *authorized* by certificates, copyrights, patents, and judicial review, ultimately guaranteeing rights of *ownership*. To lend a solemnity to their dissembling, authorities (be they the state, the church, or the academy) erect a field of scholarly inquiry that uses specialized language to obscure the conflict it is trying to elide. In his *Jargon of Authenticity*, Adorno systematically dissects the method and the goal:

> That which is empty becomes an *arcanum*: the mystery of being permanently in ecstasy over some numinous thing which is preserved in silence. . . . That is what is being exploited by language, and what becomes the schema of the jargon of authenticity. Its dignified mannerism is a reactionary response to the secularization of death. Language wants to grasp what is escaping, without believing it or naming it. Naked death becomes the meaning of such talk, a meaning it would have only in something transcendent. The falseness of giving meaning, nothingness as something, is what creates the linguistic mendacity.[29]

The inhabitants of the "New World" Columbus "discovered" knew well where such authenticity leads. As Buffy Sainte-Marie sang, "My country 'tis of thy people you're dying."

The entire authenticity project would eventually collapse into incoherence. Among the most compelling reasons were that music-making simply defied all the categories and significations generated by theorists. In spite of the profound and ever-present effects of racism, musicians of all ethnicities continued to interact, cross-pollinate, and share the joys of music-making itself. In spite of the machinations of the music industry, the enduring effects of mass migration from Europe and Africa to the Americas continued to be expressed in such diverse forms that they could never be completely erased by Tin Pan Alley, minstrelsy, or any other manufactured imitation. As a rallying point for resistance to the draft and imperialist war, music would become the champion of human liberation, creating a context that made it abundantly clear that there were great musicians in every ethnic group and that, pale imitations notwithstanding, they all had soul.

It would not take long for the music industry to restore "order." The brief opening created by the combination of a mass movement and musical innovation would close soon enough, but not before the impact of the black liberation struggle on music was felt by musicians everywhere. The great triumph for black music was that it liberated everybody. Breaking the mold meant that musicians in genres as varied as country, salsa, and Mexican music were emboldened to challenge the status quo, and, to provide but a few examples, Loretta Lynn, Rubén Blades, Los Tigres del Norte, and Creedence Clearwater Revival all seized the opportunity to make music for everyone.[30]

CHAPTER 5

If You're Going to San Francisco: What One Song Tried to Usurp

"Led by our shepherds, we never found
ourselves in the company of freedom
except once—*on the day of its burial*."
—Karl Marx, *Introduction to a Critique
of Hegel's Philosophy of Right*, 1844

"Walked past the wig store
Danced at the Fillmore
I'm completely stoned
I'm hippy and I'm trippy
I'm a gypsy on my own
I'll stay a week and get the crabs and
Take a bus back home
I'm really just a phony
But forgive me
'Cause I'm stoned"
—The Mothers of Invention,
"Who Needs the Peace Corps?" 1968

"If you're going to San Francisco," wafted across America's airwaves in May 1967, instructing listeners to "be sure to wear some flowers in your hair." With the sincerity of a penitent and the solemnity of a priest, the song had you reaching for your staff and a chain of daisies to set out on a pilgrimage to the holy city. As was its purpose. Composed by John Phillips and produced by Lou Adler, "San Francisco (Be Sure to Wear

Flowers in Your Hair)"[1] was an advertising jingle for a music festival they were organizing in Monterey, California, just south of San Francisco.[2] The song itself was a wistful paean to a hippie Neverland bearing scant resemblance, musically or lyrically, to what was erupting in the real San Francisco at the time.

Coming hot on the heels of the Week of Angry Arts and the Spring Mobilization Against the War, as well as preparations for Vietnam Summer and a huge antiwar demonstration in San Francisco on April 15, 1967, "San Francisco" was derisively mocked by anyone even vaguely associated with what the song purported to represent. Indeed, Phillips and Adler were viewed by members of San Francisco's burgeoning music scene as slick sharks from Los Angeles seeking to co-opt and commercialize all that these musicians held dear. Nevertheless, even a silly song can raise a serious question. What, in fact, *had* made San Francisco's reputation? What attracted such interest that not only music industry moguls but all the machinery of the corporate media was mobilized (and has been ever since) to invent a narrative that could not only be sold as entertainment but also be inscribed in the collective consciousness as historical fact?

Before examining the specific reasons Phillips, Adler, and their coterie of industry heavies descended on San Francisco, however, it's worth asking a further question: Why *did* so many young people flock to San Francisco at this time? Previous chapters have explored some of the historical reasons for San Francisco's reputation but what could explain this sudden influx? The answer is inseparable from the massive escalation of the war in Vietnam and the equivalent rise of violent urban unrest that led *Newsweek* to dub the summer of 1967 the "Summer of Discontent," a far cry from the Summer of Love.[3] All of this must also be carefully disentangled from the narrative manufactured by corporate media using wisps of disinformation, rather than simply misrepresenting what actually occurred.

Locating the Local

Given that the prevalent image is one of a mass migration to an empty place whose principle attraction was quaint architecture that no one lived in, it is first necessary to establish that San Francisco's reputation was founded on a local basis. Not that all participants were born and raised there, but the activities that would bring the city its notoriety were conceived and carried out as decidedly local affairs, presented to a local audience and supported by a local network of friends and associates. Because this was an ongoing and increasingly frequent sequence of events, artists, musicians, political activists, and journalists and filmmakers began to come to the city to join in a vibrant exchange between the inside and the outside. Between the summer of 1965 and the summer of 1967, all the principle features of what made San Francisco an epicenter of renaissance and revolution were in full bloom. The system's prime objective became to crush or co-opt this force; had it not been remarkably unsuccessful at doing so, at least for several years, there would be nothing to speak of at present.

It is also of no small importance that army personnel were processed through California on their way to and from the battlefields of Vietnam. Between 1965 and 1968, 222,750 soldiers passed through the Oakland Army Base en route to the Pacific.[4] During the Vietnam War, the Oakland Army Base was the largest military port complex in the world. During the first eight years of the war, more than thirty-seven million tons of cargo to and from Vietnam passed through the base.[5] This brought a large number of young soldiers, sailors, and airmen into direct contact with opposition to the war at its fiercest; it also afforded many of them their first opportunity to identify with those of their own age group who were growing their hair, wearing colorful clothing, and getting high. *Sons and Daughters,* a documentary film made in 1966 by Jerry Stoll, examined the situation and spread the word.[6] The film makes several crucial links between the students marching from UC Berkeley to the Oakland army terminal and their generational counterparts being sent to Vietnam. It also made clear the strategic location of the many defense plants and the army terminal, as well as drawing attention to the overarching importance of the growing opposition to the war. Footage of the action in Berkeley and Oakland is alternated with scenes from the war in Vietnam, with parallels also drawn between Vietnam and the large number of Asian Americans living in the Bay Area. Not coincidentally, *Sons and Daughters* includes a soundtrack made by the Grateful Dead in collaboration with Jon Hendricks, who sings both the title track and another song entitled "Fire in the City."

I am not aware of any attempt to estimate the number of GIs who were among the denizens of the Haight-Ashbury, but innumerable anecdotal references suggest that there were thousands over the war years, and at least dozens, if not hundreds, by 1967. More importantly, by 1967, the influence of radical ideas within the army was getting out of hand as far as the authorities were concerned; the mutinies and fraggings had already begun.[7] There can be little doubt that from the government's perspective, the sensitive nature of the army base made it crucially important that it be monitored and protected. Under no circumstances could the Bay Area be ignored; indeed, every effort had to be made to defuse or derail opposition in the region.

Meanwhile, the Central Valley of California was the site of a great movement to organize farmworkers. In 1965, the United Farm Workers Association launched a massive campaign, including the world-famous grape boycott, which depended to a large extent on organizing efforts in the Bay Area. Such efforts included the long-forgotten publication of a newspaper that at its peak had a readership of more than twenty-five thousand and was the link between the Student Nonviolent Coordinating Committee (SNCC), the UFWA, and the antiwar movement. Appropriately named *The Movement*, this newspaper carried not only news of the struggles being waged but also of important artistic developments, with a particular focus on radical theater.[8] It also carried timely reporting on what was happening in the Haight-Ashbury, not in isolation from but connected to what was happening elsewhere in the Bay Area. Reports, for example, of the numerous assaults on people in the Haight-Ashbury mounted by the San Francisco Police Department linked the repression in that neighborhood to the violence meted out to antiwar demonstrators in Oakland or young people in the Mission District. It should be further noted that *The Movement* and the farmworkers struggle exerted a profound influence in the Mission District and those musical and artistic expressions that sprung into life there at this time.[9]

None of this is to say that the launching of the *Berkeley Barb* and the *San Francisco Oracle* at approximately the same time (1965–1966) were not of tremendous importance and more specific to the constituencies that would later be called the counterculture. The evidence presented by these publications make one thing overwhelmingly clear: from the beginning, what characterized the era was an interweaving of the political and the cultural, not mutually exclusive but mutually *dependent* as sites of conflict and creative exploration. *The Berkeley Barb* certainly made the necessary connections. From the Vietnam Day Committee, to the United Farm Workers, to SNCC, and urban unrest, from the Merry Pranksters, the Acid Tests, the Trips Festival, and Mime Troupe Benefits, the *Barb* reported on the connections and mutually reinforcing effects.[10]

MOVEMENT

SEPTEMBER 1968   VOL. 4 NO. 8

20¢

HAIGHT STREET BLUES P. 3
WILDCATS IN CHICAGO P. 6
CUBAN POEMS, PHOTOS P. 8

HUEY'S TRIAL BEGINS!

photo by Stephen Shames

by Karen Wald

Oakland, California --

Outside the Alameda County Courthouse disciplined Black Panthers, men and women, lead a demonstration of thousands. Free Huey! Set our warrior free! Inside the seventh floor courtroom sits Huey P. Newton, Minister of Defense, charged with first-degree murder. But even as Huey Newton sits in the courtroom, it is America on trial.

Since July 15, the first day of the trial, the Oakland Courthouse has been a scene from a police state. Armed, riot- helmeted guards stand guard at the doors, letting in only those with suitable identification and official business. On the first day twenty deputies stood in the hall outside the courtroom. Since then, between twenty and forty riot police are held in readiness in the basement.

Members of Huey Newton's family were forced to be fingerprinted and photographed before being allowed to enter the courtroom. Lately the cops have searched every person entering the courtroom. The police state atmosphere has incurred the wrath of the press and this, combined with favorable impressions of Huey Newton from interviews, has helped make the mass media coverage relatively fair up to now.

Focus On Politics

In Defense Attorney Charles Garry's opening statement, he explained to the jury the entire history of the Black Panther Party, the Party's Ten Point Program, and described their organizing in the black community.

Given the tone of the previous two weeks of pre-trial motions and jury selection, all aimed at exposing the judicial system and understanding white racism, it came as no surprise that the focus of the defense, at the outset, would be on politics.

Before the first juror was asked a question, Garry moved to quash the entire master panel from which a jury is chosen. The motion was based on the racism inherent in whites and the lack of ghetto and poor representation on a jury selected from voter registration lists.

Garry also pointed out in his motions that a jury selected by a system which allowed the exclusion of those opposed to capital punishment would necessarily result in a "hanging jury" more ready to convict a black man than to acquit

him. Garry hammered not only at the racial composition but the economic class bias of the jury panel.

Expert Testimony

Garry's pre-trial motions were based on several days of expert testimony by social scientists. Dr. Jan Dizard of U.C. cited a study he had made of Oakland and various national studies to indicate that voting lists are a discriminatory method for jury selection.

Floyd Hunter, nationally prominent sociologist who is presently engaged in a study of Oakland's power structure, tried to explain the reasons for the discouragement of black people with government and the standard political processes, and outline the differences between the West Oakland ghetto and East Oakland.

Jury Commissioner Schnarr was convinced of the method's fairness but his testimony revealed that "no response" was the chief eliminator of prospective jurors, from people who had moved or could not be located. Excuses for non-service came most often from persons who would suffer severe economic hardship; the poor are thus exluded.

Judge Monroe Freidman took a consistantly myopic view of the testimony. He constantly asked that the sociologists confine themselves to only Alameda County, and voter registration. "If any black people are prevented from registering to vote in Alameda County, I want to know about it", said the Judge. He didn't want to know about much else, or he would have listened to some of the psychological and sociological factors which effectively prevent black registration.

Capital Punishment

Dr. Hans Zeisel, of the University of Chicago, has done numerous jury studies. He testified that opposition to capital punishment had been increasing among all people, but that race remains a major differentiating factor in opinions on capital punishment; black people tend to oppose it. Those who favor capital punishment are more likely to oppose open housing or move out of an integrating neighborhood.

He added that those in favor of capital punishment were more likely to vote "guilty" on the first ballot in criminal cases and would need less proof to arrive at a guilty verdict.

Laughter broke out in the courtroom at one point when Zeisel was asked by the somewhat disconcerted judge, "Do you think white jurors would wrongfully convict a Negro defendant?" Zeisel, who had been trying to avoid strong condemnations and stick to clear evidence, said, "It's been rumored to have happened."

Zeisel's testimony on capital punishment included a description of what has been termed the "authoritarian personality". His testimony was followed by Nevitt Sanford, psychologist from Stanford, an originator of the authoritarian personality test. He testified as to the linkage between pro-captial punishment and prejudice.

While the judge again ignored this testimony and it provided no immediate answers as to how to keep racists off juries, it remains an important point for appeal. Large numbers of prospective jurors were eliminated "for cause" on the basis of their opposition to capital punishment and nearly all prospective black jurors who were eliminated for "cause" were challenged because they opposed the death penalty.

White Racism

Perhaps the most penetrating and precedent-setting testimony was given by Robert Blauner, sociologist from U.C., who studies racism. Blauner's testimony, widely reported as were the others, was education in its most practical sense.

Blauner distinguished between objective and subjective racism. Objective racism is an inescapable, structural and institutional part of this society; subjective racism is a question of attitudes. "Living in this (objectively) racist society", he said, "it is not possible for white people to be free of subjective racism."

Garry asked, "How do I find a juror who is not racist to the extent that he will prejudge a black defendant?"

The most feasible way", Blauner testified, "would be not to have whiteson the jury." (Exactly what the Panthers and Garry have argued from the beginning). If this was not done, Blauner suggested, there might be ways to eliminate the most serious racists. The judge asked, "Is there a test?".

Screen For Racists

Blauner came up with the following four points.

(1) A white juror should have knowledge of black history and culture.
(2) He should be aware of his own prejudices and be working to overcome them, rather than being unaware or indifferent.
(3) He should have personal experience with black and minority people—have lived a more equalatarian than segregated life.
(4) He should be actively concerned with changing the racist structure of society--in his job, his personal life--in some way making a commitment to change.

In response to a question from DA Lowell Jensen, Blauner stated that although theoretically racism could be found in blacks as well as whites, in reality whites in our society have a "monopoly" on it because of the objective situation.

Blauner, like Bernard Diamond, criminologist, doctor, law professor, and psychiatrist from Berkeley, responded to DA questioning that he, like everyone else, has some amount of racism in him.

CONTINUED ON PAGE 12

THE MOVEMENT PRESS
449 14TH STREET
SAN FRANCISCO, CA. 94103

The *Barb* was one of the first and most radical of all the underground papers, a phenomenon that quickly spread throughout the country. In 1966, five papers with an estimated readership of fifty thousand were organized in the Underground Press Syndicate. According to a *Washington Post* article of July 6, 1970, by the summer of 1970, there were two hundred such papers with six million readers. There were also five hundred underground newspapers in high schools. Liberation News Service began in 1967 and by 1970 furnished more than four hundred underground media outlets with weekly bulletins on progressive movements worldwide. Simultaneously, *The Black Panther* newspaper was by March 1969 distributing thirty thousand copies a week throughout the United States. Clearly, this underground press had a role in motivating many people to come to the Bay Area.[11]

The Haight

The Haight-Ashbury became both a center of activity and cultural reference point for specific reasons. Word of mouth and the Blue Unicorn coffeehouse had attracted several different yet overlapping social currents to the Haight-Ashbury by 1965, spurring the opening of the Psychedelic Shop, a couple more coffeehouses, and some hip clothing stores, which created a center of social and commercial activity on Haight Street itself.[12] Chet Helms and the Albin brothers had launched a series of public jam sessions in the ballroom of an old mansion at 1090 Page Street that the Albins rented from their uncle. The San Francisco Tape Music Center had occupied a building on Divisadero since 1961. The Both/And jazz club had opened up across the street in 1965. And a group of former SNCC activists had started a school called the Haight Ashbury Settlement House on Cole Street the same year. These public establishments drew attention to themselves and inevitably became magnets for both new arrivals to San Francisco and Bay Area residents seeking lively places to congregate.

The locals included the Family Dog crowd, the San Francisco Mime Troupe, the Tape Music Center group, and an assortment of artists, poets, and musicians connected with San Francisco State College. Even before the Haight had any particular reputation, these people had been drawn together by a series of increasingly large events akin to roving parties held in different parts of the city. The Longshoremen's Hall was the site of many of the seminal events that launched the hip community, ranging from the Family Dog's first shows in 1965 to the Trips Festival in January 1966. Other locations, including the California Hall and the Mime Troupe's Howard Street studios, also played host to such gatherings. Initially no one neighborhood or venue was the sole focus of attention or activity. What was key were the ideas and the sense of adventure people brought with them wherever they gathered.

Nevertheless, a variety of factors encouraged a growing number people to open businesses in the Haight and to move into or hang out in the neighborhood; rent was cheap, it was near Golden Gate Park, and the successful Freeway Revolt had imbued the Haight with a vague aura of "cool."[13] By mid-1966, the momentum had grown to a point where the hip community was self-aware enough to create an organization and launch a newspaper: the Haight Independent Proprietors (HIP) and *The San Francisco Oracle*. From that point on, a platform existed for propagating the ideas that would attract more and more people to the hitherto unremarkable neighborhood.[14]

These developments led to the Human Be-In of January 1967, held in Golden Gate Park. The poster for the Be-in is most instructive. Announcing a "Gathering of the Tribes" for a "Pow Wow" and sporting an Indian motif illustrated by a brave on horseback holding an electric guitar, most of the poster was devoted to the names of speakers: poets Allen Ginsberg and Gary Snyder, psychologist and LSD propagandist Timothy Leary, and antiwar activist Jerry Rubin among others. Down in the lower left hand corner was written "All San Francisco Rock Bands." Obviously, the main attraction was not particular bands let alone stars. Rather, it was noteworthy individuals representing varied viewpoints who were calling this convocation. Not only was the Be-In the culmination of an extraordinary year of intense activity, it put before the people of the Bay Area an image of themselves. That such a large gathering could be convened was numerically significant but far from unique, since there had already been demonstrations of similar size. What distinguished the Human Be-In was that it deliberately set out to articulate a vision for transforming the world. No doubt this effort was torturously conflicted. There could be no mistaking the differences between the emphasis Gary Snyder, for example, placed on the need for young people to leave the city and go back to the land and the emphasis Jerry Rubin placed on intensifying struggle against the war in Vietnam. Insurgent poets and playwrights such as Lawrence Ferlinghetti and Michael McClure could not be confused with psychedelic sloganeer Timothy Leary. Nonetheless, the "Gathering of the Tribes" was an explicit attempt to join together the disparate strands of radical opposition broadly grouped under the banners of the New Left/antiwar movement and the more vaguely defined consciousness-expanding, New Age spiritualism, that was *later* named the counterculture. This was a landmark event compelling everyone to take notice. The authorities certainly did, the police making one of their many sweeps of Haight Street the night of the Be-In.[15]

Free Fairs

The genesis of the Haight-Ashbury and the counterculture lies deeper still in the social fabric of San Francisco. Threads of local politics, arts, and organization were being woven together with those of national and international scope. Much of what would soon make San Francisco an epicenter of worldwide revolution began on a neighborhood level in conflicts over city government policy like the Freeway Revolt. The redevelopment controversy was another. But the spark that ignited a powder keg, leading to the Human Be-In, the Monterey Pop Festival, and even Woodstock and Altamont years later, was the battle over arts funding in San Francisco.

From the formation of the Artists Liberation Front (ALF) and the Diggers in mid-1966 to the Free Fairs in October the same year, a series of events organized by artists, actors, musicians, and political activists filled the calendar and kept the growing number of new bands playing regularly. Indeed, one defining feature of the Sixties has it origins in the long series of free concerts in the Panhandle during this period. In subsequent years, they would move on to Speedway Meadow and the Polo Fields. Ralph Gleason's description captures the ambience: "The Free Fairs featured rock bands, from which came the practice of free music in the parks, a whole new idea to this generation. Poets gave open readings. Jazz musicians jammed on the grass. Kids ran all over the place and at times there were whole sections set off for kids to play with paint or mud."[16]

This historic sequence of events was inspired by the formation of the ALF in an attempt to implement a strategy based on the principle of diffusion, championed by poet Kenneth Rexroth.[17] Rexroth argued that instead of (indeed in opposition to) constructing opera houses and museums that centralize control and enforce the professionalization of art-making, art and art-making should be brought to the neighborhoods to directly engage the residents and to put the tools of art-making into their hands, thereby enabling a "people's art." As Rexroth explained, "Now, the simplest thing that they could do is open the playgrounds of the schools and open the school auditoriums for cultural use. The important thing in this city is to get the Art Festival diffused over the city, to get music, to get all this stuff out into the city, because we are facing a cultural crisis. We are facing the absolute schism between what's called the Establishment and the Disestablishment. And the artists' community is going over to the Disestablishment."[18] Inspired by the ALF, four Free Fairs were organized: in the Mission on October 1, the Tenderloin on October 8, the Haight-Ashbury/Panhandle on October 15, and in Hunters Point on October 22.

Several highly charged events were interspersed between the fairs. On October 2, the ALF held a rally on the steps of City Hall to protest the police murder of Matthew Johnson in Hunters Point on September 27, unleashing several days of rioting. A memorial service was also held in Hunters Point on October 2, attended by the ALF and what grew to a crowd of more than a thousand people. On October 6, the Love Pageant Rally was held in the Panhandle to mark the day that LSD was made illegal. This event was also a direct outgrowth of a September 16 antifascist rally and march that had begun at the 1500 block of Haight Street and proceeded to the Park Police Station to protest a particularly outrageous drug bust. Between September 16 and October 6, curfews were imposed in the black neighborhoods of Hunters Point and the Fillmore district and in the Haight-Ashbury.[19] At the third Free Fair, held on October 15 in the Panhandle, the police arrested two of the event's organizers, Yuri Toropov (also the manager of a band, Sopwith Camel) and Arthur Lisch (a member of the Diggers). As Gleason recalled it: "And for producing this urban miracle, the cops arrested Yuri Toropov and jailed him until 5AM without a phone call to a lawyer. Is this REALLY the city that knows how?"[20] (The last comment was in reference to a silly Establishment slogan intended to draw attention away from San Francisco's growing reputation as a haven for lunacy.)

If following this sequence of events is dizzying, imagine what it was like to be directly involved! Extraordinary as it was, it typified an era.[21] Some of the most innovative musical and artistic experiments of the period were born from the interweaving of creative effort and intensifying local and international political conflicts. Of course, there were many other things going on simultaneously, including all the tripping, partying, and hanging out that are more commonly associated with the Sixties in San Francisco. But the frequency of actions involving hundreds and sometimes thousands of participants made them a vital thread in the fabric of daily life. Most importantly, their grassroots, neighborhood orientation produced a sense of community that included not only the Haight but also the Mission, the Tenderloin, and other San Francisco neighborhoods. This would result in one of the most enduring legacies of the period; neighborhood associations mobilizing local residents for political action expanded dramatically, and they continue to be a feature of Bay Area politics to this day.

The song "San Francisco" was intended to usurp the mass uprising that was gaining strength in numbers and nurturing revolutionary aspirations. A reporter from *Ramparts* magazine wrote of the Love Pageant Rally that along with banners, flags, chimes, feathers, costumes, etc., were "photos of Ho Chi Minh and Lenny Bruce." He concluded that "if this movement ever catches on, it could be the single most subversive influence on Western Civilization since Gutenberg."[22] Indeed, in a direct rebuttal to the vultures already positioning themselves to exploit it, on November 18, one George Metevsky (probably Diggers founder Emmett Grogan), wrote in the *Berkeley Barb*:

> We're not foiled anymore by the romantic trappings of the marketeers of expanded consciousness. Love isn't a dance concert with a light show at $3 a head. It isn't an Artist Liberation Front "Free" Fair with concessions for food and pseudo psychedelia. It is the SF Mime Troupe performing Free Shows in the parks while it is being crushed by a furious $15,000 debt. It is Arthur Lisch standing under a blue flag in Hunters Point scraping rust off the tin-can memorial to Matthew Johnson from two to five everyday. It is free food in the Panhandle where anyone can do anything with the food they bring to each other. It is Love. And when love does its thing it does it for love and separates itself from the false-witness of the Copsuckers and the Gladly Dead.[23]

Or as the Communication Company wrote on May 17, 1967:

> Revolution for $3.50 is an impossibility.
> Revolution is free because it's yours.
> Watch out. Here come the creeps.[24]

The Artists Liberation Front, Teatro Campesino, and the Diggers

Local, community-based efforts were not easily suppressed *or* co-opted by the system. Indeed, police harassment, corporate media scorn, and other attempts to squelch these endeavors only spread the sparks rather than extinguishing them. The formation of the Artists Liberation Front, Teatro Campesino, and the Diggers are among the best examples.

The Artists Liberation Front grew out of a confrontation with prominent businessmen convened by the mayor as the Art Resources Development Committee of the San Francisco Cultural Board. This gathering of bigwigs was crashed by members of the San Francisco Mime Troupe in full commedia regalia and playing musical instruments. Mime Troupe director Ron Davis read a statement that said in part:

> Money For Art
> Money For People
> Money For Culture!
> No Buildings!
> People Make Art
> Artists Are People
> Support the Artists![25]

Naturally, the artists were escorted from the building, while the bigwigs resumed eating.

The following day, Ron Davis shared a panel with Kenneth Rexroth as part of the "Campus and Community Day" symposium held at San Francisco State College. (It was here that Rexroth made his aforementioned appeal to young artists to take art out into the neighborhoods as an act of a cultural diffusion.) A short time later, a meeting was held at the Mime Troupe's Howard Street studios. In attendance were a wide assortment of musicians, poets, painters, dancers, producers, and directors—in short, a cross-section of the community of practicing artists in San Francisco. The meeting was chaired by Assemblyman Willie Brown, and among those present were Lawrence Ferlinghetti, Kenneth Rexroth, Bill Graham, and Ralph Gleason. It was there that the Artist Liberation Front was founded, "dedicated," in Ron Davis's words, to the artists' "collective defense and offense." The ALF immediately took up Rexroth's proposal, calling for what became the Free Fairs, discussed above. Most significant, however, was that a highly effective means of mobilizing cultural resistance was developing. This, combined with its neighborhood focus, gave it far greater influence than any appeal to corporate media or Establishment cultural outlets could have achieved. This was a stunning rebuke to those who claimed (and still do) that you had to "work within the system" to get your point across. That this rebuke was delivered by the artists doing the most innovative work in theater, music, dance, and painting made it all the more compelling. Indeed, the rebellion went beyond the artistic merit of the artists and their works to the more difficult question of the role of art in society, and whether it served or hindered the struggle for liberation.

Certainly not all those involved were as consciously revolutionary as Ron Davis and the San Francisco Mime Troupe. No doubt, many who participated in the Free Fairs and the almost daily musical events held at one or another venue for the next several years were seeking adventure, experience, or enlightenment of some kind without consciously joining the movement. But this only serves to highlight the fact that the Mime Troupe, with its contentious, polarizing director, was among the most influential groups, both artistically *and* politically, in San Francisco at the time. It also indicates the reach of this influence. Musicians, for example, might have been blissfully ignorant of how the music business functioned or deliberately apolitical in their artistic practices, but they could not ignore their audience's belief that fighting the system or otherwise trying to change the world was fundamental. Marty Balin once said that when Jefferson Airplane was preparing to sign with RCA Victor, "I realized we were working for the enemy."[26]

The Mime Troupe inspired numerous other important theatrical and political projects, including Teatro Campesino and the Diggers, both motivated by the antiwar movement, black liberation, and the farmworkers struggle led by Cesar Chavez and the United Farm Workers. Luis Valdez was a young actor who'd joined the Mime Troupe in 1964. As Ron Davis explained, "Then he disappeared one day and turned up with one of the most important theatrical inventions of the 1960s. He put together a group that combined theatre and organizing, workers and culture, performance and lessons. His base was the Delano grape strike, 'la causa,' and his first skits or *actos* were done for striking grape pickers."[27] Teatro Campesino went on to so deeply inspire other theater groups that Valdez is often referred to as the "father of Chicano Theater."

The close connection between the Bay Area and the Central Valley, both geographically and politically, made it inevitable that this symbiosis would develop. A survey of the Avalon and Fillmore posters now coveted by collectors and fans reveals a significant number of concerts that were benefits for the United Farm Workers. Even more important, the farmworkers' campaigns led to a marked increase in cultural and political activity among Chicanos and other Latino people in the Bay Area, especially in the Mission District. The flowering of many Teatros modeled on Teatro Campesino and of graphic arts, particularly the outdoor mural and the silkscreen poster, mark the era as much as famous musical groups like Santana and Malo, who were themselves directly connected to these unfolding events.[28]

The Diggers also evolved out of the Mime Troupe. Several founding members including Peter Berg, Peter Cohon (later Coyote), Judy Goldhaft, and Emmett Grogan had been actors, dancers or, scriptwriters involved in numerous Mime Troupe plays and had been particularly instrumental in founding the ALF. There were debates within the Mime Troupe and ALF concerning what constituted political theater, ultimately leading the Diggers to formulate a strategy focused on literally using the world as a stage. Identifying themselves as "life actors," the Diggers played on themes of anonymity as opposed to personal fame, money as an unnecessary evil, and, above all, the concept of "free" (as in the free city, free frames of reference, and "it's free because it's yours"). With numerous tracts and interventions over the course of two years, the Diggers effectively demolished notions regarding "hippies," hip merchants, hip proselytizing (including Tim Leary and the *Oracle* newspaper), and even hip musicians, like the newly famous and now wealthy Jefferson Airplane. Their Death of Money Parade, Intersection Game, Invisible Circus, and Death of Hippie/Birth of Free were public events that not only involved hundreds of participants but inspired heated debate throughout the Bay Area. As the Digger Archives relate:

> Their most famous activities revolved around distributing Free Food every day in the Park, and distributing "surplus energy" at a series of Free Stores (where everything was free for the taking). The Diggers coined various slogans that worked their way into the counterculture and even into the larger society—"Do your own thing" and "Today is the first day of the rest of your life" being the most recognizable. The Diggers, at the nexus of the emerging underground, were the progenitors of many new (or

newly discovered) ideas such as baking whole wheat bread (made famous through the popular Free Digger Bread that was baked in one- and two-pound coffee cans at the Free Bakery); the first Free Medical Clinic, which inspired the founding of the Haight-Ashbury Free Medical Clinic; tie-dyed clothing; and, communal celebrations of natural planetary events, such as the Solstices and Equinoxes.[29]

Indeed, one such solstice event was held in Golden Gate Park only four days after the Monterey Pop Festival. It was a daylong celebration in Speedway Meadow, featuring some of the bands who had just performed in Monterey. Thousands of young people attended what was essentially an event of their own making, thus begging the question, "Who needs Monterey Pop?"

Did the song "San Francisco" convey any of this? Did wearing flowers in your hair accurately symbolize what people in San Francisco were doing? Did the rhythm or melody capture the nature and intensity of activity? The sheer number of events was remarkable. "There was one point where we did—I think it was called Vietnam Summer—we did 28 gigs in one month. And they were all benefits for the opposition to the Vietnam War," recalls Bill Champlin of the Sons of Champlin.[30] Most of these were outdoor rallies, but some took place at venues as disparate as the Muir Beach Tavern and the Irwin Street Warehouse. The historical record is preserved in the posters announcing these events, conclusively proving that spontaneous, popularly organized activities were so numerous and vibrant as to undermine the self-importance so crucial to selling spectacles like the Monterey Pop Festival. Furthermore, the uncompromising stance of groups like the Mime Troupe profoundly embarrassed many less committed and less visionary artists, particularly among musicians, who by mid-1967 were already facing the snares and delusions of the system, albeit in the guise of carefully cultivated "hipness." In fact, it was precisely at this time that "Hip Capitalism" made its appearance. Henceforth the battle would be fought on two fronts: against the system in its blatant, repressive form and against its surrogate disguised as a promoter of the revolution. The best example of this phenomenon is none other than "rock impresario" Bill Graham. Graham's career, like that of so many other key figures in Sixties San Francisco, began with the Mime Troupe.

Bill Graham Presents

"Bill Graham first came to the Troupe as an aspiring actor," remembers Saul Landau, who at the time collaborated closely with Ron Davis. "Although he had no talent, which he made apparent every time he would get on the stage. But it didn't stop him. And he was good at business."[31] Graham took over as business manager of the Mime Troupe in 1964. As Ron Davis explained, "Although he stood aside from our political direction, his isolation made him a good front man and sometimes a more energetic publicity seeker than a radical could be."[32] Davis recalled Graham's visible entrepreneurial excitement when he took up the challenge: "Anyone can sell Coca Cola, wanna try selling radical theater?"

From the outset, Graham insisted that promotion for the Troupe's performances should say "Bill Graham Presents," to which Davis acceded. Graham did his job well, garnering publicity for the Troupe and rallying support during the fracas surrounding performances in city parks. After Davis's notorious arrest in August 1965, the first "Appeal" was held at the Mime Troupe's Howard Street studios.[33] An estimated one to two thousand people were in attendance, and within months the Bay Area music scene underwent a transformation. The Appeals (there were to be three such benefit concerts) were crucial in catapulting Graham from obscurity to rock impresario, leading him to part ways with the Mime Troupe in February 1966. Davis recalls the final break: "There was one more appeal, Appeal III, January 14, 1966, for more 'legal defense' funding. It netted little money and lots of lost time. Graham was hot to go for more money, and we ended our working arrangement one day when, on the phone, Graham said, 'Ron, the Mime Troupe can sponsor another rock show. . . . We can make a lot together.'"[34] Even if Appeal III didn't net much, Bill Graham Presents had struck gold. As Saul Landau recalled, "Bill saw the opportunity. He didn't know shit about any of these groups. I don't think he could carry a tune. But he saw a thousand people show up to hear these new bands. In his mind, he turned it right into cash. Within six months, he was a millionaire."[35]

It goes without saying that no artistic or social movement on the scale of that in San Francisco in the Sixties was the result of any one person or group. Nonetheless, the role Graham played was pivotal—for contradictory reasons. On the one hand, his organization and promotion effectively drew together disparate elements from poster designers, light show operators, musicians, and other performers. He was certainly not the only one doing this, but he did it consistently and efficiently. On the other hand, he made no bones about the fact that he was a businessman and his purpose was above all pecuniary; indeed he was notoriously ruthless in pursuit of his acquisitive aims. The fact that he became such a dominant figure says as much about the forces that opposed him as it does about his own abilities. In the swelling ranks of the movement, there was a broad range of views regarding capitalism, music, work, and organization. There was little consensus between the explicit anticapitalism of activists such as the Diggers and the vague free-spirited idealism common to many more recent dropouts. In consequence, no organized force was equipped to mount a sustained critique of or effective resistance to Graham.

Early on, Graham attracted a lot of support because of the heat he was taking from the San Francisco Police Department and the court battles he waged to obtain his dance hall permit. Furthermore, he fostered friendly relations with the businesses in the black neighborhood surrounding the Fillmore. He even developed a working relationship with the Black Panther Party when their offices opened up down the block, allowing the Panthers access to the Fillmore for their own events. But perhaps the most important thing Graham did to silence his critics and earn the grudging support of many musicians was the programming of the Fillmore shows. As mentioned above, Graham was clueless when it came to the music scene; it's difficult to imagine a more unhip individual running a venue like the Fillmore. Yet Graham turned his ignorance into his advantage by listening attentively to musicians, actors, poets, and artists, then implementing their suggestions with unfailing precision. The fact of the matter is that Graham was not only ignorant of the music he was promoting, he was also a novice when it came to the workings of the music industry. Had he gotten his start in Los Angeles or New York, it is unlikely he would have weathered the competition from already established promoters. But in the 1960s, there was no precedent for what was unfolding in the Bay Area, nor was there any significant music industry presence to capitalize on it in San Francisco. Yet.

Opposition to Graham

Graham did not simply waltz his way to dominance, however. From the very beginning, he faced competition and deliberate opposition from other promoters and even loose groupings of musicians. The years between the first Fillmore show in December 1965 and the collapse of the Wild West Festival in 1969 saw a series of running battles against Graham's developing monopoly.[36] The first involved Chet Helms, who had appropriated the name Family Dog from its founders and launched the Avalon Ballroom to provide an alternative to the Fillmore. Helms was a genuine "freak" who'd been involved with the scene since its inception, hosting LEMAR (Legalization of Marijuana) meetings at the Blue Unicorn, jam sessions at the Albin brothers' place on 1090 Page Street, and managing Big Brother and the Holding Company. Helms was no less ambitious than Graham, but he would try (and fail) to walk the tightrope between "New Age entrepreneur" and cultural revolutionary.[37]

Next, the Grateful Dead and a loose grouping of other bands took over the Carousel Ballroom on Market Street and attempted to run it in opposition to Graham. As Bill Champlin, whose band was involved, relates, "Because everybody was beginning to realize that Bill's making all the money. And that's where the Diggers came in and were getting more and more pissed off."[38] This effort lasted a year, after which, amidst mutual recriminations (particularly between the Diggers and the Dead), the musicians threw in the towel. Naturally, Graham stepped in, renamed the Carousel Fillmore West and continued his march of conquest.

Summarizing Graham's role, Joel Selvin, a columnist for the *San Francisco Chronicle*, remarked, "You can't tell the story without the Diggers being front and center because they were sort of the philosophical forefront of the movement, trying to take the philosophy into action where the rubber meets the road. Bill was like the 'imperialist exploiter' who had come to the small Caribbean island to rip it off for its resources and build his big mansion on top of the hill. The Diggers were the tribe."[39] By 1969, with the world tuned to San Francisco's seemingly endless supply of great bands, there was one last, fateful attempt to wrest control from Graham. However, after the collapse of the Wild West Festival (discussed further in Chapter 8), Graham had no serious competition anywhere in Northern California. He went on to systematically impose the stadium concert model of music presentation, a model diametrically opposed to the festivals in public parks that had been the heart and soul of the San Francisco renaissance.[40]

Graham was aided in his pursuits by two contradictory factors: fracturing of the communal spirit that initially characterized the scene and the simultaneous belief that the scene was too strong to be impacted.

First, in contrast to the unifying spirit and sheer excitement produced by the music and the movement, divisions were beginning to appear among musicians and the community from which they'd come. "The scene kicked in and it lasted about a year and a half where people really were sharing with each other, all that peace and love everybody was talking about, and then along came meth," recalled Bill Champlin. Methedrine's appearance on the scene was in sharp contrast in both social and chemical effects to those of pot and psychotropics. It was manufactured and distributed by drug dealers with more connections to established criminal enterprises than to anything remotely hip. In contrast, pot dealing was part of the economy of a subculture, a network of psychedelic Tupperware parties, decentralized and small scale, something anybody could be involved in and many were. Speed was altogether different. Not only was its economy the domain of gangsters, meth bred paranoid fantasy and aggressive violence far different from the mellow or contemplative effects of marijuana or LSD. The band Mad River provided ironic commentary on this development in their song "Amphetamine Gazelle." And Blue Cheer, perhaps the world's first heavy metal band, could always count on an audience of speed freaks for their displays of bruising bravado. But methedrine was only part of it. As Bill Champlin adds:

> The San Francisco scene, just in terms of the musicians to each other, it played out really the opposite of what everyone was talking about. The Dead were at one point really cool. But I just kinda lost it on most of that royalty stuff. And you look at these guys now, and they really are royalty. You almost expect to see a crown and a cape. Even at the time, I remember thinking, "This is not what LSD's telling us to be. This hierarchy bullshit, this is the thing that we're not supposed to be involved in."

Was this simply a matter of naiveté or unbridled ego, the unintended consequence of surprising success?

From the Monterey Pop Festival onward, the music business would intensify its efforts to gain control of something that had initially eluded its grasp. While many were aware that this was happening, resistance to it was theoretically lame and practically impotent. Clouding the issues further was the fact that in purely musical terms, the Monterey Pop Festival was an exciting affair, rich in quality and diversity. From Ravi Shankar to Jimi Hendrix, from Hugh Masekela to Country Joe and the Fish, this was unusual for festivals of the time that centered around jazz or folk or some other musical style. But such diversity was the norm in San Francisco and directly responsible for the programming of Monterey Pop. It remained the norm until Graham successfully mounted the stadium rock concert beginning in 1973 with "A Day on the Green" at the Oakland Coliseum. While this is getting ahead of our story, it's important to note that the changes wrought by "Hip Capitalism" did not occur overnight. Rather, they were insidious and gradual, exploiting the very enthusiasm that had developed in opposition to the ethos of money and power underlying capitalism in any form.

The second factor was the sense of invincibility. Side by side, the music and the movement were attracting millions of young people. Far beyond Haight Street, San Francisco, or even California, revolution appeared to be imminent, there seemed to be no way that a Bill Graham or any businessman could prevent its advance. Though, in hindsight, this was hopelessly naive, such views were nonetheless a factor in the outcome of events. Confirming them further was the fact that the whirlwind blew full force well beyond 1967 and Monterey Pop. Indeed, 1969 marked the recording of some of the most enduring music of Bay Area–based groups as well as many of the most noteworthy political struggles.

While it is common to view two festivals, Woodstock and Altamont, as marking the apex and nadir of an era, the truth is otherwise. For one thing, groups like Sly and the Family Stone, Creedence Clearwater Revival and Tower of Power were just producing their best work and continued to do so for some years to come. For another, the attitudes and practices associated with San Francisco were having a powerful impact on musicians from elsewhere. Two examples from a far broader field are Delaney and Bonnie and War. These groups' melding of black, white and, in the case of War, Latin influences, was a musical triumph and a conscious attempt to unleash the spirit of celebration and community. They would in turn exert a reinvigorating influence on the Bay Area. Indeed, even a cursory glance at music recorded between 1969 and 1975 reveals such a breadth and depth of creativity, musicianship and social engagement on the part of bands from the Bay Area and those influenced by them that it is impossible to view Altamont or 1969 as "the end."[41]

All of this, however, created an atmosphere that made it possible to ignore the machinations of the music industry and of people like Bill Graham. Even today, many people view such institutions and individuals as necessary evils to be frowned upon but tolerated. At the time, the sheer quantity of great new music and the regularity with which it was being produced, along with the parallel increase in political struggle, caused many people to fail to see what was happening right before their eyes.[42]

Revolution

Perhaps the most stunning example of how the song "San Francisco" completely distorts what was attracting worldwide attention to the Bay Area was an event almost coincidental with the song's appearance. On May 2, 1967, eleven days prior to the release of "San Francisco," thirty Black Panthers (twenty-four men and six women) marched into the California State Capitol building armed with shotguns and rifles. The Panthers had come to denounce a new bill being proposed that would explicitly forbid what they were doing at that very moment: state law allowed an adult citizen to carry a shotgun or rifle if it was in plain sight. (It was not legal to carry a concealed weapon without a license.)

The Black Panther Party had been founded in October 1966, the Panthers had started to patrol the Oakland ghetto, following the police, while armed with law books and shotguns. The tactic required strict adherence to the law: how far to stand from a cop making an arrest, what a bystander could say aloud to those being apprehended, how to hold a weapon without appearing to threaten a police officer, and so forth. Not only did these patrols address a deep grievance felt by all black people, they served to consolidate an organized force around the Panthers' Ten-Point Program. In directly confronting the humiliating brutality of the police, the Panthers correctly assessed the mood of the black community and exposed the vulnerability of the state at what appeared to be its strongest point: the monopoly of violence. Their uniforms, their weapons, and their program combined to make the Panthers a liberating army in the eyes of the black community.

Naturally, this enraged the police. Law enforcement agencies throughout the state clamored for this glaring loophole in existing law to be closed. "Negroes with guns" was so terrifying a prospect that even the right-wing gun lobby, in Sacramento on the same day to protest the bill, were silenced by the state of emergency the Panthers' presence created. Here was political theater at its grandest and most deadly accurate. It was a publicity stunt that struck the ugly, guilt-ridden nightmare buried in white Amerika's racist heart.

Within hours, Bobby Seale's statement to the press was making its way around the world. With one bold, brilliantly executed action, the Black Panther Party became a force in international affairs. Young black people began flooding Panther offices, new chapters were set up in cities across the country, and the BPP founders Huey Newton and Bobby Seale were fast becoming household names.

Two major events in October occurred as a direct result. Stop the Draft Week, launched by white radicals attempting to stop draftees from being inducted into the armed forces, turned into a full-scale riot when police attacked demonstrators. It led to the arrest of the Oakland 7 on conspiracy charges, creating a *cause célèbre* in the Bay Area. The second major event was the arrest of Huey Newton on charges of murdering a police officer. The entire Bay Area immediately understood that the state was out to forcibly crush the Panthers. The result was a massive international campaign, to "Free Huey," the first of a long series of such campaigns that continue to this day (e.g., Free Leonard Peltier). These two events, Stop the Draft Week and the Free Huey campaign, coincided with the formation of the Peace and Freedom Party, as an attempt to find an organizational form for people who were not black to participate in the struggle for black liberation while linking it with the ongoing antiwar movement.

Thus, within a year of its founding, the Black Panther Party was playing a leading role not only in the black community but in the movement as a whole. This was partly inspired by symbolism and imagery, including the black panther itself, and partly by the novelty and daring of the Panthers' theatrical enactments of the black masses rising up against injustice. By 1967, the idea of peacefully reforming the system was being rejected outright, not only in black ghettoes across the country but also by young white people, who were dropping out in ever-increasing numbers. The emergence of the Panthers produced a series of sudden and far-reaching cultural shifts. Phrases such as "right on," "off the pig," and "power to the people" were coined—or at least popularized—by the Panthers and rapidly gained widespread use. The word "black" replaced the word "Negro" at this time and this was accompanied by the conceptualization of a black colony invaded by an occupying force, in the form of the police. Young white people had long been heavily influenced by black speech, so these linguistic developments quickly migrated into the New Left and the counterculture. Most significantly, the Panthers made the usage of such new terminology explicitly revolutionary, inter-nationalist, and socialist. The banner unfurled by the Panthers marked a historic turning point in the United States and the world.

The Free Huey campaign was a monumental organizing drive, attracting the support of millions of people and accelerating the growth of the Black Panther Party itself. The Panthers built on the rapid increase in their membership by launching their survival programs, especially the Free Breakfast for Children program. Also known as "serve the people" programs, these quickly mobilized a mass base of support in black communities throughout the country. To a certain extent they paralleled what the Diggers had initiated in the Haight. In a manner similar to the Haight Ashbury Free Medical Clinic, the Panthers organized health clinics and, an ambulance service, as well as establishing the first liberation schools. But in the Panthers' case, these programs had a much greater impact than their white counterparts, reaching millions of black people, and were eventually so established that they became models for government-supported projects in later years.[43]

For black musicians in particular, the Panthers became a force that could not be ignored, and which many openly supported. Musicians as diverse as James Brown, Chaka Khan, Natalie Cole, the Impressions, Aretha Franklin, and Marvin Gaye would all, at one time or another, publicly stand with the Panthers, performing at benefit concerts, donating money, and in some cases actually joining the Party. "There's a recording," reports Black Panther historian Billy X Jennings, "of a 1970 concert at USC, where Jimi Hendrix is saying, 'This is the Black Panther Party national anthem,' and he broke into 'Voodoo Chile.' And not only that, he has a relative, a cousin, used to be a Party member in Seattle. The founder of the Party in Seattle, Aaron Dixon, says Jimi Hendrix, Jim Morrison, people like that came through the Party offices, and I told you about James Brown, in Winston-Salem, couldn't spell 'ambulance,' and so someone spelled it out for him, and he made out a $5,000 check for the Party's ambulance service."[44] And as we've seen with Jim Morrison, support wasn't confined to black musicians.

Pianist Alberto Gianquinto, who performed with Santana in their first formation and was himself a revolutionary, brought his politics into the group and the scene surrounding them. This is evident in the song Gianquinto composed with Carlos Santana, "Incident at Neshabur," a tribute to Toussaint L'Ouverture and a crucial battle in Haiti's revolution.[45]

Gianquinto's influence led Santana to play an important benefit concert for the Panthers. "We did the Black Panther benefit and we were sympathetic because Alberto got us into it," recalled Santana drummer Michael Shrieve.[46] And they weren't alone. "The Escovedo family," comments Billy X Jennings, "always supportive, for a long time, starting with Pete through Sheila, Coke Escovedo; I have pictures in our archive of them doing a radiothon for the Party."[47] Other examples of this widespread support included Country Joe and the Fish dedicating their second album to the Panthers, the Grateful Dead playing a benefit concert for them along with many songs and other musical expressions inspired by and dedicated to the Panthers.

At this point, no one from the teenage runaway to the Establishment news reporter could possibly be unaware of the alternately ominous and inspiring presence of the Black Panther Party in the Bay Area, even in the Haight itself. There were Party members in the student body at Polytechnic High School, the large, predominantly black school on Frederick Street, directly across the street from Kezar Stadium. There were members active in the Fillmore district and in the housing projects on Potrero Hill. Their influence was amplified by the house meetings organized by the Party; tens of thousands of leaflets were distributed on city buses offering to have Party representatives speak to private gatherings in people's living rooms.[48] All of this is relevant, not only because it exposes the duplicity of endeavors like the Monterey Pop Festival and the song "San Francisco" but because it sheds light on the reality they were designed to obscure.

From our vantage point, fifty years later, it might seem predictable that the music industry would attempt to co-opt and suppress popular creativity and resistance, which makes it all the more necessary to underscore the fact that no one at the time viewed the outcome of events as a foregone conclusion. Besides, what the "powers that be" have spent fifty years trying to bury is so much more intriguing and inspiring than anything they've concocted that every effort to rediscover it will be richly rewarded.

Pop Goes the Weasel

If more evidence is needed to make the point, it can be found in the story of the Monterey Pop Festival itself. Not only was it a calculated move to make a lot of money, Monterey Pop was a deliberate attempt to incorporate San Francisco's music scene into the structures of the music industry. The Diggers directly addressed this in public pronouncements decrying the "old star/management/booking agency syndrome" and predicting that Monterey Pop would be a "rich man's festival."[49] The Diggers were not just carping from the sidelines, either. They were drawn into the affair by Derek Taylor, publicist for the Beatles, hired by Phillips and Adler, who sent out a stream of press releases including inferences that the festival was a charity event intended to raise money for the Diggers, among others. To make matters worse, Adler and Phillips had called the managers of all of the most important local bands, telling them that no one was getting paid because it was a benefit concert and insisting on waivers for film rights. In fact, the festival organizers were desperate. In spite of a stellar international line up, they could not proceed without the San Francisco bands. What's striking here is that except for Jefferson Airplane, whose "White Rabbit" had gained national notoriety, even the bands who had made records were not well known outside the Bay Area. Nonetheless, it was self-evident that the world was so keenly aware of the social and creative turmoil in San Francisco that the city's presence on the program was indispensable.[50]

In his autobiography, John Phillips wrote: "Haight-Ashbury was becoming the universal hippie Mecca for both the drug and rock cultures. Musicians saw themselves as organic post-capitalist advocates of 'power to the people.' They wanted to co-opt—that was the word then—the event to feed 'their' people in the Bay Area."[51] Obviously, "they" were the Diggers, but "they" also included many of the bands with whom Adler and Phillips were compelled to meet in an all-out effort to salvage the situation. At various junctures—Taylor in a confrontation with the Diggers, Adler in another confrontation with the musicians—the events' organizers were on the verge of throwing up their hands. An appeal was made to Ralph Gleason, perhaps the only "straight" person respected by San Francisco's bands, to persuade the musicians to participate. Gleason was not immediately supportive, requiring not only that the festival be genuinely nonprofit but that moneys go to designated projects. Given what Gleason later wrote in his column, it is clear he was given such assurances:

> The artists are performing for free at the festival, with the net profits going to a foundation which the festival committee is

establishing which will endow scholarships and engage in other long range activities for the betterment of pop music. One immediate specific project, Phillips said, yesterday, [Friday, April 20, 1967] would be to guarantee money for food for the Diggers in San Francisco to distribute during the summer months to aid in caring for the expected deluge of hippies to the city.[52]

Not only was this patent nonsense (and, apparently Gleason was taken in by the sweet talk), what actually happened was quite the opposite. First, no money was ever given the Diggers. Second, big money was made not from the festival itself but from the movie of the festival and an album that was made from live recordings of Otis Redding and Jimi Hendrix, the rights to which had been negotiated in horse-trading between Albert Grossman and Warner Brothers Records.[53] In fact, a great deal of money changed hands at Monterey, the details of which are unimportant, since they simply reflect common music industry practice. What is important is that behind the scenes, managers and record companies began to systematically integrate the bulk of the San Francisco music scene into the corporate machine. The process would take some time to complete and would involve considerable conflict, but it remains the case that the Monterey Pop Festival was a turning point in this regard.

This brings us full circle to the larger questions posed at the beginning of this chapter. It should be abundantly clear that what began in San Francisco with the Family Dog and the Mime Troupe Appeals catalyzed a sequence of events that by the end of 1966 were attracting international attention and many outsiders to the area. These events were quintessentially local endeavors, all were integrally linked to the antiwar, black liberation, and farmworker movements, and all were intrinsically multidisciplinary affairs, integrating music with theater, poster art, light shows, and dancing. At the same time, the cultural dimensions of marijuana, LSD, and other psychotropic drugs became indissolubly linked with a multifaceted assault on convention that could not be explained by the drugs' chemical effects alone. While the corporate media distorted beyond recognition what actually transpired, this nonetheless initially resulted in amplifying the very effects the system was attempting to suppress. The movement's increasing momentum and the extent of the still unfolding musical renaissance was so great that the attention brought to them by corporate media and the music industry only increased their attraction, redoubling their subversive effects. The next few years would witness, not the demise, but the full flowering that had begun in 1965.

CHAPTER 6

Songs of Innocence and Experience: Music's Rivalry with the State

In Autumn of 1967, the *American Scholar* published an essay by Ralph Gleason that sought to explain not only the violent turmoil engulfing America but also the disturbing turn evident in popular music. Gleason began by quoting Plato, who had said in *The Republic*, "the musical modes are never changed without change in the most important of a city's laws."[1] Gleason invoked Plato to support his contention that music was undermining the authority of the state, and that neither the Establishment nor the "square left" got it. Furthermore, Gleason argued, this was because, "At this point in history, most organs of opinion . . . are in the control of prisoners of logic. . . . They complain because art doesn't make sense! Life on this planet in this time of history doesn't make sense either—as an end result of immutable laws of economics and logic and philosophy."[2] Gleason's claims not only offended conservatives, they also rubbed his left-wing constituency the wrong way. People of every persuasion viewed art and politics as separate spheres, perhaps overlapping, but in any case neither equivalent nor equally important in the governance of society. Gleason was challenging everyone with an unsettling indictment. Some viewed this position as an endorsement of antisocial nihilism, others as the abdication of politics altogether. Most failed to grasp that beneath the turmoil of the present lay an ancient conflict (even Gleason himself did not fully grasp it). This, as Plato had instructed, is music's rivalry with the state.

Gleason's position does not appear to have influenced historical inquiry or analysis. While others have certainly made reference to Plato's remark, specifically relating it to music in the Sixties, few have drawn the conclusions that Gleason did. Indeed, the very concept of art or music being in conflict with the state is largely absent in discourse about the Sixties. Most often, that conflict is conceived of as cultural, not political, and is certainly not cast as a battle over law or government policy. To my knowledge, this line of inquiry has only been fully developed by Kenyan author Ngugi wa Thiong'o, who published *Penpoints, Gunpoints, and Dreams*, in 1998.[3] Ngugi's seminal work is based in part on a thorough reading of Plato, drawing out the implications in postcolonial Africa. This may explain why inquiry in the United States or Europe has failed to do so. It is perhaps more obvious in totalitarian regimes that art is at war with the state than it is in liberal democracies which maintain the appearance of a separation between state functions and industrial functions, between guarantees of free speech and free enterprise and the control of art's production and distribution. I will endeavor to show that such claims are bogus.

No Business Like Show Business

The rivalry between music and the state was evident in the attitude music industry professionals expressed toward what was happening in San Francisco. Contrary to what one might assume given the enormous profits generated by the music made there, many in the industry loathed everything about the Bay Area. This can only be explained by a brief overview of how the industry was constituted in the middle of the 1960s. The corporations, personalities, social networks, and political sympathies, that suddenly found themselves confronted with Jefferson Airplane, the Grateful Dead, and Country Joe and the Fish were the product of an earlier period that was substantively different. Jerry Wexler is a typical example. He produced Ray Charles, Aretha Franklin, and many other black artists, making him one of a small number of white New Yorkers who had the privilege of contributing to this timeless music, with its roots in the South. But Wexler was not just some white guy from New York.

"It's a pretty good bet she was a card-carrying member of the Party," Wexler wrote of his mother. "She was one of those self-taught Jewish New Yorkers who would congregate in cafeterias like the Automat or Bickford's to drink endless cups of coffee and argue over Lenin and Trotsky."[4] Born in 1917, Wexler grew up surrounded by the sounds of jazz and blues that were the pulse of the Harlem Renaissance. His role models were producer John Hammond, "with his brush haircut, Brooks Brothers tweed, button-down Oxford shirt, and intellectual-radical periodicals—*New*

Masses, Masses and Mainstream, The Worker—tucked under his arm," and "a Brooklyn bartender, a jazz scholar with an Irish dock-workers' accent who, when drunk, wept for the brave Spanish rebels while swearing vengeance on the head of Franco." Wexler himself became a model whose stamp was not only on the music he produced and popularized but on an attitude shared by many of his peers. This attitude combined music and politics in peculiar mixture, as Wexler describes:

> My political leanings have always been left, quite left. So naturally, my sympathies were very, very liberal and progressive and certainly addressed the concerns of discrimination and oppression of Black people. However, politics were out the window when we made records. We were in the entertainment business. I found that groups or singers who had a hit with a politically sub-toned song or recording became trapped in that vein and found themselves going down slower, as they say in the blues. If you make that your main object, I think you're doomed.

This attitude, articulated by an avowed leftist, was prevalent in the music industry, regardless of the civil rights movement and the success of Bob Dylan. Fundamentally, this position was an acceptance, if not an endorsement, of capitalism and liberal democracy within which reforms could be made but revolution was neither possible nor desirable. Furthermore, there was nothing inherently bad about entertainment. From Wexler's point of view, "entertainment" was a more or less neutral term which, far from determining the content or merit of musical expression, was open to be molded by talent and taste. Indeed, the common good, such as it was, would ultimately be served by high-quality production and wide dissemination. This attempt to reconcile art with commerce could be defended on the basis of works like *West Side Story* (which topped the popular music charts for fifty-four weeks in 1957–1958),[5] the cultivation of artists like Duke Ellington, Billie Holiday, and Ray Charles, and the gradual improvement of conditions for black people in America, as reflected in *Billboard* magazine's dropping of the designation "race" for its black music charts in 1949.

Wexler recalls:

> The editors were looking to change the name of a weekly record chart that was increasingly sounding awkward and wrong: race

music. We used to close the book on a Friday and come back to work on a Tuesday. One Friday, the editor got us together and said, "listen, let's change this from race records." A lot of people were beginning to find it inappropriate. "Come back with some ideas on Tuesday." There were four guys on the staff, one guy said this and one guy said that, and I said, "rhythm and blues" and they said, "oh, that sounds pretty good. Let's do that." In the next issue, that section came out as "Rhythm and Blues" instead of "Race."

This was also the period of McCarthyism and the witch-hunt. Pete Seeger's was only the most notorious of many cases in which music and musicians were targeted for their political affiliations, song lyrics or behaviors (especially race mixing) deemed unacceptable by ruling dogma.[6] Certainly, the pioneers of rhythm and blues, rock 'n' roll and subsequent developments in recorded music were fully aware that if they wanted to work they would have to obey certain rules. Regardless of the fact that some record companies such as Columbia and Atlantic had highly placed individuals steeped in Popular Front politics,[7] they were in no position, theoretically or practically, to do more than "do some good." The balance of forces always favored wealth and power, including the exploitative techniques and oppressive machinery necessary to acquire them. Indeed, what kept people like Wexler going was a genuine love of music and an admiration for the gifts of its greatest practitioners. This combined with a fervent hope, an evangelical predisposition born of left-wing backgrounds, that bringing this great music (particularly black music) to the attention of the American public would expose the great injustices on which America was built and lead to their correction in some indefinite future.

Cheap Thrills versus Divine Madness

In this context, the attitudes shared by participants in the music scene in San Francisco were shocking. It was unimaginable that musicians of consequence would be emerging from a community so dazed and confused that they thought they could eliminate the evils of war, racism, and poverty *in one generation*. How could anything of merit be produced by people who thought drugs brought enlightenment, and enlightenment made them superior judges of music? It's not surprising that many years later Wexler would attack internet file-sharing with the dismissive remark: "Why should music be free? It originated from some brainless hippie attitude. The San Francisco thing: free music in the park and all of that crap. But that's over." The point, which Wexler failed to grasp, was that *free* was what people wanted to *be*. Obviously, money didn't free anybody, it enslaved *everybody*. Yet, coveting its blindness, the music industry declared that anyone who could *see* must be crazy. Scurrying about in their suits, and psychosis, industry reps couldn't grasp how repulsive they appeared. Of course music should be free.

The problem, however, went deeper than dollars or dress. One could be deeply moved by the music Wexler produced, while at the same time rejecting both the motives for producing it and the criteria by which it was judged. Buried within their irreverence, iconoclasm, and rebellion young people were seeking from music something altogether different than what Wexler intended them to find. The romantic ideal was firmly established in their consciousness, and music was the gateway to the infinite, the sacred, the *true*. This was not a musical movement per se, but an ethos which music expressed. That indeed made them freaks. They were *inviting* the divine madness Socrates had spoken of so long ago. That "possession by the Muses, which takes a tender virgin soul and awakens it to a Bacchic frenzy of songs and poetry that glorifies the achievements of the past and teaches them to future generations."[8] But what is the divine? Giambattista Vico described the divine as the power of divining, "which is to understand what is hidden *from* men—the future—or what is hidden *in* them—their consciousness." (italics in the original).[9] As to God (who was, in any case by the Sixties, long since dead), the questions music posed were precisely those that religion had surrendered to the state. The best religion could offer was comfort, not revelation, and music erupted with oracular gesture and Delphic prognostication to challenge a Christianity that had been the handmaiden of imperial conquest, genocide, and slavery.

If it was not clear to Jerry Wexler's generation, it was abundantly so to Jerry Garcia's: the rational and irrational had changed places. If duck-and-cover drills in public schools were deemed a rational response to nuclear attack, then the irrational was actually rational. If the achievements of science resulted in the destruction of the planet, then sense is nonsense, making nonsense sense. But there was more to it than blatant contradictions of logic. A more subtle and sinister substitution was at work.

Delusion took the place of divinity, and technology the place of consciousness. America's answer to the death of God and the insanity of mutually assured destruction was Mickey Mouse and Disneyland. Such substitutions, moreover, made dupes of the American people, but dupes of a special kind. In this case, the dupe is not an innocent victim, but is complicit with his or her own deception. Instead of Kierkegaard's *leap of faith,* a suspension of disbelief, not a conscious choice, but a choice to remain unconscious. This was facilitated, indeed made possible, by the expropriation of the utopian imaginary of fairy tales—such as the Pied Piper, Jack and the Beanstalk, or Snow White—that convey and keep alive the dream of justice.[10] Recall that in most fairy tales the protagonists are poor people who use their wits to overcome a stronger, malevolent foe. Making these stories the basis for his empire, Walt Disney was not only making tons of money, he was erecting an impenetrable barrier between dreaming the good and making that good a social reality. The only choice available was that between undiluted drudgery and occasional relief. You can be "realistic" and unhappy or you can, at least while visiting Disneyland, enjoy some innocent delights. Thus, gullibility is to be preferred, since questioning only produces unhappiness.

That fine old American tradition, the medicine show, based its popular appeal precisely on this gullibility. Everyone attending a medicine show knows that snake oil will not cure what ails them but nevertheless enjoys the excuse an elixir gives for consuming alcohol. Such loony leaps of faithlessness were a constant in American culture. This is clearly evident in the constant evocation of mania. "Beatlemania," "dance craze," even "fan" (short for fanatic) are examples of techniques employed especially by the music industry to exploit this gullibility while fending off the enduring fascination with what is divinely inspired. If one were to actually seek prophecy (*mantic* in Greek) it was because it "is more perfect and more admirable than sign-based prediction, in both name and achievement, madness (*mania*) from a god is finer than self-control of human origin."[11] *Mantic* (divination, prophecy) has nothing to do with *romantic*, which is derived from the word *romance*, originally a description of vulgar French as opposed to Latin (hence the Romance languages). The substantive (as opposed to etymological) linkage between mantic and romantic is the infinite appearing to the mind of the lover or the artist. This process is subverted by the substitution of a medicine show for divine madness. Snake oil is a fake not because it deceives the ignorant but because it is complicit with the desire of the drunk to pretend they didn't knowingly consume alcohol. But the consumption of alcohol is a substitution of chemically induced madness for the madness legitimated by divine origin. Intoxication instead of inspiration.

The music industry was incapable of grasping what music itself was capable of doing. What young people were deriving from rock music—and especially one of rock's principle ingredients, black gospel music—was the ecstatic experience. This did not require belief in Jesus. Exhilaration was evoked by the rhythm and shout-singing of the congregation—in this case, the band and the audience. The entry into the body—both the individual body and the social body—of this spirit was an empirical fact. Every participant, musicians and audiences alike, shared the experience that made it so. Its effect was not reduced by it being, in many cases, a commercial product. The power of this experience, connecting body and soul with the divine, exposed the pathos and banality of commerce itself.

Furthermore, as the freaks knew well, the shrill alarums about drugs were utterly hypocritical. Not only were adults imbibing alcohol in copious amounts, the pharmaceutical industry was dosing the populace with cures for depression—"mother's little helper"—barbiturates, and speed. In contrast, psychotropics (peyote, mescaline, psilocybin, and LSD) were traditionally linked to enlightenment. Societies spanning the globe had long used drugs to gain access to the infinite. Aldous Huxley's *Doors of Perception* was on every freak's reading list, even before "turn on, tune in, drop out" became a pop catchphrase. That this was already common knowledge by the mid-1960s is evident in one song—"White Rabbit." This psychedelic anthem deserves special attention since it brought together the fairy tale imaginary with the command to expand one's consciousness. By invoking *Alice's Adventures in Wonderland* to encourage everyone to "feed your head," the song simultaneously exposed the hypocrisy of prevailing attitudes about drugs and celebrated the freedom that expanded consciousness proffered. Being hip meant, above all, not being conned.

When all else failed, there remained one more arrow in the quiver of the freak: irony. At once invincible and incomprehensible to music industry hacks, irony exposed the fraudulence of their very reason for being. Contrary to the hippy-dippy flower child image pasted over the lens of inquiry, San Francisco's music abounded in irony. The names of bands like the Charlatans, the Great! Society, or Big Brother and the Holding Company make this abundantly clear. The title and cover of Big Brother's most famous album introduce the subject graphically. *Cheap Thrills*, designed by underground comix pioneer R. Crumb, is the perfect example of ironic self-mockery, a key weapon in the arsenal of the freak. Even without the guidance of a Socrates, being hip depended on critical faculties capable of evaluating one's own consciousness. This might not provide all the answers, but at least it warded off the gullibility in which the general populace was guiltily wallowing.

Romantic, Didactic, and Classic

While casual reference is often made to romanticism, little attention is paid to the specific content of the term as it applied to San Francisco in the Sixties. Romanticism covers a broad and contradictory set of notions and works that run from Jean-Jacques Rousseau to Percy Bysshe Shelley, from Johann Gottfried Herder's German nationalism to Harry Smith's *Anthology of American Folk Music*, with stops along the way to visit Ralph Waldo Emerson, Henry Thoreau, and Walt Whitman. But as far as the Sixties were concerned, three romantic principles were so widely shared that they were characteristic, or emblematic of the *zeitgeist*.

First, feeling, emotion, *soul* trumped intellect, rationality, or reason. This was of special import for music, of course. But passion was held in higher regard than calculation and, in any case, was considered more honest.

Second, the church and the state were arbitrary devices of human (and therefore flawed) invention. Nature, particularly wilderness untrammeled by civilization, was not only where beauty originated but also where the sacred was most accessible. The contrast between this and electric guitars was extreme, and many chose to follow the lead of the New Lost City Ramblers back to the sylvan glades of Appalachia. For most, however, the contradiction could be resolved by living communally, perhaps in the country, while still enjoying the big beat of the ballrooms.

Third, the possession of objects prevented being possessed by spirits. Hoarding *things* was opposed to gaining experience. Above all, the infinite and eternal lay within, in one's consciousness, and not without, in one's position in the rat race.

These principles provided a moral compass rather than a theoretical program, but they nonetheless guided action. Specifically, they informed what became a full-scale assault on romanticism's two competitors in the arts: didacticism and classicism. Didacticism was the guiding principle of the Old Left in the United States, which viewed the role of music and art as primarily educational. Education served to improve the understanding and unify the efforts of working people, urban and rural alike, by using folk forms created directly by the people themselves, infusing them with lyrical or imagistic content that corresponded to working people's collective interests. There is a very long tradition of such work dating back to Irish revolutionary songs, the songs of Joe Hill and the Industrial Workers of the World, and, for that matter, every revolutionary movement in history. Indeed, this was a major element in Teatro Campesino's practice with farmworkers.

The one thing didacticism and romanticism agreed upon was that classicism was the enemy. Classical was not in this sense confined to the European canon but was a way of incorporating music of any kind into the structures of rule, of making it both a servant of hierarchy and a purely aesthetic pleasure.

Prior to the Sixties, classicism dominated through Hollywood films, the Broadway musical, and the popular songs of Tin Pan Alley. Classicism corresponds to the refinement of form, the professionalization of performance, and the institutionalization of artistic production. Its purpose was to confine artistic expression to personal gratification and to provide diversion from the alienation produced by life under capitalism. Its greatest servants were the critics and journalists who extolled not only the "great works" but also the superiority of the classical mode of creation and apprehension of art. As a rule, this corresponded to commercial success, but it rested on an ideological bedrock that made the consumption of art equivalent to the consumption of medicine. It was, above all, therapeutic—an exalted form of pain relief. Using philosopher Alain Badiou's schema, the three aesthetic modes corresponded to education (didacticism), therapy (classicism), and truth (romanticism).[12]

What is most compelling about the Sixties is the complete triumph of romanticism over its rivals. Old hierarchies were shattered and assumptions of superiority upended, as "high" and "low" art ceased to be meaningful categories. The most exciting and novel works were being produced outside the boundaries set by classicism's arbiters of taste.

Furthermore, romanticism elevated what otherwise might be ethical matters into social concerns that became rallying points for millions. Of course, there were still plenty of works of a classical nature being produced. But classicism had been dealt a crippling blow that could only be addressed by a wholesale renovation of technique.

Rock Music Journalism: The New Classicism

These conditions gave rise to rock journalism in general and *Rolling Stone* in particular. Founded in San Francisco in 1967 by Jann Wenner and Ralph J. Gleason, the magazine modeled itself after underground newspapers like the *Berkeley Barb* while focusing on cultural affairs, especially rock music. Gleason's prestige was crucial to *Rolling Stone*'s future. Almost immediately, however, disputes between Gleason and Wenner led to Gleason's acrimonious departure. "He battled with his protege over editorial issues and personnel matters," wrote Joel Selvin in a retrospective on Gleason.[13] Things went so far that shortly prior to his death, "Gleason began frustrating, infuriating negotiations with Wenner to sell back his stock in Rolling Stone. 'Do me a favor,' Gleason said to a mutual associate he bumped into on the streets of Berkeley. 'The next time you see him, punch him in the nose for me.'" The details of such disputes are less important than what is a clear distinction between the strategy Wenner followed and what Gleason's life had been dedicated to. Wenner made rock journalism the "new classicism," forging a close alliance with the music industry which proved to be highly lucrative for all parties. But it didn't stop with business, as *Rolling Stone* became a mouthpiece for the Democratic Party, not only championing rock's return to the cultural mainstream but encouraging the view that politics consisted of supporting the system.[14]

Was Gleason complicit in this? What distinguishes his work from that of Wenner? Here's what he himself wrote: "Press parties and junkets are an abomination, a device to substitute money for intelligence and to buy the press' cooperation with jet flights, free booze and the rest. Were I in charge of any rock paper I would forbid the staff to attend press parties and insist that any interview which has to include a flight to Vegas and one or two days at the Century Plaza is no interview at all." This appeared, ironically enough, in *Rolling Stone*.[15] Second, Gleason was associated with radical politics both before and after the founding of *Rolling Stone*. Alvah Bessie, a writer blacklisted by the Red Scare, recalled Gleason greeting him by announcing, "I'm a fan of yours. I used to read your stuff in *New Masses* when I was growing up in New York."[16] Leonard Feather, while fact-checking an *Encyclopedia of Jazz* entry on Gleason, had a conversation that closed with Gleason saying, "Please don't forget to include that I was on the White House Enemies List. That's the honor I'm most proud of." While never openly affiliated with any political organization, it's evident from his close association with artists, such as photographer and social activist Jerry Stoll, that Gleason was actively sympathetic to left-wing politics. The terms in which he defended the Free Speech Movement make this abundantly clear:

> In the face of a university which abandoned its nerve center to armed policy, on the first university campus outside Mississippi to be taken over by the cops, dragged to jail by cops who removed their badges so as not to be identified, in the face of a torrent of apoplectic outrage from the elders of the tribe who felt their positions threatened, this generation has stood up and continued to speak plainly of truth.[17]

This did not prevent Gleason from making some questionable choices, some of which put him at odds with radicals. Gleason, for example, defended Bill Graham, championed the Wild West Festival, and gave his blessing to the Monterey Pop Festival. With all his enthusiasm for the "San Francisco sound," he was largely uncritical when it came to the music industry. If anything, Gleason was a romantic. His conviction was that music was a powerful and autonomous force. Even if the means of its propagation were in the hands of capitalists, they were ultimately incapable of suppressing music's liberating effects. Furthermore, revolution meant overthrowing the government, not the music business.

Prisoners of Logic versus Visions of the Future

Gleason's "prisoners of logic" remark bears closer scrutiny because it was made in the context of a major public debate. The debate had been sharpened, if not initiated, by Herbert Marcuse's widely influential book, *One Dimensional Man* (1964). Marcuse had a large following among college students, broad influence in the New Left and was embroiled in controversies which kept him in the headlines. *One Dimensional Man* analyzed how the system used "technological rationality" to transform Reason from liberator of consciousness into "labor-saving device," providing leisure time devoid of thought. "Theoretical and practical Reason, academic and social behaviorism meet on common ground: that of an advanced society which makes scientific and technical progress into an instrument of domination."[18] This was manifest not only in the threat of nuclear annihilation but the advance of automation. The insanity of Mutually Assured Destruction had its immediate corollary in the robotization of work, a vision being widely promoted by its proponents in industry and government. Together, these strategies were consigning humanity to servitude in a "Warfare/Welfare State."[19]

This was specifically linked to art by means of *repressive desublimation*. "Man today can do *more* than the culture heroes and half-gods; he has solved many insoluble problems. But he has also betrayed the hope and destroyed the truth which were preserved in the higher culture."[20] While the "higher culture" was no doubt a bourgeois culture, it nonetheless retained "a rational, cognitive force, revealing a dimension of man and nature which was repressed and repelled in reality." Repressive desublimation gutted art of any oppositional or critical capacity. Furthermore, this was not confined to the United States; it was a characteristic of the Cold War between the United States and the USSR. "The greatness of a free literature and art, the ideals of humanism, the sorrows and joys of the individual, the fulfillment of the personality are important items in the competitive struggle between East and West. They speak heavily against the present forms of communism, and they are daily administered and sold."[21] Against this, "art contains the rationality of negation. In its advanced positions, it is the Great Refusal—the protest against that which is."[22]

The Great Refusal thus embraces art's rivalry with the state. But the Great Refusal is predicated on more than opposition to or criticism of the state's present failures. Rather, the Great Refusal implies an affirmation of the future. The divine, in this sense, has nothing to do with God or theology. It is not an entity, but the power (as Vico pointed out) to *foretell*. Art and science vie in the quest to unlock the secrets of the universe. Not a religious submission to mystery, but the bringing to human consciousness those truths that set us free. While science had undoubtedly produced many stunning results, it nonetheless foretold a grim future of unfreedom manifest in nuclear annihilation and slavery to machines. Art, on the other hand, still retained the power of imagination, which in turn allied itself with the one indispensable element of revolutionary politics: *the world to come*.[23]

From Plato's *Republic* to the *Communist Manifesto*, from Thomas More's *Utopia* to William Morris's *News from Nowhere*, visions of a world transformed have guided human thought and the struggle to fulfill thought's potential. Call it heaven on earth or call it communism, this future is irrepressible because the future itself is the province of the mind. Not that consciousness is only to be found in the future, but that only in consciousness is the future to be found. Yet the very conceiving of it makes the future more than an object for contemplation. The future becomes the embodiment, in thought, of thought's own capacity to change the world. This capacity, in turn, makes the demand that consciousness not only free itself but also guide the liberation of all humanity. The struggle to realize this in social practice is what comprises history. But history demonstrates that this struggle must be directed by the future, or history will endlessly repeat itself. And therein lies the seed of art's conflict with the state. Who has the vision, who truly sees, and above all, who can articulate humanity's liberation? Is it the poet or the philosopher? Who will reveal or produce the truth? Who knows the way to the world to come?

By the Sixties, one thing was abundantly clear: the Soviet Union was not the Promised Land. If anything, the Soviet Union had betrayed a great revolution. When people spoke of the system, it included the Soviet Union as a necessary complement to U.S. imperialism. But even as millions became increasingly aware of what they were fighting against, the example of the USSR obscured the vital question of what people were fighting *for*. This was further complicated by the examples of China, Cuba, and Vietnam—Third World countries that, at the very least, had freed (or were freeing) themselves from imperialism, and therefore deserved support. But even in these cases, the question of the future was muddled by turning an idea into a place. The Promised Land was a country, an actual place, we in the United States (or Europe) could actively support and even emulate. This meant the future as an idea and a guide was left empty of creative content. Revolutionaries could easily envision the future in negative terms, compiling a list of all the systemic evils that would be negated by a revolution. But that only presented the future as what *would not be*. This abandoned to the artist the more important task of imagining and articulating what human liberation would look like—not only a beacon of light but a new society that would be illuminated by that light.

As a consequence, divisions appeared that would widen as the Sixties unfolded. Not only were there splits between the Old Left and the New Left, between the civil rights struggle and Black Power, between reformists and revolutionaries, there was also a sharpening divide between those who viewed art as a weapon of political struggle and those who viewed art as the instrument of change in *opposition* to political struggle. We will explore this more fully in later chapters. What is important here is to note that even as the movement grew, eventually mobilizing tens of millions of ordinary people in opposition to the system, the rivalry between art and the state manifested itself also as a rivalry between art and those who sought to overthrow or radically transform the state. Many were convinced, for example, that music would make the revolution. On a mundane level, this might seem absurd, but in the midst of great turbulence involving increasing state violence directed at protest of any kind, it is not so easy to dismiss the wish that somehow the world would be inspired by joyful sound to lay its weapons down. Besides, everyone from the imperialist to the revolutionary sought to win the war for hearts and minds. What few were able to grasp was the dialectical connection between envisioning a future and its ultimate achievement in social practice. Or, as Ngugi wa Thiong'o so clearly expressed it in *Penpoints, Gunpoints, and Dreams*, to "sleep not to dream but dream to change the world, to change the conditions that confine human life. This is the mission of art, and it is often in conflict with the state as we have known it up to now."[24]

It must not be forgotten, however, that in the ferment of the Sixties, art's rivalry with the state made art an ally of popular and revolutionary movements. This was not limited to agitprop theatrical performances, protest songs or revolutionary anthems, and graphic or literary depictions of political events. Indeed, a distinguishing feature of the Sixties is that the terrain on which art fought the state most often, and perhaps most effectively, was not overtly political, except insofar as state repression made it so. Of course, overtly political art abounded, and the era produced innumerable examples of art that spread the word, rallied the oppressed, and exposed the hypocrisy and destructiveness of the system. Some unabashedly political art was both innovative and timeless, exerting a widespread influence felt to this day. But the main threat posed by art in general, and music in particular, was throwing into chaos and disorder aesthetic hierarchies, educational priorities, and Enlightenment epistemologies. Upending high and low led to the collapse of ranking itself—at least according to the criteria established by the state. Art proclaimed itself the harvester of dreams and legislator of ideality—at once the champion of futures foreclosed by the state and of the practices that could make such futures present.

CHAPTER 7

The Underground Is on the Air: Radio, Recording, Innovation, and Co-optation

With a few notable exceptions, by 1967 AM radio was an arid terrain dominated by corporate shills.[1] What comfort or consolation teenagers might have once derived from rock 'n' roll or rhythm and blues stations was increasingly diluted by dumb patter, silly ads, and constricted playlists. Only two years before, Top 40 radio still retained a vibrancy due to the content provided it by the British Invasion and extraordinary works of black music, particularly rhythm and blues and soul. But the speed with which events unfolded was manifest in music to such an extent that the structures created by the music industry for the promotion and sale of its product were at best woefully inadequate, at worst embarrassing anachronisms. It began to dawn on people that what was really happening in music was *not* on the radio!

Launched in 1949, KPFA was the pioneer of public radio in the United States and had a disproportionate influence in the Bay Area, particularly on those musicians interested in noncommercial or "authentic" music. Most importantly, it welded together the disparate strands of oppositional politics throughout the darkest hours of the Cold War and McCarthyism. That it endures to this day, while KMPX, KSAN, and their "underground" progeny do not, casts light on certain illusions that will become apparent as our story unfolds. Nevertheless, the birth of KMPX in San Francisco in 1967 was groundbreaking in ways that differed from KPFA. Most obviously, KPFA was a noncommercial, listener-sponsored station and KMPX was owned by a corporation, sold air time to make a profit and was never, even in its most radical and outrageous phase, independent of the legal and financial structures that govern commercial media in the United States. This makes what transpired over the course of several years all the more anomalous and subversive. Along with the vast proliferation of underground newspapers, KMPX was an incursion into territory dominated by the system, and like its print media siblings, it thrived in direct proportion to the size and consciousness of its audience.

In a little-known book entitled *Hip Capitalism*, author Susan Krieger carefully documents the rise and fall of KMPX/KSAN, examining the contributions of many individuals, especially those of Tom Donahue. The book began as Krieger's doctoral dissertation in communications at Stanford University, which she was attending in the 1970s. Its original title was *Cooptation: A History of a Radio Station*.[2] I call attention to this book not only to credit it as a source but to highlight how the crucial role of radio stations is largely absent from most accounts of the era. While plenty of ink has been devoted to Donahue, KMPX, and freeform radio, such "legend and lore" of San Francisco in the Sixties obscures as much as it reveals and provides little substantive documentation. Donahue's induction into the Rock and Roll Hall of Fame, for example, is recognition of some vague socio-cultural importance, while inadvertently presenting a classic case of cooptation. If nothing else, this episode and Krieger's account put the lie to a fundamental premise of the "official story" promulgated by the rock music establishment: namely that San Francisco's renaissance was essentially *apolitical*, its inspiration aesthetic or hedonistic, not remotely concerned with power, as in Power to the People.

As both titles of Krieger's study suggest, struggle raged from the birth to the demise of freeform radio. Conflicting agendas might at one time flow together and at another rip acrimoniously apart. The very words "hip" and "capitalism" were heavily loaded. So were others such as "revolution" or "liberation," as used in everyday conversation. What lent them weight was far from academic hair splitting. These were "fightin' words," by which one could be branded a hero or a villain. Having had some experience with vilification at the hands of capitalism in its normative, unhip mode, Tom Donahue found himself uniquely situated on a battlefield.

Donahue had come to the Bay Area from Philadelphia, an escapee from the payola scandal. In the early 1960s, several well-known DJs, the most famous being Alan Freed, had not only seen their careers go into decline but had found themselves threatened with fines and jail sentences for accepting bribes (payola) from record companies in return for playing particular records. The story of payola is beyond the scope of this book, but suffice it to say that from its inception, the music business in the U.S. employed song-plugging and all the devious methods selling entails.[3] The indictment of certain DJs for what was and remains a standard industry practice was ultimately a ploy designed to placate conservatives seeking to suppress rock 'n' roll and the deviant behavior of white youth.[4]

In 1961, Donahue landed a job at a Top 40 AM station, KYA, and quickly became one of a handful of hip DJs that included his partner in other music-related ventures, Bobby "Tripp" Mitchell, and Russ "the Moose" Syracuse. From their influential position, Donahue and Mitchell went on to become concert promoters, which in turn led them to start a record company, the aforementioned Autumn Records, to take advantage of the growing quantity of local talent in the Bay Area and the corresponding absence of record companies interested in recording it. Success in San Francisco did not, however, completely erase the taint of corruption attached to Donahue. As Krieger writes, "He had never fully renounced his associations with payola practices in Philadelphia and he seemed to take pride in viewing himself as one of the 'lepers of the industry.' He was a grown man who had been playing music for kids before that had a cloak of intellectual respectability."[5] Though he eventually sought and gained official clearance of all of the FCC charges, there was a certain disturbing quality about Donahue, something that made "respectable" people uneasy—the hint, as Krieger put it, "that somewhere, near to the core, he was a dangerous man."[6]

Politically speaking, none of this made Donahue more than a left-leaning liberal, but his encounters with the social milieu of San Francisco definitely pushed him in an increasingly radical direction. There was also a basic honesty that forced Donahue to rebel against the absurdities of radio programming in America, subsequently leading him to write a highly influential essay entitled "AM Radio Is Dead and Its Rotting Corpse Is Stinking Up the Airwaves." From his perspective, it was clear that the real corruption in society started at the top with those who controlled everything and that what was happening in his newfound home was only the healthy response of idealistic young people. He once quipped on air, "The news today, friends, is obscene, dirty, immoral, filthy, smutty news. But if you cook up a brownie, it doesn't taste all that bad. Meanwhile, the Vietnam War is still going on, and, man, that's obscene."[7]

At the same time, expressing a notion shared by likeminded people in or around the music business, Donahue said in one interview, "The Establishment will probably end up financing the revolution."[8] What he meant was that the corporate minions running record companies and radio stations were so out of it that they couldn't grasp the radical changes in popular consciousness being wrought by the very products they purveyed. Support for this sentiment was everywhere in evidence, particularly in the immediate and unexpected success of KMPX. But it reveals a flaw as well, one that would prove decisive in the years to come. Donahue and others thought that co-optation went both ways—that the revolution would co-opt the Establishment, taking over from inept, dimwitted managers before they realized what was happening.

Freeform Radio

Larry Miller, a DJ who had relocated from Detroit, was the first to broadcast his own favorite records on KMPX, an eclectic mix of folk, classical, jazz, and some rock. He was first to play entire albums—the latest Bob Dylan release, for example, which he might follow with Ravi Shankar or Sun Ra. Miller was hired for $45 a week in February 1967 to hold down the midnight to six slot on what was otherwise a foreign language station. To the surprise of his employer, Leon Crosby, whose Crosby-Pacific Broadcasting Company owned KMPX, Miller attracted a sizable following. This was no small feat given that this was a virtually moribund station, and many people didn't even have FM receivers in 1967. Miller worked almost alone, handling everything from selling air time to buying the records he played on his show, and even cleaning up the 50 Grant Street studio.

Simultaneously, Donahue had been searching for a chance to experiment with radio since two other pioneering ventures—Autumn Records and Mother's, discussed in Chapter 3—had come to a premature end. Apparently Donahue didn't know about Miller's show, didn't even have an FM radio, but had been given a tip that he should contact the management of KMPX to see if they were interested in his vision for a new kind of programming. Ralph Gleason, with whom Donahue had shared a cordial relationship for several years, provided the tip. Gleason knew that Donahue had been in the thick of things since arriving in San Francisco, displaying a rare combination of integrity and daring in all his dealings around town. Even if his forays proved commercially unsuccessful, Donahue gambled with his own resources, guided by his good taste in music and his distaste for "conventional wisdom." Hiring a nineteen-year-old black kid from Vallejo (Sly Stone) to produce records for Autumn had been a particular stroke of genius.

Within two weeks of his April 7 debut in the eight to midnight slot that preceded Miller's, Donahue was overwhelmed with listener response. Letters poured in, the phone rang off the hook, and people started dropping by the station with decorations and other gifts. Unprepared for the speed with which an audience was gathering, Donahue and the station's owners didn't even have a rate card for the air time they were selling. Donahue scrambled to meet the response, while simultaneously assembling an assortment of industry veterans, dope dealers, and (long before affirmative action) female engineers. In fact, Donahue went so far as to announce on air that he was looking for engineers, but that he only wanted to hire women. His sales staff consisted of Milan Melvin, Chandler Laughlin, and Jack Towle, all of whom were pot dealers, which in Donahue's eyes made them perfectly suited to approach local merchants like the young owners of the North Face outdoor clothing store or Don Wehr's Music City. The methods chosen and the constituent individuals involved were direct extensions of a large and expanding community that defined itself according to specific cultural and political criteria. This did not exclude wildly contradictory positions; it embraced them. Combining New Age spiritualism and "back to the land" communalism with black radicalism and a general anticapitalism, a plethora of people overflowing with ideas gathered under a glowing, multicolored umbrella, intoxicated not only by the drugs and music but also by a spirit of insurgency that was palpable.

Charting the course of this endeavor is therefore to follow many of the main trends in music and politics as they unfolded in the Bay Area. The rapid evolution from a general and unfocused antiauthoritarianism to more clearly articulated positions in subsequent years, particularly as expressed on the news programs of Scoop Nisker and Dave McQueen, not only paralleled developments in society at large, it *shaped* them. Originally, it was driven by a new approach to broadcasting recorded music. Playing the Beatles' *Sgt. Pepper* album in its entirety a day before its release had thousands of young people glued to their radios. Launching Moby Grape's debut album by playing it nonstop did too. Soon this became the norm. Interspersed with announcements as personal as requests for rides to Mendocino and as public as ones about antiwar demonstrations or Digger happenings, KMPX transformed radio into a gathering point and bulletin board of unprecedented quality and scope. Never before had any radio station, including KPFA, been such a center of cultural life. Of course, it couldn't last. Not only was the system constantly wielding the twin blades of coercion and co-optation but, internal to the movement and the diverse forms of cultural opposition, divisions were appearing that would ultimately break apart what had begun as a unifying force.

In the years between 1966 and 1973, as far as KMPX and KSAN were concerned, it was by no means a foregone conclusion that the revolution would end in defeat. The very reason to call attention to this anomaly in the annals of radio history is that it reveals how the crisis confronting the system unleashed a response among the populace the system could not initially contain. Even after a strike against KMPX's management was brought to an unsuccessful conclusion, Donahue and most of his crew moved on to an even larger corporation, Metromedia, to begin their experiment anew under the call letters KSAN. If anything, programming became even more adventurous, and definitely more radical. A perfect example was the case of avowedly revolutionary DJ, Roland Young, who became the focus of heated controversy that eventually led to his firing on phony charges of inciting violence—for a *report* on a speech by the Black Panthers' David Hilliard, in which Hilliard rhetorically threatened the life of the president.[9]

People from a much broader spectrum than could be called countercultural routinely tuned in to Nisker's and McQueen's newscasts. Particularly during the Chicago 7 trial and subsequent Angela Davis case, KSAN was relied upon by revolutionaries as a trustworthy source of information as well as crucial outlet for their views. Scoop Nisker summed up the prevailing mood in a piece he wrote shortly after he was forced to resign from KSAN for encouraging listeners to attend an antiwar demonstration, thus breaking a taboo for an "objective" newscaster. Nisker's piece appeared on the front page of the *San Francisco Good Times*:

> In general, we must understand that the media controls America by controlling the images which shape the thinking and the desires of the people. The administration knows this fact well. We must get the new images on the air and on the screen. The truth about alternative ways of living and thinking, who we are and the truth about

our struggle against the corrupt violent death-oriented country we live in. Our truth. Our objectivity. Right now the media are political prisoners. Free the media! Free the imagination![10]

Which is to say, first of all, that what gave KMPX its immediate success was the same community that made the Fillmore a success. A community, moreover, that was thriving before the Human Be-In of January 1967, before Larry Miller's first broadcast in February, and well before corporate media or the music industry caught on. It was, however, plagued from the start by weaknesses dialectically connected to its strengths, leaving it ultimately defenseless against co-optation, albeit in hip guise. An advertisement aired on KSAN perfectly illustrates the conundrum: a couple is talking about where they want to buy records, one says to the other, "Darling, where else would I shop for my records? Only Leopold's has X-69. Now, when I spend my record dollar, I don't want it sitting in the pocket of some fat capitalist, I want it recycled! And that's what X-69 does—it recycles the money into the pockets of community groups. So take it from me, darling, I wouldn't be caught dead in another record store, no matter what hypes they used."[11]

33⅓ Revolutions per Minute

Needless to say, radio has relied on music to attract listeners from the first broadcast to the present day. But the music upon which KMPX/KSAN relied was undergoing a transformation that in turn gave underground radio its identity and purpose. Underground radio's identity was partly the result of playing entire records—not just singles—and of combining many styles of music, mixing the wildly experimental with the more familiar. But the format change also formed a symbiosis with developments in music that preceded it. Indeed, the sounds music was capable of incorporating were very quickly increasing in number and diversity. Pioneers of the recorded medium were to be found in both the popular and avant-garde fields, ranging from rock 'n' roll groups to classically trained composers. No doubt technology played an important role in this, as the medium of tape made recording much easier to manage and experiment with than had older methods of direct to disc and copper wire, or, in the case of Conlon Nancarrow, sophisticated reworkings of the player piano. But the innovations in technology were driven by the creativity of musicians, who were forcing technology to catch up.

Gathered around the San Francisco Tape Music Center, the San Francisco Conservatory of Music, and Mills College were composers who sought new possibilities by incorporating amplifiers, microphones, loudspeakers, and tape recorders into their compositions. This can be distinguished from the well-established practice of recording compositions performed independently of recording as such (recording a live concert, for example). Such experimentation was by no means confined to the Bay Area, but specific innovations made there by composers such as Terry Riley, Steve Reich, Morton Subotnick, Ramon Sender, Pauline Oliveros, and others gained international renown. Subotnick, Sender, and Oliveros were undoubtedly among the pioneers of electronic music, inspired by the work of Bay Area native Henry Cowell, who a generation before had written *New Musical Resources* and commissioned Leon Theremin to build the world's first drum machine, the Rhythmicon. Steve Reich's "Come Out" and "It's Gonna Rain" are well known examples of compositions based entirely on recorded sound. They also express Reich's political concerns: "Come Out" was composed to benefit the Harlem Six, and "It's Gonna Rain" was inspired by the Cuban Missile Crisis.

At the other extreme, Terry Riley's "In C" is performable without electricity by any ensemble of musicians capable of producing the fifty-three short, numbered musical phrases that make up the piece. A groundbreaking work of minimalism, "In C" was first performed by Reich, Subotnick, Oliveros, and others in 1964. It was subsequently recorded and released in 1968 to widespread acclaim. Riley had been experimenting with tape loops since the tape recorder became available in the 1950s, and the combination of electronics and minimalism opened fertile ground for the next generation of musicians, including Pete Townshend of the Who and Brian Eno. It's not surprising that the first synthesizer was invented by Don Buchla, who was commissioned to do so by Subotnick and Sender. Interestingly, Buchla's first synthesizer was not designed for recording purposes but for live performance, since it enabled the performer to control a wide range of electronically produced sound through means such as touch-sensitive plates. (Eventually, this would lead back to conventional keyboards for ease of use.)

Marginal as any avant-garde may be, the Bay Area encouraged collaborations that might well have been viewed as pandering to popular taste or as an inexcusable compromise of aesthetic principle in New York or Los Angeles. Steve Reich composed music for the Mime Troupe, for example. The same is true of Phil Lesh of the Grateful Dead, who was first involved Mills College scene before ever taking up the bass and rock 'n' roll. Peter Albin recalls Chet Helms introducing members of Big Brother to people from the Tape Music Center, which prompted Ramon Sender to experiment with sending Jim Gurley's electric guitar through a ring modulator. "Ramon thought he could do something with the band at the Trips Festival he was organizing for January 1966 at Longshoremen's Hall. We performed at the Trips Festival. A few songs. Ken Kesey cut us off saying we didn't sound good."[12] This humorous anecdote is relevant here, because the Trips Festival was based far more on the experimental music of the Tape Music Center and the light shows developed by visual artists who were associated with them, than it was on rock 'n' roll. From the very start, the San Francisco musical renaissance found a crucial source of its inspiration in the innovations made far away from the popular arts, yet connected to them by the common determination to challenge convention and test the limits.

It is well known that the Beatles were in the forefront, not only of the transformation of popular music but, more specifically, the transformation of recording into an art form independent of live performance. Prior to Sgt. Pepper, and for some time thereafter, recorded music relied almost entirely on a performance by a musician or group that was in all essential features the same as would be presented on a concert stage. The advent of multi-track tape recorders was an indispensable part of the Beatles' creative breakthroughs, since it enabled the composition of a single piece out of many performances none of which had to be recorded at the same time. "The conceptual breakthrough had been made with three-track," recalls producer David Rubinson, "with selective synchronization and punching in, time and space change, since everything did not have to be done at once."[13] But as Rubinson is quick to point out, this was not simply a technological change. "Follow the logic. The producer had all the power. Suddenly changes in a performance could be made that at least in theory gave the artist input, though, at first, not a lot." The Beatles were in the extraordinary position to give a lot of input. Combined with the introduction of the *four*-track machine and the best microphones, preamplifiers, and mixing consoles in the world, the Beatles had the opportunity to make unprecedented use of the recording studio, turning it into a musical instrument of a new type.

These changes, however, were predicated on others. "Had there been no rock 'n' roll, there would have been no rush to make the tech breakthrough," Rubinson points out. "There was this 'fuck you' attitude, 'Yes, I'm turning it up and I'm doing it wrong on purpose, not the way *you* did it. I'm making this so you hate it!' That demanded the tech breakthrough. There wasn't *enough* technology to match the creativity of the people." This is confirmed by engineer Paul Stubblebine: "There were still fights over the technology. Basically, how loud could you play in the studio. I came from the band perspective, the live perspective. They didn't want a limit on how loud they could play. They wanted to be able to roar; to get their tones and their energy."[14]

"Then," Rubinson adds, "the black musicians said, 'How about us?'" Among the first to do so was Sly Stone who, along with Rubinson, was one of only a handful of producers in the Bay Area. In fact, Sly had produced a variety of styles from rhythm and blues ("C'mon and Swim") to Beatles-influenced rock ("Laugh, Laugh") as well as his own "Underdog" on the first Sly and the Family Stone album, *Whole New Thing*. Just as the Beatles found themselves in a unique position due to their unparalleled success, Sly found himself in a unique position because he was in the Bay Area at a crucial moment in history. In Sly's case, this moment afforded him an opportunity denied most black musicians at that time; it enabled him to combine musical elements he might not have been exposed to, let alone encouraged to use, in other parts of the United States. As Jerry Slick, drummer of the Great! Society recalls, "Sly was producing us. Here were these white kids from the peninsula. Here was Sly, a consummate musician, who could play any of our instruments better than we would ever be able to *in our entire lives*. Still, he was impressed with our tunes. The fact that we had written some songs. This was at a time when he was a DJ, he was playing in cover bands in North Beach. I don't think he was doing any composing at that point [1965]."[15]

Slick went on to point out what was an important development, "Sly overdubbed a lot of drum parts, even had his friend Billy Preston come in and play kick drum on a cardboard box." This marked a major change in the process of recording. As Rubinson explains:

> The musicians were taking control of the means of production. If you view this as a Marxist paradigm, you see where this is heading. The means of production were in the hands of white record

companies, the producer who was sent in to tell Louie Armstrong or Bessie Smith what to do. But the rockers broke that. "Get these record company people out of here. Get these honkies *outta* here!" Then there was a paradigm shift. The means of production were being taken over by the workers, in a sense, and that's where Sly came from, because Sly said, "Hey, if Jefferson Airplane gets to mix their own record and work 20 hours on one song, I want that, too."

Two points bear repeating. First, before this, there was no music industry to speak of in the Bay Area. There were only a few recording studios, designed for advertising and augmented by a bit of jazz or folk. Much of the seminal music that made San Francisco's reputation was in fact recorded in Los Angeles. "Up until 1969, there were no rock 'n' roll studios in the Bay Area," recalls Paul Stubblebine. Indeed, Rubinson's arrival in San Francisco from New York was a revelation to a young man trained in the great recording studios of Columbia Records, a milieu which encouraged the notion that outside of a few special cases like Memphis or Detroit, everything worth recording came to or from New York.

The second phenomena was related to the first: with the corrosive influence of the music industry at a minimum, musical expression was led by the instincts and passions of musicians themselves. The results were, of course, a large and diverse body of timeless work. Citing only a few well known examples is sufficient to make the point: Tower of Power, Santana, Sly and the Family Stone, the Doobie Brothers, Azteca, Malo, and Creedence Clearwater Revival are only a small sample of the groups that made important records. Joining them from genres more diverse are Denny Zeitlin, the Jerry Hahn Brotherhood, the Fourth Way, and Taj Mahal, all of whom were in one way or another nourished by what was happening in the Bay Area. (In Taj Mahal's case, the story is complicated by a landmark lawsuit he filed and won against none other than Bill Graham, which we'll explore further on.) Contrary to the myths upon which the music industry justifies its existence, the renaissance in the Bay Area came about largely due to the creativity of musicians and the encouragement they received from an aroused populace, not from bean counters and bagmen in LA. As Stubblebine put it, "The Sons were signed to Capitol. The second album was cut in LA where we were welcomed by the staff engineer proudly saying, 'A lot of hits have been recorded in this studio!' And we thought, 'How crass! Commercialism, boo.' The Sons, even more than most bands, were idealistic. We wanted to make great records, and if the world loved 'em, great, but we're not going in to cut a hit. We're going in to record this manifesto which is gonna help the world change."

David Rubinson's role in this is important for reasons similar to Tom Donahue's role in underground or freeform radio. Rubinson initially came to San Francisco in 1965 at the behest of Columbia Records to produce a recording of comedy team Burns and Schreiber at the hungry i. He'd gotten the gig at Columbia in part because of his OBIE award-winning production of Mark Blitzstein's musical *The Cradle Will Rock*. Once in San Francisco, however, Rubinson encountered the Mime Troupe. "I saw the Troupe perform," he recalls, "and met Ronnie and Bill Graham. I wanted to produce the Troupe in New York! I was around for the bust, and then attended the first benefit, which completely blew my mind. People were free, politically astute, the music was wild—besides, nothing was happening in New York. Folk was a benign 'We Shall Overcome' music; it was *Sing Out* and Dylan, but it wasn't a street thing. The Mime Troupe was the catalyst, for me and for a lot of things." That Rubinson went on to produce some of the most important records of the era— the Chambers Brothers, Taj Mahal, Malo, Tower of Power, the Pointer Sisters, Moby Grape, and many others—testifies to this fact. But achieving such results was an uphill battle against the entrenched viewpoints of his superiors in New York.

There were, of course, the perennial conflicts pitting craft against commercialism. Now, however, the problem was being exacerbated by the resistance of an old guard, who were still respected for the music they had produced, but who looked upon San Francisco with disdain. Yet such disdain could not withstand rapid developments in music itself, which were forcing this confrontation. The tension could not simply be reduced to crazy hippies versus wise guardians. Many of the most brilliant innovations were being made by black musicians, who could not be branded as irresponsible middle-class brats. As Rubinson saw it, "It was a crusade—not only to change the world but to change the grownups. Change the way they looked at things, change the results of how they looked at things—it had to change, it was not sustainable." Rubinson therefore found himself in the role of "running interference," as he put it, between the artist and the record company. In an unequal battle, the only power Rubinson had was his own convictions and the support of the

BAY AREA FRIENDS OF SNCC *
&
MARY ANN POLLAR PRESENT

A
SNCC
BENEFIT CONCERT

★ THE
★ FREEDOM
★ SINGERS
★ OF
★ ATLANTA,
★ GEORGIA

SATURDAY / OCTOBER 5 / 8:30 P.M.
BERKELEY COMMUNITY THEATRE • GROVE & ALLSTON WAY •
ADMISSION: $2.00 / INFORMATION: OL3-6328
TH3-8361
TICKETS: DOWNTOWN CENTER BOX OFFICE, S.F. / HUT T-1
S.F. STATE / RECORD CITY, CAMPUS RECORDS, ASUC BOX OFFICE,
REID'S RECORDS, BERKELEY / BELL'S COLLEGE BOOK SHOP, PALO
ALTO / KEPLER'S BOOKS, PALO ALTO & MENLO PARK •

* STUDENT NONVIOLENT COORDINATING COMMITTEE

1963 SNCC benefit

BAY AREA STUDENTS DISCUSS PLANS FOR CUBA TRIP
Christian Raisner, left, said travel ban "legally is a myth"

Forty persons from the Bay area, mostly students, have already signed up for the trip, Raisner said. They must put up $100 for travel expenses within this country, but the rest of the tab will be picked up by the Cuban Federation of University Students, he said.

Raisner, a senior at San Francisco State College, was flanked at yesterday's session by three veterans of last year's Cuban trip: State College students Eric Johnson, 20, and Luria Castell, 20, and San Francisco artist Robert Kaffke, 35.

They charged that persons who made the trip last year have been harassed by the FBI and State Department and have received threatening anonymous letters and telephone calls.

Three New Yorkers who made the trip were indicted by a Federal Grand Jury last September on charges they conspired to organize the project and for leaving and entering the country without valid passports. Their cases are pending.

San Francisco Examiner, March 20, 1964, San Francisco State College students charged harassment by the FBI for a trip to Cuba in 1963 (Luria Castell is speaking)

BILL GRAHAM PRESENTS

A SUNDAY AFTERNOON WITH

THE JEFFERSON AIRPLANE AND

THE HEDDS APRIL 3

FILLMORE AUDITORIUM

FILLMORE & GEARY STS.

2 p.m. to 6 p.m. $2.00

1965 Jefferson Airplane and the Hedds (Note the pre-psychedelic lettering)

20¢

THE MOVEMENT

published by the
STUDENT NONVIOLENT COORDINATING COMMITTEE
of california

OCTOBER 1966   VOL. 2 NO. 9

IN THIS ISSUE..

HOW TO RESEARCH A RURAL COMMUNITY
TORTURE IN SOUTH AFRICA
THE "POWER AND POLITICS" MEETING

HUNTERS POINT - COPS SHOT INTO COMMUNITY CENTER SHELTERING 200 CHILDREN

SAN FRANCISCO -- On Thursday September 27 about 4 o'clock in the afternoon, Matthew Johnson, 16, was shot in the back and killed by a policeman. The officer had stopped the car Johnson and a friend were riding in: he thought they looked suspicious.

The policeman, Alvin Johnson, 51, ordered the two out of the car and told them to raise their hands. Matthew Johnson

YOUNG HUNTERS POINT man watches burial of Johnson.

began to run down a hill with his hands raised. The officer says he fired three warning shots before hitting Johnson. A witness claims that all the shots were aimed at the boy.

At the time of the shooting the officer did not know that the car was stolen. The owners reported it as stolen several hours later.

HELP EXPORT THE MOVEMENT

Several revolutionary groups have written to us requesting subscriptions to THE MOVEMENT. We need some help if we are to send them copies. Airmailing one copy of the paper to Cuba costs 39¢, to Tanzania 75¢, to the National Liberation Front 45¢. It's important that they know what is happening inside this country. Can any of our readers send us a contribution toward the postage needed to mail THE MOVEMENT to these groups?

Soon after the shooting, the windows of a Rexall Drug Store were broken by an angry group of young Negro men. Further down the street, around the Bayview-Hunters Point Community Center, several young men together with some of the Center's community workers and Youth For Service, began to organize what later was called the Peace Patrol. This was only hours after the initial attack on the drug store. That night the Patrol numbered 50.

Early Wednesday morning several radio broadcasts reported that violence had broken out in the Fillmore District. However, one of THE MOVEMENT staff went down there and reported that only a few windows were broken and that all the streets leading into Fillmore between Geary and Haight Streets were completely cordoned off by the California Highway Patrol. All was quiet. The radio reports during the week were full of hysterical announcements of new "violence" and "riots." Checking them out, THE MOVEMENT found most of them not to exist or to be local fistfights between highschool students.

On Wednesday the 28th, the Peace Patrol demanded a meeting with Mayor Shelley, Governor Brown, Assemblyman Willie Brown, Assemblyman John Burton, and Congressman Phil Burton. The meeting was to be in Hunters Point. Only one of the Burtons showed up.

Downtown, a group of Hunters Point residents did meet with the Mayor that afternoon. Their meeting was interrupted by reports of more violence along Third Street.

The Peace Patrol had asked the police to get out of Third Street and to block off the street so no traffic would pass through. The Patrol had little success in stopping people from throwing rocks and bottles at passing cars, since the police would not block off Third Street and let the Patrol deal with their people.

Then a policeman was hit with a rock as he passed by in a squad car. He cried out, "I'm hit, I'm hit." The driver of the car called into headquarters, "My buddy is hit." He did not clarify what he meant by "hit."

At this time there were over 500 people on Third Street, mostly young people.

The police assumed he was shot and at 5 pm closed off Third Street to all traffic. Then they marched up to the Community Center, firing over the heads of the crowd.

All this time the Peace Patrol was trying to clear the streets. Some used bull horns and all wore black armbands.

COPS FIRE INTO CENTER

When the police reached the Community Center, one officer yelled, "There's a gun in there somewhere; they're firing at us!" On television and in the newspapers people saw the police fire into the building.

More than 200 children were in the Center at that time. This was not reported by any of the news media.

THE BODY OF MATTHEW JOHNSON, 16, shot to death by a San Francisco policeman, is carried out after funeral services. 1000 attended the Hunters Point funeral.

In a MOVEMENT interview with Harold Brooks, Director of the Center, he pointed out that the shooting lasted 7 or 8 minutes. "Minutes before," Brooks recalled, "the kids were in the windows. The police must have known they were in there."

Only three newspapers have interviewed Brooks or anyone else in the building at that time, THE MOVEMENT, The BERKELEY BARB, and the NATIONAL GUARDIAN. None of the Establishment press mentioned the number of children in the building.

"The children didn't expect the police would fire," Brooks said. "When the firing broke out, bedlam followed, until I got them to lie down. I went out the front door to get them to stop firing and let the kids out."

"After the kids got out, the police came looking for cocktails and guns. They didn't find anything."

Seven people were wounded outside the building at that time. Six were clearly marked Peace Patrol members. One, Adam Rogers, standing a block off Third Street, was telling people to get off the streets with a bull horn at the time he was wounded in the back. He kept screaming, "Why did they shoot me?"

The police later agreed to keep off

A few minutes later a squad of police closed off the street. They started grabbing people and putting them in a bus. About 70 were picked up. The police only went for hippies with long hair and sandals, students with beards, and Negroes, whether or not they were demonstrating.

One of THE MOVEMENT staff who looks like the all-American boy was pushed out of the way by a cop so he could arrest a hippie. A couple who had been shopping and had grocery bags in their arms were arrested. The charges were violating curfew, being a public nuisance, and inciting to riot.

The police entered some stores and pulled people out to arrest them -- again, only Negroes, students and hippies.

The police claim on their records that all the people were arrested at Haight and Cole. As far as we know, 70 were arrested at Clayton, some at Masonic and none at Cole. Clearly the police were trying to cover up the fact that they made no loudspeaker announcement of the curfew time. The newspapers and television said that the curfew was in the Fillmore and Hunters Point, not in the Haight-Ashbury or the Western Addition. The police have tried to claim that the Haight-

> **THE SEVERAL HUNDRED PEOPLE ARRESTED IN HUNTERS POINT AND HAIGHT-ASHBURY DISTRICTS OF SAN FRANCISCO, CANNOT, BEING POOR, AFFORD THE EXPENSES OF THEIR BAIL AND COURT COSTS.**
>
> **WE ASK OUR READERS TO SEND URGENTLY NEEDED MONEY FOR THEIR DEFENSE TO THE COUNCIL FOR JUSTICE, THE COMMITTEE OF VOLUNTEER LAWYERS HANDLING THEIR DEFENSE. MAKE CHECKS OUT TO CFJ BAIL FUND AND SEND TO 449 14th STREET, SAN FRANCISCO, CA 94103.**

Third Street entirely on Saturday night. Saturday night the Patrol would keep the peace.

CURFEW RAID IN HAIGHT-ASHBURY

Meanwhile, on Thursday night in the Haight-Ashbury district, some middle-class students and hippies demonstrated against the 8 p.m. curfew and the presence of the National Guard in the city. They demanded the withdrawal of the police and the Guard from Fillmore and Hunter's Point in solidarity with the Negro people.

At ten minutes to eight, according to Pete Robinson, a community worker at Hamilton Methodist Church, a police officer stepped out of his car and said, in a conversational tone, that there was a curfew and people should go home. He did not use the loudspeaker on the car.

Ashbury is part of the "Greater Fillmore," an area unknown to San Franciscans. But then the police have been aching to get their hands on those hippies for a long time.

A map published by the CHRONICLE showed the Western Addition curfew area gerrymandered around all areas with a large Negro population. St. Francis Square, a mostly white middleclass housing project, was excluded even though it lies in the middle of the Fillmore district.

One resident said that it would be impossible to move around the area without a map. Step across the wrong street and you're under arrest.

No daily newspapers were delivered in any of the curfew areas, even during the day, while the curfew lasted.

"Now Matthew Jones won't have to fight in Vietnam," said one of the signs carried by the Haight Street Demonstrators.

The Movement newspaper front page, October 1966 (Note "Curfew Raid in Haight-Ashbury" subhead in lead story)

134

1967 Straight Theater opening, with a representative sample of the San Francisco music scene at that time

1967 Benefit for Berkeley Strike Committee

1967 Week of Angry Arts—Spring Mobilization to End the War in Vietnam (Note: Quicksilver, Big Brother, Sopwith Camel, Country Joe and the Fish, Grateful Dead—the same groups that opened the Straight Theater)

1967 Vietnam Summer benefit

1967 Vietnam Summer benefit

1967 Vietnam Summer

1967 benefit for Quaker medical relief for North Vietnam

1967 Benefit for the Valley Peace Center

1967 benefit for Proposition P, a San Francisco initiative stating official opposition to the War in Vietnam (it was voted down). Note: although added too late to be included in the poster, this author's band, The Threshold, opened this show.

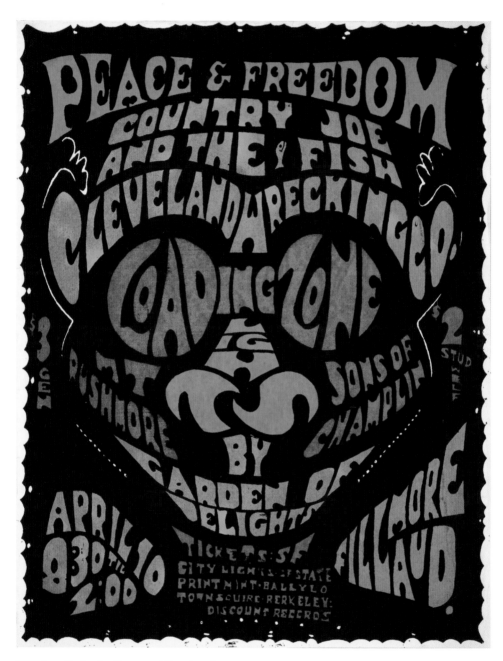

1968 Benefit for the Peace and Freedom Party

1969 Detroit's MC5 played the Straight Theater—one of the last shows at the Straight, which closed in 1969

Circa 1969

1969

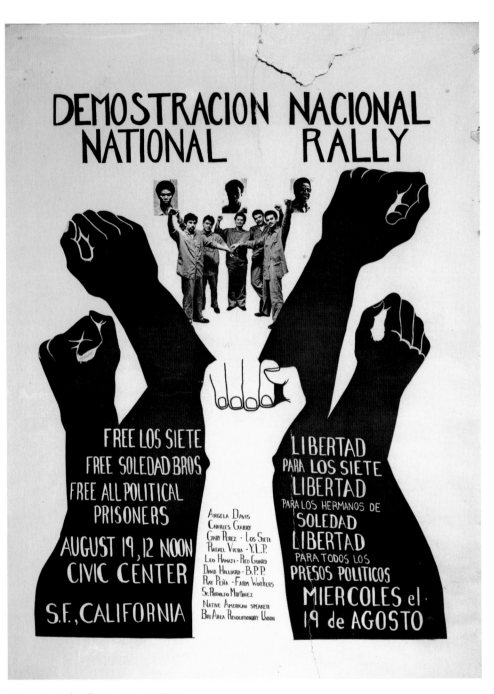

1970 National Rally to Free Los Siete

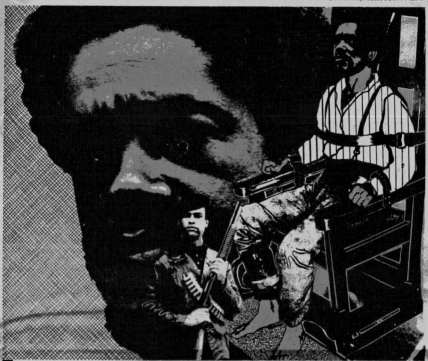

Where is Freedom when a peoples right to "Freedom of Speech" is denied to the point of murder? When attempts at "Freedom of the Press" brings bombings and lynchings?

Where is Freedom when the right to "peacefully assemble" brings on massacres? Where is our right to "keep and bear arms" when Black People are attacked by the Racist Gestapo of America? Where is "religious freedom" when places of worship become the scene of shoot-ins and bomb-ins? Where is the right to vote "regardless of race or color" when murder takes place at the voting polls? Are we free when we are not even secure from being savagely murdered in our sleep by policemen who stand blatantly before the world but yet go unpunished? Is that "...equal protection of the laws"? The empty promise of the Constitution to "establish Justice" lies exposed to the world by the reality of Black Peoples' existence. For 400 years now, Black People have suffered an unbroken chain of abuse at the hands of White America. For 400 years we have been treated as America's foot-stool. This fact is so clear that it requires no argumentation.

REVOLUTIONARY PEOPLE'S CONSTITUTIONAL CONVENTION

PLENARY SESSION
TEMPLE UNIVERSITY
GYMNASIUM

SEPTEMBER 5–7
PHILADELPHIA,P.A.

Black Panther newspaper, August 29, 1970

149

1970 Viva Los Siete

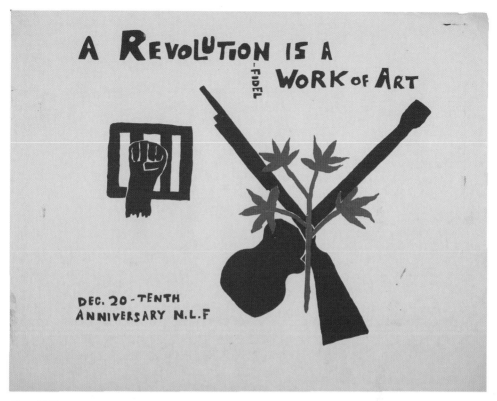

Circa 1970

Circa 1971 Alcatraz Indian Land poster

Circa 1971 Detail of Alcatraz Indian Land poster showing that Creedence Clearwater Revival donated $15,000 to the Alcatraz Indians

REVOLUTIONARY INTERCOMMUNAL DAY OF SOLIDARITY FOR

BOBBY SEALE
CHAIRMAN OF THE BLACK PANTHER PARTY
Political Prisoner

ERICKA HUGGINS
BLACK PANTHER PARTY
Political Prisoner

ANGELA DAVIS
Political Prisoner

RUCHELL MAGEE
Political Prisoner

FRIDAY, MARCH 5TH, 1971
7:00 PM to 11:00 PM
OAKLAND AUDITORIUM ARENA
10 – TENTH STREET
OAKLAND, CALIFORNIA

And POST-BIRTHDAY CELEBRATION For HUEY P. NEWTON
MINISTER OF DEFENSE
AND SUPREME COMMANDER
OF THE BLACK PANTHER PARTY

SPEAKERS:
Huey P. Newton
Kathleen Cleaver
COMMUNICATIONS SECRETARY
BLACK PANTHER PARTY

Plus Revolutionary Singing By
The LUMPEN
Of The Black Panther Party
backed by THE FREEDOM MESSENGERS
• Also THE VANGUARDS •

Music By
The Grateful Dead

TICKETS ARE AVAILABLE AT THE FOLLOWING LOCATIONS:

TICKETS $2.50   At Door $2.50

BAY AREA: BLACK COMMUNITY INFORMATION CENTER   WEST BERKELEY BRANCH, B.P.P.
1690 10th ST., WEST OAKLAND   2230 10th ST. WEST BERKELEY   IN LOS ANGELES CALL: (213) 635-2586
                                                                       BERKELEY N.C.C.F.
                                                                       3106 SHATTUCK AVE.
BLACK PANTHER PARTY CENTRAL DISTRIBUTION   RICHMOND BRANCH, B.P.P.   BERKELEY   EAST OAKLAND BRANCH B.P.P.
1336 FILLMORE ST., SAN FRANCISCO   425 CHESLEY ST. RICHMOND   1321 99TH AVENUE EAST OAKLAND
              FOR   FURTHER   INFORMATION   CALL   (415) 465-5047   -5048   -5049

1971 Revolutionary Intercommunal Day of Solidarity

154

FEB. 28

Herbie
Hancock

Taj
Mahal

Malo
AND
Maya
Angelou

IN
CONCERT
for ANGELA

at the BERKELEY COMMUNITY THEATRE
ALLSTON & GROVE
tickets at TICKETRON
information: 922-5800

Feb. 28
MONDAY 7:30 pm

1972 Concert for Angela Davis

1972 Farmworkers benefit

1972 Justice for Farmworkers

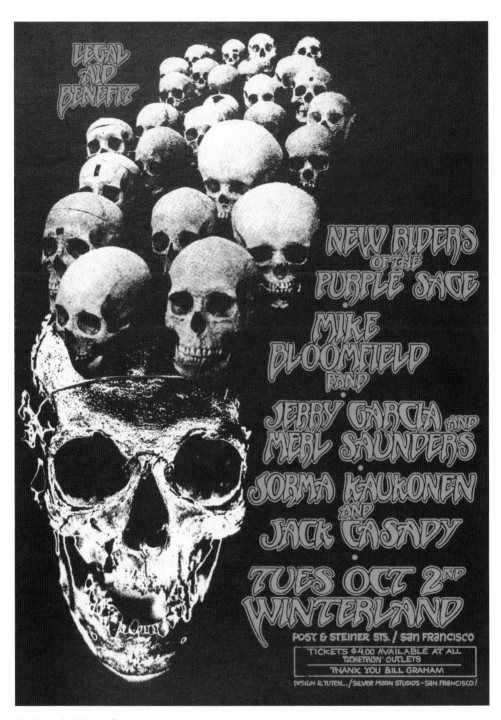

1973 Legal Aid Benefit

1974 United Farm Workers benefit

Above and right: 1974 United Farm Workers benefits featuring major Latin-rock bands characteristic of the era

A BENEFIT CONCERT FOR THE FARMWORKERS

EL
CHICANO
AZTECA
SAPO

RICHMOND CIVIC
AUDITORIUM 6:00pm
McDonald & Civic Ave.

SUNDAY
MARCH 17

CESAR CHAVEZ special guest

$4.00 adv.
$4.50 door

Sponsored by
UNITED FARMWORKERS of AMERICA • S.A. GUADALUPANAS • CHICANO STUDENT UNION de CCC
• UNITED COUNCIL FOR SPANISH SPEAKING ORGANIZATIONS

TICKETS — San Francisco (outside in 2544 mission) Oakland (Mel Thrams) Berkeley (Cody's Books) Richmond-San Pablo (A&L Records, el portal center)
Antioch (Rock Bottom Records) Vallejo (Eucalyptus Records) all Macy's Outlets
Labor Donated

161

1974 benefit for Books Behind Bars

record-buying public. But while that public was expanding exponentially, it was also increasingly unwilling to purchase anything it considered anathema to its ideals. The broad social context within which developments specific to music-making were taking place was no longer one the music industry could easily ignore *or* control.

This explains Donahue's view that the Establishment would finance the revolution. While this appears woefully naive from our present perspective, it was a serious issue at the time. Millions were convinced that the revolution was advancing on all fronts, bringing together disparate elements in an overwhelming force. The Panthers certainly said so, the Peace and Freedom Party said so, as and so did the farmworkers, the newly formed Vietnam Veterans Against the War, and other movement organizations. The rancorous splits and political infighting would emerge soon enough, but in 1967–68, it still appeared that unity was not only desirable but should be everyone's overriding concern. Hindsight is ill-suited to explain this, since it was precisely the visionary, consciousness-expanding, liberating revolution that was creating the conditions. In other words, the opening that people saw was at least in part created by their seeing it.

It did not appear, for example, that the music industry was preventing the message from being delivered. Wasn't Bob Dylan on Columbia? Joan Baez on Vanguard? Phil Ochs on A&M? Richie Havens on Verve? What difference did it make that money was going into the coffers of big corporations if the music was enlightening the people? While anyone close enough to the workings of the business had plenty of horror stories to tell about corrupt, exploitative practices, this did not lead to the same conclusions that many drew regarding newspapers, television, or other corporate media. While, by 1967, millions of people had come to realize that the underground press was providing the only reliable information, they did not extend that logic to the music industry.

One reason for this was that since its inception the music industry had carefully crafted an image of political nonalignment, subservient only to the marketplace, never dictating but always responding to "popular demand." The fact that minstrel shows, coon songs, and degrading images of black people were the basis on which the music industry was built was overlooked. That Tin Pan Alley's deliberate purpose was to *replace* the authentically popular with a copyrighted substitute was simultaneously well documented and carefully obscured. As we saw above, the law that established the modern music business was passed in 1909 and supplemented by a 1917 Supreme Court decision, but these facts were largely unknown to musicians or the general public. What the general public knew was that there were exemplary individuals who inspired trust and respect, such as a Leonard Bernstein or a Harry Belafonte. It was well known and applauded that some famous musicians, actors, and industry representatives had publicly supported the civil rights struggle and the antiwar movement. Marlon Brando had openly supported the Black Panther Party!

Compounding the problem was the ignorance and poverty of most musicians. Recording was a specialized skill that cost money. Producers and engineers played a vital role in navigating complicated equipment and imponderable contracts. Musicians wanted to play, and they wanted to get their music out to as wide an audience as possible, so it was easy to be convinced that the record company (as sleazy as many of its representatives undoubtedly were) was actually helping them reach their goal. This contributed to the widely held view, at least in San Francisco, that, as Bruce Barthol of Country Joe and the Fish put it, "If these hippies can sell records, that'll show those motherfuckers. The fact that we did was a big surprise."[16]

Hip Capitalism: *Reductio ad Absurdum*

The time it took for the music industry to recover from its surprise and reassert its control was all the time Bill Graham needed to establish himself as a major figure within it. Though he played only a small role in the Monterey Pop Festival (he secretly invested $10,000, when it was not yet clear how such involvement might affect his reputation), Graham witnessed the proceedings with both satisfaction and admiration.[17] Satisfaction, because he knew he was in the perfect position to control the Northern California market for live concerts that suddenly appeared more lucrative than he'd ever dreamed. Admiration, because there was much to be learned from the big-time sharks who had come into his territory, revealing to Graham's perceptive eye the secrets of their success. In particular, Graham watched in awe at how Albert Grossman seemed to dominate the backstage proceedings at Monterey. Not only was he impressed with the money and influence being traded at lightening speed, but he saw in an instant the crucial gap between the altruism of the San Francisco bands and the way they had been cajoled into playing at the festival in the first place.

As he publicly declared when interviewed by Ralph Gleason not long after, Graham firmly believed he *understood* the bands, *understood* the San Francisco scene, even *understood* the Diggers and the Panthers. On the other hand, the bands also *understood* Graham, because what they all wanted was fame and fortune; they just didn't want to dirty their hands getting it. Graham didn't mind getting his hands dirty. In fact, he relished the role of the tough, two-fisted scrapper nobody could put one over on.[18]

Between 1966 and 1969, Graham not only firmly established Bill Graham Presents as the dominant music promoter in the Bay Area, he formed a booking agency, a management company, a record company, and a merchandising arm. The fact that there were conflicts of interest inherent in this didn't matter to him, until he was challenged by one perceptive client—Taj Mahal. What mattered was control of all aspects of uncharted territory. Graham had learned from Grossman that you made up the rules as you went along. More importantly, you cultivated an image of wise counsel, of defending the artist *against* the music industry. The music industry itself was behind the times and not yet structured to accommodate either the quantity or the quality of growth in its own domain. That the numbers were staggering was no doubt wonderful, but that so much great music was flowing through the Fillmore alone could not be accounted for by anything the industry had itself initiated. Quite the contrary.

Graham was more aware of these stunning implications than any of his counterparts in New York or Los Angeles. This was indeed a renaissance; it was not a result of the industry's conventional wisdom at all. Furthermore, if the industry were to apply standard operating procedures, it would kill the goose laying the golden egg. This meant that a successful operator needed to appear to be the provider and guarantor of the artists' *freedom*. No more telling musicians what to do—onstage or in the studio. No more telling musicians what they could or could not say in lyrics, onstage, or in interviews. No more dress codes, no behavior monitoring, or otherwise appearing judgmental or *parental*. All of that was out. From now on, it was cultivating the creativity of the "artist," elevating their status from entertainer to "visionary," promoting their gifts as magical and mysterious, to be treasured and worshipped like icons in a shrine. The crucial distinction between Jerry Wexler and all that he represented was this: Graham was *not* in the entertainment business. Graham was producing "art." His idol was impresario Sol Hurok. What Graham had learned from Grossman was that there was a higher mountain to be scaled than mere commercial success. Wexler and his ilk sat atop a lower peak. The ultimate in Graham's eyes was the glory of enlightening the world with his discovery and promotion of "genius"! Entertainment was for chumps. The leap from the Mime Troupe to Albert Grossman gave Graham a vision of the commanding heights and a goal worthy of his talents. That was Graham's strategy—and it worked.

Here it is important to recall one of the Black Panthers' most provocative inventions: the "pig." Originally, this derogatory term was used to brand the police, to delegitimize their authority and ridicule their brutality. But the term quickly caught on and was subsequently also employed by millions to identify male chauvinists and capitalists as well as the police. Graham was frequently called a "capitalist pig," and he hated it. Not only did he bridle at the term, he emphatically and repeatedly railed against it being applied to him. In fact, so frequently did he talk about it in interviews and other public venues, that he brought to mind Shakespeare's quip, "The lady doth protest too much, methinks." For indeed Graham was a capitalist pig. His alternate use of bullying tactics and craven pleas was legendary. His unscrupulous pursuit of gain made him a caricature of himself. Fond of saying, "It's not the money, it's the *money*!" he was the archetypical demon driven by forces reason must struggle to comprehend. "He had a refugee's need for material possessions and security. When he died, they found shit buried in his back yard. He was pathetic, he was not a civilized human being, he was a money-grubbing European refugee, and he never lost those habits, no matter what," recalls Joel Selvin, adding, "At a certain point acquisitiveness is sated. The need for glory never is. And Bill's need for glory and approbation was fucking *endless*, and I know because I'd get these phone calls after he read a headline of an article I'd written!"[19]

Graham was offended by being called a "capitalist pig" not because of the moral implications or even personal affront. Rather, Graham was offended because "capitalist pig" spoiled the image he needed to maintain. He had to make himself appear to be indispensable to a community of which he was not a member, while all the while subverting the aims and aspirations of that community and the musicians who'd sprung from it. This was tricky, but, as previously noted, Graham saw the gap between musicians' altruism and their desire to play music, and drove a giant wedge through it by being the loudest voice shouting, "We are important! Don't let them tell you any different! We are important!" Meaning, of course, that he, Bill Graham, was important.

"There's a certain level. . . . Let's say he went past that line of just straight, hard business and got greedy," remembers Taj Mahal, "He wanted the 10 percent for the booking agency, the 15 percent for the management—which he would push up to 20 percent, if he could—so now, we're talkin' 30 percent of what you're making."[20] In his obsessive drive to monopolize, Graham overlooked the fact that not all musicians were willing to ignore injustice. Taj continued: "When my brother and I started making inquiries, they couldn't say, because they knew what the outcome of it was going to be." So the brothers got the runaround, "It was like, 'Why should we tell a couple of *schwarzers*?' The business is cutthroat, but the point is Graham had some guys who were stand-up human beings looking him eye to eye, while he was mistreating us. He had the management over *here* and the agency over *here*; whatever was coming in from me here could also be distributed to anybody else without me knowing, so I ended up in some ways being the draw for a lotta groups that weren't doing good—so a long story short, we filed a lawsuit, and we won."

Was this a landmark lawsuit? "Yes," said Taj, "That's where the division between management and booking was established. But that was just the beginning. Anywhere else this guy [Graham] figured he could block me, he did. So, essentially, after that, I basically stopped playing in this country. I started playing over in Europe." This forgotten incident needs to be recalled for three reasons. First of all, Taj Mahal is a master of his craft, beloved by his audience and respected by his peers. He had no need to be anointed by a kingmaker, which Graham considered himself to be. Second, this was not an exception; it was the rule for how Graham conducted business. One incident illustrates this well. Fulfilling a lifelong ambition to act, Graham was cast for the role of Lucky Luciano in the film *Bugsy*. He noticed, as he said himself, that "there were distinct similarities" between mafia practices and his own.[21] Third, his highly touted "innovations" were in fact a means to more effectively exploit music and musicians. They were crucial in domesticating what had momentarily been wild and free. It's true that Graham made many charitable donations (the Haight Ashbury Free Medical Clinic is one well-known beneficiary), but charity is a characteristic means of maintaining control. As an old Inuit adage puts it, "Gifts make slaves like whips make dogs."

The fact that these are all symptoms of capitalism and that Graham was simply playing the game better than his contemporaries does not absolve him of responsibility. In the context of a revolutionary upheaval, during which choices not predetermined as to their outcome could indeed be made, Graham's were ultimately reactionary. They played a crucial role in the *counterrevolution*. This element arose even before the Sixties had run their course, first as a distracting nuisance later as a debilitating influence. Above all, it maintained the appearance of coming from *within* the movement as part of the force for changing the world. This is why it remains so important to expose Graham's actual legacy. As a rock impresario, he undoubtedly fulfilled his dreams, but as a historical figure his role was to reestablish an illusion at precisely the moment music was shattering it. Just as the truth dawned on a generation that "everything they taught us was a lie," Graham used that awakening to create a semblance of it. As Ludwig Feuerbach put it more than a century before: "In these days illusion only is sacred, truth profane. Nay, sacredness is held to be enhanced in proportion as truth decreases and illusion increases, so that the highest degree of illusion comes to be the highest degree of sacredness."[22] Not only did Graham "highjack a movement," as Digger Peter Berg once said, but he secured the willing participation of many musicians in the forging of their chains.

It bears repeating that the great majority of musicians at the time were not revolutionaries, or even politically active. But music was. It is difficult to imagine fifty years after the fact, but music posed a threat to the social order precisely in the manner described by Plato in *The Republic*, and for the same reasons. Does this mean that there was one song or one scale or one rhythm that repeated often enough would cause the walls of the Pentagon to crack? Obviously not. So, why the reaction? Why the effort to crush and to co-opt? Why not simply ignore it? The answer lies in how the sound affected consciousness.

At a critical juncture, music *as such* entered into consciousness as an enlightening substance. In so doing, music manifested the infinite as a revelation. This is not identical to God or the sacred in religious terms. Rather, music presents a truth, the fundamental premise of philosophy, without which there can be no philosophy. In the absence or abandonment of philosophy, music took up the role of teacher, akin to

Pythagoras speaking to the *akousmatikoi*, preparing them to become the *mathematikoi*. The fact that musicians themselves were rarely capable of articulating this verbally is beside the point. Musicians were not the teachers; at their best, they were the students. The truth music taught had the twofold significance of exposing the mediating effect of money and the *im*mediate effect of a disturbance of the air. Not a sign in place of the signified, no "sacred illusion" in place of "profane truth." Rather an experience, one that desacralized illusion.

CHAPTER 8

1968 and Beyond: Culture, Counterculture, and Revolution

How do we remember 1968? Is it the Tet Offensive, when the National Liberation Front launched a coordinated assault across the length and breadth of southern Vietnam, leading ultimately to the defeat of the United States? Is it the assassinations of first Martin Luther King and then Robert Kennedy, dashing all hope of nonviolent political change? Is it the violent confrontation in Chicago between police and demonstrators at the Democratic National Convention—where, as the demonstrators loudly and rightly proclaimed, "The whole world is watching"? Do we remember Prague Spring—the rising of young Czechs demanding radical reform, only to be met by Soviet tanks? Is it the May events in Paris, where massive student protests led to even more massive strikes of French workers, nearly toppling the government? Perhaps it's the Mexican Olympics: Tommy Smith and John Carlos raising clenched fists in defiance of the U.S., for whom they'd ostensibly won their medals, or the giant protests of Mexican students and workers, brutally suppressed only days before the Olympics began.

Or is it all these events and many more that we remember simply as 1968, the year of a worldwide and world-historic revolution? Many books titled simply *1968* suggest that people will make the connection and draw the conclusions. As world-systems theorist Immanuel Wallerstein wrote: "There have only been two world revolutions. One took place in 1848, the second took place in 1968. Both were historic failures. Both transformed the world. The fact that both were unplanned, and therefore in a profound sense spontaneous, explains both facts—the fact that they failed, and the fact that they transformed the world."

If 1848 marks the rising of the dispossessed—the wretched of the earth—to throw off the yoke of ancient despotisms, then 1968 marks the explosion of deferred dreams. If 1848 recalls the specter of communism haunting Europe, of fallen monarchs, rising proletarians, romantic poets and enslaved nations yearning for freedom in the "springtime of peoples," then 1968 recalls the outraged response of the young to the broken promises of liberal democracy on the one hand and of social-democracy and Soviet communism on the other. This was not only impatience but disbelief in the claims made on both sides of the Iron Curtain that, in the wake of World War II, dreams of peace and freedom, of "liberty, equality, and fraternity" would at long last be realized. Two decades had passed and the rulers, communist and capitalist alike, had failed to deliver. If that were not enough, the United States (with the acquiescence of the Soviets) was suppressing liberation movements in the former colonies of Europe. A great wave of revolution was sweeping the "Third World" from China to Vietnam, from Algeria to Cuba. These revolutions (and others less successful) were made, moreover, against the advice of the Soviet leadership bent on maintaining the status quo agreed to with the United States at Yalta. But 1968 went one step further: Prague Spring on the one hand and the Great Proletarian Cultural Revolution on the other proved beyond doubt that simply overthrowing a government and expropriating the property of the rich does not end class conflict. Rather, conflict simply migrates into the ruling party, now the Communist Party, and the same hierarchical and oppressive structure that was the target of revolution in the first place is restored in a new guise.

In this broad context emerged three interrelated questions that to a large extent dictated what transpired as result of 1968. First, the question of culture, which was so closely interwoven with revolution that it became hard to distinguish where one ended and the other began. Second, the emergence of new movements and organizations representing excluded "minorities" and women, challenging notions that their demands should be subordinated until "after the revolution" or submitted to the will of majorities and existing political parties, be they communist, social democratic, or liberal. Last but not least, there is the central but often overlooked role of the breakdown of the armed forces in Vietnam and how this, perhaps more than any other single factor, propelled the Sixties past 1969. Indeed, the changes in consciousness for which the Sixties is most notable occurred within the ranks of servicemen and women, and these mostly young people were drawn from "America's Heartland," returning there with revolutionary ideas.

Culture and Revolution

Perhaps never before have the questions of culture and revolution been so tightly interwoven as they were in the Sixties. In part, this was due to the Great Proletarian Cultural Revolution launched in China in 1966 and to the struggles of black, brown, red, and yellow peoples to define their own identities against those constructed for them by Hollywood, the music industry and white supremacy in general. It was no doubt crucial for the first blows struck by women's liberation to attack cultural expressions of male chauvinism since these were accepted, even by revolutionaries, as norms to which everyone unquestioningly adhered. But the linkage between culture and revolution was made more broadly still and not only by theorists or advocates of cultural strategies directed toward revolutionary ends. Rather, it was young people's wholesale rejection of the most cherished notions held by their *parents* that led Theodore Roszak to coin the term "counter culture" in 1968.[1] A half-century later, this neologism (now one word, counterculture) has come to mean long hair, colorful clothing, hedonistic practices involving sex and drugs and vacuous notions of peace and love. As one recent study points out, "Historians of the 1960s have been complicit in this restrictive assignation of the term 'counterculture.' In any number of tomes published since the mid-1980s, the counterculture is accorded the requisite chapter wherein cultural revolt is extracted from (and then reinserted within) the rest of 1960s history."[2] That this does not at all correspond to Roszak's writing or what the counterculture consisted of in practice is simply one of the most glaring examples of how the Sixties have been distorted by defenders of the status quo.

In fact, the term "counter culture" was preceded by "contraculture," coined by sociologist J. Milton Yinger to distinguish a sociological phenomenon from the more familiar "subculture." Subcultures evolve practices by which members separate and protect their cohesion from the dominant culture. Yinger's argument was summarized by Braunstein and Doyle: "A contraculture represents a full-fledged oppositional movement with a distinctively separate set of norms and values that are produced dialectically out of a sharply delineated conflict with the dominant society. Unlike subcultures, a contraculture aspires to transform values and mores of its host culture. If it is successful, it *becomes* the dominant culture."[3]

This is certainly what Roszak had in mind when he wrote, "I am at a loss to know where, besides among these dissenting young people and their heirs of the next few generations, the radical discontent and innovation can be found that might transform this disoriented civilization of ours into something a human being can identify as home."[4] Furthermore, Roszak concluded, "If the resistance of the counter culture fails, I think there will be nothing in store for us but what anti-utopians like Huxley and Orwell have forecast—though I have no doubt that these dismal despotisms will be far more stable and effective than their prophets have foreseen."[5]

Lest there be any doubt, Roszak makes explicit the *political* content of his definition:

We grasp the underlying unity of the counter cultural variety, then, if we see beat-hip bohemianism as an effort to work out the personality structure and total life style that follow from New Left social criticism. At their best, these young bohemians are the would-be utopian pioneers of the world that lies beyond intellectual rejection of the Great Society. They seek to invent a cultural base for New Left politics, to discover new types of community, new family patterns, new sexual mores, new kinds of livelihood, new esthetic forms, new personal identities on the far side of power politics, the bourgeois home, and the consumer society.[6]

Finally, Roszak emphasizes the salient characteristic of the counter culture, its disaffiliation:

No doubt, as the local city fathers fear, these youngsters learn all sorts of bad habits on the avenue—but they probably take their corruption indiscriminately from SDS handouts and psychedelic newspapers without much awareness of the difference between dropping out and digging in for the political fight. It all boils down to disaffiliation for them—and the distinctions are of secondary importance.[7]

This is undoubtedly how many young people—not only white but Asian, Latino, Native, and black as well—chose to separate themselves from the dominant "straight" culture and seek means of identifying themselves and fellow outlaws in society at large. Nonetheless, even in the stereotypical image of a young white kid leaving affluent middle-class surroundings, two components of "countercultural" thinking were full of revolutionary implications.

One was communalism. Communes and collectives typified the era, mobilizing hundreds of thousands. They were intensely political in the strict sense that politics poses the question: Who decides? Most important, they sought to create alternatives to the institutions that, even if nominally "democratic," only served to reinforce the system. Communalism insisted that nothing short of a wholesale social transformation, particularly as this applied to war, capitalism, the family, and humans' relationship with nature, was worthy of the name *change*. Communalism led further to the back-to-the-land movement, self-reliance, organic farming, and so on. Examples of this widespread trend include Morning Star Ranch, initiated by Lou Gottlieb, and The Farm, which grew out of Stephen Gaskin's Monday Night Class at San Francisco State College. Communalism had powerful effects that continue to be felt today, especially in the environmental movements.

The other component was anticapitalism. The counterculture defined itself against the deification of money, the hoarding of wealth, and the obsession with private property. The "revolt against the Technocracy" was directed not only at machines but also at the profit motive commanding their manufacture.[8] This produced rancorous divisions within the counterculture itself, as "hip capitalists" began exploiting the potential of a rapidly expanding market. Nonetheless, from the outset, the counterculture's cardinal principle was disdain for what society held most sacred. This, too, has had lasting impact and certainly cannot be reduced to fashion statements or mindless pleasure seeking. Indeed, it cannot be reduced to culture at all, even with the prefix "counter" attached to it. This raises other questions about terminology, and how to define culture as opposed to art and/or politics, which we will revisit further on. What's important here is that the counterculture was a battleground of contending ideas about culture and about revolution.

Woodstock and Wild West

Woodstock occupies an exalted position in Sixties legend and lore. On August 15–18, 1969, five hundred thousand people attended an event that not only featured some of the greatest musicians of the era but one that purported to convey a message of peace from the young generation to the world. Joni Mitchell wrote the song "Woodstock," underscoring this point, and Abbie Hoffman wrote the book *Woodstock Nation* to make the political implications explicit. The name Woodstock would thereafter symbolize the idea that music could bring about social trans-formation. Woodstock's unprecedented success, moreover, validated its claims. In this sense, Woodstock deserves its status as a high point of an era. It undoubtedly gave voice to a fervent belief, shared by mil-lions, that music could bring about a revolution without recourse to violence. It was here that music as an *instrument* of change reached the apex of its social influence—a position from which it would gradually retreat in the face of mounting evidence to the contrary, but that was yet to come. The film of the event not only confirms that these were the aspirations shared by participants but also supports the reasoning behind them with exemplary performances and commentary. It opens with Richie Havens singing an impassioned "Freedom" and concludes with Jimi Hendrix's extraordinary performance of the "Star-Spangled Banner." Smack-dab in the middle is Country Joe McDonald leading the crowd of half a million in singing a rousing version of "The Fuck Cheer," followed by the "I-Feel-Like-I'm-Fixin'-to-Die Rag"! (Also quite reveal-ing is the scene of Bill Graham—who actually had nothing to do with Woodstock—waxing eloquent about crowd control, using the metaphor of army ants to describe the public and how trenches need to be dug to contain them. Obviously full of himself, he goes on to unveil a strategy he would employ very effectively in the years to come.)

The greater significance of Woodstock lies not, however, in the dreams it conjured, but in the conflicts of which it was a product and to which it added fuel. Utopian imagining was a crucial component of the Sixties in general, but it was already in full effect *before* Woodstock and would not cease being so for many years thereafter. The conflicts Woodstock brought to light were between the usual suspects of the music industry and corporate media, on the one hand, and the growing insurgency of increasingly radicalized youth, on the other. But they also included the system as a whole and diversifying social movements extending far beyond the constituency attending Woodstock. In other words, the Vietnam War and increasing state repression of dissent versus a growing movement that now included Third World and women's liberation.

Caught in the middle were many liberals and leftists, young and old alike, some with ties to the media and the music business, who hoped that they could navigate the murky waters of commerce to achieve a higher purpose: the greater diffusion of the music and the message of the young. They hoped that this could somehow transcend the limits set by the system. Perhaps the clearest example of this is a festival that never happened. Reporting on the debacle for *Ramparts*, Joan Holden of the San Francisco Mime Troupe wrote, "The media orgy at Woodstock almost drowned out the earlier event, or rather non-event, that brought it all back home to San Francisco, where a group of prominent rock businessmen blamed threats of violence from left-wing hippies for the cancellation of the 'Wild West' Festival."[9]

Band manager Ron Polte's idea was to have a giant three-day extravaganza, August 22–24, 1969, at numerous sites in Golden Gate Park, including big names at Kezar Stadium. Holden reported, "Its promoters had described Wild West as a rebuke to the commercialism of the other rock festivals, a non-profit celebration for the community."[10] Some events would be free, while others would charge admission, but it was never clear where any profits from what the organizers claimed would be both "a party and a spiritual statement" would go.

Convened for the event and leading the effort was the San Francisco Music Council, which included Tom Donahue, Bill Graham, Ralph Gleason, David Rubinson, and Frank Werber—i.e., the movers and shakers of the San Francisco music scene. In an attempt to broaden its appeal and prevent it from becoming just another Bill Graham production, Barry Olivier from the Berkeley Folk Festival was invited in as the director. Those involved were surprised to find that their idea was not welcomed in all quarters. While they had expected opposition from City Hall, they had not counted on the animosity of the Mime Troupe, the Haight Commune, and community organizers in the Fillmore and Mission districts.[11] Few, if any, could accurately gauge the effects of 1968, a year of worldwide revolution, and even Gleason and Donahue, used to being in the forefront of social trends, found themselves left behind by the rapidly changing popular mood. The violent repression visited on young people from Paris to Prague to Mexico City to Haight Street had swept away whatever illusions might have remained that "All You Need Is Love." Music's importance was greater than ever, but less as a plea for peace and more as a demand for justice.

Furthermore, the Wild West Festival organizers were caught in a crossfire that included a strike by light show operators against the Family Dog and Bill Graham—fueled by the bitter acrimony that lingered after the failed attempt by local bands to run the Carousel Ballroom in opposition to Graham and by a growing distrust in appeals to a nonexistent "community" by way of phony spirituality. It became painfully evident that a division had opened between those who saw the musical renaissance as a spiritual and even political revolution and those who viewed revolution as a struggle to overthrow the system. One group believed that music would somehow transcend violence and racism and change the world through simple celebration. Frank Werber is even purported to have said, in reference to Wild West, "This *is* the revolution!"[12] In stark contrast, opponents of the festival knew that 1968 had been a pivotal year and that San Francisco was part of a worldwide revolutionary upsurge not represented by music alone.

As Holden explained, "Hip culture, biggest of contemporary fads, instantly produced a thriving capitalist class. This aided the development of an ardent revolutionary minority, and battles between those to whom a 'revolutionary life-style' means socialism and those for whom it means profit has become as much a part of the Scene as love-ins."[13] As an example of the "revolutionary minority," Holden cites "The Haight Commune, which represents 22 'families' of 10–30 members each." A leaflet from the Haight Commune articulated their position:

> When our attempts to live and to create freedom and common experience begin to succeed, the pimp merchants of bread and circuses converge on the source of this success, turn the people's artists into whores and slaves, slick-package a shit version of our expression, and hustle it back to us for incredible profits.
>
> When our culture clearly opposes this system of exploitation it is crushed.
>
> When our culture begins to liberate people from their unfreedom it is rapidly remolded into more chains by the existing furnaces of corrupt power and decadent values.

Our talents/creativity/energy are like any natural resource. We can be destroyed by the money-crazed tyrants of business just like any other resource on the planet (a forest, a mine, a river, etc.). . . . Or The Resource Of The People's Lives Can Be Used To Make Life Itself A Better Experience For All The People.

Holden continues, "The mandate to 'do your own thing' has run out for the radicals, and it is not uncommon to see them excoriated in hip publications with all the vehemence, and in the terms of, the far right. . . . As times get heavier, more and more of the beautiful people are finding that what they mean by 'revolution' is groovy vibrations. . . . *This is it!* was the message from Woodstock: Paradise Now, the Aquarian Age— look no further, and *don't bring me down!*"[14] Polarization had come to a head.

The Good, the Bad, and the Stubbornness of Facts

The Making of a Counter Culture was published in 1969, a fact that makes it apparent that no one used "counterculture" to identify themselves or events in which they were participating until the beginning of the 1970s. Roszak himself admitted forty years later that he "had a precise but far-too-narrow definition in mind. I meant the rebellion against certain essential elements of industrial society: the priesthood of technical expertise, the world view of mainstream science and the social dominance of the corporate community—the military-industrial complex, as Dwight Eisenhower called it." He added, "Yet it was among women and various embattled minorities that the enduring political ideals of the period were forged: participatory democracy, consciousness raising, communitarian sharing and open institutions that permitted personal authenticity. No matter how zany things might get in the streets, there was high moral purpose behind the antics."[15]

Roszak is, of course, referring to what occurred after 1968. His favorable take on this period contrasts sharply with many other accounts that make a distinction between the "good" and "bad" Sixties, as in: before and after 1968, or before and after Woodstock. It is often asserted that up to this point, peaceful protest against war and racial discrimination sought to "heal the nation" and make America live up to its promises. Afterwards, there was a turn to violent confrontation, separatism, and decadence. As Jason Ferreira points out:

Scholars focus most exclusively on the period between the founding of the New Left in the early 1960s, characterized by an emphasis on participatory democracy, and 1968, when the Movement
allegedly fell into a steep decline and became increasingly disor-
ganized and obsessed with revolutionary violence. In other words,
a "good" Sixties and a "bad" Sixties is constructed with 1968 serving
as the watershed moment in which "years of hope" degenerated
into "days of rage."[16]

This narrative unravels, however, when confronted with the proliferation
of revolutionary ideas among society's dispossessed. Ferreira continues:
"In fact, 1968 serves as a 'take-off' point rather than a concluding moment
for social movements within communities of color."[17] This is clear in the
case of the Black Panther Party, but the Panthers were not alone. The
period is remarkable for the Indian occupation of Alcatraz and the birth
of the American Indian Movement (AIM), Los Siete de la Raza, the San
Francisco State strike, Third World liberation, women's liberation, gay
liberation, and on and on. While the war in Vietnam and opposition to
it continued to be the overriding issue (the one around which all other
struggles united), a significant change had also occurred; by this point,
many people not only opposed the war but also consciously supported
the Vietnamese. This in turn gave rise to the embrace by young radicals
of political revolution, the Vietnamese, Cuban, and Chinese varieties,
in particular. A revival of Marxism-Leninism was afoot. Popularized
initially by the Panthers, Marxism-Leninism, and in some quarters,
Maoism, gained legitimacy as the Vietnamese, the Cubans, and the Great
Proletarian Cultural Revolution grew in prestige in direct proportion to
the disastrous policies of the United States and the USSR.[18]

Ample evidence for this can be found in underground and revolutionary publications, but it is even confirmed by mainstream sources,
including the various polls and commissions conducted on behalf of the
government and major media outlets. In *The Changing Values on Campus*
(1972), pollster Daniel Yankelovich reported that, in 1968, 368,000 people
strongly agreed with the need for a "mass revolutionary party" in the
United States. By 1970, Yankelovich found that more than a million
people considered themselves "revolutionaries." In early 1971, the *New
York Times* reported that four out of ten students (over three million
people) thought that a revolution was needed in the United States, and

sociologist Seymour Lipset concluded that 75 percent of all students (about six million people) endorsed the need for "fundamental change" in the nation.[19]

As George Katsiaficas reported in his groundbreaking study *The Imagination of the New Left*:

> Two years after the French May, the United States experienced what is today regarded as its worst political crisis since the Civil War. The first general strike of students in the history of the United States was not the usual springtime festivities: At Kent State and Jackson State Universities, six students were shot dead. . . . The nationwide student strike of May 1970 was the high point in the development of the student New Left in the U.S. and, as such, reflected both its limitations and its strengths.[20]

The available data unquestionably reveals the advance of a truly mass movement, with a strong revolutionary component, and certainly not the dissipation and disintegration often ascribed to the period. But what is most often buried by the "good" Sixties/"bad" Sixties myopia is the GI and veterans movement and how the revolt in the armed forces radically reshaped the American landscape.

GI and Veterans Movements

First, it must be recalled that the GIs were completely unprepared for what they encountered in Vietnam. They had been told by their superiors that they were liberators and were shocked to discover that, to the Vietnamese, they were hated oppressors. Black GIs in particular were confronted by an "enemy" who forthrightly appealed to them on the basis of solidarity with the struggles of black people in America. Patrols began encountering signs planted in the jungle by the Viet Cong addressed to black GIs. These became so famous that their message was enunciated by none other than heavyweight champion Muhammad Ali when he declared, "No Viet Cong ever called me nigger!"[21]

Combined with the racism endemic to the armed forces, these revelations inspired rebellion. Furthermore, divisions within the ranks between "lifers" and "grunts," between officers and enlisted men, many of whom were conscripts, increased in frequency and hostility. Not surprisingly, opposition had its cultural (and especially musical) expression. Indeed, if more proof were needed of music's subversive effects, one need look no further than how music was used by rebellious soldiers. Two outstanding books of the period, *Soldiers in Revolt* and *Turning the Guns Around*, record how this transpired. In *Soldiers in Revolt*, David Cortright, who served in the army, observes:

> The division within the enlisted ranks is perhaps most evident in what, for lack of a better term, may be called a GI counterculture— a community of shared values and expressions antithetical to military standards. As within civilian society, a new consciousness emerged within the services, expressed in cultural idioms and an anarchic indifference to authority. Black and white GIs, searching for an identity apart from their role in the military, formed buddy groups of "brothers" and "freaks." In the totalitarian environment of the military, solidarity was expressed symbolically through long hair and afros, rock and soul music, beads and black bracelets, peace signs and clenched fists.[22]

Another army vet, Larry G. Waterhouse, adds:

> A "youth culture" rebellion outwardly characterized by long hair, drug use, open sexuality, and rock music, born of the growing alienation of youth from the goals and values of the society as a whole, reinforced a revolutionary commitment for many. The cultural revolution cut across class lines, reaching far beyond the young educated whites who were its prototypes in the eyes of the mass media. Young people on all levels of society began to try to redefine themselves in nonoppressive ways and advanced hundreds of programs and theories designed to reform or revolutionize the United States. And the steadily escalating war, with its seemingly endless repercussions in domestic life, was the driving force behind this great radicalization.[23]

From the point of view of the military, this was disastrous, leading to the famous report by combat veteran Col. Robert D. Heinl Jr., "The Collapse of the Armed Forces," published in the *Armed Forces Journal*. Heinl wrote: "By every conceivable indicator, our army that now remains in Vietnam is in a state approaching collapse, with individual units avoiding or having refused combat, murdering their officers and non commissioned officers, drug-ridden, and dispirited where not near mutinous."[24] Given the class and ethnic makeup of the armed forces generally, and the army in particular, the threat this posed would not be confined to Vietnam, but would be diffused throughout American society by returning service-men and women. The volatile combination of urban rebellion, campus unrest, and the radicalization of working-class youth of all ethnicities in the armed forces was responsible for the growing sense that revolution was both the only solution and an imminent prospect.

Dozens of films, from *Platoon* to *Apocalypse Now*, portray the twin phenomena of demoralization of the troops and the special significance of music in the bonding of disillusioned young men. What is not por-trayed, however, is the militant resistance that was ultimately responsi-ble for the breakdown of the armed services and the role of music in that resistance: not as a soundtrack to despair, but as the sound of defiance.[25] Perhaps filmmakers and others grappling with the Vietnam War were simply baffled by what was an unprecedented phenomenon. There were no preexisting coordinates by which to apprehend, let alone gauge, such a powerful and widespread response from rank-and-file soldiers or to grasp that radicalization took place in Vietnam and inside the military. But this only reveals a deeper failing: there is scant reference to the draft, either in films about Vietnam or in subsequent literature. It is remark-able that so little attention has been paid to a policy that affected every American male of a certain age. Though historical, journalistic, and artis-tic documents acknowledge that the draft occurred, few examine its consequences or the significance of the basic fact that the armed forces filled their ranks largely through coercion, not patriotism.

The Draft

Conscription was a fact of life for the American teenager. As a young man's eighteenth birthday approached, so did registration, the draft phys-ical, and induction. Families, classmates, employers, and friends were all drawn into a vortex that, by 1965, had both a long history and an ominous future. The U.S. military had filled its ranks with conscripts since the Civil War. World War I and World War II had seen extensive use of the Selective Service System, as had the Korean War. But when Lyndon Johnson com-mitted American ground forces to Vietnam in 1965, "draft calls soared from 100,000 in 1964 to 400,000 in 1966 enabling U.S. forces there to climb from 23,000 military advisers in 1964 to 543,000 troops by 1968."[26] For most young people, this forged an indissoluble link between the draft and Vietnam. This was no "urban myth," either. In spite of the fact that draftees made up only 16 percent of actual military personnel, they "made up the bulk of the infantry riflemen in Vietnam (88 percent, in 1969) and accounted for more than half the army's battle deaths."[27] A deadly conveyor belt carried its human cargo to and from the war in increasing numbers, with the body bags and the wounded grimly reminding new inductees of what awaited them. Furthermore, it escaped no one's notice that a disproportionate number of draftees and casualties were from the working class, black, white, Chicano, and Native American families. In 1967, black people, 11 percent of the U.S. population, accounted for 16 percent of the army's casualties in Vietnam (15 percent for the entire war).[28] Student and other deferments were readily available to those with the social networks and financial means to get them, so the speed with which the war escalated ensured that a generation was forced to simultaneously confront class privilege, racial oppression, and imperialism.

Opposition developed almost as rapidly as the expansion of the draft. Under the slogan "Hell No, We Won't Go," first popularized by SNCC, opposition to the draft led the movement from protest to resistance—as a riotous confrontation at the Oakland Induction Center in 1967 announced. This resistance was so effective that "what to do about the draft" became a decision, not a foregone conclusion, and an essential component of being a young American between the years of 1965 and the war's end ten years later. (The government announced there would be no further draft calls in 1973).

Draft resistance forever altered perceptions of war, the government, the military, as well as the role of the United States in perpetuating colonialism in a new guise, specifically in taking over from the defeated French in Indochina. Whatever reservoirs of faith, filled during World War II and the fight against fascism, were poisoned forever for a generation of Americans. While it is an axiom of power that to rally a population, a government need only target a foreign foe, this proved to be false in the case of the United States and the Vietnam War. In fact, quite the opposite happened. The sustained militant confrontation that occurred was the result of multiple injustices, combined with the disproportionate number of young people in the general population—young people, moreover, who were driven into a war they played no part in deciding to fight.[29]

In reply to government propagandists' harangues about "supporting our troops" came the reply from these very troops: "U.S. Out of

Vietnam." This was given its most articulate expression by Vietnam Veterans Against the War (VVAW) and such powerful demonstrations as Dewey Canyon III in Washington, DC, during which hundreds of combat veterans threw their medals on the Capitol steps.[30] Militant resistance within the armed forces themselves altered the terms of political conflict. Such massive protest demolished government claims to represent a "silent majority" of patriotic Americans against a handful of ungrateful, unwashed "outside agitators." Never in living memory had the government and its mouthpieces in the media appeared so isolated and unrepresentative. It is difficult to exaggerate how broadly and deeply this affected the American people, but along with losing the war, the U.S. government lost any sense of unified national purpose. It would take decades for the state to overcome the "Vietnam Syndrome," if indeed, it really has done so.

In documenting this confrontation, we must never lose sight of the central and decisive role of the Vietnamese people and their struggle for liberation. The Vietnamese were the fulcrum of history, creating a moment to which the entire world was forced to respond. They not only proved to be the military nemesis of both French and American imperialism but also obliterated the West's claim to moral, intellectual, technological, and spiritual superiority. A small Asian country, deeply impoverished by colonialism and war, was nonetheless capable of achieving a higher standard of civilization than the French or the Americans. As Ho Chi Minh wrote: "Under the mask of democracy, French imperialism has transplanted in the country of Annam the cursed system of the Middle Ages. . . . The Annamese peasant is crucified by the bayonet of the capitalist civilization at the cross of prostituted Christianity." The Vietnamese proved, to quote the Black Panthers: "The spirit of the people is greater than the Man's technology."

Reprise: Culture and Revolution

Taken together, all of this raises a basic question: Did the counterculture exist? Is Roszak's term of any usefulness? After all, counterculture is almost exclusively used in reference to the Sixties and has never become a universal sociological term in the manner of "subculture." Given his own criticism, it would seem that, seen from today, Roszak would have applied the term to "women and embattled minorities," rendering it virtually indistinguishable from "political movement." This poses yet another question: Is culture no more than the domain to which we retreat when we are defeated politically? It would appear that art, science, and politics are sufficient to describe the categories of conflict alternatively designated as cultural or ideological. Culture seems of greatest import when oppressed groups are actively resisting domination by force, whether it be military, legal, or political force, which is, moreover, greater then the oppressed groups possess. Why is culture substituted for the frank admission that we are oppressed and exploited and must gather our strength for resistance, and ultimately a great struggle for liberation?

To answer these questions, we must first acknowledge that the Sixties were marked by not one but several distinct political strategies aimed at changing the world. Different levels of commitment corresponded to the dynamics of a truly mass movement and cannot be reduced to a question of the counterculture versus politics. For one thing, people sharing the same clothing styles or musical tastes were on all sides of the political divides. For another, throughout the Sixties, artistic expression generally aligned itself with the movement. No doubt, Hollywood and the music industry maintained their dominance over popular culture with their pro-imperialist and counterrevolutionary agenda. But the spirit of revolution permeated the atmosphere and the most innovative techniques and novel forms of expression were in the hands of "cultural workers," collectives, and iconoclasts. This broad alliance of art with left-wing politics broke down only after the defeat of the revolution, the decline of the mass movement, and the end of the war in Vietnam.

Was there no distinction then between the New Left and the counterculture, the movement and the freaks? Certainly, and it increased as the Sixties advanced. But this was a difference in political strategy and philosophical outlook, of *how* to change the world, not between engagement versus escapism. As Marvin Garson put it in the countercultural *San Francisco Express Times*, "Our purpose is to abolish the system (call it the Greed Machine, capitalism, the Great Hamburger Grinder, Babylon, Do-Your-Job-ism) and learn to live cooperatively, intelligently, gracefully (call it the New Awareness, anarchism, the Aquarian Age, communism, whatever you wish)."[31] In fact, the New Left and counterculture shared claims regarding the *future*, envisioned as communistic and egalitarian rather than capitalistic and hierarchical. Achieving this future furthermore required a revolution of some kind, not reforms of the current status quo. For the freaks the "future is now"; for the New Left, the future is soon, or as it was widely believed by 1969: "Revolution in Our Lifetime." But who was in which group at what time fluidly changed, affinities continuing side by side with mutual nonrecognition, even mutual contempt, throughout the period. Yet as conflicts intensified and casualties mounted, lines were drawn with greater urgency.

After the killings at Kent and Jackson State and the murder of George Jackson and many Panthers, committed revolutionaries held "hippies" in disdain for their evacuation into rural communes and Aquarian Age mysticism. The feeling was mutual, in that large sections of the counterculture viewed "political" revolutionaries as bringing down the "heat" on everybody and in any case consciously disagreeing with the strategy and tactics for revolution. Such distinctions mattered little to the system, however.

In the military, on the campuses, in the streets or out in the country, agents of the law were as likely to come down on a freak as a militant. In what was turning into civil war, the Man was indiscriminately hostile to whomever he perceived as a threat. The result was that an enduring, if distrustful, rapport was maintained throughout the Sixties, no matter how blurry the lines, appearing in common efforts from benefit concerts to rallies and demonstrations. Besides, there was no simple badge of identification in either the movement or the counterculture. Certainly the latter was predominantly (but by no means exclusively) white. Certainly, the movement included many more people of color. But afros got bigger and black dress more flamboyant as the years progressed, while many of the most political white youth continued to wear "hippie" garb. And of course, the first thing many returning GIs of all nationalities did was grow their hair!

If there is any usefulness to the counterculture designation, it lies in defining certain alignments that otherwise defy categorization. These did begin to break down after Woodstock, which explains the attraction of the "good" Sixties/"bad" Sixties scenario. In other words, Woodstock was the dream, Altamont was the nightmare, and then came Charles Manson.[32] The fact that the Rolling Stones were responsible for hiring the Hells Angels as security at Altamont makes them complicit in the murder of a young black man that occurred while they were performing a few feet away. But such stupidity and irresponsibility can be attributed to rock stars generally and not to a counterculture or political movement.

Furthermore, the "dream turned to nightmare" view corresponds to the steady co-optation of music and musicians and not, therefore, to their audiences or to youth in general.

In June 1968, *Life* magazine published an issue dedicated to "The New Rock." A photo of Jefferson Airplane graced the cover, and most of the stories inside were about bands from the San Francisco Bay Area. The reporting, which included a piece by Frank Zappa, displaying his usual wit and insight, was surprisingly knowledgeable for such a mainstream publication. But this giant spread in the most widely read magazine in America was already out of date. No doubt the bands profiled were among the most popular of the period and all would make a lasting musical impact. Certainly, the focus on bands from San Francisco accurately portrayed the Bay Area as the center of creative explorations in music, a fountain pouring forth a plethora of local talent that made it a magnet for musicians from all over the world. Yet, by the time *Life* published its story, both the music being made and the people making it were changing, and the period between 1969 and 1975 would prove to be the high point of the San Francisco renaissance.

Four Bay Area groups—Sly and the Family Stone, Santana, Tower of Power and Creedence Clearwater Revival—prove the point, not because they were unique but because they were representative of a much larger number, comprising a socio-musical trend. All of the groups were influenced by what was going on at the Fillmore and the Avalon, and all were intimately familiar with the diversity and experiment that characterized the music played there. But all were decidedly different, as well. With the exception of Creedence, these bands were of mixed ethnicity, playing music that was "integrated," which is to say a mixture of rock, blues, soul, Latin, and jazz. In the case of Creedence, folk and country elements were added to the mix. But these are only the most obvious, external features of a more profound change

More significantly, these bands attracted working-class audiences. Creedence in particular brought the new sensibility thriving in the Bay Area to working-class youth, and were especially popular among GIs. Moreover, explicitly political lyrics were woven into a general expression of youthful concerns, not isolated or pigeonholed as "protest" songs. Sly's album *Stand!* is perhaps the best summation of popular attitudes made during the Sixties, while Creedence clearly articulated an anti-authoritarian position from the perspective of white working-class kids.

While these groups were undoubtedly successful in commercial terms, music industry promotion cannot alone account for such success. By 1969, the music industry was only *beginning* to restore its control over music production. Distribution was always tightly controlled and without it, no group or musician could hope to reach the audiences that flocked to hear bands such as these. But the music-making process was still, to a large extent, in the hands of musicians (especially *bands*) who were products of communities being radicalized by unfolding events. In other words, Sly and Creedence were not "prophets" or "messiahs." Rather, they spoke with the voice of the people from whom they had come and for whom they performed.

The significance of these groups is greater than either their musical achievements or their political views. They challenge the orthodoxy of the last half-century of Sixties narratives, demonstrating a radical change in consciousness among working-class people of all ethnicities. Given that the most common reference points for sweeping changes in American culture are "The New Rock" and, above all, Woodstock, this is not mere oversight. Exemplified by sitcoms like *All In the Family*, the working class has been portrayed as the "the silent majority" in support of government policies, patiently tolerating the "zany antics" of raging radicals and drug-crazed freaks. Throughout the Culture Wars that followed the defeat of the revolution, this notion was systematically reinforced. The existence and popularity of groups like Creedence refute such claims, exposing the counterrevolutionary agenda of those making them.

In this light, one more crucial aspect of the question deserves attention: the deliberate attempt to obscure the fact that the association between culture and revolution, as it was understood in the Sixties, was originally made by revolutionaries. V.I. Lenin may well have been the first to use the term "cultural revolution," in the 1923 essay "On Cooperation": "The organisation of the entire peasantry in co-operative societies presupposes a standard of culture among the peasants (precisely among the peasants as the overwhelming mass) that cannot, in fact be achieved without a cultural revolution. . . . In our country the political and social revolution preceded the cultural revolution, that very cultural revolution which nevertheless now confronts us."[33] This theme was subsequently taken up by theorists in Algeria, Cuba, and China.

In 1959, Franz Fanon articulated the need for colonized people to wage war on the cultural front to first and foremost decolonize their minds.[34] In 1965, Che Guevara clearly stated the need to create a new socialist man and woman, a transformation in consciousness, without which socialism would be a hollow shell.[35] Finally, the Chinese Communist Party defined the purpose of the Cultural Revolution as rooting out of the ideology of the bourgeoisie in art, literature, and habits of thought.[36]

The influence of these ideas in the United States was considerable. Indeed, the identification of culture with revolution, or with changing the world, reflects just how influential (especially after 1968, when the problem of "after the revolution" came vividly into focus). On the one hand, Fanon's ideas clearly applied in the Third World, where people were still fighting to free themselves from U.S. imperialism. On the other hand, leaders of successful revolutions were admitting that seizing state power was not enough. If anything, seizing state power only led to a growing struggle to change the consciousness of the people. Failure to do so was evident in the Soviet Union, and rejection of that failure was manifest in Prague Spring. So, in a perhaps inarticulate way, the counterculture was saying: it does no good to have a political revolution without a transformation of consciousness. Indeed, the change of consciousness must precede a revolution in order to ensure its integrity and long-term viability.

Opponents of these ideas argued that without a political revolution and the seizure of state power, you could never prevent the co-optation and degradation of what popular, oppositional culture spontaneously produced. In short: revolt is not revolution, and change is not necessarily liberation.

CHAPTER 9

Power to the People: Nations, Classes, and Listening to the People

"**P**ower to the People" was among the most widely used slogans of the Sixties. Coined by the Black Panther Party, it marked the apex of a trajectory from Freedom Now through Black Power to All Power to the People. Songs by the Chi-Lites and John Lennon, an album by saxophonist Joe Henderson, and, most recently, a compilation CD entitled *Power to the Motown People: Civil Rights Anthems and Political Soul 1968–1975* all attest to the breadth of its appeal. But these are only prominent symbols of a far more profound phenomenon. Power to the People expresses the radicalization of popular consciousness that defines the Sixties. Confronting the twin problems of what constitutes power and what constitutes the people, Power to the People pointed beyond the rights and entitlements *granted* by the state to the *exercise* of authority by the people, with all their class and ethnic diversity, in their respective communities and workplaces.

Elaborating on its defining characteristics, then-imprisoned Black Panther leader Ericka Huggins wrote:

> We cannot allow our children, be they Black, Mexican, Indian, Japanese, Chinese or White to be miseducated and degraded in America's degenerate school system. We cannot allow any more lynching, bombing and racial ignorance down South or up South.
>
> We cannot allow unions, any longer, to drive the working class—the working class must drive the unions. Our fight must be endless to organize the workers of this country, to overhaul and change every assembly line in every factory.
>
> We cannot allow the reformists to clean up the surface while the inner structure rots. We need a revolution![1]

Linking means and ends in a dialectic of liberation, Power to the People was both a guiding principle for political organizing and a strategic goal. If the revolution of 1848 gave us "Proletarians of the World, Unite," then the revolution of 1968 gave us "Power to the People"; each focused on the universal aspirations of the particular historical moment from which it arose.

Prospects for Revolution

When Mao met Nixon in Beijing in 1972, the two governments issued a joint communiqué. For their part, the Chinese stated: "Countries want independence, nations want liberation and the people want revolution."[2] If revolution seemed imminent in 1972, that was the result of more than 1968 or America's impending defeat in Vietnam. Large numbers of people were becoming convinced that revolution was the only solution. The great uncertainty lay not with revolution's desirability but with its possibility. Could the people be welded together into a force capable of wresting power from the system? Could the consciousness and organization be forged that would end oppression and exploitation for good? Answering these questions required revolutionaries to join popular struggles and to seek through these struggles, to raise consciousness and build organization for revolution.

From this perspective, it was necessary to examine the phenomenon of popular consciousness itself. If it is self-evident that the people must liberate themselves, it is above all necessary to gauge the prevailing attitudes and ideas held by the people. Today, the extent to which revolutionary ideas were embraced by the populace is a cardinal question for any evaluation of the Sixties. Determining what people thought cannot, however, rely on elections, opinion polls, or even census data since many of society's members are not accounted for by these means. Simple answers to questions framed by pollsters and politicians tell us little about people's views on subjects like overthrowing the government or changing the world. Not only are such questions never asked, they are forbidden. They are in every sense, *unthinkable*. Yet they were very much on people's minds.

Music, however, can provide us with some answers. While explicitly revolutionary songs do *not*, in fact, characterize the Sixties, appeals for unity in opposition to war, poverty, and oppression certainly do. Such appeals were not confined to the "Give Peace a Chance" variety, either.

They were far more often linked to the conditions faced by the people in their daily lives, indicting the Man, or the system, as the source of misery. James Brown's albums *Hell* (1974) and *Reality* (1975) typify the lyrical terrain shared by the most influential black artists of the period. But the lyrics aren't the key. The evidence is in the music itself, both its formal characteristics (diverse influences, inventiveness, novelty) and its sonic characteristics (timbre, volume, instrumentation, experimentation, etc.).

Even after it was apparent that music could not, by itself, change the world, let alone *be* the revolution, music continued to play a vital role in the struggles for liberation that did not cease in 1970 or 1971. Music gave voice to themes that emerged most forcefully *after* Woodstock and the mass marketing of the "rock revolution." Broadly speaking, these themes were connected to a new kind of unity among a newly constituted people and a determination to "make a change." When Oscar Brown Jr. sang, "What you mean, '*we*,' white man?" in 1974, he humorously summarized how attitudes *had* changed regarding who the "American people" actually were.[3]

Listening to the People

In the ghettos and barrios, housing projects, and trailer parks, in labor camps and coal mining towns, live people who don't vote, don't get interviewed, and for all practical purposes, are only counted when they are needed to fight wars or provide labor. They nevertheless have thoughts that are expressed largely through music. Listening, in this sense, means listening not only to hit songs by famous groups, not only to rock music or any other *category* established by the music industry, but to the broad range of music that people made and heard. Stylistic categories, sales figures, chart-rankings, or the opinions of self-interested critics hinder an accurate assessment of what "the masses" actually thought. But if we hear past these limitations, we can hear a unifying theme running through a vast number of musical works. We will also hear how music, in the broadest sense, continued to be revitalized (and to revitalize the movement), even as the music industry was reasserting its control.

Four examples should suffice to make the point. Redbone, a funk-rock band made up of Hispanic and Native American musicians, released the album *Potlatch* in 1970. On this album (incidentally, a commercial hit), were songs such as "Alcatraz," "Judgment Day," and "Bad News Ain't No News at All," dealing not only with particular struggles, such as the

Indian occupation of Alcatraz, but with all the social and political conflicts that Redbone and their audience were affected by or involved in.

A second exemplary group is War, who say of themselves, "Our instruments and voices became our weapons of choice and the songs our ammunition. We spoke out against racism, hunger, gangs, crimes, and turf wars, as we embraced all people with hope and the spirit of brotherhood. It's just as apropos today."[4] War's albums *The World Is a Ghetto*, *Deliver the Word*, and *Platinum Jazz* are only part of a large corpus that summarizes the musical and political attitudes and viewpoints of the Sixties. That War was embraced by youth of all ethnic groups is in itself an important dimension. But that War made musical links between diverse styles or genres, including jazz, Latin, funk, and rock, evoked the unity and solidarity shared by a large segment of those involved in making music at the time.

The third example is the Pointer Sisters song "Yes We Can Can," which characterizes the breadth and depth of such aspirations in geographical as well as musical terms. The Pointer Sisters came from West Oakland, but the song came from New Orleans; it was written by Allen Toussaint and originally recorded by Lee Dorsey. Produced by David Rubinson in 1973, the group, the song, and its sources are both a wonderful musical expression of what the Sixties were all about and a damning refutation of many misconceptions fostered since. Not only did the Pointer Sisters defy industry norms of what black musicians could or should do, but Allen Toussaint and his compatriots completely demolished the line between "political" and "apolitical" music. Indeed, most people didn't even use the term "political" to describe their music, referring instead to "music with a message." Message music, in fact, *predominated* (at least in New Orleans), as is evident if one listens to the work of The Meters, Dr. John, and Allen Toussaint himself. In the broad ranks of an ethnically divided working class, these appeals for unity and a higher purpose were the norm, not the exception.

Malo, from San Francisco's Mission District, displayed the musical and sociological origins of a significant trend. Musically, the band incorporated a range of influences from Afro-Cuban to jazz to rock. Sociologically, they came from an ethnically diverse barrio that included native-born and immigrant musicians unwilling to accept the rigid formulas imposed by the music industry. While one of the band members, Jorge Santana, is related to a "star" (his brother, Carlos), Malo was always more closely associated with the "street" and with the cholos and lowriders, than were more famous groups. They were also more closely identified with the Mission District and its peculiar mix of Mexican, Central American, and Caribbean populations. This mixture spawned the unifying identifier: La Raza, inclusive of all people from the Spanish-language Americas. It also spawned the hybrid music that wedded Caribbean (specifically Afro-Cuban) with Mexican influences (particularly the trumpet playing of Luis Gasca).[5]

To these examples must be added a fifth that might, at first glance, appear anomalous, but on closer inspection is highly relevant: Johnny Cash. As early as 1964, Cash had taken controversial positions with the release of a single "The Ballad of Ira Hayes" and the album *Bitter Tears: Ballads of the American Indian*. His two prison albums, *Johnny Cash at Folsom Prison* and *Johnny Cash at San Quentin*, were overt expressions of solidarity with society's downtrodden, a point Cash made explicit in his song "Man in Black":

> I wear the black for the poor and the beaten down,
> Livin' in the hopeless, hungry side of town,
> I wear it for the prisoner who has long paid for his crime,
> But still is there because he's a victim of the times.

The significance of Cash's role is made all the greater by the fact that the music industry in Nashville was notoriously right-wing and provided vocal support for government policy in Vietnam and for the repression of dissent. Cash's unparalleled stature put the lie to the industry's claim to represent "the working man" (meaning white workers). Cash's association with the likes of Pete Seeger and his collaboration with artists such as Peter LaFarge, who were both clearly left-wing in their political sympathies, was consistent with Cash's understanding of the attitudes shared by his own constituency. Were Cash alone in this, he would perhaps be an anomaly. But there were others, the most famous of whom are Kris Kristofferson and Willie Nelson, whose left-leaning politics became increasingly evident at a time when the Sixties were little more than a memory.

In, *Listen, Whitey!*, Pat Thomas presents evidence for yet another dimension of the Sixties that contradicts prevailing notions.[6] The period's leading jazz musicians were swept up in the ferment, giving articulate expression to the movements' most advanced ideas. This was by no means an underground subculture of hipsters and aficionados, but representative of the main currents of jazz. Jazz was enjoying the same renaissance of creativity and innovation as rock, soul, and funk, and experiencing its greatest popularity at the same time. From Archie Shepp to Rahsaan Roland Kirk, from Ornette Coleman to the Art Ensemble of Chicago, from the Last Poets to Gil Scott-Heron, jazz undertook a profound exploration of consciousness-raising through music that is inspiring in its ambition. Albums such as *Black Unity*, *Freedom and Unity*, *Volunteered Slavery*, *Ghetto Music*, *The Panther and the Lash*, and *Attica Blues* characterize a trend among jazz musicians to comment on and contribute to the struggle for liberation. Lest there be any doubt, Charlie Haden's and Carla Bley's Liberation Music Orchestra made it explicit. "Song for Che" was among their most memorable compositions.

While all of this is simply undeniable in the face of the facts, it has nonetheless been buried historically. This historical burial has been accomplished by either marginalization (the impression that such music was not widely listened to) or by segregation (the insistence that rigid formal characteristics isolated jazz in a ghetto of its own making). The music industry and rock music journalists who insist on maintaining the supremacy of "rock" at the expense of music as a whole have thereby created a false impression of what actually made up the music of the Sixties. An egregious example is *Rolling Stone*'s "100 Greatest Artists of All Time". While the title's claim could be dismissed as mere P.T. Barnum-esque hyperbole, its purpose is nonetheless to marginalize and segregate music that does not meet with the approval of the "gatekeepers."

Marginalization and segregation are justified by rock's larger audience, sales figures and, therefore, its greater social significance. But this overlooks the fact that during the Sixties, jazz was neither marginal nor segregated, being frequently included in the varied assortment of music people listened to. If anything, the broadening of the jazz audience is a hallmark of the Sixties, not in competition with rock or any other form, but simply as music being creatively explored. As Black Panther historian Billy X Jennings remembers:

> Albert "Big Man" Howard, original founder of the Party with Huey—went to Merritt—but jazz was his thing. So I'm listening to this Kool and the Gang record, and Big Man comes in, slips on some John Coltrane—and it blew me back. Then he goes on

to explain what's going on in that music. Next he starts playing Pharaoh Sanders and telling me the story behind that. And he taught me the ability to visualize what was being told, what is happening in a song, in a piece of music.[7]

Billy went on to present a long list of jazz musicians who openly and defiantly supported the Panthers, including Max Roach, Freddie Hubbard, McCoy Tyner, Abbey Lincoln, and Oscar Brown Jr. Even Miles Davis would say, "I am not a Black Panther or nothing like that," only to add, "I don't need to be, I was raised to think like that."[8]

Where did these ideas come from and, aside from music, how were they propagated? It is certainly not the case that musicians were theorists or, in most cases, politically active. If anything, musicians responded to what they perceived to be the thoughts and feelings of their audiences. What were these thoughts and feelings? Answering this question requires examining the conditions that gave rise to Power to the People and the particular struggles guided by that principle.

The Future Foretold

In *The Souls of Black Folk* (1903), W.E.B. Du Bois prophetically claimed: "The Problem of the twentieth century is the problem of the color-line— the relation of the darker to the lighter races of men in Asia and Africa, in America and the islands of the sea."[9] Du Bois made clear who had drawn that line in the first place: "Some day the Awakening will come, when the pent-up vigor of ten million souls shall sweep irresistibly toward the Goal, out of the Valley of the Shadow of death, where all that makes life worth living—Liberty, Justice and Right—is marked 'For White People Only'."[10] Nearly sixty years later, following two world wars and the Russian and Chinese Revolutions, it had become abundantly clear that Du Bois was right.

At first glance this might appear to contradict the classic Marxian division of proletariat and bourgeoisie, of "proletarians of all countries, unite." But as the Russian Revolution of 1917 showed, *proletariat* as a concept could not be so firmly wedded to the industrial worker that its emancipatory political content is erased. Indeed, "proletariat" was a Roman word describing "men of no property," a class excluded from governance, because "They had not even the minimum property required of the lowest class. Their sole possession was their children, *proles*;

hence the name."[11] Marx had made his interpretation explicit when he wrote, "The *head* of this liberation is *philosophy*, its *heart* is the *proletariat*. Philosophy cannot be realized without abolishing the proletariat and the proletariat cannot be abolished without realizing philosophy."[12]

As became increasingly evident, the peasantry and a vast and growing number of propertyless laborers congealing around trade routes and urban agglomerations (but *not* always or even mainly employed in the dark, satanic mills of capitalism) were in fact the proletariat of the world as it was outside of Paris, London, Chicago, and Berlin. The Chinese Revolution proved this beyond a doubt, and all subsequent revolutions were to display these dynamics, with two exceptions, France in 1968 and Portugal in 1974, neither of which were successful in bringing about an end to capitalist rule. Furthermore, British and American imperialism created and propagated the fallacious concept of race to justify slavery in the Western Hemisphere, and to share "the white man's burden" with the working classes of the metropole, in order to align them with this "civilizing" mission and divide them from an international "brotherhood of toil."

At the dawn of the 1960s, this was no longer tenable. As was enunciated most strikingly by Frantz Fanon in *The Wretched of the Earth*, colonization took place not only on the territory and on the backs of the colonized; it depended on the colonization of the minds of the dispossessed. To break this mental slavery and to assert one's capacity for humanity was, therefore, to render *human* both oppressor and oppressed alike. The violence this necessitated did not implicate the oppressed in moral turpitude; on the contrary, revolutionary violence was the purgation of the disease of injustice. As Sartre wrote in his preface to the book, "We have sown the wind; he is the whirlwind. The child of violence, at every moment he draws from it his humanity. We were men at his expense, he makes himself a man at ours: a different man; of higher quality."[13]

The Black Panther platform and program and All Power to the People sought to address the forces of state, nation, and class as they clashed geopolitically within and outside the United States. In the United States, white people constituted a large majority and black people a distinct minority, but one becoming increasingly aware that the *world's* majority was colored, with Europeans a small minority. Throughout Africa, Asia, and Latin America, great masses were stirring, encircling their colonizers, forcing the populations of Europe, North America, and

Australia/New Zealand to make profound moral and political choices. Indeed, the Panthers' genius was to envision an internationalist unity of all the people, while simultaneously waging an anticolonial struggle against the white power structure in the most powerful imperialist country of all. This struggle was based on the recognition that the white power structure was incapable of "integration," since it depended on black subordination to maintain its rule over all members of society, including poor whites. As mentioned earlier, it was only in 1967 that the Supreme Court heard the *Loving v. Virginia* case and struck down the laws against interracial marriage still enforced by sixteen states.

The Panthers' response was a radical intervention in the deadlock produced by racism as they encouraged unity with all people, including whites, at the high point of Black Power nationalism and separatism. Maintaining a principled independence based on the right of self-determination, while uniting all the forces arrayed against U.S. imperialism, was no easy task. Indeed, it was ultimately unsuccessful. But the composition of the people demanded the attempt. In 1960, the U.S. census used "White," "Negro," and "other" as racial categories. At that time 159,467,000 were counted as White and 20,540,000 as Negro. As already noted, the world population was strikingly different, with Asia's 1,849,000,000 alone dwarfing North America's 219 million. By the time human population had crossed the 3 billion mark in 1965, more than two-thirds lived outside Europe and North America.[14]

W.E.B. Du Bois became a communist, and the Black Panthers advocated revolutionary socialism under the banner of Marxism-Leninism. The Panthers also played a key role in popularizing Mao Zedong's thought and restoring revolutionary honor to Marxism in the United States. The Communist Party and the Trotskyist Socialist Workers Party claimed the mantle of Marxism-Leninism, but their relationship to the New Left was tormented, undermined by their Old Left baggage, their reformist organizing strategies, and dubious analyses of the Third World revolutions from which the younger generation of radicals and revolutionaries drew so much inspiration. The CP and SWP certainly opposed the Vietnam War; the SWP, in particular, played a vital role in organizing the huge antiwar demonstrations characteristic of the era. But not only did these organizations cling to outmoded analyses and discredited policies, they were largely unsuccessful in capturing the imagination of the young, especially in oppressed communities. The Panthers, with all their flaws and contradictions, provided a revolutionary spirit combined with innovative thinking that addressed the needs of oppressed people living in "the belly of the beast."

The People Redefined

The Panthers inspired a wave of radical organizing throughout the United States. By 1968, an awakening of unprecedented scale was challenging every premise of America's self-image. As is demonstrated by two of the most important battles of the Sixties, the San Francisco State strike and the Indian occupation of Alcatraz, this was no longer confined to civil rights, or even to Black Power. The San Francisco State strike, which lasted from November 6, 1968, until March 20, 1969, began when an English instructor, George Mason Murray (also Black Panther minister of education) was fired on dubious charges unrelated to his qualifications. The strike, however, immediately put forward a larger agenda that led to the formation of the Third World Liberation Front (TWLF). The TWLF not only united students and led the battle against the institution, it also began organizing support in the black, Asian, Latino, and Native American communities in the Bay Area. These efforts had consequences far beyond the confines of the campus, including sweeping changes in curricula at universities across America. According to San Francisco State's current website: "Students, faculty and community activists demanded equal access to public higher education, more senior faculty of color and a new curriculum that would embrace the history and culture of all people including ethnic minorities. As a result, the College of Ethnic Studies was instituted in 1969 and hundreds of other higher educations institutions across the country followed SF State's lead."[15]

The strike was brutally attacked by the police and vilified by corporate media. The public was instructed to view the students as rabidly antiwhite, separatist, and violent. The radicals, it was claimed, were disrupting the education of the majority of hardworking students, with no agenda other than to destroy. In response, George Mason Murray told a reporter:

> Listen to this: freedom is a state not limited to a particular culture,
> race or people, and therefore, the principles upon which a struggle
> for human rights is based must be all inclusive, must apply equally

for all people. Freedom, equality is not relative. For example, the struggle at San Francisco State is based upon three principles: 1) a fight to the death against racism; 2) the right of all people to determine their economic, political, social and educational destines; and 3) the right for the people to seize power, to carry out all their goals, and to answer all their needs. In short—All Power to the People. These are principles that all human beings can fight for, and the fight is being waged by Black, Brown, Red, and Yellow students, and workers, as well as progressive whites.[16]

San Francisco State student Richard Oakes carried these ideas into the Indian occupation of Alcatraz that followed the San Francisco State strike. LaNada Means, another leader of the occupation, had earlier been active in the Third World Liberation Front at Berkeley and, like many of her generation, was developing in a radical direction. In one sense, Indian claims were distinct in that native tribes had treaties with the U.S. government recognizing them as nations. Power to the People, in this case, could literally mean seizing land ostensibly guaranteed them by treaty with the U.S. government—the legal premise on which Alcatraz was occupied. Yet, in a more fundamental sense, Indians shared with other oppressed peoples both a common enemy and a common demand for freedom and self-determination. Given that an earlier attempt to take over Alcatraz (see Chapter 1) occurred at the beginning of the Sixties, a comparison can be made illustrating the development of strategy and tactics of the movement overall. The 1964 takeover lasted hours. The second was a true occupation, lasting from November 20, 1969, until June 11, 1971. The first was a symbolic act designed to raise public awareness. The second launched a movement that galvanized Indians of All Tribes, the American Indian Movement, and broad popular support for years to come. Indeed, present-day Indigenous peoples' struggles, especially in the Western Hemisphere, have been to a great extent inspired by Alcatraz.

Above all, these struggles sought to enunciate and enact a transformative vision of popular will and legitimacy in opposition to a state that had long claimed to be "of the people, by the people, for the people." In a world convulsed by revolution, it was possible to completely reconfigure the people as a multiplicity of histories and cultures with the destiny of a shared humanity.

The Revolutionary People's Constitutional Convention

"In a world of racist polarization, we sought solidarity," wrote Kathleen Cleaver many years later. "We organized the Rainbow Coalition, pulled together our allies, including not only the Puerto Rican Young Lords, the youth gang called the Black P. Stone Rangers, the Chicano Brown Berets, and the Asian I Wor Kuen (Red Guards), but also the predominantly white Peace and Freedom Party and the Appalachian Young Patriots Party."[17] Practically speaking, all these organizations provided mutual support in the face of government attacks and organized in their respective communities to broaden the appeal of revolutionary ideas. This strategy culminated in the Panther-initiated Revolutionary People's Constitutional Convention, held in Philadelphia in September 1970. This almost forgotten event is important for several reasons. First, the range of organizations and individuals participating included not only the aforementioned groups but also representatives of the women's and gay liberation movements. Second, the content of the deliberations and the ambitious program proposed as a result challenges the oft-repeated charge that no practical suggestions for change were ever made by radicals in the Sixties. Finally, the convention can, in hindsight, be seen as the apex of Panther influence and leadership within the broad forces of the New Left and the movement. Estimated attendance ranges from 5,000 to 15,000, with the *New York Times* claiming there were 6,000 people inside and another 2,000 outside. The summary of the convention's conclusions made in the *Black Panther* newspaper (circulation: 100,000 per week, at this time) is worth quoting at length:

> Taken as a whole, these reports provided the basis for one of the most progressive Constitutions in the history of humankind. All the people would control the means of production and social institutions. Black and third world people were guaranteed proportional representation in the administration of these institutions as were women. The right of national self-determination was guaranteed to all oppressed minorities. Sexual self-determination for women and homosexuals was affirmed. A standing army is to be replaced by a people's militia, and the Constitution is to include an international bill of rights prohibiting U.S. aggression and interference in the internal affairs of other nations.... The present racist legal system would be replaced by a system of people's courts where one

would be tried by a jury of one's peers. Jails would be replaced by community rehabilitation programs.... Adequate housing, health care, and day care would be considered Constitutional Rights, not privileges. Mind expanding drugs would be legalized. These are just some of the provisions of the new Constitution.[18]

The significance of the RPCC and its constitution is not limited to words on a page, provocative as such words may be. They express not only ideas or theories but also years of daily, practical organizing. Contrary to the image of revolutionary work as either endless, fruitless talk or, conversely, the oiling of rifles and construction of bombs, most revolutionaries or radicals were committed to daily community and workplace organizing. Although on-campus activity continued, following the San Francisco State strike, greater emphasis was placed on organizing oppressed people where they lived and worked.

Serve the People

Inspired by Mao's famous injunction that revolutionaries should "serve the people," the Panthers initiated a series of programs designed both to meet the material needs of the black community and to provide political education. The first of these was the Free Breakfast for Children Program, quickly implemented throughout the United States by all sixty-eight chapters of the Party. Community health centers, liberation schools, legal services, and prison visitation programs soon followed. Not surprisingly, these programs were greeted with enthusiasm by the black community, garnering support from many noteworthy musicians, including Aretha Franklin and James Brown. Perhaps more significantly, they earned the grudging respect of many liberals who otherwise frowned on the Panthers' politics. Indeed, the programs became so effective that they attracted the attention of J. Edgar Hoover, who instructed his FBI to attempt to shut down the Free Breakfast for Children Program, in particular.[19] Since churches had long provided food for the poor, the issue was obviously not the breakfast, but rather the politics being served. As Eldridge Cleaver clarified:

Breakfast for Children pulls people out of the system and organizes them into an alternative. Black children who go to school hungry each morning have been organized into their poverty, and the Panther program liberates them, frees them from that aspect of their poverty. This is liberation in practice. . . . If we can understand Breakfast for Children, can we not also understand Lunch for Children, and Dinner for Children, and Clothing for Children, and Education for Children, and Medical Care for Children? And if we can understand that, why can't we understand not only a People's Park, but People's Housing, and People's Transportation, and People's Industry and People's Banks? And why can't we understand a People's Government?[20]

The example set by the Panthers inspired similar efforts in Chicano/ Latino, Asian, Indian, and poor white communities. An example from San Francisco's Chinatown illustrates a much wider phenomenon found in cities across the United States during the Sixties.

As a direct outgrowth of the student strike at San Francisco State College and subsequent struggles to establish ethnic studies programs at Bay Area colleges and universities, young activists sought to deepen their political involvement. As Steve Yip recalls, "We were feeling empowered by these victories on campus that had resulted in the first university ethnic studies programs in the U.S., and we now hungered for greater social change. The newly founded Asian Studies introduced us to many revolutionary writers of the day, especially the works of Mao."[21] This led not only to intense study of Mao's philosophical works, such as *On Contradiction* and *On Practice*, but inspired these young people to heed Mao's call "to go among the laboring people, to go 'serve the people' and learn the theories and methods of changing the world." Yip explains how he and his comrades "opened the doors of the Asian Community Center in one of the many basements of the International Hotel. A little more than a month later, we each pitched in $50 to stock and open Everybody's Bookstore in one of the I-Hotel's walk-in-closet-sized storefronts."

The programs launched ran the gamut from film showings to free food. The emphasis was on literature from China (especially Marxist classics and the works of Mao), as well as news about the Cultural Revolution in China, and liberation struggles everywhere, including in the United States. These programs galvanized both immigrant and U.S.-born members of the Chinese and Filipino communities. After a year of such activity, Wei Min She was formed with the goal of waging anti-imperialist struggle. The significance of this move was twofold, concentrating the experience of a generation of Asian radicals that had far-reaching effects well beyond the Sixties, and exemplifying the nature of revolutionary work in the Sixties overall.

> When we opened the doors to the Asian Community Center and Everybody's Bookstore, the block-long I-Hotel complex on San Francisco's Kearney Street was a seething hotbed of Asian youth radicalism. Besides the Asian Community Center and Everybody's Bookstore, it was also home to a multitude of political and cultural rebels: the Chinatown Draft Help/Asian Legal Services; the Red Guards/I Wor Kuen/Chinese Progressive Association; the Kearney Street (artists) Workshop; and the I-Hotel Tenants Association. The battle against the eviction/demolition of the I-Hotel went through many tense twists and turns that lasted from 1969–1977.[22]

Yip also recalls the intense struggles that pitted revolutionaries against reformists, and nationalists against internationalists. These were far from academic debates; they arose out of conflicts between workers and employers in Chinatown itself. In practice, what characterized revolutionary politics was its direct engagement with the struggles of the people, combined with an effort to find the means to end exploitation and oppression altogether. As Bobby Seale put it, "It's impossible for us to have control of the institutions in our community when a capitalistic system exists on the outside of it, when in fact the capitalistic system was the very system that enslaved us and is responsible for our continued oppression. So if we want to develop a socialistic system within the black community, we're saying it's also going to have to exist in the white community."[23] Obviously, this applied in particular ways to all the communities of color in the Bay Area, but the class divisions that emerged in each particular community could not be adequately addressed, let alone overcome, by simply appealing to ethnic or national unity. This was a major factor in the rapid growth of the New Communist Movement at this time. Numerous organizations were part of this development. Perhaps the largest and most influential of them was the Bay Area Revolutionary Union, with which Wei Min She allied itself.

The essential point, historically, is that what the Panthers initiated and what Power to the People expressed, required nothing less than the overthrow of the system. Achieving that aim meant confronting the divisions sown by the system as it pitted workers of different nationalities against each other and making expressions of solidarity of paramount importance. Yip recalls, for example, the strike of Chinese electronics workers at a small factory called Lee Mah:

> We began mobilizing broadly in the Chinese community with car caravans and cultural events, unleashing the anger many felt about the discrimination faced by the whole community. We also mobilized rank-and-file workers of all nationalities to join and support the Lee Mah workers. White strikers from other Bay Area electronics factories, Black, Latino and white workers from the post office, city bus drivers, Chinese garment and restaurant workers would join the picket lines and support activities.[24]

Not the Usual Suspects

The overwhelming majority of Sixties histories focus on a specific and limited set of organizations and individuals, leaving the impression that these were the most important or had the greatest impact at the time. Time frames are often confusing or contradictory, some claiming that everything ended in 1969, others that it did so in 1971 or in 1973, and so on. The "usual suspects" must include the Panthers, whose influence was too great to ignore, but invariably go on to emphasize the Weathermen (or Weather Underground), Jerry Rubin, Abbie Hoffman and a few other notables who made headlines at the time. But the writers of headlines are not the makers of history—unless, of course, we allow ourselves to believe that they are. Not only were there many historical actors, but some with the greatest influence, largest numbers, and most enduring effects were erased from the historical record. By 1971, even the Black Panthers were eclipsed as government repression and internal division crippled the organization. While it took another ten years for the Panthers to completely shut down, their ability to lead, especially in the path-breaking and innovative manner they had done until 1971, was rapidly diminishing. The movement, however, was reinvigorated by many of the groups mentioned above, as well as Vietnam Veterans Against the War and, especially in Detroit, the League of Revolutionary Black Workers. Without great contortions of logic one can also not evade the eruption and enduring impact of women's liberation.

It is true that by 1973 there were many indications that the movement could no longer mobilize throughout the country on the same scale it had previously. The reasons for this were readily apparent: the gradual winding down of the Vietnam War, the end of the draft, and numerous small but important concessions made to various constituencies within the broader movement. The Twenty-Sixth Amendment securing voting rights for all citizens eighteen years and older was passed in 1971. This not only addressed the outrageous fact that young men could be drafted but could not vote, it also led to many black people being elected to political office. By 1970, the Indian termination policy was being phased out, just as the Environmental Protection Agency was being launched. *Roe v. Wade* guaranteed abortion rights in 1973. In short, the federal government moved to placate popular demands, deliberately severing the bonds between revolutionaries and their mass base of support.

Nevertheless, it is not a quibble over dates or about the factors leading to decline that makes a radical reappraisal of the period 1968–1975 so necessary. For one thing, the San Francisco Bay Area remained a hotbed of radical activity far longer than elsewhere in the country. Recognition of the groups and ideas written out of the historical record is all the more important since their influence was considerable years after the Sixties came to an end. For another, the system's crisis was deepening, convincing many that what the movement faced was a temporary lull and not irreversible ebb. No doubt some recognized that a critical impasse had been reached and wrote accordingly. But such views were not a movement "consensus" so much as a basis for intense debate. Independent but partisan publications of the Sixties such as *Ramparts* and *The National Guardian* make them valuable historical resources today. *Ramparts* closed its doors in 1975, but in its final issue, Noam Chomsky's analysis of U.S. defeat in Vietnam clearly defined both an end point and pursuant tasks. In 1973, it was not clear that the revolution of 1968 had been decisively defeated; indeed, it took at least until 1980 for this conclusion to be unavoidable and recognized by virtually everyone.

It is important, at this point, to return to the question of music, the music industry, and how this part of the Sixties was marked by deepening conflict, not by the sudden "disappearance" of revolution, politics, or music's subversive influence. After all, *Fight the Power* was released in 1975, *Takin' It to the Streets* in 1976, and *Go for Your Guns* in 1977, to name just a few prominent examples of music with a political edge that was widely popular. The liner notes to Gil Scott-Heron's 1974 release, *Winter in America*, are worth quoting at length, since they more accurately convey the contradictions than do assessments made by most historians or music journalists.

> At the end of 360 degrees, Winter is a metaphor: a term not only used to describe the season of ice, but the period of our lives through which we are traveling. In our hearts we feel that spring is just around the corner: a spring of brotherhood and united spirits among people of color. Everyone is moving, searching. There is a restlessness within our souls that keeps us questioning, discovering and struggling against a system that will not allow us space and time for fresh expression. Western icemen have attempted to distort time. Extra months on the calendar and daylight saved what was Eastern Standard. We approach winter the most depressing period in the history of this industrial empire, with threats of oil shortages and energy crisis. But we, as Black people, have been a source of endless energy, endless beauty and endless determination. I have many things to tell you about tomorrow's love and light. We will see you in Spring.[25]

Power to the People versus the "Rock Revolution"

Anyone can claim the mantle of revolution. And in the Sixties, everyone did. By 1971, even President Nixon was calling for a "new American revolution," exhorting Americans in his State of the Union Address to make "a revolution as profound, as far-reaching, as exciting as that first revolution almost 200 years ago."[26] Nixon was, of course, trying to capitalize on general sentiment, but he was also imitating a strategy effectively developed by the music industry. Rock and revolution had been made synonymous not only by continuous linkage of the two words in advertisement but also by a quasi-sociological "analysis" meant to give the appearance of a "real" phenomenon, not merely a corporate marketing strategy. *Rolling Stone* was the preeminent vehicle for such views, announcing in a full-page *New York Times* ad, "If you are a corporate executive trying to understand what is happening to youth today. . . . If you are a student, a professor, a parent, this is your life because you already know that rock 'n' roll is more than just music; it is the energy center of the new culture and youth revolution."[27]

While such ploys were obviously aimed at co-opting and disarming a threat, the more significant point is what that threat actually consisted of. In musical terms, Power to the People signified the fulfillment of the wild dreaming unleashed at the Fillmore and Avalon at the beginning of the Sixties. Not "rock" as a classical form, rigidly defined and basically white, but rock that broke all stylistic and genre constraints to explore and unleash music's power to inform and inspire. These qualities persisted long after the music industry and its mouthpieces had turned the "rock revolution" into charity concerts and endorsements for the Democratic Party. What continued beneath the hype and hoopla was fueled by continued political struggle, as well as by the force of music itself.

Power to the People is the quintessential *democratic* demand, and it was this demand that defined the revolution of the Sixties. The challenge it posed to America's conception of itself as a nation (a nation born of a revolution no less) was both fundamental and glaringly obvious. If the Sixties accomplished nothing else, they exposed forever the fact that it is precisely this demand to which the U.S. government cannot accede, since the concentration of power in the hands of a privileged few is what the American state was designed to protect.

CHAPTER 10

Humanhood Is the Ultimate: Women, Music, and Liberation

The women's movement did not begin in the Sixties. In the heat of the French Revolution, Mary Wollstonecraft and Olympe de Gouges argued for the equality of women as both the logical extension of revolutionary principles and as a practical necessity for the emancipation of humanity. Wollstonecraft's *Vindication of the Rights of Woman* and de Gouges's *Declaration of the Rights of Woman and the Female Citizen* argued for the education of women and for women's full participation in the governance of society. Moreover, both explicitly linked women's emancipation to the abolition of slavery, forming an indissoluble bond between two great strands of struggle that emerged as an inevitable consequence of the cluster of revolutions (American, French, and Haitian) that marked the end of the eighteenth century. Throughout the nineteenth century, these links were made stronger, as abolitionists, feminists, and socialists joined forces in common cause. Sojourner Truth and Harriet Tubman, for example, were leaders of both abolitionist and suffragist movements during and after the Civil War.

Yet legal rights alone were only one dimension of what grew into a wholesale assault on capitalism and imperialism. The growing influence of Marxism combined with the organization of women workers to make the emancipation of women inseparable (in theory, at least) from the emancipation of the proletariat. The workers' movement brought forth women leaders, including Emma Goldman, Lucy Parsons, and Elizabeth Gurley Flynn, and inspired both notable songs, "Bread and Roses" among them, and commemorative events like International Women's Day. This led Irish revolutionary socialist James Connolly to make his oft-quoted statement, "The worker is the slave of capitalist society, the female worker is the slave of that slave." Connolly drew the following conclusions:

> Down from the landlord to the tenant or peasant proprietor, from the monopolist, and from all above to all below, filtered the beliefs, customs, ideas establishing a slave morality which enforces the subjection of women as the standard morality of the country.
>
> None so fitted to break the chains as they who wear them, none so well equipped to decide what is a fetter. In its march towards freedom, the working class of Ireland must cheer on the efforts of those women who, feeling on their souls and bodies the fetters of the ages, have arisen to strike them off, and cheer all the louder if in its hatred of thralldom and passion for freedom the women's army forges ahead of the militant army of labor.[1]

By the end of World War II, however, the Russian Revolution and decades of socialist agitation among the proletariat throughout the world showed that the principles expressed by Connolly were at best unevenly and inadequately applied. In 1947, Simone de Beauvoir set herself the task of writing *The Second Sex*, not only to discover how bourgeois society kept women in chains but also to uncover why women remained a subjugated subspecies of humanity even in the Soviet Union and other nominally socialist countries. As she said in a 1976 interview:

> It is true that equality of the sexes is impossible under capitalism. If all women work as much as men, what will happen to those institutions on which capitalism depends, such institutions as churches, marriage, armies, and the millions of factories, shops, stores, etc., which are dependent on piece work, part-time work, and cheap labor? But it is not true that a socialist revolution necessarily establishes sexual equality. Just look at Soviet Russia or Czechoslovakia, where (even if we are willing to call those countries "socialist," which I am not) there is a profound confusion between emancipation of the proletariat and emancipation of women. Somehow, the proletariat always end up being made up of men. The patriarchal values have remained intact there as well as here.[2]

The Second Sex is among the most profound and influential books of the twentieth century. In it, Beauvoir dissects a fundamental problem in the struggle for human emancipation:

Quite evidently this problem would be without significance if we were to believe that woman's destiny is inevitably determined by physiological, psychological, or economic forces. Hence I shall discuss first of all the light in which woman is viewed by biology, psychoanalysis and historical materialism. Next I shall try to show exactly how the concept of the truly feminine: has been fashioned— why woman has been defined as the Other—and what have been the consequences from man's point of view. Then from woman's point of view I shall describe the world in which women must live; and thus we shall be able to envisage the difficulties in their way as, endeavoring to make their escape from the sphere hitherto assigned them, they aspire to full membership in the human race.[3]

The full impact of *The Second Sex* was not felt, however, until the revolution of 1968. As Beauvoir herself said, "Then came 1968, and everything changed. I know that some important events happened before that. . . . But it was within the anti-imperialist movement itself that real feminist consciousness developed." Women had,

joined the marches, the demonstrations, the campaigns, the underground groups, the militant left. They fought, as much as any man, for a nonexploiting, nonalienating future. But what happened? In the groups or organizations they joined, they discovered that they were just as much a second sex as in the society they wanted to overturn. Here in France, and I dare say in America just as much, they found that the leaders were always the men. Women became the typists, the coffee-makers of these pseudorevolutionary groups. Well, I shouldn't say pseudo. Many of the movement's male "heavies" were genuine revolutionaries. But trained, raised, molded in a male-oriented society, these revolutionaries brought that orientation to the movement as well. Understandably, such men were not voluntarily going to relinquish that orientation, just as the bourgeois class isn't going to voluntarily relinquish its power. So, just as it is up to the poor to take away the power of the rich, so it is up to women to take away power from the men.

And that doesn't mean dominate men in turn. It means establish equality. As socialism, true socialism, establishes economic equality among all peoples, the feminist movement learned it had to establish equality between the sexes by taking power away from the ruling class within the movement, that is, from men.[4]

This explains why, in spite of the women's movement's long and noble history, women's liberation was such a profound shock to the movement of the Sixties. This shock was felt in all quarters of the New Left, but also among those who viewed themselves as "cultural revolutionaries," and whose focus was on music, consciousness expanding, or on other forms of opposition to the system that were not explicitly or conventionally political. Shocking as it undoubtedly was, feminist consciousness spread rapidly within the movement and in society at large. A gauntlet was thrown down:

> Traditional womanhood is dead.
> Traditional women were beautiful . . . but really powerless.
> "Uppity" women were even more beautiful . . . but still powerless
> Sisterhood is powerful!
> Humanhood is the ultimate![5]

While criticism of male chauvinism within the movement was crucial, the main target of women's liberation was always the system responsible for all forms of oppression. Though marked from its inception by wide diversity and contradictory views, the women's movement shared basic unity in opposition to the Vietnam War, in support of Third World liberation struggles, and the fight against poverty. All but forgotten in most accounts of the Sixties was the growth of the National Welfare Rights Organization, which pointedly linked poverty with the oppression of women. "Welfare Is a Women's Issue" was the title of a widely read essay by NWRO leader Johnnie Tillmon. In it, she argued that the system depended first and foremost on the unpaid labor of housework and child rearing. It followed, therefore, that welfare should be viewed as a means of recompense, not a charitable donation to the poor. This was and remains one of the most revolutionary contributions of the Sixties. The depth and breadth of its influence is indicated by the fact that the NWRO had at least twenty-two thousand members, 90 percent of whom were black women, in a nationwide organization.[6]

While historical attention has most often focused on specific issues, such as abortion, maternity leave, equal pay, gender quotas, and the battles waged to improve women's status *within* capitalism, the demand that women be compensated for hitherto unpaid, yet vitally necessary labor, challenged the very foundation of the system. Indeed, it is often overlooked that the general tenor of the women's movement in the Sixties was consistently radical in two senses. First, equality was something the rigidly hierarchical system could never provide; second, all the traits commonly defined as "feminine," such as caring, sharing, nurturing, and healing, are practical tasks and moral virtues upon which society depends for its very existence. They are also diametrically opposed to the conquest and domination that self-evidently characterized U.S. imperialism.

Like black and Third World liberation only a short time before, women's liberation exposed both a glaring injustice of epochal proportions and a glaring weakness in the system's claims to legitimacy. Not one, but *all* of the claims made by liberal democracy were exposed as a fraud, thus undermining authority in every conceivable situation. Permeating every personal and social relationship, women's liberation produced jarring effects that were simultaneously threatening and inspiring. The magnitude of these effects raises questions for any evaluation of the Sixties, even those that are not specifically devoted to the subject of women's liberation.

The women's movement casts division of the "good" and "bad" Sixties (i.e., before and after 1968) in an entirely different light and exposes the fallacy of dividing overlapping and mutually reinforcing events into discrete compartments. Counterculture, New Left, Black Power, antiwar, and women's liberation, can all be pigeonholed and stereotyped, rather than being viewed as components of an all-embracing movement to change the world. As Kathleen Cleaver pointed out in the essay "Women, Power, and Revolution":

> It is important to place the women who fought oppression as Black Panthers within the longer tradition of freedom fighters like Sojourner Truth, Harriet Tubman and Ida Wells Barnett, who took on an entirely oppressive world and insisted that their race, their gender, and their humanity be respected all at the same time. Not singled out, each one separate, but all at the same time. You cannot segregate out one aspect of our reality and expect to get a clear picture of what this struggle is about.[7]

It is certainly not the case, as some have suggested, that women's liberation weakened the movement.[8] By exposing the facile and hypocritical character of what had only a short time before been viewed as revolutionary, feminism (especially what was called radical feminism at the time) strengthened the resolve and clarified the vision of those seriously devoted to change. This included, of course, challenging the subordination of women within organizations and campaigns, the dismissal of women's ideas and creativity, as well as their relegation to menial tasks. But feminism went further still, by directly confronting male supremacist logic and behavior in regards to the very categories by which liberation had been earlier defined. More specifically, the "sexual revolution," "consciousness-expanding," and the fields of music and the arts were all subjected to withering criticism that has never ceased.

Precisely because of its radical nature, feminism is the best example of how the history of the Sixties has been distorted. Though an enormous amount of literature is devoted to the subject, including books written by feminists and scholars of women's history, a peculiar separation or marginalization of the subject persists, not only perpetuating the relegation of half of humanity to substrata within academia but also sowing confusion in any attempt to come to grips with the ultimate defeat of the revolution of 1968. When, for example, we consider the co-optation of music, it is often overlooked that this co-optation was in large part accomplished using male supremacist ideology and tactics. It is furthermore overlooked that the music industry was to a great extent responsible for propagating male supremacist ideology, side-by-side with minstrelsy and the degradation of black people, in the first place. Women music-makers, in particular, paid the price.

By employing a feminist critique, it is possible to unearth how the music industry was built by fostering an image of "the feminine," and how the industry subsequently reconstructed itself amid the storms of the Sixties by appropriating "sex, drugs, and rock 'n' roll."

Women, Music, and the Music Industry

In the 1930 book *Tin Pan Alley*, Isaac Goldberg wrote:

> Our popular song, in its industrial phase, begins largely under the influence of women. It is women who sing songs in the home. It is women who play them on the piano. The men, as it were,

serve only as the page-turners, unless it be to chant a sour note or two in the amateur quartet of club or street-corner. Women, in the Harrisian age [Charles K. Harris, noted songwriter], were women—still ingenuous, still untainted by sophistication and adulterated modernism. They rocked the cradle instead of the boat, and ruled the world.[9]

This contrasts markedly with another point Goldberg makes in the same book:

Woman has always been the inspiration of song rather than the writer of it. By nature, by convention, even in these days of toppling social values, she is the passive, rather than the active, voice of love. Or so, in her elemental strategy, she would have us believe. Whatever the cause of this relative silence, it can have no specific relation to Tin Pan Alley as such, for the place of woman in the music of the world, as in the more consciously artistic music of America, is small. She is the executant, not the creator.[10]

Taken together, the two remarks only make sense in the warped world created by the music industry itself. On the one hand, women sang and played music. On the other, it was their "femininity" to which Tin Pan Alley appealed, by constructing a "femininity" that appealed to Tin Pan Alley.

David Suisman elaborated on this process in *Selling Sounds*:

John C. Freund, editor of *The Music Trades and Musical America*, estimated that women were responsible for 70 to 75 percent of all money spent on music. Beginning in the 1890s, when New York department stores opened music counters, publishers such as Joseph W. Stern and M. Witmark and Sons sent representatives to give song demonstrations in those overwhelmingly female sanctuaries and subsequently made the department stores a prime outlet for Tin Pan Alley sheet music. . . . In this respect, Tin Pan Alley was part of the consumer economy generally structured around women already.[11]

Obviously, this had far-reaching consequences not only for the commercialization of music but also for the construction of the social roles and ideals to which women and men should aspire.

The efforts of the music industry were not made on an empty, uncontested field, however. Among the common people, especially in the South, women were full participants in the music-making process, as composers, instrumentalists, band leaders, and singers. As many recordings, films, and photographs of women playing religious and secular songs, lullabies, and political anthems can attest, women made music in church, at social gatherings, at home, and professionally before the rise of the music industry, and for decades thereafter. Sister Rosetta Tharpe, for instance, not only exemplifies this widespread phenomenon, she can legitimately be considered the founding *mother* of rock 'n' roll! Tharpe's guitar playing is extraordinary, making her a pioneer of the electrified version of that instrument.[12] Another example is Sarah Ogan Gunning, who, by the 1930s, was already writing innumerable songs about her life in the coal fields and as a fighter for the working class. Her great song, "I Hate the Capitalist System," undermines many of the claims made by the music industry and its mouthpieces regarding women, authenticity, workers' struggle, and the history of American music.[13] While this would appear to mightily contradict Goldberg's assessment, it does so only in the sense that Tharpe, Gunning, and women generally continued making music in spite of Tin Pan Alley and in direct confrontation with its basic tenets, which Goldberg nonetheless accurately summarized. Goldberg's assessment was true insofar as Tin Pan Alley was concerned, but Tin Pan Alley's dominance was never complete, nor was it ever capable of destroying the evidence of its duplicity.

Even *within* the confines of the music industry, the role of women musicians was extraordinary. Two studies, *Jazzwomen* by Sally Placksin and *Blues Legacies and Black Feminism* by Angela Davis, make abundantly clear that not only were there many women involved in all aspects of music-making, but that women performers actually predominated in the blues and other areas of music directed at an untapped market of black consumers in the first two decades of the twentieth century. Davis writes, "Black women were the first to record the blues. In 1920, Mamie Smith's version of Perry Bradford's 'Crazy Blues' . . . was so popular that 75,000 copies of the record were sold within the first month of its release." Davis adds, however, "That women were given priority over men as recording artists attests to the reductive marketing strategies of the then-embryonic recording industry, strategies we still see today in the industry's efforts to categorize—or, in effect, to segregate culturally—different genres of music that in fact claim an increasingly diverse listening public."[14]

This was by no means limited to black people but extended to musicians and audiences still making music in the "old" way: the multifaceted music categorized by the music industry first as "hillbilly," and later as "country." Among the first "stars" to emerge was the Carter Family, featuring the highly influential guitar playing of Maybelle Carter. Women were also among the most important musical voices of the workers movement in the 1920s, 1930s, and 1940s, with Aunt Molly Jackson, Florence Reese, and the aforementioned Sarah Ogan Gunning being prime examples. But there is more to this than the fact that women performed alongside men.

Women's contributions to music are fundamental in strictly musicological terms. The *sound* of American popular music is as much a result of women's role in making it as any other factor. This cannot be understood solely as biological difference in the sense that women's voices are as a rule higher than men's. Rather, women shaped the very forms of musical delivery through a concentration of social relations as expressed in music-making processes. Perhaps this is most obvious in church music, but it is also evident in many regional communities, for example, the Gullah and Geechee people of the Sea Islands.[15] In any case, women's role in music-making stands in stark contrast to the fact that women were nowhere to be found in the ownership or administration of the music industry, let alone in the development of its strategy and tactics. As successful as such strategy and tactics were, however, they had to change in the face of popular revolt.

Rock and Revolt

Revolt in the Sixties led to the music industry's abandonment of the Tin Pan Alley model, opportunities for bands to compose their own material, and the jettisoning of bourgeois "femininity" for sex, drugs, and rock 'n' roll. Music production (that is, composition, performance, and recording) had been seized to a considerable extent by bands consciously rebelling against the rigid formulas imposed by the music business. But this seizure of the "means of production" did not include the means of distribution and promotion, by which the music industry continued to exert control. The manufacture of celebrity, a function basic to the industry's existence, remained firmly in the grip of the largest record companies: Columbia, RCA, Warner Brothers, and so forth. Now, however, the star had to be created out of the raw material provided by genuine popularity that was gained in the context of genuine youth rebellion: "street credibility," as it's come to be called. Instead of the old and outmoded industrial model whereby performers were groomed to sell Tin Pan Alley's formulaic "hits," the industry cultivated "authentic" artists ("geniuses," "visionaries," "messiahs") from among those who had established a base of popularity on the strength of actual musical achievement. Prior to the emergence of women's liberation, the rock star could cut a rebellious figure, while simultaneously exalting male supremacy. This was given greater encouragement by vague and confused notions of sexual liberation, freedom from "straight" society's repressive mores, and the shocked response of authorities to youthful promiscuity. Yet this alone would not account for the music industry's full-blown strategy of domination.

The rock star is, above all, male, servicing the lust of groupies and female disciples, who, worshipping superior cocksmanship as much as musical talent, assign *themselves* a subservient role. Women musicians could be stars, too, but only as the "chick" singer, embodying male sexual fantasy, not as a composer or an instrumentalist, let alone band *leader*. The music industry itself was not only a "boys club," made up mainly of men, but was thoroughly male supremacist in its outlook. Of course, there were many outstanding women musicians, some of whom composed music as well as played instruments, but they were nonetheless subordinated in an industry that based itself on promoting exploitative stereotypes of women and girls. By the time Aretha Franklin released her anthem "Think,"[16] it was clear that sexism was as much at the core of music industry practices as racism was. Indeed, the tactics employed by the music industry in the years after the Monterey Pop Festival boiled down to showering musicians with money, sex, and drugs; transforming them into an aristocracy that lorded it over demented minions; thereby reinforcing discipline in a new guise.[17]

Discipline was maintained by three principle means: legal, journalistic, and outright repression. The legal means were mainly contractual, tying up musicians in endless and costly court proceedings.[18] But legal means also included drug busts and the excuse this gave police to harass and intimidate musicians on a continuous basis. Indeed, enforcing drug laws provided the system with a perfect cover when carrying out political repression.

Journalistic discipline was exercised through the rock music press. Publications like *Rolling Stone* ensured that musicians conformed to standards set by the industry, articulating and refining these standards in a language suited to popular consumption. One glaring example was the issue of *Rolling Stone* devoted to "The Groupie." Not only did this issue celebrate the degrading role women were encouraged to play, *Rolling Stone* took out a full-page ad in the *New York Times* to announce it, arrogantly proclaiming, "This is the story only *Rolling Stone* can tell because we are the musicians, we are the music, we are writing about ourselves."[19] This statement had its corollary: rock critics were not only consumer guides, they told musicians what would gain recognition and what would not. By the early 1970s, rock music critics had anointed themselves "gatekeepers" and arbiters of popular taste and were, moreover, almost exclusively male.

Legal and journalistic means were the predominant tools for in enforcing discipline, but when these were not sufficient, repression was employed. This was obviously directed toward politically radical musicians, but extended to any musician refusing to toe the industry line. Thus, for example, artists such as Buffy Sainte-Marie and Nina Simone were effectively driven out of the U.S. market while others were "quietly" marginalized by limiting promotion and distribution of their recordings or possibilities to perform. While this was not conducted as openly as it had been during the McCarthy period, blacklisting and persecution were far more widespread than is often acknowledged, as we shall see in the next chapter.

At this juncture, the feminist perspective clarifies what might otherwise appear to be unrelated or contradictory phenomena. Women's liberation challenged fundamental premises of countercultural rebellion, specifically as they dealt with sex, drugs, and rock 'n' roll, exposing the exploitation that hid beneath a veneer of "free love," "consciousness-expanding," and youthful transgression.

Sex, Drugs, and Rock 'n' Roll

Feminism exposed how once-radical ideas can be turned into their opposite. As originally conceived, the now-ubiquitous phrase "sex, drugs, and rock 'n' roll" held dangerous connotations for the system. To the uptight WASP mind, sex meant the death of the family. Drugs meant the death of the self. Rock 'n' roll meant the death of civilization. To the young, conversely, it was crystal clear that stodgy old white men were *afraid* of sex, drugs, and rock 'n' roll. It was not that they held any wisdom or concern for the greater good; it's that in their paranoid fantasy of hoarding their possessions, maintaining their privilege and keeping young people in line, they were the very definition of "old." There was thus complete congruity between appearance and substance: old, white, short-haired, stiff, authoritarian versus young, multi-ethnic, long-haired, loose, *free!* To counteract this required more than brute repression. In fact, it could not be counteracted at all if it were treated as a political problem. The initial response of the system, therefore, was to identify sex, drugs, and rock 'n' roll as *pathologies* of which society had to be purged.

It need hardly be said that power must reassert both its military/ police force and its moral force, i.e., its claims to legitimacy. It will thus always seek to pathologize political opposition, prescribing medical treatment for a malady suffered by individuals. More specifically, the U.S. government used psychoanalytic models to supplement the outmoded Red Scare techniques discredited along with McCarthyism, which proved to be startlingly ineffective when confronted with the sudden growth of interest in the Cuban, Vietnamese, and Chinese revolutions.

Accordingly, hysteria, which had previously been used in ad campaigns aimed at mobilizing teenagers (Beatlemania, dance "craze") was now treated with an air of seriousness as it applied to "sex, drugs and rock 'n' roll," treated as threats to one's health. That outbursts of unbridled hedonism were hardly unique to this era was blithely ignored. Many periods throughout history (the Roaring '20s of jazz and prohibition, Weimar Germany as illustrated so well by *Cabaret,* come to mind) have celebrated amorous pleasure seeking, intoxication, and contemporary artistic trends. The film *Reefer Madness* (1936),[20] with its titillating warnings of "drug-crazed abandon" and "women cry for it, men die for it" sounds remarkably similar to films made in the Sixties, such as *The Trip,* with its tag-line of a Lovely Sort of Death.[21] That in any case people would challenge prevailing codes of behavior is not extraordinary nor is it explanatory as regards actually novel developments in art and politics. Indeed, what "hysteria" obscures is that the pursuit of *freedom* as a political, artistic, and social principle was the driving force of the Sixties. Fighting for freedom created social spaces for the coexistence of many practices, especially anything held in disrepute by the authorities. "The enemy of my enemy is my friend," was how revolution of a political type could be easily confused with any expression of disobedience.

But there is more to be untangled from the sex, drugs, and rock 'n' roll hysteria. Each of these terms designates a particular social practice that, lumped together in a catchy slogan, effectively legitimates authority's reaction to them. Sex was a site of insurgency against a repressive, hypocritical set of norms already being exposed by Freudian psychoanalysis, Dr. Benjamin Spock's *Baby and Child Care* and the *Kinsey Report*. Furthermore, the women's movement challenged everyone and everything from Miss America and *Playboy* to the sexism of revolutionaries and rock 'n' rollers. The revolution began with certain old ideas regarding race and gender still firmly in place. Women's liberation seized the opening created by national liberation and in a very short time altered the landscape irreversibly. By 1970 no one could avoid it. To reduce these broad social conflicts to "sex" is of course to trivialize them. More importantly, it is to definitively separate them from their actual goal, which was above all to discover, to invent, and to unleash freedom

The same can be said about drugs, with specific attention to psychotropics (LSD, peyote, mescaline, etc.) that for a time appeared to hold the promise of mystical or revelatory illumination. "Consciousness expanding," however, gave way to "consciousness raising" precisely at the point when radical feminism exposed the fact that the former never seemed to expand beyond a self-centered male guru and certainly did not include awareness of the oppression of women. In actuality, the drug with the greatest significance and influence during the Sixties was the contraceptive known as "the pill." Control over pregnancy, offered young women by the pill, had a much greater societal impact than any comparable effects due to mind-altering substances.

Most strikingly, however, rock 'n' roll (along with sex and drugs,) was reduced to a sound track for deviant behavior. There is, of course, some truth to this, but it is precisely the inclusion of rock 'n' roll in this trinity of sin and vice that lends the saying its credibility. "Sex and drugs" alone sounds merely clinical or medical, and carries no connection to a place and time (San Francisco in the Sixties) with which it is always associated. Used in this manner, music in general—and rock in particular—is returned to its cage as entertainment that revels in transgression, naughtiness, and disobedience as *affect*, rather than as a serious threat to authority. No doubt, scandalizing the bourgeoisie, inverting beauty and ugliness, and redefining obscenity could still produce a charge. But sex, drugs, and rock 'n' roll ultimately announced the arrival of a new regime in which fornication and inebriation would be openly promoted and exploited without recourse to coded speech or fear of legal restriction.

Putting this in contemporary perspective, Beth Bailey writes:

> The lure of sexual transgression as a key to human liberation is a powerful strand of twentieth-century American thought, from Henry Miller to Robert Crumb to Gangsta Rap. Too often, as the experience of America's 1960s counterculture shows, the transgressive does not serve cleanly as a path to liberation; it is also a form of exploitation of those with less power, often within the sub/counterculture itself. That is a lesson worth remembering, as too many academic champions of cultural rebellion today embrace the transgressive, without adequate concern for the proximate targets of that transgression.[22]

Feminism brought to light the fact that music should not and *could* not be a male preserve—indeed, that music does not belong to anyone. Rather, human beings belong, not to, but *in* and *through* music. That this fundamental belonging, this sense and need for togetherness, felt by everyone, could be perverted and sullied by the denigration of women was both deeply hurtful and highly illuminating. It exposed the contradiction staring everyone in the face: on one side, music as a joyful, unifying force; on the other, music as a tyrant, capable of inflicting the most painful wounds and enforcing the most oppressive divisions.

Class, Race, and Gender

Women's liberation burst forth at a pivotal moment: of crisis for the system and the apex of size and influence of the movement. The years between 1970 and 1973 witnessed countless acts of resistance from the Attica prisoners' revolt and the Chicano Moratorium to AIM's Trail of Broken Treaties and the confrontation at Wounded Knee. The Soledad Brothers and Angela Davis trials were world-famous, eliciting many musical expressions of solidarity, including songs by such luminaries as Bob Dylan and the Rolling Stones. It is particularly important to note the large-scale involvement of jazz musicians in projects such as Archie Shepp's *Attica Blues* and in groups such as the Liberation Music Orchestra that overtly expressed revolutionary politics. (This key development is examined in greater detail in the previous chapter.) The antiwar movement was so large that, according to opinion polls, it could claim to represent the will of the majority of American people. But this was not confined to a single issue. At the time, the spread of revolutionary ideas among broader sections of the population appeared inexorable. The significance of women's liberation, in this context, lies in the reshaping of consciousness among the broad masses of people. Posing the most fundamental questions of liberty, equality, and justice for all, women's liberation raised the stakes, marking the culmination and high point of the Sixties overall. It also laid bare the limits that had been reached.

In 1848, *The Communist Manifesto* called on proletarians of the world to unite. In 1903, *The Souls of Black Folk* declared the problem of the twentieth century to be the problem of the color-line. In 1949, *The Second Sex* focused attention on the subjugation of women. Class, race, and gender were questions the Sixties forcefully raised anew but could not answer.

CHAPTER 11

The Future Foreclosed: Counterrevolution and Defeat

When did the Sixties end? How do we define victory and defeat? Why have all the conflicts buried along with the Sixties erupted anew? On the one hand, the answer is simple: the system's crisis poses and answers all of these questions. From the system's perspective, the dates, victory and defeat, as well as the obstacles that must be thrown in the path of new anti-systemic movements are clear enough. On the other hand, the answer is complex, multifaceted, and contradictory, the subject of debate and critical analysis for four decades. Lessons continue to be drawn from the last great revolutionary upsurge and may only be considered settled questions when the system has been overthrown. From the perspective of music's rivalry with the state (the fundamental premise of this book), however, certain landmarks are discernible. The dynamics of aesthetics and politics, the philosophical dimensions of which were never adequately addressed in the Sixties, provide a schematic by which events and outcomes can be evaluated. More specifically, the mechanisms of co-optation and repression visited upon the movement as a whole, and on music and musicians in particular, reveal both defining characteristics of the Sixties and the means by which the "restoration of imperial command" was accomplished.

In the last edition of *Ramparts* magazine, published in 1975, Noam Chomsky contributed an essay entitled "The Remaking of History." He began, "American imperialism has suffered a stunning defeat in Indochina. But the same forces are engaged in another war against a much less resilient enemy, the American people. Here, the prospects for success are much greater." Pointing out that even as it suffered defeat in Vietnam, U.S. imperialism had brutally imposed dictatorships in Indonesia, Brazil, Chile, and the Dominican Republic, Chomsky continued:

> Apologists for state violence understand very well that the general public has no real stake in imperial conquest and domination. The public costs of empire may run high, whatever the gains to dominant social and economic groups. Therefore the public must be aroused by jingoist appeals, or at least kept disciplined and submissive, if American force is to be readily available for global management.
>
> Here lies the task for the intelligentsia. If it is determined that we must, say, invade the Persian Gulf for the *benefit of mankind*, then there must be no emotional or moral objections from the unsophisticated masses, and surely no vulgar display of protest. The ideologists must guarantee that no "wrong lessons" are learned from the experience of the Indochina war and the resistance to it.[1]

While his main focus was the "remaking" of the past, Chomsky nonetheless exposed a glaring contradiction in the present: the Vietnamese victory over American imperialism contrasted sharply with the state of the movement. The end of *Ramparts* was itself an indication of the impasse. The system's crisis was one thing: 1973 bore witness to the oil crisis, Nixon's cancellation of the convertibility of the dollar into gold, and the end of the Bretton Woods System by which the world had been organized since World War II. In 1974, Nixon resigned. In 1975, the United States was finally driven out of Vietnam. Yet the people did not rise and the government did not fall. Instead, the movement found itself in disarray.

At this juncture, Herbert Marcuse delivered a speech at the University of California entitled "The Failure of the New Left?" Punctuated with a question mark, Marcuse was clearly addressing a widely shared view while challenging conclusions being too hastily drawn. He began by clarifying what distinguished the New Left in the first place:

> It has re-defined the concept of revolution, bringing to it those new possibilities for freedom and new potentials for socialist development that were created (and immediately arrested) by advanced capitalism. As a result of these developments, new dimensions of social change have emerged. Change is no longer defined simply as economic and political upheaval, as the establishment of a

different mode of production and new institutions, but also and above all as a revolution in the prevailing structure of needs and the possibilities for their fulfillment. This concept of revolution was part of the Marxian theory from the outset: socialism is a qualitatively different society, one in which people's relationships to one another as well as the relationship between human beings and nature is fundamentally transformed.[2]

This was not an attempt to elide the present, disorienting situation much less to offer a pep talk to discouraged activists. An accurate appraisal was required, one that could precisely define the characteristics of opposing forces, not in isolation but in mutual interdependence. In this context, *counterrevolution* was as much responsible for current conditions as any shortcomings of the New Left.

Now we come to the second point concerning whether the New Left has really failed. This question has to be answered on several different levels. In part, the movement was co-opted or openly suppressed by the establishment; in part it destroyed itself by failing to develop any adequate organizational forms and by allowing internal splits to grow and spread, a phenomenon that was linked to anti-intellectualism, to a politically powerless anarchism and a narcissistic arrogance.

The suppression of the movement by the existing power structures took many forms. It was violent, but also, so to speak "normal": infallible, scientific mechanisms of control, "black lists," discrimination at the work-place, an army of spies and informers—all of these things were set up and mobilized as instruments of repression, and their effectiveness was enhanced by the Left's continued isolation from the rest of the populace.[3]

Counterrevolution was therefore understood as qualitatively different than the aberrations of an otherwise democratic process by which the popular will would sooner or later be represented. Counterrevolution was a strategy of domination and control, its co-optive or propagandistic methods complimented by and ultimately dependent upon brute force. Failure to grasp the implications of this (at the time and ever since) has made systematic efforts on the part of the state appear to be anomalous, disconnected occurrences attributable to rogue agents or overzealous security forces. The evidence, some of it only recently discovered, shows otherwise. Before turning to that evidence, however, a further distinction needs to be made.

While the movement did not and *could not* achieve its aims, the causes and consequences of this cannot be found in one year or even one decade. In every important detail, the same questions confront us today. Rather, the future as it was envisioned and as it was foreclosed is the ultimate determining factor, both in consciousness and in social practice, of the Sixties and its outcomes. The future, in this sense, was neither part of a temporal sequence nor a vague, unattainable dream. Least of all, was the future a predetermined "given," the inevitable outcome of historical processes. The future was the *motive*, infusing every thought and deed with *purpose*, every present sacrifice with *justice*, and every personal and social relationship with greater import than narrow self-interest or the satiation of animal appetites. Therefore, the terms of both the struggle and its history are set by the future, not the present or the past. It is fruitless, in fact, to make any evaluation of victory or defeat, of strength or weakness, much less right or wrong, without acknowledging that the future beckons and threatens in equal measure. For the hoarders of wealth and power the future always harbors danger. For the oppressed, for those who have nothing but their discipline and their imagination, the future will always harbor the possibility of emancipation.

Counterrevolution

> "Just because I'm paranoid doesn't
> mean they're not out to get me."
> —Lenny Bruce

Many studies have documented the FBI's systematic efforts to undermine and ultimately destroy the movement and its constituent organizations. One recent book, *The Burglary: The Discovery of J. Edgar Hoover's Secret FBI*, describes how antiwar activists, mostly pacifists, formed a Citizens Committee to Investigate the FBI.[4] On March 8, 1971, some members broke into the unprotected offices of the FBI in Media, Pennsylvania, and took all the files. The mass of documents revealed the existence of a J. Edgar Hoover–inspired Counter Intelligence Program (COINTELPRO) and of a Security Index (SI) with the names of tens of thousands of people on it. The documents were subsequently sent to media outlets, including the *Washington Post* and Liberation News Service (itself a target of COINTELPRO), which, over the course of five years, finally unraveled the whole sordid tale. Virtually every civil rights, student, and antiwar organization was a target, as were long-standing civil liberties groups like the ACLU and the National Lawyers Guild. All of the organizations of the New Left, the Black Panthers, the American Indian Movement, and the Young Lords, as well as numerous newly emerging communist groups, such as the Revolutionary Union, had been surveilled, infiltrated, and manipulated.[5] As is now well known, COINTELPRO was responsible for assassination, incarceration, and the sowing of violent discord within and between the most effective organizations of the period, especially targeting the Panthers and AIM. Literally thousands of dedicated activists and revolutionaries were either killed, spent many years in prison, or had their work sabotaged and their personal lives destroyed by the U.S. government.

The Burglary makes special note of the fact that Hoover had files on "an endless roll call of the best novelists, nonfiction writers, poets, essayists and playwrights, including Nobel laureates,"[6] concluding that this was a result of Hoover's distrust of intellectuals. While Hoover's personal phobias were no doubt a factor, the more sinister fact is that the FBI deliberately sought to discredit and derail the careers of many artists, popular musicians among them. To this day, the extent of the FBI's efforts has still to be fully explored. But there is enough evidence to prove that "popular taste" or lack of artistic merit had nothing to do with what put many musicians "out of business."

Phil Ochs was the target of an FBI investigation that lasted more than ten years. His FBI file was four hundred pages long and included the FBI's suggestion that he be arrested as a subversive. In *Parental Advisory: Music Censorship in America*, Eric Nuzum writes, "In a query into Ochs's involvement in several anti–Vietnam War protests, longtime FBI director J. Edgar Hoover said Ochs was 'potentially dangerous; or has been identified as a member or participant in Communist movement; or has been under active investigation as member of other group or organization.' Hoover also cited Ochs's past conduct and statements as showing a 'propensity towards violence and antipathy toward good order and government.'"[7] Other examples include the Last Poets and the Fugs. In the case of the Last Poets, FBI operations led to the imprisonment, on dubious drug charges, of group member Umar Bin Hassen. In the case of the

Fugs, "people would call in bomb threats," says Fug Ed Sanders. "They would raid my bookstore. Somebody sent me a fake bomb. Right-wing nurses picketing us. We would get thrown out of theaters. Carnegie Hall wouldn't rent to us. We played Santa Monica Civic and they wouldn't rent to us again. We were always in trouble. . . . So we ran a close ship. I learned that James Brown wouldn't let his band carry drugs, and I did the same thing, because I knew how close we were to being arrested at any point."[8] Lest these be viewed as isolated incidents, confined to monitoring or harassment, the case of Buffy Sainte-Marie illustrates the scope of U.S. government attempts to suppress dissent among musicians.

Buffy Sainte-Marie was not only an exceptional songwriter and committed activist but the victim of direct intervention by the president of the United States. As recounted by Richie Unterberger in his book, *Turn! Turn! Turn!*, Sainte-Marie reported:

> By the late '60s, like Eartha Kitt, Taj Mahal and other outspoken artists of color, I was pretty much hamstrung by the Lyndon Johnson blacklist. . . . A radio broadcaster named Joe Forester in Toronto made me aware of the situation. He surprised me by beginning what I thought was to be a routine interview with a ten-years-too-late apology for having gone along with a request from the Lyndon Johnson White House ten years before to suppress my music, which "deserved to be suppressed."
>
> This was a huge surprise to me. Until Joe brought up this mystery I had figured that American show biz is fickle, and that music tastes change with the times, and that my continued success in other parts of the world was what was pretty amazing. After Joe's on-air apology to me, I received a similar one from a DJ in Cleveland, and from time to time broadcasters have mentioned it. At the time I reviewed my FBI files from the period and although there were a lot of pages to go through, there was so much crossed out in fat indelible marker that there was nothing to be learned about this matter or anything else except that they kept files on me and corresponded with other people. Conversations with long-term friend Taj Mahal (with whom I attended college) let me know I wasn't the only one who had experienced blacklisting. I really have no idea of how big a deal it was, but I've always wished someone had the time to investigate it properly.[9]

In another interview, with *Indian Country Today*, Sainte-Marie made clear how all this connected and what was at stake. Concerning AIM's occupation of Wounded Knee and the shoot-out with FBI agents at the Jumping Bull residence at Pine Ridge, on June 26, 1975, Sainte-Marie states, "That is where Leonard Peltier's troubles began. Who recalls that on that day one-eighth of the reservation was transferred in secret—*on that day*. It was the part containing uranium. That is what never seems to be remembered."[10] This is in reference to Pine Ridge Tribal Chairman Dick Wilson being in Washington on June 26, 1975, signing away one-eighth of the reservation's lands to the Department of the Interior, a fact corroborated by *The Nuclear Resister*.[11]

Calling attention to this case is important not only as evidence that in the "land of the free" the government used such methods to silence opposition but also to expose the hoax that even Buffy Sainte-Marie found herself taken in by. Like most artists, she attributed her declining popularity to fickle fate, not the deliberate sabotage of the government in collusion with the music industry (in this case broadcasters). Few musicians were even vaguely aware that music journalists were complicit in fostering such illusions, steadfastly denying any political implications, instead emphasizing aesthetic or personal factors in musicians' success or failure. Who among rock journalists deigned to consider the reasons for Sainte-Marie, a well-known and respected artist, being "mysteriously" absent from the music scene in the 1970s? While rock's arbiters of taste were busy promoting their view of what the public should listen to, few if any rose to defend musicians under government attack.

In his doctoral thesis, "'Must Be the Season of the Witch': The Repression and Harassment of Rock and Folk Music During the Long Sixties," completed in 2013, Daniel A. Simmons drew a number of stunning conclusions from exhaustive research. He begins by confirming how little has been written about the subject.[12] This is startling, given that the McCarthy era and, the blacklisting of the Hollywood Ten, Pete Seeger, and Paul Robeson, to name only a few famous examples, were common knowledge in the Sixties. Why, then, has it taken almost fifty years to fulfill Buffy Sainte-Marie's wish that someone "investigate properly" the repression meted out by agents of the state in collusion the music industry? Why have journalists and historians failed to even ask the pertinent questions?

Simmons does acknowledge works such as *Acid Dreams: The Complete Social History of LSD, the CIA, the Sixties, and Beyond*,[13] which explore the government's harassment and repression of the counterculture. But he goes further to say:

> By situating its central focus and primary analysis on all aspects of folk and rock music (instead of just rock's connection to LSD, the main subject of Lee and Shlain's study), this dissertation extends the discussion that the cultural reasons for the harassment or repression extended towards some rock and folk musicians included more than just an attack on the psychedelic counterculture or a crackdown on drug use. It also demonstrates how the FBI and other law enforcement agencies sought to destroy the antiwar movement and the anti-imperialist demands of leftist revolutionaries, targeting groups that demanded the overthrow of racism, imperialism, and capitalism.[14]

Simmons makes an additional distinction between his study and the substantial literature devoted to the government's efforts to destroy opposition, from SDS to the Black Panther Party, from the New Mobilization to End the War in Vietnam and AIM.

> My study ventures into grounds uncharted by Garrow, Churchill and Vanderwall, Davis, and Cunningham by examining how some rock and folk musicians directly or inadvertently supported political radicals and revolutionaries, consequently leading these musicians to the attention of law enforcement officials, including the FBI. I argue that while there was no "COINTELPRO-ROCK" OR "COINTELPRO-FOLK," the FBI, in addition to other federal agencies and local officials nonetheless exerted harassing or repressive acts for political and cultural purposes (many of which varied by degree and meaning). Most studies on the FBI's federal acts of repression have concentrated solely on the doings of the Bureau. I extend the analysis by examining the FBI alongside other federal agencies and local law enforcement officials, many of whom worked alone, as for instance, the vice squad officials assigned to a concert. This is especially important, because while some musicians were harassed by such varied law enforcement entities as narcotics officials or FBI agents, they were often unable to define their antagonist.[15]

Ultimately, two interrelated conclusions can be drawn from the voluminous data. First, judging by the government's response, the threat posed by the movement and by music was both larger and more explicitly political than has previously been thought. Nationwide, multi-agency repression was neither a paranoid fantasy on the part of radical leftists nor was it the obsession of isolated (and soon to be discredited) sociopaths like Hoover and Nixon. Surveillance, harassment, and repression were a measured response calculated to fit the size and scale of the opposition, especially as it was expressed in public appearances, such as benefit concerts, demonstrations, and music festivals. This demolishes certain tropes that have plagued Sixties scholarship overall, especially regarding the utopian character of the revolt. Utopia is unconquerable by armies, ungovernable by tyrants, and unexploitable by capitalists, hence the danger it poses when it grips the imagination of the people. In most accounts of the period, this is turned on its head to support the claim that musicians caused their own victimization. They willfully broke drug laws, performed lewd and lascivious acts, and were intoxicated with their inflated social importance (which they owed to the music industry's promotion).

Secondly, a more nuanced, dialectical analysis of the relationship between co-optation and repression must be made. It can no longer be maintained that co-optation alone was responsible for the defeat of the revolution or the reassertion of control by the music industry. The evidence clearly points to another conclusion altogether, to co-optation and repression as interdependent elements, with each guaranteeing the other's effectiveness. Co-optation could not succeed without the fear and intimidation produced by repression, certainly not to the extent it undoubtedly did. At the very least, evidence shows that authorities had no confidence that the co-optive and propagandistic machinery of the music industry or the mass media would be sufficient to quell the threat. Similarly co-optation not only serves to dupe and delude the "masses," making them complicit in their own enslavement, but serves a more pressing task of concealing the coercive force that lurks in the shadows, employed judiciously but enough to secure obedience.

The success of these strategies perhaps explains why, until Simmons's doctoral thesis, the thought never occurred to journalists or historians. Starting from flawed premises (such as America's constitutional guarantee of free speech, or that co-optation is a noncoercive practice functioning exclusively through the workings of the "free" market), it is inconceivable that far more violent and anti-democratic means were systematically employed. Yet the evidence suggests another explanation, one that even Simmons does not take into account: music's rivalry with the state.

The suppression or co-optation of music was always intent on making music a servant of the state and not its rival. Of course, in the American context, this did not just mean aligning music with the U.S. government or with politicians and political parties; it has always been necessary for the state to maintain the illusion that people are being served, their desires met, their will expressed. This not only shifts the blame for the manifest crimes committed in their name onto the people but renders the tools most readily available to them, namely the popular arts, inoperative or ineffective. Crushing and co-opting can therefore be seen not only through the effects on musicians, as important as these effects may be, but on the reduction of popular participation in music-making altogether. Elimination of arts education in public schools, public funding for art-making in general and the utter destitution of the common good as a guiding principle are one dimension of this.

But even in terms of "pop" music, or music composed, performed, and recorded within the framework of commercial exchange, the purpose of co-optation and repression is to ensure that music *as such* is never heard. Only categorized, packaged, and above all sterilized music is allowed. Music must be purged of its infinite, boundless possibility and confined to authorized, certified norms. Warring national, generational, gendered, stylistic identities must be pitted against music's universal content that pulses through diverse forms of expression. Above all, none should experience music's capacity to herald the good, the beautiful, and the true. The power to determine these coordinates of consciousness is jealously guarded by the state. To rule is to dictate what constitutes the good, the beautiful, and the true. Which is why the state as we have known it until now has always feared the critique, the ridicule, and the stirring of the oppressed that music can produce.

Daze on the Green

In 1973, Bill Graham launched a concert series called "A Day on the Green" at the Oakland Coliseum. This innocuous title cloaked an event of considerable significance. Less than a decade before, Golden Gate Park had been the site of dozens of free concerts. Almost every week for a few years, the Panhandle, Speedway Meadow, the Polo Fields, and occasionally other locations, saw bands performing to the large and growing throng that came to participate in what many thought was a new world being born. Throughout the period, ever-increasing numbers attended rallies, marches, and demonstrations against the war in Vietnam, the biggest of which ended at Kezar Stadium and always included musical performances. By the time Woodstock happened, there was already a well-established precedent of large outdoor festivals combining music, diverse cultural activities, and politics. Large antiwar demonstrations and concerts in Golden Gate Park continued, including the largest ever on April 24, 1971, where over 150,000 were in attendance. Moreover, concerts in the park, demonstrations over a widening range of social issues and the general climate of confrontation with the system had in no sense abated by the time Graham held the first Day on the Green. But staging these events was more than simply a matter of moneymaking and efficient crowd control. The stadium concert was designed to provide the appearance of "festival" while channeling a herd of onlookers into a sports complex where they could be charged high prices to surrender their rebellious spirit. The festival with which the Sixties had begun was perverted, the connection between the musicians and the communities from which they'd come was severed, and the hypnosis of the spectacle replaced the liberation of consciousness.

Graham was not alone in this and was joined by many musicians and their own networks of friends and supporters. Santana and the subsequent career of Journey are an example of this. Santana was a quintessentially San Francisco band. Multi-ethnic and multi-talented, its members came from the Mission District and the suburbs, inspired by what was going on at the Fillmore and Avalon, partaking of the sounds and the sights, the psychedelics and the social turmoil characteristic of the period, including playing a famous benefit for the Black Panthers. After making two path-breaking albums that rank among the best of the period, they began to break up due to drug abuse and intense touring. When the band fell apart, three of its members were pulled together by their manager, Herbie Herbert, and what came to be known as corporate rock was born. From 1973 onward, Journey pioneered everything that was antithetical to their roots. Budweiser commercials and stadium spectacles (it would be a stretch to call these musical performances) paved the way for the demise of an ethos.

San Francisco still retained its aura as the center of musical innovation for a few years. But this reputation now served as camouflage for the corporate takeover being spearheaded there. Some Bay Area musicians were certainly aware of this and responded with disdain. Tower of Power, for example, released, *What Is Hip?*, in 1973, posing a question many were asking. Singing, "What is hip today, may become passé," the band challenged underlying assumptions about hipness itself. Pointing the finger at poseurs and phonies pimping (to use the term in its Sixties sense) on the spirit of the times, Tower closed with the timely advice "think about it, y'all." When in the same year Jamaica's Wailers released *Catch a Fire* and first toured America opening for Sly and the Family Stone, milestones were laid. The Wailers were harbingers of the future; Sly and the Family Stone, touring in support of their final album, would soon be gone. Music continued to be a vital force within a society still very much in turmoil. But the signs were everywhere that San Francisco was being eclipsed creatively and that music no longer provided the undiluted, untainted voice of the millions struggling to change the world.

An outcry was raised and it would be a mistake to think co-optation was passively accepted as a *fait accompli*. An essay collection, *Side-Saddle on the Golden Calf* (1972),[16] presented a wide range of commentary that today serves to remind us that the corporate takeover of rock music was still a contentious subject, not a settled issue. In his contribution, "Rock for Sale," journalist Michael Lydon wrote:

> But rock 'n' roll musicians are in the end artists and entertainers, and were it not for all the talk of the "rock revolution" one would not be led to expect a clear political vision from them. The bitterest irony is that the "rock revolution" hype has come close to fatally limiting the revolutionary potential that rock does contain. So effective has the rock industry been in encouraging the spirit of optimistic youth take-over that rock's truly hard edge, its constant exploration of the varieties of youthful frustration, has been ignored or softened.[17]

In "Altamont: Pearl Harbor to the Woodstock Nation," Sol Stern quotes Jann Wenner: "Rock and roll is the only way in which the vast but formless power of youth is structured, the only way in which it can be defined or inspected. The style and meaning of it has caught the imagination, the financial power and the spiritual interest of millions of young people." Stern retorts, "This is the kind of obscurantist rhetoric that *Rolling Stone* still uses to push the idea that rock, only rock, is the revolution, and to put down the many attempts to unite it with a wider political perspective."[18] The appearance of these essays in widely read magazines from *Ramparts* to *Scanlan's* to *Esquire*, suggests the controversy was not confined to academics, let alone to political radicals. Taken collectively, they confirm both the significance of music as an autonomous force—independent of the music industry—and the struggle underway to unleash or contain its revolutionary potential.

Twenty-five years later, the results were still being debated. *The Mansion on the Hill* by Fred Goodman (1997) addresses these developments from within the music industry.[19] Divided into books one and two, *The American Revolution* and, *The Mansion on the Hill*, Goodman revisits familiar territory, accepting conventional wisdom regarding the "rock revolution" hype and its dismal aftermath. But Goodman goes further than most accounts documenting the process by which rock journalists, record company execs, and some musicians collaborated to consciously and systematically make rock serve the system. Perfecting techniques pioneered in San Francisco by Graham, the charity concert was used to create the appearance of "political activism," stadium/corporate rock joined to produce the appearance of "festival," and rock entrepreneurs personally and professionally aligned themselves with politicians and policy makers in waging campaigns bent on restoring America's much-tarnished image. By 1976, Jimmy Carter's election campaign exploited connections with impresarios and rock bands to guarantee not only Carter's election but the institutionalization of rock as the voice of the Democratic Party.

Yet, along with all the lurid details, *Mansion* questions whether this was inevitable. Goodman says at the outset:

> If the acquisition of wealth and influence is rock's ultimate meaning, then the most meaningful figure it has produced is the billionaire mogul David Geffen. Indeed, it's more than ironic that Geffen's appreciation of the dollars-and-cents value of the music has placed him in a position to exert a greater influence and power over society and politics than the artists—it may be the measure of a profound failure by the musicians and their fans.[20]

Goodman, nonetheless, suggests an alternative. His inspiration for writing *Mansion* was a statement made by Arlo Guthrie at the ceremony inducting Arlo's father, Woody, into the Rock and Roll Hall of Fame. As Goodman recounts: "Stepping to the Waldorf podium to acknowledge his father's enshrinement into the Hall, the gray-haired songwriter looked out on the tuxedoed crowd that claimed Woody Guthrie as its own. 'I don't know where Woody would be tonight if he were alive,' Arlo said with a small grin when the applause died down. 'But I can guarantee you he wouldn't be here.'"[21]

This example is more significant than Goodman may fully have realized. It proves not only that co-optation is not all-powerful or irresistible but that effectively resisting it brings greater honor and influence than could ever be imagined by the cretins and sycophants guarding a privileged elite. The fact that Woody Guthrie is only one of many musicians who have resolutely stood against oppression, exploitation, and war, exposes the vacuity of the arguments made to justify submission and the duplicity of those making them. Furthermore, Guthrie's legacy was an inspiration for the most stunning rebuke to cynical music industry hacks ever made. In the Sixties' wake arose a challenge heard round the world.

No Future

You knew the Sixties were over when "God Save the Queen" hit the airwaves. "No Future," sang the Sex Pistols, angrily denouncing not only England's "fascist regime" but the illusions to which the preceding generation (the "Children of the Future") had succumbed.[22] Rock 'n' roll is dead, the Pistols exclaimed, their mockumentary film, *The Great Rock 'n' Roll Swindle*, only a belated funeral for a decaying corpse. Lest the point be missed, the Clash followed with "Hate and War," indicting not only these scourges of human history but also blatantly attacking the "peace and love" with which San Francisco in the Sixties would forever be associated. Long hair and long guitar solos, psychedelic paraphernalia and New Age mysticism, rock royalty and political pretension were all scornfully ridiculed. Punk boldly reasserted music's power to challenge authority (indeed, music's rivalry with the state), exposing the link between that state and the corporate rock that had by 1977 co-opted music's anti-authoritarian mission. When the Sex Pistols crashed and burned at Winterland in San Francisco (a Bill Graham production, no less) Johnny Rotten exhorted the crowd with, "Ever get the feeling you've been cheated?" Rotten was referring to the short set his band performed, but his question became legendary, because it was an indict-ment: not only had the revolution been defeated, it had been *betrayed*.

Punk, ska, and reggae emerged together in the UK and Jamaica in the few short years before the Thatcher/Reagan axis began the "res-toration of imperial command." This musical insurgency provided a point-by-point critique of the musical counterrevolution being carried out in San Francisco. Against stadium/corporate rock, there was Rock Against Racism, a series of festivals and events rallying youth to fight Britain's National Front. Contributing mightily to this movement was the Two Tone ska revival and the unity forged between punk, ska, and reggae bands against the racist division of "white" rock versus black music. Finally, young women vastly expanded their role in music-mak-ing against the industry's male supremacist strategies. Especially in punk and New Wave, women began to assert their independence and creativity as composers, instrumentalists, and band leaders, going far beyond anything accomplished during the Sixties proper. Needless to say, these developments were themselves circumscribed and ultimately co-opted or suppressed. Yet they succeeded in exposing many of the fal-lacies and illusions by which the previous generation's noblest aims were subverted.[23] They furthermore challenge all subsequent accounts, in particular those promoted by rock journalists and revisionist historians, that portray the Sixties as no more then the hedonistic outburst of ego-driven reprobates, or, conversely, the naive self-delusion of dreamers. By specifically targeting San Francisco and its rock royalty, punk, ska, and reggae reasserted the very musical and social themes of diversity, unity, revolution, and liberation that had made the city's reputation.

Today, this eruption both complicates and illuminates Sixties schol-arship. The Sixties did not end in one decisive battle. Nor did they slowly dissipate into the ether. It only became apparent through a series of cam-paigns, each one holding the promise of rejuvenation, that the system's overthrow was not imminent and the movement was no more. Perhaps, given the high concentration of radical groups and revolutionary ideas in San Francisco, the flame burned longest there. Who can forget the struggle to defend the International Hotel, or the militant demonstra-tions of Iranian students leading to the overthrow of the Shah, or the cel-ebrations of African Liberation Day and the struggle against apartheid? Who was not inspired by the victory of the Sandinistas in 1979? And how could anyone not feel the sense of a revived movement with the explosion of gay pride, and the election and subsequent assassination of Harvey Milk? Certainly, the White Night Riots that followed the acquittal of Milk's murderer gave every indication that militant opposition to the system was still very much alive. In fact, for many in San Francisco, the end of the Sixties was only clearly marked when histories began to appear in the mid-1980s. Only then could the end of the Vietnam War, the beginning of the first serious crisis of capitalism since World War II and the cumulative effects of co-optation and repression, be identified as the conclusion of a historical sequence. Not a bang *or* a whimper, but an end, nonetheless.

This compelled a recognition of defeat, a recognition that the counterrevolution had succeeded and that there would be hell to pay. Perhaps inevitably, many who were still politically active resisted an acknowledgement of defeat, causing even more of the rancor and sectarianism that had contributed to undermining the movement's effectiveness. Yet acknowledging defeat is not to succumb to defeatism, rather it is to find a new beginning.

Endings and Beginnings

Reflecting on the moment decades later, philosopher Alain Badiou wrote:

> The years that followed 1980 remind one of what Mallarmé rightly said about those that came after 1880: "A present is lacking." Since counter-revolutionary periods resemble one another far more than revolutionary ones, we should not be surprised that after the "leftism" of the sixties, we now revisit the reactive ideas that emerged in the wake of the Paris Commune. This is because the interval between an event of emancipation and another leaves us fallaciously in thrall to the idea that nothing begins or will ever begin, even if we find ourselves caught in the midst of an infernal and immobile agitation.[24]

The system's apologists, especially those in the music industry, have never ceased to remind us that we lost because we were wrong. The accommodation they preach is based not only on a "remaking of history" but on a foreclosure of the future. This of course makes the task of accurately assessing the errors, shortcomings, and self-sabotage that weakened revolutionary forces more difficult. It was, after all, those weaknesses that the counterrevolution exploited to insure its victory.

The difficulty can only be overcome by firmly grasping that any critical analysis must be a beginning, and a new beginning, at that, one not only cognizant of experience but also of the future not yet written. "Where there is oppression, there is resistance" is a truth that even the system's apologists are forced to accept, if only to deny its more significant corollary: where there is resistance, there is nourished the seed of humanity's liberation.

Humanity's liberation is the *not yet* explored so deeply by philosopher Ernst Bloch. The *not yet* is the wellspring of art. Instead of the "infernal and immobile agitation" provided by the system's hirelings, it is a quest for the world to come. This quest goes further than pathos and deeper than exposé, providing an antidote for the poison proffered by defenders of the status quo. It is not only the Great Refusal but the Great Affirmation: there *is* a better way. The revolution forged an indissoluble link between art-making practices and an aesthetics of liberation, an aesthetics in the precise sense that the beautiful is *shaped* in a struggle to realize an ideal of justice and equality in human being. Triumphing over classicism, the revolution succeeded not only in ushering forth innumerable great and enduring works, it provided criteria for the production and judgment of the sublime. Instead of *repressive desublimation* (to use Marcuse's terminology), the liberation of wonder, that is, the rational and imaginative exploration of the infinite.

If anything, the failure of the revolution was a failure to grasp this role of aesthetics in liberating consciousness, indeed the *leading* role of aesthetics in imagining a future. Not, therefore, a collapse of aesthetics into politics or, conversely, a Nietzschean elevation of the poet over the philosopher, but a thorough repudiation of the notion that life is "nasty, brutish and short," in which our senses are a prison from which the only escape is momentary pleasure and death. The revolution fell prey to its own tacit acceptance of the "realism" imposed by the system, an abandonment of the task of elaborating in political terms what the system's replacement might look like.

It is not without irony that we find ourselves today confronting all those questions posed but not answered by the revolution. In a speech delivered in April 2014, Immanuel Wallerstein remarked, "The most noticeable thing about antisystemic movements in the second decade of the twenty-first century is the degree to which the debates that embroiled them in the last third of the twentieth century, once exorcised in the world-revolution of 1968, have returned to plague them, virtually unchanged."[25] The question posed by Marcuse, "The Failure of the New Left?," is returning as well. Above all, it is clear that the failure was not a failure to fight but a failure to win. History may be "remade" by the victors, but that cannot guarantee victory's permanence. In spite of a decades-long interregnum, the system's victory remains temporary and provisional. The question thus becomes: How do we *win*?

While the challenges we face may remain unchanged, a new opportunity is presented in the utter failure of the system to deliver on its promises. This is nowhere more evident than in the domain of art. It is more urgent than ever that the lessons of defeat be transformed by the unleashing of creativity and the imagination, by firmly establishing what Jacques Rancière calls the aesthetic regime of art.[26] Art's emancipatory mission must be reaffirmed.

No doubt the artist is confronted with enormous obstacles, not the least of which are cynicism and despair. To be a voice in the wilderness is no more appealing than to be a voice in the crowd at a football game. To make a contribution, to make a difference, to make history, these are goals worthy of the artist. In their place are offered opportunities to make a name for oneself, to be acclaimed and fêted by agents of the state. It's called a "career," and it's the booby prize for which you surrender your life. In this situation, it is perhaps best to recall the words of surrealist poet André Breton, who in 1944 wrote:

> One must go to the depths of human suffering, discover its strange capacities, in order to salute the similarly limitless gift that makes life worth living. The one definitive disgrace one can bring upon oneself in the face of such suffering . . . would be to confront it with resignation . . .
>
> There is, in fact, no more barefaced lie than the one that consists in asserting, even—and above all—when faced with an irretrievable situation, that rebellion is good for nothing. Rebellion is its own justification, completely independent of the chance it has to modify the state of affairs that gives rise to it. It's a spark in the wind, but a spark in search of a powder keg.[27]

I would only add that whether the powder keg is the explosive force of art itself or that latent power of the people who, enlightened and inspired by art, might liberate themselves matters little here. The metaphor is apt in that it reminds us of a potential that is always present, that has at times been realized, and may yet again be realized—depending, that is, on what we do!

Glossary of Terms

The *system* not only referred to capitalism or to economics. The system represented the constellation of forces that dominated and controlled all aspects of social life, from sexual mores to the oppression of black people, from the exploitation of labor to the suppression of student protest. Above all, it was not confined to the United States but included the Soviet Union as well. The system was everything that kept people down and it had to be overthrown or radically transformed; it could not be reformed and preserved. Furthermore, it was doomed.

The movement was a direct outgrowth of the civil rights and antiwar movements that gave it birth but it was also the grandchild of the labor movement and the peace movement of an earlier generation. It was an all-encompassing term that invited people in without requiring membership cards or dues. Thus, by 1967, a supporter of the farmworkers and an organizer of draft resistance or a GI coffeehouse would consider themselves part of the movement. For the millions swept up in this great undertaking, the system was the enemy; the war in Vietnam, the oppression of blacks and Chicanos, and the alienation of youth were just the most grievous signs of its depraved nature. By 1970, women's liberation, environmentalism, and the struggle for gay rights grew out of and in turn radically transformed the movement itself.

Consciousness expansion came into wide use in the years between 1965 and 1970 referring to everything from LSD to Nietzsche to Buddha to Mao. Women's liberation inspired the even more widespread use of the term "consciousness *raising*." In any case, this was no ivory tower, academic debate. This was a serious pursuit by large numbers of ordinary people coming to grips with philosophical, political, and spiritual questions that inevitably erupt when people aspire to more than merely improving their lot within an oppressive social order. And people did, generally, aspire to more. The idea of a revolution of some kind ushering in a truly different world had fired the imaginations of many who thought at the time that their victory was both assured and imminent. That they (we) were wrong about this does not alter the point.

Liberation was originally inspired by the independence movements that swept Africa and Asia in the early Sixties. The right of nations to self-determination was part of the UN Charter signed in 1948 and was given significance by the collapse of Europe's colonial empires in the face of popular revolt following World War II. But the greatest spur to widespread use of the word came from the National Liberation Front in Vietnam. As resistance to the war merged with the struggle of black people for civil rights, both movements moved from focusing on specific targets to a wholesale assault on the system in the interest of people's liberation everywhere. Thus the civil rights movement gave way to the struggle for black liberation.

Inventory of Falsehoods

First, there was no "San Francisco sound." Even though Ralph Gleason's enthusiastic boosterism led him to use the term, he would be the first to admit that it has been construed in a manner other than he intended. Declarations of a "sound" of a city are often of dubious musical or historical value. In the case of Detroit, Memphis, Chicago, or New Orleans there might be some merit in using the term, since a cohesive musical style and tradition did develop (albeit for different reasons in each case). In the case of Detroit, a small group of inspired musicians, calling themselves "The Funk Brothers," became broadly influential through the intrinsic quality of what they created in combination with the popular success of Berry Gordy's marketing of the "Motown Sound." In the case of New Orleans, this was a more generic process spanning more than a century in which a combination of African and European influences produced a distinctive local music.

But San Francisco never had any single, defining musical style, certainly not one that originated there. In fact, it was the absence of any *one* sound that opened a space for the diversity that came to be identified with San Francisco. Such diversity was only possible because of what many musicians have emphasized since: the audience was decisive. This public welcomed anything it perceived as authentic, innovative, wild, and free regardless of its stylistic particularity. What had hitherto been sharp, apparently irreconcilable, divisions between folk, jazz, rhythm and blues, and rock music underwent an alchemical transformation. Everything is permitted where God is dead, and if rock 'n' roll was anything, it was the slayer of gods. Present, even, were the works of contemporary composers such as Moondog (Louis Hardin), Morton Subotnick, and Terry Riley. What happened as a result was more than the creation of a large body of work. Instead of one sound or genre, music as such was elevated to the position formerly held by poetry as the queen of all the arts. To paraphrase Shelley, music became the unacknowledged legislator of the world.

Second, there was no "Summer of Love."[1] This was a media creation that passed into popular usage the same way Tampax became the generic name for a sanitary napkin. Journalists and publicity agents (is there really a difference?) repeated this phrase so often that it became a common referent; it was a short, easy way to identify a time and place without doing the hard work of chronicling what actually transpired, thereby preventing its lessons from being learned. A large migration of young, mainly white, high-school and college-age people did come to the Bay Area in 1967.attracted by its growing reputation; along with the tour buses, many subsequently found themselves wandering up and down Haight Street.

The Diggers, the Family Dog, *The Oracle* newspaper, and the Straight Theater did use the phrase in a press release of April 5, 1967, to announce a series of celebratory events and community activities, including sweeping the streets. But love had a lot less to do with this than is commonly believed. The press release and coinage of the phrase were an attempt to give some direction to what had exploded in January of that year at the Human Be-In, when at least twenty thousand people had attended a "Gathering of the Tribes" in Golden Gate Park. The local organizations had to deal with the response of the authorities, including repeated instances of police violence. In 1967 alone, the police carried out several massive sweeps down Haight Street, beating and arresting everyone in sight, sending plenty to the hospital, and charging anyone they chose with "assaulting a police officer."[2] The stakes were raised higher since plans were afoot for a giant festival (the Monterey Pop Festival) that, along with the song "San Francisco (Be Sure to Wear Flowers in Your Hair)," released in May 1967, sought to capitalize on a growing anti-authoritarian sentiment. The festival itself generated bitter controversy that was nonetheless overshadowed by the music performed there. Indeed, in musical terms, Monterey Pop was a brilliant representation of what San Francisco's openness and creativity had inspired. But, along with the police and their repression, the music industry was moving in, forming the second jaw of a steel trap.

To put this in its broader context, it is doubtful that these events would have occurred, or caused more than a ripple, were it not for the ferment in society arising from the civil rights and antiwar movements. The Human Be-In was a conscious attempt by its organizers to unite the overtly political movement with the nascent, and as yet unnamed, counterculture (often referred to at the time as the "socially hip movement" or "hip community").

The "Summer of Love" and its abiding image of a pilgrimage to a psychedelic Lourdes furthermore obscures the intensely local phenomenon of San Francisco in the Sixties, its driving personalities and participants coming from within the Bay Area as much as from without. Most importantly, the "Summer of Love" designation cannot be applied to the extraordinary growth in size and influence of the Black Panther Party, founded across the bay in Oakland in 1966. The connection, for example, between the San Francisco Mime Troupe, the Diggers, and the Panthers was not simply a temporal coincidence. The people involved met, exchanged views, mutually influencing and supporting each other. Such activity took place in Oakland, and in the Mission, Fillmore, and Tenderloin neighborhoods, not only in the Haight-Ashbury.

Third, there was no "hippie movement" or "hippie revolution." The term "hippie" was considered a pejorative and was not used by anyone considering themselves "hip." The origin of the term is instructive, however, since it illustrates how naming and authority are mutually dependent.

A coffeehouse called the Blue Unicorn opened its doors on the north side of San Francisco's Panhandle in 1963. Its claim to fame was the cheapest food and coffee in town, so it naturally appealed to those with little money, such as the artists, and students, housepainters, and cab drivers who frequented the place. The Blue Unicorn's reputation steadily grew until it came to the attention of one intrepid reporter for the *San Francisco Examiner*, Michael Fallon, who announced its existence to the world on September 6, 1965, in an article entitled "New Haven for Beatniks." Perhaps it's a coincidence that the article was published at the height of the battle raging over a planned freeway through the Panhandle that would run past the Blue Unicorn. This battle became known as the Freeway Revolt. *The San Francisco Examiner*, owned by the family of William Randolph Hearst, supported building the freeway. Could this have been the ulterior motive for drawing attention to an otherwise innocuous business Establishment?

Among the ideas fueled by caffeine and conversation was "The Unicorn Philosophy," courtesy of owner Bob Stubbs. An excerpt quoted by Charles Perry in *The Haight-Ashbury*, reads as follows: "It is nothing new. We have a private revolution going on. A revolution of individuality and diversity that can only be private. Upon becoming a group movement, such a revolution ends up with imitators rather than participants.... It is essentially a striving for *realization* of one's *relationship* to life and other people."[3] "Nothing new?" "Revolution"? "Private"? That wouldn't by any chance be an effort to fend off the authorities, who unsurprisingly descended on the Blue Unicorn shortly after Fallon's piece was published?

It is certainly a favorite tactic of authorities to harass or shut down anything even mildly subversive, particularly if it just happens to be in the path of their bulldozers. So San Francisco's Public Health Department cited the Blue Unicorn, forcing it to close. Was this just coincidence or was it because that there had been weekly meetings sponsored by LEMAR (legalization of marijuana) and the Sexual Freedom League at the coffeehouse for at least a year? After a month, the Unicorn reopened, and managed to stay afloat for some time. But by then, the vultures had smelled blood. Something was happening and Mr. Jones didn't know what it was. So the best thing to do was to give it a derisive name, "hippie," and spread that name far and wide.

What "hippie" sought to ridicule was real enough, however. Young people started growing their hair long, wearing colorful clothing, listening to rock music, smoking marijuana, dropping acid, and calling themselves "heads" or "freaks." They also began calling each other brothers and sisters. "Hippie" was always viewed as the straight world's appellation of scorn. Indeed, "hippie" was usually accompanied by "get a haircut" or "take a bath," often followed by harassment and physical abuse at the hands of the police.

In any case, the real news was not the Blue Unicorn. It was the launching of the Haight Ashbury Neighborhood Association and its successful mobilization to oppose the freeway. What would have become of San Francisco in general, and the Haight in particular, had that freeway been built? Contrary to manufactured myth, by 1967, the Haight-Ashbury was a battleground, the site of low intensity civil war. Many, if not most, people spoke in terms of the movement in the broadest sense ("counterculture" had not been coined yet), meaning everything from opposing the war in Vietnam to the struggle for civil rights or, for that matter, the farmworkers. The Diggers' "Death of Hippie/Birth of Free" march down Haight Street in 1967 was one of many events that drew a line between the system's machinations and the people's aspirations. Digger interventions played a decisive role in articulating the explicitly anticapitalist views shared by a large and growing number of young people. Their Free Store, Free Frames of Reference, free food, and the regular distribution of mimeographed messages were rallying points aimed at turning a spontaneous outpouring of rebelliousness into a conscious attempt to change the world.

Fourth, "peace and love" did not characterize daily activity, nor did it reflect prevailing Sixties attitudes on Haight Street, or anywhere else for that matter. Certainly, many championed the *ideals* of peace and love, but at the time these were highly charged political terms, not abstractions floating in the ether. Peace meant opposition to the war in Vietnam. Love meant opposition to the brutality of the police in particular, and authority in general. Macho images such as the jock, the drill sergeant, or the cowboy were love's targets, since it embarrassed them profoundly.

Furthermore, violence and brutality of a political nature had, by 1965, become commonplace in American life. Not only were black people everywhere being attacked, whether by southern racists or the cops, but so were young whites protesting against the war. As mentioned earlier, Haight Street itself was attacked on several occasions by the San Francisco police. Besides, this was the era of the occupation and of demonstrations to free political figures, such as Huey Newton, imprisoned by the system.

Fifth, the term "counterculture" was misused. Theodore Roszak's book remains important to this day; even if one disagrees with his conclusions, one has to take into account the broad influence of the work and the importance of the author's subject matter. For example, the social critics that focus his discussion (including Herbert Marcuse, Paul Goodman, Norman Brown, and Allen Ginsberg) give us some indication of just how widely read such writers were. Leveling a sustained attack on the technocracy is also instructive, not only in terms of the arguments, many of which remain valid to this day, but also as an indicator the prevalence of such views at the time.

The way in which the term "counterculture" became pervasive is another matter altogether. I question it on two grounds: 1.) All oppositional movements develop "cultural" expressions that reinforce solidarity while critiquing the dominant or oppressive culture. Certainly, black people developed a culture counter to the dominant one, and Roszak goes to great lengths to point out that it would take another book to adequately address what was happening with black youth; and 2.) its attempt to circumvent class, ethnic, or gender identifiers is both useful and problematic. It is certainly true that young people of all ethnicities, classes, and genders (including gays and lesbians) were among those who fit into the category "counterculture." But, as subsequent events would demonstrate, it was a designation that was easily manipulated for contradictory purposes. Indeed, it provided the very tools by which co-optation and commodification was achieved. Even at the time, the counterculture was frequently pitted against the movement, both as a description of constituencies and as a social vision. This was certainly not what Roszak intended, as is clear, if one reads his book. From the outset, Roszak identifies the counterculture as a resistance movement, in some ways even more revolutionary than its conventionally political counterpart. He explicitly discredits attempts to categorically separate the two in any case. Roszak sought to provide a means by which serious discussion of a social phenomenon could be joined without falling into the pitfalls of doctrinaire Marxism or of classic liberalism. Few from the Old Left or Johnson's Great Society had anticipated, let alone adequately responded to, the demands of youth as a social force. Citing Marcuse, in particular, speaks both to Marcuse's exceptional influence as well as the content of that influence, namely the necessity of revolutionary social transformation. and its re-envisioning by the New Left.

Sixth, the claim was wrong that the whole thing was white and middle class, for all intents and purposes conforming to Ronald Reagan's portrayal. This is perhaps the most common of all assumptions about the Sixties today, and it is false on several counts. From the outset, people from all social classes, including the children of wealth and the children of workers, were drawn to the movement. Furthermore, countercultural and movement influence spread simultaneously with resistance to the draft and opposition to the war in Vietnam. Soldiers and draft resisters were drawn into "countercultural" activities in increasing numbers, identifying with the music, the attitudes, and the politics expressed. This ultimately amounted to millions of people, most of whom were not from well-off backgrounds, and many of whom were black, Latino, Asian, or Native American. It was not long, in fact, before young workers of all nationalities were adopting the ways and means associated with their generation and rejecting, to one extent or another, the modes and manners of their forbears, particularly those of organized labor. The composition of the milieu is not, however, the only issue; there are two other problems with the "white, middle class" characterization.

Race was the social fault line cutting across and to a large extent determining all others in the United States. The ghettoes (including San Francisco's Hunters Point, which exploded in 1966) were in flames. The mood among black people generally was growing increasingly militant. Nowhere was this more clearly demonstrated than at Polytechnic High School on the edge of the Haight-Ashbury district itself. The school was predominantly black, and there was an uneasy but thought-provoking relationship between these young people and the burgeoning street scene through which they walked every day on their way to and from school. This resulted in innumerable petty confrontations, some violent, some merely verbal taunts, but there was no way "hippies" on Haight Street could ignore or be ambivalent toward race. Nor, for that matter, could young black people fail to be influenced by something that was obviously exciting and was meeting with extreme repression at the hands of their own enemies, the cops.[4]

Finally, the whole concept of "middle class" has to be critically evaluated. At best, it is a rough description of income, occupation, and perhaps educational level. But that has little value in determining the participants in the movements of the Sixties, let alone their motivations. Above all "middle class" is a political designation invented to combat the Marxian concept of the proletariat or working class, whose historic mission was to eliminate classes altogether.

Originally, the term was used in Europe to designate the position of the bourgeoisie between the aristocracy and the laboring classes.

Following World War II, it became the a crucial component of a social model that the ruling class in the United States used to defend its power against revolution. In any case, among dropouts, freaks, and radicals, "middle class" was a term of derision, not an expression of aspiration.

Seventh, the mountain of mystification surrounding drugs needs to be addressed. LSD and a group of plants with psychotropic properties were used, because they produced experiences akin to revelation as recorded by mystics and religious seekers. At the very least, these drugs made users contemplate the nature of perception and think about thinking, that most philosophical of preoccupations. Marijuana is in a special category, both connected to these hallucinogens, but also independent from them. Its lineage was different, as it was popularized by black jazz musicians and the hipness associated with them. Together, marijuana and the psychotropics have to be distinguished from all other drugs, including speed, heroin, cocaine, barbiturates, alcohol, caffeine, and nicotine that were in use before and since the Sixties for other reasons, reflecting no change whatsoever in the status quo.

The most damning indictment of the "Summer of Love" nonsense is that, by 1967, LSD and pot were being systematically replaced by speed and junk. Anyone who was there at the time remembers the case of Superspade, a black pot dealer, whose murder and that of another dealer that very summer, attracted nationwide attention. An article in the August 18, 1967, issue of *Time* magazine reported, "Says Dr. David E. Smith, founder of a Haight-Ashbury medical clinic that ministers to bad-tripping hippies: 'Amphetamines are the biggest drug problem now in the Haight.'"[5] The article concluded with this retrospectively hilarious quotation: "In an effort to restore peace and quiet, if not sanity, a hippie house organ called *The Oracle* editorialized: 'Do not buy or sell dope any more. Let's detach ourselves from material value. Plant dope and give away all you can reap. For John Carter and William Edward Superspade Thomas—may their consciousness return to bodies that will not want for anything but the beauty and joy of their part in the great dance.'"[6]

While LSD in particular had important social effects, encouraging users to reexamine their most cherished beliefs and practices, leading many to reject the prevailing views of a corrupt, hypocritical, consumerist society, it can nonetheless be flatly stated that drugs were mainly important as agents of social bonding, not for their chemical effects. Indeed, taken as a generic designation, "drugs" can never be separated from other factors, such as therapeutic aids, or in the case of "the pill," its effect on sexual practices and women's consciousness. The pill, in fact, had the most far-reaching consequences of any drug associated with the Sixties.

Dropping Out

Dropping out, made famous by the slogan "turn on, tune in, drop out," had many dimensions, from attitude to lifestyle to strategy for social change. However, one key element was the social phenomenon of the teenage runaway. The teenage runaway was furthermore closely associated with the Summer of Love, the Haight-Ashbury, and the counterculture in general. But what was this phenomenon, exactly, and what made it significant? "The FBI reports the arrest of over ninety thousand juvenile runaways in 1966; most of those who flee well-off middle-class homes get picked up by the thousands each current year in the big-city bohemias, fending off malnutrition and venereal disease," wrote Theodore Roszak, quoting, among other sources, a September 15, 1967, *Time* magazine article on the subject.[7] That this was neither confined to the United States nor directed toward San Francisco alone is confirmed: "The immigration departments of Europe record a constant level over the past few years of something like ten thousand disheveled 'flower children' (mostly American, British, German, and Scandinavian) migrating to the Near East and India—usually toward Katmandu (where drugs are cheap and legal) and a deal of hard knocks along the way." Roszak concludes, "Certainly for a youngster of seventeen, clearing out of the comfortable bosom of the middle-class family to become a beggar is a formidable gesture of dissent. One makes light of it at the expense of ignoring a significant measure of our social health."[8]

The authorities in San Francisco didn't make light of it. They sounded the alarm. In 1967, Police Chief Thomas Cahill explicitly warned that "law and order will prevail. There will be no sleeping in the park. There are no sanitation facilities and if we let them camp there we would have a tremendous health problem. Hippies are no asset to the community. These people do not have the courage to face the reality of life. They are trying to escape. Nobody should let their young children take part in this hippy thing."[9] Cahill's remarks, however, came after the fact and were, to a large extent, part of a campaign being orchestrated by the very Establishment from whom young people were running away.

When the Health Department, for example, investigated living conditions in the newly notorious Haight-Ashbury (no similar investigations were planned for the black ghettos of the Fillmore district or Hunters Point), they found nothing out of the ordinary. After visiting 1,400 residences they found only sixteen in which people fitting the description of hippies could be cited for violations.[10] Longtime Haight residents were outraged by the Health Department's actions. Led by the Haight-Ashbury Neighborhood Association, fresh from the victorious Freeway Revolt, they denounced the city's "gratuitous criticism of our community." They accused officials of "creating an artificial problem" and of being motivated more by "personal and official" prejudice, rather than by legitimate concern. The head of the Health Department, the hilariously named Dr. Ellis D. Sox, had to back off. "The situation is not as bad as we thought," he said. "There has been a deterioration [of sanitation] in the Haight-Ashbury, but the hippies did not contribute much more to it than other members of the neighborhood."[11] This was not, Dr. Sox maintained, a deliberate campaign against weirdos, when everyone knew that was precisely what it was.

Two more points about runaways: first, the numbers have to be put in perspective and qualified by what constitutes a runaway as opposed to an adult participant in the same activities; secondly, there were always conflicting agendas within the Haight-Ashbury, and the Bay Area at large, particularly as regards the organization and mobilization of these youth. The HIP merchants and the *Oracle*, for example, were only two of several groups with conflicting agendas contending for the allegiance of the young.

In terms of the numbers, estimates have been proposed suggesting that as few as fifty thousand and as many as a hundred thousand young people flooded into San Francisco between the summers of 1966 and 1968. Reports claimed that the hippies numbered three hundred thousand nationwide and that enclaves could be found in many cities across the country. The purpose of these reports, however, was not to quantify a population, but to construct a *type* that could be marginalized and isolated.

There were at least as many, if not more, young people from local high schools and even junior high schools who participated in the Human Be-In, to use only one noteworthy event as an example. Young people flocked to San Francisco from other parts of the Bay Area, swelling the ranks of gawkers and idlers on Haight Street on a regular basis. They might have been juveniles, but most of them were not runaways.

Actual runaways were by definition a temporary phenomenon since their approaching adulthood meant they would soon no longer be their parents' responsibility. More importantly, what brought them together in the Haight-Ashbury as opposed to, say, San Diego was more than their status as runaways, which could apply to any minor leaving home against the wishes of their legal guardians. Obviously, a combination of factors, including dreams, drugs, the draft, distance from families, and alluring rumors led them to seek security in numbers or solidarity in tolerance. No doubt the most gullible actually believed the song "San Francisco," just as some thought the Monkees were a real band who actually played their instruments. But the phenomenon, such as it was, could no more be attributed to music industry hype than could resistance to the war in Vietnam. Ultimately, the runaway was one manifestation of a much larger and more fluid situation. That runaways posed a threat to the system was beyond doubt, but it soon became clear that they also posed a challenge for revolutionaries.

Roszak put the question provocatively: "The adolescentization of dissent poses dilemmas as perplexing as the proletarianization of dissent that bedeviled left-wing theorists when it was the working class they had to ally with in their effort to reclaim our culture for the good, the true, and the beautiful. Then it was the horny-handed virtues of the beer hall and the trade union that had to serve as the medium of radical thought. Now it is the youthful exuberance of the rock club, the love-in, the teach-in."[12]

APPENDIX II

San Francisco Census Data 1960, 1965, 1970

(Source: U.S. Bureau of Labor Statistics. Note the spelling and terminology used to identify ethnic groups and occupations. Also note the decline in San Francisco's population between 1950 and 1970, and the steady growth in the Bay Area. —MC)

1965 Population: 750,500
                                        (1.4% increase over 1960)

San Francisco City and County: 740, 316
White: 604,403
Negroe: 74,383
Other: 61,530

Bay Area:*   2,783,359
White: 2,436,665
Negroe: 238,754
Other: 107,940

San Francisco
Male 14 years and older: 287,720
Female 14 years and older: 303,452

---

* "Bay Area" includes Alameda, Contra Costa, Marin, Napa, San Francisco, San Mateo, Santa Clara, Solano, and Sonoma counties.

Labor Force
Male:	226,280
Female:	141,722
Manufacturing:	54,467
Construction:	14,049

San Francisco Population from 1950–1970
(note the steady drop in population in San Francisco and the steady growth in the Bay Area—MC)

1950:	775,357
1960:	740,316
1970:	715,674

San Francisco/Oakland:*

1950:	2,135,934
1960:	2,648,762
1970:	3,109,519

24% growth between 1950+1960
17% growth between 1960+1970

Spanish population of SF 1970:
Mexican:	27,487
Puerto Rican:	5,037
Cuban:	1,282
Other:	35,827

Spanish population of Oakland:
Mexican:	24,168
Puerto Rican:	13,887
Cuban:	1,720
Other:	8,435

---

* "San Francisco/Oakland" includes Alameda, Contra Costa, Marin, San Francisco, and San Mateo counties.

San Francisco Bay Area Work Force 1970:   1,267,643
Manufacturing: 211,280
Construction: 68,210
Railroad: 9, 179
Trucking/warehousing: 18,563
Other Transport: 47,918

San Francisco Only:
Manufacturing: 37,341
Railroad: 2,515
Trucking/warehouse: 3,366
Other Transport: 14,947
Construction: 12,189

Longshoremen, Warehousemen, Teamsters
1960
Longshoremen: 3,493 + 9 (female)
Teamsters: 2,120
Warehousemen: 7,065

1970
Longshoremen: 2,642
Warehousemen: 4,692
Freight handlers: 6,676
Stock handlers: 6,640 + 997 (female)

Production Worker's Average Weekly Earnings, San Francisco/Oakland
1964:
126.01 dollars

The Record Deal—Standard Industry Practice in the Twentieth Century

(Throughout the twentieth century—indeed, into the twenty-first—the record business followed practices established in the days of sheet-music sales which were, in turn, protected by legal statutes enacted by Congress. To this day, the general public, including many music critics, knows little about the contracts and laws that actually governed, and continue to govern, the production and distribution of music. Indeed, many musicians are blissfully unaware of what their rights and obligations are in a hierarchy ostensibly devoted to their craft. The following data is presented to show how, even in the revolutionary Sixties, control over music and musicians was maintained by contractual arrangements enforced by industry practices and courts of law. With the advent of the internet, some of these practices and corresponding laws have been modified in ways that won't concern us here, but suffice it to say their fundamentally exploitative nature remains unchanged.

The data and analysis were provided by producer and manager, David Rubinson, in an interview with this author. They have been confirmed by other experts I consulted as well as by my own experience as an artist, manager, and producer.)

1. All recording and publishing/songwriter contracts were Personal Services agreements and companies based their agreements on this model.

2. All contracts were exclusive, meaning:
A – The company owned the exclusive rights to the services rendered by the artist.
B – While the company could not force the artist to perform, it could prevent and enjoin the artist from performing services for others. Thus,

control over the rights to the artist's works and/or performance rested with the entity (record company or publisher).

3. All contracts were based on a formula derived from the era of printed sheet music (music "publishing") and the first 78 rpm records (1900s), when recorded performance was quantified in terms of a printed sheet of music, or recorded "sides," as in one side of a shellac (later vinyl) platter or record. Records were usually packaged and sold in sets ("albums"), with a cardboard outer cover and paper sleeves for each of the platters. The definition of services was given as a minimum number of sides, and later "albums," that the performer was contracted to provide.

4. All contracts paid the artist a royalty based on the retail price of the sides or albums *minus* the packaging costs, breakage (78 rpm sides were fragile), and returns of unsold merchandise. *All recording costs* and many marketing expenses were also recouped by the record company *prior* to the artist receiving any royalty payments on sales.

5. In record company accounting, for purposes of recoupment of all of these costs, all contracts computed an "artist" royalty rate (usually between 3 and 10 percent of retail price). It was from that "artist's" royalty alone that the artist recouped the costs of recording and packaging. This is a crucial point because 100 percent of the money received from record sales went to the record company whereas only 3–10 percent, were credited to the artist for recoupment of costs.

Hypothetically, John Artist might be entitled to a 10 percent royalty rate, which might amount to approximately $1 per record sold at $10 retail. Given recording costs of $100,000—and 100,000 records sold—since John only recouped the costs at his $1 per record "artist" royalty rate—not the $10 per record the record company was earning—the record company would recoup all of its costs at 10,000 records sold (100,000 sales multiplied by $10 per record) but John would not recoup until 100,000 records were sold (100,000 sales multiplied by $1 per record). This meant that the record company received income on 90,000 records sold while paying John nothing. In general, a vast number of record contracts were "unearned," meaning that costs were *unrecouped* at the artists' royalty rate.

General comment: This was and remains a plantation system. Recording artists were and are equivalent to sharecroppers or slaves.

Ownership of capital and control of the channels of marketing and distribution enable the record and publishing companies to compel the artist to hand over the lion's share of the goods and services he or she produces (in this case composition and performance) in order to be able to produce their work, to continue producing, and to have any access to distribution. This is not fundamentally different from cotton or tobacco, gold or copper or any other industrialized crop except that in order to sell the musical composition and/or performance, notoriety has to be created for the artist (as a brand or trademark) thereby increasing demand in the marketplace. The result is that with rare exceptions, musicians have usually derived the greatest portion of their income from live performance fees, not from recordings, augmented by songwriter royalties from the licensed use of their copyrighted works (fees paid by radio, filmmakers or advertisers). Furthermore, other participants in the system such as managers, agents, accountants and attorneys derived their percentages and fees from the *gross* earnings of the artist, before expenses. The plantation analogy held for virtually every aspect of the music business until the recent breakdown of the monopoly that came with the growth of the internet, and the advent of cheap high quality home recording.

Nevertheless, these changes, including the promise of greater creative freedom, quickly revealed their limitations. Promotion and distribution remain in the hands of those with the capital and political clout to dominate all channels of communication. It is beyond the scope of this book to go into the ramifications but it is important to emphasize that, though the music industry is changing, these changes do not benefit most musicians, and least of all do they represent a "victory" for the revolution of the Sixties.

APPENDIX IV

Revolution (the movie)

Filmed in 1967 and released in 1968, *Revolution* disappeared almost immediately, never to be seen again. The only traces it left were a brief mention in Ralph Gleason's *The Jefferson Airplane and the San Francisco Sound* and some passing references in unrelated interviews by participants in its making it. So obscure is *Revolution* that even filmmakers well-acquainted with the expansive archive of photographs, posters, articles, recordings, and films from the era, have never heard of it.[1] No doubt this is partly a result of the film's poor cinematic quality. *Revolution* is a docudrama weaving together interviews, live concert footage, and scenes from the Haight-Ashbury with the fictional story of its main character, Today Malone. It collapses in lengthy sequences attempting to portray an acid trip, along with tedious forays into experimental film techniques that were already dated when they first appeared. What the film omits is as noteworthy as what it contains: there is no mention of the "Summer of Love," or the song "San Francisco (Be Sure to Wear Flowers in Your Hair)," or, for that matter, the Monterey Pop Festival, all of which were purported to be "big news" at the time the film was being shot.

Inadvertently, the film reveals the blind spots of its makers when constant reference is made to white middle-class youth, while virtually every scene includes blacks, Chicanos, and other people of color. Indeed, the film's first interview is with a black man at the Diggers' Free Store on Frederick and Stanyan, in the Haight. His statement is worth quoting in full:

> A Digger is a person that they label—whatchacallit—beatnik, you
> dig?, *Beatnik*, people with an unconventional generation—they

didn't know what was happening, they didn't know the beatnik cared so much about humanity as they do now. Well, the Free Store to me means a great deal, because it helps out the community and it brings people together with *no profit involved.* If there was any profit involved, I wouldn't be here, because money doesn't mean that much to me. You talk about the hippie—what *is* the hippie? Where did the name come from, *hippie?* Why don't you talk about the younger generation, the people who are changing? Why don't you talk about the people who know what's happening and don't agree with the old line of thinking? Why don't you talk about the people who believe in brotherly love and nothin' else and prove it every day on Haight-Ashbury?

This statement concentrates a great deal. That it is expressed by a black person points to the necessity of exposing the racist subtext that runs through the "standard narrative" of the era. Furthermore, the statement itself serves as a concise and, accurate summary of what participants thought, especially about the labels beatnik and hippie.

In fact, the film succeeds in a manner it perhaps never intended; *Revolution* provides a relatively accurate glimpse of what was actually going on in San Francisco in 1967, at least as regards the music, the light shows, the dance, the theater, and the poster art that was bursting forth at the time. It also presents an unpretentious picture of drugs (mainly pot and LSD), sexual experimentation, and the influence of Eastern religion. Moreover, several interviews (notably those with Ronnie Davis and Lou Gottlieb) are concise expressions not only of the views of the speakers but also of a way of thinking that was widespread at the time. Finally, the film manages to capture how the Fillmore or Avalon looked from the inside. The light show dominated, you could not see the band, and the dancing was wild and free. The sense one gets is of young people thoroughly enjoying themselves, which, to a greater extent than is often acknowledged, was a major reason so many became so involved so quickly. It was not just "fun"; it was exciting!

The cast of characters includes many of the main protagonists in San Francisco at the time. The bands performing in the film or on the soundtrack include Mother Earth singing the title song, Country Joe and the Fish performing the "I-Feel-Like-I'm-Fixin'-to-Die Rag" and "Section 43," the Steve Miller Band doing, "Mercury Blues," Quicksilver

Messenger Service, with "St. John's River," and Ace of Cups, just jamming. Dan Hicks performs a humorous version of the song, "Stoned, Dead Stoned" on a park bench. While far from comprehensive, this is a representative sampling of local music, none of which bears any resemblance to "San Francisco (Be Sure to Wear Flowers in Your Hair)." Proving the point is Mother Earth's rendition of the title song: a rhythm and blues/jazzy hybrid (in 5/4 time!) with anthemic lyrics that crudely but clearly summarize prevailing notions about what was happening and why it was a revolution. "We want more than the laws allow" and "Mr. General, you can keep your war, we won't play no more" are representative samples.[2]

Herb Caen, a journalist for the *San Francisco Chronicle* (the man who coined the term "beatnik" and popularized the word "hippie") is interviewed about LSD (he never tried it) and pot (he smoked it and had for a long time). The Reverend Cecil Williams is interviewed, along with a nun and another priest, all expressing sympathy with the hippies and decrying official brutality, especially that of the police department. Then there's Chief Thomas Cahill of that very police department offering his justifications coupled with representatives of San Francisco's Health Department and General Hospital, Dr. Ellis D. Sox and Dr. Barry Decker, respectively.

Also interviewed are anonymous representatives of the Haight-Ashbury Job Co-op, the Free Medical Clinic and the Sexual Freedom League. Finally, there's the Anna Halprin dance company onstage at either the Fillmore or the Avalon (not specified in the film) shrouded in the light show of Glenn McKay and Jerry Abrams. Set against a backdrop of San Francisco (Ocean Beach, Seal Rock, Golden Gate Park, and the Haight-Ashbury), the film focuses on the Summer Solstice celebration held in Speedway Meadow four days after the Monterey Pop Festival. The contrast between the film of the Monterey Pop Festival and *Revolution* is readily apparent.

Sociologists, psychiatrists, Health Department officials, and the police reveal the utter confusion with which the Establishment confronted a resistance movement. The fact that this movement was composed of different and contradictory streams was initially a strength enabling it to thrive as long as it did. While characterized by dilettantism in regards to Eastern religion, the youthful participants were nonetheless enthusiasts in the original sense of the word, which is to say, "god inspired." The wholesale rejection of capitalism, Christianity, and nationalism are accompanied by a zealous embrace of the opposite: sharing, direct personal contact with the divine, and humanity as one. Rejection of marriage, the nuclear family and the macho image of masculinity are expressed by affirming sexual love unbound by child bearing or exclusive monogamy and by men with the capacity to appreciate beauty and tenderness. Rejection of alcohol is coupled with the affirmation of marijuana and psychotropic drugs. The film's portrayal of such attitudes is incomplete but reasonably accurate.

The interview with an anonymous volunteer at the Haight Job Co-op highlights the problems activists were facing:

> People are pouring into the scene so fast that it's very difficult to turn 'em all on, because what you're trying to turn 'em on to is freedom. If it's free, if everyone really has the room to do their thing, something really fine will come out of it. But in learning how to do your thing, you make mistakes. You really just fuck everything up, and this is the danger of, like, 100,000 people coming to San Francisco this summer. Maybe there'll be street riots, which is not good. Maybe we'll have that sort of problem.
>
> The other sort of problem is that we're getting successful enough now that we're gonna have to integrate back into society. The music is the best example: we're all making a lot of money. Like Donovan said, "beatniks getting rich." Well, the rock bands in the San Francisco area are going to make more than a million dollars this year. And this brings a lot of problems with it. We're rapidly moving into the entire Establishment and it's a question of whether we're going to turn them on or they're gonna turn us off.

Ronnie Davis's mile-a-minute improv-rap, which was said to have had the audience in stitches at the film's San Francisco premier, provides more striking insights. Ronnie later explained that he'd been approached by the filmmakers and told he could say anything he wanted to—in one minute.[3] So, shortly before going onstage to perform L'Amant Militaire with the Mime Troupe, Ronnie ranted:

> I wrote an article called "Guerilla Theater," in which we talk about getting people from the community who are dropouts, who dislike the society: the Old Left, the New Left, the psychedelic left, junkies, ex-junkies, winos, dropouts, psychotics, people who are

really disenchanted with what happens. They join us. They help us do shows. There's a whole noncommercial underground—not underground, everybody profits off the underground at this point. It's very open, 'cause this is like a middle-class country—but the dropouts, the hippies, the beatniks, and the professional dropouts. In other words, we work hard, and we're professional dropouts, dropouts from middle-class ideology, success ideology—we not only criticize it, we live it, we *do* it! Different than you [to the camera crew] who watch and "understand" the hippie scene, who "understand" the avant-garde. The difference is the avant-garde *does* it. The new person is not one who simply says it's a bad society, but who proves it by his actions. It's a great difference, a great difference from a critic of this society like Noam Chomsky and other people who make films, etc., criticizes society, but don't *do* it! The difference is we do it. We live it all the time. We'll continue living it. We'll survive and work hard. We also eat less than most other people. We demand less. We don't spend $1,500 on furniture. We don't buy a stage for $10,000. We pay about $500 for it. Pay our actors $5 a performance. You can live on $25 a week, that's assuming you're doing something that's interesting. You gotta make a lotta money, mac, you gotta make a *fortune* to keep a boring job or to support a war in Vietnam that's evil, that's murderous. So we struggle in our own humble way to destroy the United States.

Whereupon, Ronnie cracks up and the camera quickly pans away.

Revolution is not a document of the quality of *Sons and Daughters* or of the more recent *Berkeley in the Sixties*. Yet it is startling, particularly when viewed by people who were active in San Francisco at the time and have had to endure five decades of distortion and outright falsification of the record. In its naive portrayal of drugs, drug-dealing, sexual experimentation, and dabbling in Eastern religion, it conveys what a day in the Haight-Ashbury of 1967 could be like. Giving some space for young people to talk about why they came to San Francisco, including addressing the moral and political questions important to them, is also useful. It may not have been the intention of the filmmakers, but, in one sense, *Revolution* lives up to its title. The film poses the question a generation was asking: how can we change the world unless we change the way we think?

Revolution
Carl Lerner – *Editor*; Jack O'Connell – *Director*; Jack O'Connell – *Screenwriter*; Bill Godsey – *Cinematographer*; Robert Leder – *Executive producer*
"Revolution" title song: words and music by Norman Martin and Jack O'Connell
Cast: Daria Halprin as Today Malone

Revolution is available at:
http://www.thevideobeat.com/beatnik-hippie-drug-movies/revolution-1968.html

Bibliography

Books

Adorno, Theodor. *The Culture Industry: Selected Essays on Mass Culture*. London: Routledge. 1991.

———. *The Jargon of Authenticity*. Translated by K. Tarnowski and F. Will. London: Routledge, 1973.

Adorno, Theodor, Walter Benjamin, Ernst Bloch, Berthold Brecht, and Georg Lukacs. *Aesthetics and Politics*. London: New Left Books, 1977.

Adorno, Theodor, and Max Horkheimer. *The Dialectic of Enlightenment*. London: Verso, 1997.

Albert, Judith Clavir, and Stewart Edward Albert. *The Sixties Papers: Documents of a Rebellious Decade*. Westport, CT: Praeger Publishers, 1984.

Ali, Tariq, and Susan Watkins. *1968: Marching in the Streets*. New York: The Free Press, 1998.

———. *Street Fighting Years: An Autobiography of the Sixties*. London: Verso, 2005.

Allen, Ray. *Gone to the Country: The New Lost City Ramblers and the Folk Music Revival*. Champagne: University of Illinois Press, 2010.

Anderson, Terry H. *The Movement and the Sixties Protest in America from Greensboro to Wounded Knee*. Oxford: Oxford University Press, 1995.

Anthony, Gene. *The Summer of Love*. San Francisco: Last Gasp, 1995.

Badiou, Alain. *The Century*. Cambridge, UK: Polity Press 2007.

———. *Manifesto for Philosophy*. Albany: State University of New York Press, 1999.

———. *Handbook of Inaesthetics*. Redwood City: Stanford University Press. 2005.

Balibar, Etienne, and Immanuel Wallerstein. *Race, Nation, Class: Ambiguous Identities*. London: Verso Books, 1991.

Beauvoir, Simone de. *The Second Sex*. New York: Vintage Books, 1974.

Beebe, Lucius, and Charles Clegg. *San Francisco's Golden Era: A Picture Story of San Francisco Before the Fire*. Berkeley: Howell-North, 1960.

Belafonte, Harry. *My Song: A Memoir of Art, Race and Defiance*. Edinburgh: Canongate, 2012.

Bendix, Regina. *The Search for Authenticity: The Formation of Folklore Studies*. Madison: University of Wisconsin Press, 1997.

Berman, Marshall. *The Politics of Authenticity: Radical Individualism and the Emergence of Modern Society*. New York: Atheneum Books, 1970/London: Verso Books, 2009.

Bernstein, David W., ed. *The San Francisco Tape Music Center: 1960s Counterculture and the Avant-Garde*. Berkeley: University of California Press, 2008.

Bloch, Ernst. *The Utopian Function of Art and Literature: Selected Essays*. Cambridge, MA: MIT Press, 1988.

Bloch, Marc. *The Historian's Craft*. New York: Knopf, 1953.

Bloom, Joshua, and Waldo E. Martin, Jr. *Black against Empire: The History and Politics of the Black Panther Party*. Berkeley: University of California Press, 2013.

Boal, Iain, Janferie Stone, Michael Watts, Cal Winslow, eds. *West of Eden, Communes and Utopia in Northern California*. Oakland: PM Press, 2012.

Boyd, Joe. *White Bicycles: Making Music in the 1960s*. London: Serpent's Tail, 2006.

Boyle, Robert. *GI Revolts: The Breakdown of the U.S. Army in Vietnam*. San Francisco: United Front Press, 1973.

Braunstein, Peter, and Michael William Doyle, eds. *Imagine Nation: The American Counterculture of the 1960s and '70s*. New York: Routledge, 2002.

Brook, James, Chris Carlsson, and Nancy J. Peters, eds. *Reclaiming San Francisco: History, Politics, Culture*. San Francisco: City Lights Books, 1998.

Brown, Elaine. *A Taste of Power: A Black Woman's Story*. New York: Pantheon Books, 1992.

Bruce, Lenny. *How to Talk Dirty and Influence People: An Autobiography*. Chicago: Playboy Press, 1972.

Brustein, Robert. *Revolution as Theater: Notes on the New Radical Style*. New York: Liveright, 1971.

Carlsson, Chris, and Lisa Ruth Elliott, eds. *Ten Years That Shook the City: San Francisco 1968–1978*. San Francisco: City Lights Foundation Books, 2011.

Clayton, Martin, Trevor Herbert, and Richard Middleton, eds. *The Cultural Study of Music: A Critical Introduction*. New York: Routledge, 2003.

Cleaver, Eldridge. *Soul on Ice*. San Francisco: Ramparts Press, 1968.

Cleaver, Kathleen, and George Katsiaficas, eds. *Liberation, Imagination, and the Black Panther Party: A New Look at the Panthers and Their Legacy*. New York: Routledge, 2001.

Cooper, John M., ed. *Plato: Complete Works*. Indianapolis: IN: Hackett Publishing Co., 1997.

Cortright, David. *Soldiers in Revolt: GI Resistance During the Vietnam War*. Chicago: Haymarket Books, 1975.

Coyote, Peter. *Sleeping Where I Fall: A Chronicle*. New York: Counterpoint, 1998.

Cushing, Lincoln. *All of Us or None: Social Justice Posters of the San Francisco Bay Area*. Berkeley: Heyday Books, 2012.

Dannen, Fredric. *Hit Men: Power Brokers and Fast Money inside the Music Business*. New York: Vintage Books, 1991.

Davis, Angela Y. *Angela Davis: An Autobiography*. New York: International Publishers, 1974.

———. *Blues Legacies and Black Feminism*. New York: Vintage Books, 1998.

Davis, R.G. *The San Francisco Mime Troupe: The First Ten Years* Palo Alto: Ramparts Press, 1975.

Debord, Guy. *Society of the Spectacle*. Detroit: Black and Red/Radical America, 1970 (unauthorized); translated by Donald Nicholson-Smith. New York: Zone Books 1995.

de Grazia, Edward. *Girls Lean Back Everywhere: The Law of Obscenity and the Assault on Genius*. New York: Vintage Books, 1993.

Denisoff, R. Serge. *Great Day Coming: Folk Music and the American Left*. Baltimore: Penguin Books, 1971.

Denning, Michael. *The Cultural Front: The Laboring of American Culture in the Twentieth Century*. London: Verso, 1997.

Doggett, Peter. *There's a Riot Going On: Revolutionaries, Rock Stars and the Rise and Fall of the '60s*. Edinburgh: Canongate, 2007.

Du Bois, W.E.B. *The Souls of Black Folk*. New York: Dover Publications, 1994.

Duncan, Isadora. *Isadora Speaks*. Edited by Franklin Rosemont. San Francisco: City Lights Books, 1981.

Durant, Sam, ed. *Black Panther: The Revolutionary Art of Emory Douglas*. New York: Rizzoli International Publications, 2007.

Edwards, Harry. *Black Students*. New York: The Free Press, 1970.

Ehrenreich, Barbara. *Dancing in the Streets: A History of Collective Joy*. New York: Metropolitan Books, 2006.

Eisen, Jonathan, ed. *The Age of Rock: Sounds of the American Cultural Revolution*. New York: Vintage Books, 1969.

Elbaum, Max. *Revolution in the Air: Sixties Radicals Turn to Lenin, Mao, and Che*. London: Verso, 2002.

Erlewine, Michael. *Classic Posters: The Interviews, Book One*. Big Rapids, MI: Heart Center Publications, 2011.

Eymann, Marcia A., and Charles Wollenberg. *What's Going On? California and the Vietnam Era*. Berkeley: University of California Press, 2004.

Fanon, Frantz. *The Wretched of the Earth*. New York: Grove Press, 1963.

Ferlinghetti, Lawrence, and Nancy J. Peters. *Literary San Francisco: A Pictorial History from Its Beginnings to the Present Day*. San Francisco: City Lights Books/Harper & Row Publishers, 1980.

Firsoff, George. *1968 Spring of Youth*. Self-published, 1980.

Foner, Philip S., ed. *The Black Panthers Speak*. Cambridge, MA: Da Capo Press, 1995.

Fortunate Eagle, Adam. *Alcatraz! Alcatraz! The Indian Occupation of 1969–1971*. Berkeley: Heyday Books, 1992.

Fraser, Ronald, ed. *1968: A Student Generation in Revolt*. New York: Pantheon Books, 1988.

Friedan, Betty. *The Feminine Mystique*. New York: Dell Publishing Co., 1970.

Friedman, Myra. *Buried Alive: The Biography of Janis Joplin*. New York: Bantam Books, 1974.

Frith, Simon. *The Sociology of Rock*. London Constable & Robinson, 1978.

Gillett, Charlie. *The Sound of the City: The Rise of Rock and Roll*. London, Souvenir Press 1970 (rev. ed., 1983).

Gitlin, Todd. *The Sixties: Years of Hope, Days of Rage*. New York: Bantam Books, 1987.

Glatt, John. *Rage & Roll: Bill Graham and the Selling of Rock*. New York: Birch Lane Press, 1993.

Gleason, Ralph J. *The Jefferson Airplane and the San Francisco Sound*. New York: Ballantine Books, 1969.

Goldberg, Isaac. *Tin Pan Alley: A Chronicle of the American Popular Music Racket*. New York: The John Day Co., 1930.

Goodman, Fred. *The Mansion on the Hill: Dylan, Young, Geffen, Springsteen and the Head-on Collision of Rock and Commerce*. London: Jonathan Cape, 1997.

Graham, Bill, and Robert Greenfield. *Bill Graham Presents: My Life Inside Rock and Out*. Cambridge, MA: Da Capo Press, 2004

Harris, Joanna Gewertz. *Beyond Isadora: Bay Area Dancing 1915–1965*. Berkeley: Regent Press, 2009.

Heins, Marjorie. *Strictly Ghetto Property: The Story of Los Siete de la Raza*. Berkeley: Ramparts Press, 1972.

Henderson, Robbin. *The Whole World's Watching: Peace and Social Justice Movements of the 1960s & 1970s*. Berkeley: Berkeley Arts Center Association, 2001.

Hilliard, David, ed. *The Black Panther, Intercommunal News Service*. New York: Atria Books, 2007.

Hirshey, Gerri. *Nowhere to Run: The Story of Soul Music*. Cambridge, MA: Da Capo Press, 1994.

Ho, Fred, ed. *Legacy to Liberation: Politics and Culture of Revolutionary Asian Pacific America*. Oakland: Big Red Media/AK Press, 2000.

Hobsbawm, Eric. *Interesting Times: A Twentieth-Century Life*. New York: Pantheon Books, 2002.

———. *Uncommon People: Resistance, Rebellion, and Jazz*. New York: The New Press, 1998.

Holt, Sid, ed. *The Rolling Stone Interviews: The 1980s*. New York: St. Martin's Press, 1989.

Hunt, Andrew E. *The Turning: A History of Vietnam Veterans against the War*. New York: New York University Press, 1999.

Jackson, George. *Soledad Brother: The Prison Letters of George Jackson*. London: Jonathan Cape/Penguin Books Ltd. UK, 1970.

Jacoby, Annice, ed. *Street Art San Francisco: Mission Muralismo*. New York Abrams Books, 2009. (Foreword by Carlos Santana.)

Johnson, Bruce, and Martin Cloonan. *The Dark Side of the Tune: Popular Music and Violence*. Farnham, UK: Ashgate Publishing Ltd., 2009.

Johnson, Heather. *If These Halls Could Talk: A Historical Tour through San Francisco Recording Studios*. Boston: Thomson Course Technology PTR, 2006.

Johnson, Troy R., ed. *You Are on Indian Land! Alcatraz Island, 1969–1971*. Los Angeles: UCLA American Indian Studies Center, 1995.

Jones, Charles E., ed. *The Black Panther Party Reconsidered*. Baltimore: Black Classic Press, 1998.

Joseph, Peniel E. *Waiting 'til the Midnight Hour: A Narrative History of Black Power in America*. New York: Henry Holt & Co., 2006.

Kaliss, Jeff. *I Want to Take You Higher: The Life and Times of Sly and the Family Stone*. New York: Backbeat Books, 2008.

Katsiaficas, George. *The Imagination of the New Left: A Global Analysis of 1968*. Boston: South End Press, 1987.

Kellner, Douglas MacKay. *Heidegger's Concept of Authenticity*. Ann Arbor, MI: University Microfilms, 1973.

Knight, Arthur and Kit, eds. *Kerouac and the Beats: A Primary Sourcebook*. New York: Paragon House. 1988.

Krieger, Susan. *Hip Capitalism*. Beverly Hills: Sage Publications, 1979.

Kurlansky, Mark. *1968: The Year That Rocked the World*. London: Jonathan Cape, 2004.

Lee, Martin A., and Bruce Shlain. *Acid Dreams: The Complete Social History of LSD: the CIA, the Sixties, and Beyond*. New York: Grove Press 1985.

Leonard, Aaron J., and Conor A. Gallagher. *Heavy Radicals: The FBI's Secret War on America's Maoists*. London: Zero Books, 2015.

Lewis, George H., ed. *Side-Saddle on the Golden Calf: Social Structure and Popular Culture in America*. Pacific Palisades, CA: Goodyear Publishing Co. Inc., 1972.

Louie, Steve, and Glenn K. Omatsu, eds. *Asian Americans: The Movement and the Moment*. Los Angeles: UCLA Asian American Studies Center Press, 2001.

Louvre, Alf, and Jeffrey Walsh, eds. *Tell Me Lies about Vietnam: Cultural Battles for the Meaning of the War*. Knowlhill, UK: Milton Keynes/Philadelphia: Open University Press, 1988.

Major, Reginald. *A Panther Is a Black Cat: An Account of the Early Years of the Black Panther Party—Its Origins, Its Goals, and Its Struggle for Survival*. Baltimore: Black Classic Press, 2006.

Marcus, Greil. *Like a Rolling Stone: Bob Dylan and the Crossroads*. New York: Public Affairs 2006.

Marcuse, Herbert. *Counterrevolution and Revolt*. Boston: Beacon Press, 1972.

———. *An Essay on Liberation*. Boston: Beacon Press, 1969.

————. *One-Dimensional Man*, London: Sphere Books, 1968.

————. *Reason and Revolution, Hegel and the Rise of Social Theory*. Boston: Beacon Press, 1960.

Marqusee, Mike. *Wicked Messenger: Bob Dylan and the 1960s*. New York: Seven Stories Press, 2005 (originally published as *Chimes of Freedom: The Politics of Bob Dylan*. New York, The New Press, 2003).

Marx, Karl. *Economic and Philosophic Manuscripts of 1844*. Moscow: Progress Publishers, 1959.

————. *Grundrisse*. London: Penguin Books, 1993.

McCarthy, Jim, and Ron Sansoe. *Voices of Latin Rock: The People and Events That Created This Sound*. Milwaukee: Hal Leonard Corp., 2004.

McNally, Dennis. *A Long Strange Trip: The Inside History of the Grateful Dead*. New York: Broadway Books, 2002.

Michaels, Leonard, David Reid, and Raquel Scherr, eds. *West of the West: Imagining California: An Anthology*. Berkeley: University of California Press, 1989.

Miller, Jim, ed. *The Rolling Stone Illustrated History of Rock & Roll*. New York: Random House, 1976.

Morris, "Indian Joe," and Linda C. *Alcatraz Indian Occupation Diary, Nov. 20, 1969–June 11, 1971*. Self-published, 2001 (2nd ed.).

Neale, Jonathan. *The American War, Vietnam 1960–1975*. London: Bookmarks Publications Ltd., 2001.

Newton, Huey P. *War against the Panthers: A Study of Repression in America*. New York: Harlem River Press, 1996.

Ngugi wa Thiong'o. *Penpoints, Gunpoints, and Dreams*. Oxford: Clarendon Press, 1998.

Noyes, Henry. *China Born: Adventures of a Maverick Bookman*. San Francisco: China Books and Periodicals Inc., 1989.

Nuzum, Eric. *Parental Advisory: Music Censorship in America*. New York: Harper Perennial, 2001.

Palao, Alec. *Love Is the Song We Sing: San Francisco Nuggets 1965–1970*. Burbank, CA: Rhino Entertainment, 2007.

Pearlman, Lise. *The Sky's the Limit: People v. Newton: The Real Trial of the 20th Century?* Berkeley: Regent Press, 2012.

Peck, Abe. *Uncovering the Sixties: The Life and Times of the Underground Press*. New York: Citadel Press, 1991.

Perry, Charles. *The Haight-Ashbury: A History*. New York: Wenner Books, 2005.

Placksin, Sally. *Jazzwomen: 1900 to the Present, Their Words, Lives, and Music*. London: Pluto Press 1985.

Rancière, Jacques. *The Politics of Aesthetics: The Distribution of the Sensible*. London: Continuum Books, 2006.

Raskin, Jonah. *The Mythology of Imperialism*. New York: Random House, 1971.

Reich, Charles A. *The Greening of America*. New York: Random House, 1970.

Reuss, Richard A., and JoAnne C. Reuss. *American Folk Music & Left-Wing Politics, 1927–1957*. Lanham, MD: The Scarecrow Press Inc., 2000.

Richmond, Al. *A Long View from the Left: Memoirs of an American Revolutionary*. Boston: Houghton Mifflin Co., 1973.

Roszak, Theodore. *The Making of a Counter Culture: Reflections on the Technocratic Society and Its Youthful Opposition*. New York: Anchor Books 1969.

Rousseau, Jean-Jacques. *Politics and the Arts: Letter to D'Alembert on the Theater*. Ithaca: Agora Editions, 1960.

Sakolsky, Ron, and Fred Wei-han Ho. eds. *Sounding Off!, Music as Subversion/Resistance/ Revolution*. Brooklyn: Autonomedia, 1995.

Schwartz, Harvey. *Solidarity Stories: An Oral History of the ILWU*. Seattle: University of Washington Press, 2009.

Selvin, Joel. *San Francisco: The Musical History Tour*. San Francisco: Chronicle Books, 1996.

———. *Sly and the Family Stone: An Oral History*. New York, Avon Books, 1998.

———. *Summer of Love: The Inside Story of LSD, Rock & Roll, Free Love and High Times in the Wild West*. New York: Cooper Square Press, 1999.

Stansill, Peter, and David Zane Mairowitz, eds., *BAMN (By Any Means Necessary): Outlaw Manifestos and Ephemera, 1965–70*. Brooklyn: Autonomedia, 1999.

Stewart, Sean. *On the Ground: An Illustrated Anecdotal History of the Sixties Underground Press in the U.S.* Oakland: PM Press, 2011.

Stoll, Jerry. *I Am a Lover*. Sausalito, CA: Angel Island Publications, 1961.

Suisman, David. *Selling Sounds: The Commercial Revolution in American Music*. Cambridge, MA: Harvard University Press, 2009.

Tamarkin, Jeff. *Got a Revolution? The Turbulent Flight of Jefferson Airplane*. New York: Atria Books, 2003.

Tenaille, Frank. *Music Is the Weapon of the Future: Fifty Years of African Popular Music*. Chicago: Lawrence Hill Books, 2002.

Tent, Pam. *Midnight at the Palace: My Life as a Fabulous Cockette*. Los Angeles: Alyson Books, 2004.

Thomas, Pat. *Listen, Whitey! The Sights and Sounds of Black Power 1965–1975*. Seattle: Fantagraphics Books, 2012.

Thompson, Hunter S. *Gonzo Papers, Vol. 1: The Great Shark Hunt: Strange Tales from a Strange Time*. New York: Summit Books, 1979.

Trilling, Lionel. *Sincerity and Authenticity*. Cambridge, MA: Harvard University Press, 1971.

Unterberger, Richie. *Eight Miles High: Folk-Rock's Flight from Haight-Ashbury to Woodstock*. San Francisco: Backbeat Books, 2003.

———. *Turn! Turn! Turn! The '60s Folk-Rock Revolution*. San Francisco: Backbeat Books, 2002.

Utter, Jack. *American Indians: Answers to Today's Questions*. Lake Ann, MI: National Wooodlands Publishing Co., 1993.

Vico, Giambattista. *The New Science*. Ithaca: Cornell University Press, 1968.

Vilar, Pierre. *A History of Gold and Money, 1450–1920*. London: Verso, 1991.

Wallerstein, Immanuel. *The Essential Wallerstein*. New York: The New Press, 2000.

Waterhouse, Larry G., and Mariann G. Wizard. *Turning the Guns Around: Notes on the GI Movement*. New York: Praeger Publishers, 1971.

Zappa, Frank. *The Real Frank Zappa Book*. New York: Poseidon Press, 1989.

Zaroulis, Nancy, and Gerald Sullivan. *Who Spoke Up? American Protest against the War in Vietnam 1963–1975*. New York: Doubleday & Company, Inc., 1984.

Zimmerman, Nadya. *Counterculture Kaleidoscope: Musical and Cultural Perspectives on Late Sixties San Francisco*. Ann Arbor: University of Michigan Press, 2008.

Pamphlets

The New York Radical Women, *Notes from the First Year*, June 1968.

W.E.B. Du Bois Clubs of America. *FSM: The Free Speech Movement at Berkeley*. 1965.

Magazines

Indians of Alcatraz All Tribes, Vol. 1, no. 2, February 1970.

Insurgent, Vol. 1, no. 1, March–April 1965.

"The 100 Greatest Artists of All Time" *Rolling Stone* (special edition), December 2, 2010.

Film and Video

Angio, Joe. *Melvin Van Peebles: How to Eat Your Watermelon in White Company (and Enjoy It)*. HVE/Image Entertainment, 2005.

Antonioni, Michelangelo. *Zabriskie Point*. Metro-Goldwyn-Mayer, 1970.

Charles, Larry. *Masked and Anonymous*. BBC Film/Intermedia Films/Sony Picture Classics, 2004. (Film co-written by Larry Charles and Bob Dylan, under the pseudonym Sergei Petrov.)

Christensen, Eric. *Trips Festival 1966—the Movie*. Trips Festival, 2008.

Cohen, Allen, ed. *The San Francisco Oracle*. 2005

Desansart, Céline, and Alice Gaillard. *Les Diggers San Francisco*. Canal+, 1998.

Freedom Archives. *COINTELPRO 101*. PM Press, 2011.

Kitchell, Mark. *Berkeley in the Sixties*. California Newsreel/First Run Features, 1990.

Nelson, Robert. *Oh Dem Watermelons*. San Francisco Mime Troupe, 1965.

O'Connell, Jack. *Revolution*. 1968.

Payne, Roz, ed. *What We Want, What We Believe: The Black Panther Party Library*. AK Press, 2006.

Peoples, David. *How We Stopped the War*, 1967. (Follows Country Joe and the Fish on their way to an antiwar rally.)

Silber, Glenn, and Claudia Vianello. *Troupers*. Catalyst Media, 1985.

Stoll, Jerry. *Sons and Daughters*. American Documentary Films, 1967.

Wadleigh, Michael. *Woodstock: The Director's Cut*. Warner Bros., 1994.

Zagone, Robert N. *Jefferson Airplane/the Grateful Dead/Santana: A Night at the Family Dog*. Eagle Vision, 2007.

Zeiger, David. *Sir! No Sir!* Displaced Films, 2005.

Notes

Foreword

1   See Chapters 3 and 6 for details of Ngugi wa Thiong'o's thinking.
2   W.E.B. Du Bois, *The Souls of Black Folk* (Chicago: McClurg, 1903), 13.

Chapter 1

1   Pierre Vilar, *A History of Gold and Money, 1450–1920* (London: Verso 1976), 324.
2   Isadora Duncan, *Der tanz der zukunft (The Dance of the Future)* (Leipzig: Eugen Diederichs, 1903), 24–26.
3   Joanna Gewertz Harris, *Beyond Isadora: Bay Area Dancing 1915–1965* (Berkeley: Regent Press, 2009).
4   Jean-Jacques Rousseau's *Discourse on Inequality, The Social Contract*, and *Emile*, had a particular impact on artists, poets, musicians and, perhaps most tellingly, on Isadora herself—both as a dancer and as an educator. See Isadora Duncan, *Isadora Speaks* (San Francisco: City Lights Books, 1981), 55 and 81.
5   Lenore Peters Job, *Looking Back While Surging Forward* (Berkeley: Heyday Books, 1984), 66, 67, 68.
6   Duncan, *Isadora Speaks*, 61.
7   Indeed, particularly as it was developed in San Francisco, it heralded the women's and gay liberation movements that erupted half a century later. This is evident in the themes chosen by many choreographers, as well as in the artistic milieu that welcomed free spirits, women, and gay people. See Duncan, *Isadora Speaks*; Harris, *Beyond Isadora*.
8   Curt Gentry, *Frame-up: The Incredible Case of Tom Mooney and Warren Billings* (New York: W.W. Norton & Co., 1967).
9   Gewertz, *Beyond Isadora*.
10 Masha Zakheim Jewett, *Coit Tower: Its History and Art* (San Francisco: Volcano Press, 1983).
11 Joel Selvin, "Don't Let the Tweed Jackets, Trench Coat and Pipe Fool You—Ralph J. Gleason Was an Apostle of Jazz and Rock with Few Peers," *SF Gate*, December 23, 2004.
12 Interview with the author. Jerry Stoll, who died in 2004, was a world-renowned photographer and filmmaker, a lifelong political activist, and a key link between the arts and politics, particularly as they began to take on a specifically San Franciscan style. (The lettering on the cover of *I Am a Lover* uses the typeface that became known as

"psychedelic," ubiquitous on show posters for the Fillmore and the Avalon Ballroom). Not only was he the official photographer at the Monterey Jazz Festival from its inception in 1958 to the mid-1960s, taking classic photos of Billie Holiday, Louis Armstrong, Miles Davis, and many others, he went on to make outstanding films that are fundamental political documents of the Sixties, including the anti-Vietnam War film *Sons and Daughters* (American Documentary Films, 1967) and films about Daniel Ellsberg and the Black Panthers.

13 Interview with the author.

14 Michael Denning, *The Cultural Front* (New York: Verso, 1997).

15 Larry R. Salomon, "The Movement for Jobs in Civil Rights–Era San Francisco, 1963–64," MA thesis, San Francisco State University, 1994, http://online.sfsu.edu/socialj/context/context13.pdf.

16 Ibid., 91.

17 Ibid., 44.

18 Michael Erlewine, *Classic Posters: The Interviews, Book One* (Big Rapids, MI: Heart Center Publications, 2011), 12.

19 Adam Fortunate Eagle, *Alcatraz! Alcatraz!* (Berkeley: Heyday Books, 1992), 15.

20 "Sioux on the Warpath," *San Francisco Examiner*, March 8, 1964, http://online.sfsu.edu/socialj/TextScans/Sheraton11.jpg.

21 Ibid.

22 Mime Troupe founder Ron Davis wrote: "Playacting in public for the TV cameras became the main theatre. The mix began in earnest and so, too, the grand confusion. People forgot that for a theatre group, whether it be guerrilla, agitprop, or simply hysterical, *the presentation is the meat of the action*, even though the drama may be a contrived happening, not a literary story, or an adaptation of a play. The action in view is what we learn from. When we actually cross the picket line, punch the cop, throw the real firebomb, tear down the fence, sit in front of a truck, we are not doing theatre. Actors, writers, or directors who confuse theatrical representations with life will struggle desperately to approach reality and become speed freak schizophrenics." See R.G. Davis, *The San Francisco Mime Troupe: The First Ten Years* (San Francisco: Ramparts Press, 1975), 171.

23 "Pact Ends Siege at Palace," *San Francisco Examiner*, March 8, 1964, http://online.sfsu.edu/socialj/TextScans/Sheraton11.jpg.

24 William Issel, "Land Values, Human Values, and the Preservation of the City's Treasured Appearance," *Pacific Historical Review*, November 1999, http://web.uvic.ca/~jlutz/courses/hist317/pdfs/Issel%20San%20Francisco%20Freeway%20Revolt.pdf. See also "The Central Freeway and the Freeway Revolt," *Removing Freeways—Restoring Cities*, http://www.preservenet.com/freeways/FreewaysCentral.html.

25 Interview with the author.

26 The Soledad Brothers—George Jackson, Fleeta Drumgo, and John Clutchette—were charged with murdering a prison guard. Their case was made famous by the Soledad Brothers Defense Committee, organized by their lawyer Fay Stender and led by Angela Davis. Support came from many public luminaries, including Marlon Brando, Jane Fonda, Pete Seeger, Noam Chomsky, and Dr. Benjamin Spock. Stender's efforts led to the publication of Jackson's internationally acclaimed *Soledad Brother: The Prison Letters of George Jackson*. Jackson's seventeen-year-old brother, Jonathan, led an armed takeover of a courtroom in Marin County, leading to his own death and that of Judge Harold Haley. The guns Jonathan Jackson used had been purchased by Angela Davis, who was charged with conspiracy, kidnapping, and murder. See https://en.wikipedia.org/wiki/Soledad_Brothers#Soledad_Brothers_Defense_Committee.

See also Angela Davis, *Angela Davis: An Autobiography* (New York: International Publishers, 1974) and George Jackson, *Soledad Brother: The Prison Letters of George Jackson* (New York: Penguin Books, 1970).

27 Henry Noyes, *China Born* (San Francisco: China Books, 1989), 81.

28 Ibid., 82. Noyes adds that in the following fifteen years, over one million copies of the *Little Red Book* were sold.

29 Many theorists/philosophers who would be influential in the subsequent decades were barely known in the English-speaking world before the 1970s. Three notable examples, Antonio Gramsci, Theodor Adorno, and Guy Debord, are now so frequently cited in reference to the Sixties, to art and culture, and to the system's ultimate success in defeating the revolution that it might be imagined they were highly influential figures guiding the movement, but this is not the case. Indeed, Gramsci was only available in English in 1970, Debord, the same year, and Adorno in 1972. The now-famous *Society of the Spectacle* (Detroit: Black and Red, 1977, https://www.marxists.org/reference/archive/debord/society.htm), published in French in 1967, was broadly influential in France, but not in America. Gramsci and Adorno would arrive even later. On a local note, Martin Nicolaus translated Marx's *Grundrisse* in San Francisco in 1970. It was first available in English in 1973 (Penguin Books/New Left Review, 1973, https://www.marxists.org/archive/marx/works/1857/grundrisse).

30 Max Elbaum, *Revolution in the Air* (New York: Verso Books, 2002); Aaron J. Leonard and Conor A. Gallagher, *Heavy Radicals: The FBI's Secret War on America's Maoists* (London: Zero Books, 2015).

31 Refer to the bibliography for details on these books.

Chapter 2

1 Langston Hughes, *The Panther and the Lash* (New York: Vintage Classics, 1967), 1.

2 James Baldwin, *The Fire Next Time* (New York: The Dial Press, 1963), 88.

3 "Report of the National Advisory Commission on Civil Disorders: Summary of Report," http://www.eisenhowerfoundation.org/docs/kerner.pdf; "Kerner Commission," *Wikipedia*, https://en.wikipedia.org/wiki/Kerner_Commission. See also "The Great Rebellion," http://www.detroits-great-rebellion.com/Kerner-Report---The-Great-Rebellion.html.

4 "1967 Detroit Riot," *Wikipedia*, https://en.wikipedia.org/wiki/1967_Detroit_riot.

5 The Deacons for Defense and Justice was an organization formed to defend civil rights workers in the South. They grew to have twenty-one chapters in Louisiana, Mississippi, and Alabama. See "Deacons for Defense and Justice," *Wikipedia*, https://en.wikipedia.org/wiki/Deacons_for_Defense_and_Justice.

6 "Loving v. Virginia," *Wikipedia*, https://en.wikipedia.org/wiki/Loving_v._Virginia.

7 Aunt Jemima syrup and Uncle Ben's rice.

8 See "Hunters Point—Cops Shot Into Community Center Sheltering 200 Children," *The Movement*, October 1966, 1, https://libraries.ucsd.edu/farmworkermovement/ufwarchives/sncc/16B%20-%20October%201966.pdf.

9 The Panther's Ten-Point Program is available from many sources, including Huey P. Newton, *War against the Panthers: A Study of Repression in America* (New York: Harlem River Press, 1996).

10 Ben Cosgrove, "The Invention of Teenagers: LIFE and the Triumph of Youth Culture," *Time*, September 28, 2013, http://time.com/3639041/the-invention-of-teenagers-life-and-the-triumph-of-youth-culture/.

11 Michael E. Malone, and Roberts Myron. *From Pop to Culture* (New York: Holt, Rinehart and Winston, 1971), 178.

12   See Edward L. Bernays, *Propaganda* (New York: Horace Liveright 1928).

13   Michael Denning, *The Cultural Front* (New York: Verso Books, 1997), 24.

14   Maynard G. Krebs was a character on the TV show *Dobie Gillis*. Krebs was a caricature of a beatnik. As for *MAD* magazine, Theodore Roszak remarked in 1968, "The kids who were twelve when *MAD* first appeared are in their twenties now—and they have had a decade's experience in treating the stuff of their parent's lives as contemptible laughing stock."

15   Eric Hobsbawm, *Uncommon People* (New York: The New Press, 1998), 283.

16   Charlie Gillette, *The Sound of the City* (London: Souvenir Press, 1970), x.

17   Alan Freed was a DJ in Cleveland who hit upon the notion and has since been credited with the coinage. See "Alan Freed," *Wikipedia*, https://en.wikipedia.org/wiki/Alan_Freed.

18   *Father Knows Best* was a TV show portraying middle-class family life, aired alternately on CBS and NBC from 1954 until 1960. See "Father Knows Best," *Wikipedia*, https://en.wikipedia.org/wiki/Father_Knows_Best.

19   Eldridge Cleaver, *Soul on Ice* (New York: Delta, 1968), 81.

20   Steve Van Zandt's induction speech for the Hollies at the Rock and Roll Hall of Fame, New York City, March 15, 2010. See "The Hollies Rock and Roll Hall of Fame Induction 2010," *YouTube*, https://www.youtube.com/watch?v=nINruIwgEyE.

21   Little Richard, "100 Greatest Artists of All Time," *Rolling Stone*, http://www.rollingstone.com/music/lists/100-greatest-artists-of-all-time-19691231/little-richard-20110420.

22   Ibid.

23   "Almost certainly that was the result of the 'economic miracle' of the 1950s, which not only created a Western World of full employment, but also, probably for the first time, gave the mass of adolescents adequately paid jobs and therefore the money in the pocket, or an unprecedented share of middle-class parents' prosperity. It was this adolescents' market that transformed the music industry. From 1955, when rock-and roll was born, to 1959 American record sales rose by 36 percent every year. After a brief pause, the British Invasion of 1963, led by the Beatles, initiated an even more spectacular surge. U.S. record sales, which had grown from $277 million in 1955 to $600 million in 1959, had passed $2,000 million by 1973 (now including tapes). Seventy-five to 80 per cent of these sales represented rock music and similar sounds." Hobsbawm, *Uncommon People*, 283–84.

24   Eric Nuzum, *Parental Advisory: Music Censorship in America* (New York: Perennial, 2001). There are many accounts of organized campaigns to suppress rock 'n' roll, but Nuzum's book is a good place to start.

25   The Weavers included Pete Seeger and Lee Hays, composers of "If I Had a Hammer (The Hammer Song)," which was a hit for The Weavers, for Peter, Paul and Mary, and for Trini Lopez. Between 1950 and 1952, the Weavers sold over four million records and were at the top of the charts with Leadbelly's "Goodnight Irene" for fifteen weeks. See Richard A. Reuss and Joanne C. Reuss, *American Folk Music and Left-Wing Politics, 1927–1957* (Boston: Scarecrow Press, 2000), 235.

26   Joe Ferrandino, "Rock Culture and the Development of Social Consciousness," *Radical America*, November 1969. Ferrandino writes: "It is by now well known how record companies would buy rights to a song mostly from black people and then make millions off it. Billie Holiday's whole life is a testimony to this type of racist exploitation. A more obvious example (and one of *the* most famous 'cover' records) is Big Mama Thornton's 'Hound Dog' (written around 1952–53 by Lieber and Stoller). She sold her rights to the song for $500.00. Elvis Presley sold over two million copies, and Big Mama Thornton never received another penny."

27　For an excellent account of this infamous episode, see: Joe Boyd, *White Bicycles* (London: Serpent's Tail, 2006).

28　Norman Mailer, "The White Negro," *Dissent* 4, no. 3 (Fall 1957): https://www.dissentmagazine.org/online_articles/the-white-negro-fall-1957.

29　Eric Hobsbawm, *Interesting Times* (New York: Pantheon Books, 2002), 396.

30　George Lewis, *Side-Saddle on the Golden Calf* (Pacific Palisades: Goodyear Publishing Co., 1972), 226.

31　Thomas Powell, interview with the author.

32　Ibid.

33　Figures in Landon Y. Jones, "Swinging 60s?" *Smithsonian Magazine* (January 2006), 102–7.

34　See http://www.americanrhetoric.com/speeches/lbjweshallovercome.htm.

35　Interview with author. Rubinson's recollection is supported by numerous other sources, including https://en.wikipedia.org/wiki/Time_Has_Come_Today.

Chapter 3

1　The origins of rock 'n' roll are heatedly debated, but two facts are not controversial: Trixie Smith recorded, "My Man Rocks Me (with One Steady Roll)" in 1922, and later joined Sister Rosetta Tharpe in the John Hammond–inspired "Spirituals to Swing" concerts at Carnegie Hall in 1938, the year Tharpe recorded "Rock Me" for the Decca label. The song was marketed as gospel, but is musically indistinguishable from rhythm and blues or rock 'n' roll. Tharpe's lyrics, however, were predominantly religious, challenging prevailing notions that rock 'n' roll or rhythm and blues were confined to hedonism, sexuality, and inebriation.

2　Posters documenting these events are available on many websites such as: http://www.sixtiesposters.com/aorpart2.htm.

3　The Great! Society was a seminal group in two specific ways. The band included Grace Slick (later to join Jefferson Airplane), composer of the emblematic anthem "White Rabbit." Furthermore, Slick brought with her to the Airplane the other song heralding a new era, "Somebody to Love." Second, the band was produced by Sly Stone, a foundational link to all that was to follow.

4　Ralph J. Gleason, *The Jefferson Airplane and the San Francisco Sound* (New York: Ballantine Books, 1969), 30.

5　Ibid., 30–32.

6　Ibid.

7　Ibid., 3. The Family Dog consisted of Luria Castell, Ellen Harmon, Alton Kelly, and Jack Towle.

8　Gleason, *Jefferson Airplane and the San Francisco Sound,* 1–10.

9　Robert Greenfield, *Bill Graham Presents: My Life Inside Rock and Out* (London: Delta, 1992). In this notorious case, Ralph Gleason championed Graham's cause, effectively shaming the Board of Permit Appeals into reversing its earlier decision and granting Graham a permit.

10　On the W.E.B. Du Bois Clubs, see: "WEB Clubs of America," *Wikipedia*, http://keywiki.org/WEB_DuBois_Clubs_of_America. The Cuba trip was controversial, garnering much press attention; for example, see: "Students Heroes in Tour of Cuba," *Oakland Tribune*, September 7, 1963, http://newspaperarchive.com/us/california/oakland/oakland-tribune/1963/09-07/page-4.

11　David W. Bernstein, *The San Francisco Tape Music Center* (Berkeley: University of California Press, 2008), 22–23.

12　Gleason, *The Jefferson Airplane and the San Francisco Sound,* 1–10.

13 Joe Selvin, "For the Unrepentant Patriarch of LSD, Long, Strange Trip Winds back to Bay Area," *SF Gate*, July 12, 2007, http://www.sfgate.com/bayarea/article/For-the-unrepentant-patriarch-of-LSD-long-2581601.php. Owsley said: "I wound up doing time for something I should have been rewarded for. What I did was a community service, the way I look at it. I was punished for political reasons. Absolutely meaningless. Was I a criminal? No. I was a good member of society. Only my society and the one making the laws are different."

14 Interview with the author.

15 Interview with the author.

16 Lincoln Cushing, *All of Us or None* (Berkeley: Heyday Books, 2012).

17 See Chapter 5 for Gleason's exposition of this theme.

18 A few notable exceptions that prove the rule. An obscure essay published in 1988, called "Rockin' Hegemony: West Coast Rock and Amerika's War in Vietnam," written by Sunderland University professor John Storey makes the point: "The prevalence of this anti-war feeling was such that in the context of the counterculture all songs were in a sense against the war." Other such examples are to be found in George H. Lewis, ed., *Side-Saddle on the Golden Calf: Social Structure and Popular Culture in America* (Pacific Palisades, CA: Goodyear Publishing Co. Inc., 1972).

19 Examples abound, from Edgard Varèse to the Composers' Collective to John Cage, but perhaps the most pertinent examples were found among jazz artists in the Sixties (see Chapter 8 for more).

20 Ngugi wa Thiong'o, *Penpoints, Gunpoints, and Dreams* (Oxford: University Press Oxford, 1998), 37.

21 Lest there be any doubt, Tom Johnston, composer of the popular song "Listen to the Music" (1971), explicitly stated: "It was all based around this somewhat Utopian view of the world. The idea was that music would lift man up to a higher plane, and that world leaders, if they were able to sit down on some big grassy knoll where the sun was shining and hear music—such as the type I was playing—would figure out that everybody had more in common than they had not in common, and it was certainly not worth getting in such a bad state of affairs about. Everybody in the world would therefore benefit from this point of view. Just basically that music would make everything better. And of course I've since kind of realized it doesn't work that way [laughing]." See "Tom Johnson from the Doobie Brothers," *Songfacts*, http://www.songfacts.com/blog/interviews/tom_johnston_from_the_doobie_brothers/.

22 One prominent example is "I Dreamed I Saw Joe Hill Last Night," performed at Woodstock by Joan Baez.

Chapter 4

1 The original Greek *authentes* was used in two ways: "one who acts with authority" and "made by one's own hand." Common usage today expresses an opposition between the genuine and the fake, the original or the copy, lived experience versus being taught, even between the true and the false. In the Sixties, the quest for authenticity followed clear coordinates, audible in music, visible in black and white, and felt as much as thought.

2 Regina Bendix, *In Search of Authenticity* (Madison: University of Wisconsin Press, 1997), 18. Bendix quotes Mailer, citing Michael Berman (1988).

3 Doug Sahm was born and raised in San Antonio. His musical background included country, rhythm and blues, and Mexican music. The uses of instruments, rhythms, melodies, and harmonies derived from these sources came naturally to Sahm since he'd been steeped in them all his life. He sang in his own, southern-accented, voice

thereby complicating questions of authenticity. Yet he also knew who the masters of the forms he used were: Ray Charles, James Brown, and Aretha Franklin, to name but a few. He thus shared with virtually every musician an intimate knowledge of a cruel injustice.

4   Pat Thomas, *Listen, Whitey!* (Seattle: Fantagraphics Books, 2012), 11.

5   Eldridge Cleaver, *Soul on Ice* (New York: Delta, 1968), 75.

6   Thomas, *Listen, Whitey!*, 20.

7   Charlie Gillette, *The Sound of the City* (London: Souvenir Press, 1970), x.

8   As Joel Selvin wrote: "With an astute reading of the cultural climate, Sly Stone sketched the agenda of the Woodstock generation. His glitzy group boasted men and women, Black and white, putting into practice the left-wing principles of his songs." Joel Selvin, *Sly and the Family Stone: An Oral History* (New York: Avon Books, 1998), xiii.

9   Isaac Goldberg, *Tin Pan Alley: Chronicle of the American Popular Music Racket* (New York: John Day, 1930), 31.

10 Ralph J. Gleason, "Like a Rolling Stone," *American Scholar* 36, no. 4 (Autumn 1967): 555–63.

11 W.E.B. Du Bois, *The Souls of Black Folk* (New York: Dover, 1903), 7.

12 David Suisman, *Selling Sounds* (Cambridge, MA: Harvard University Press, 2002). On Ernest Hogan, the black man who composed "All Coons Look Alike to Me," see "Ernest Hogan," *Wikipedia*, https://en.wikipedia.org/wiki/Coon_song. Ernest Hogan composed "All Coons Look Alike to Me".

13 "Alexander's Ragtime Band," *Wikipedia*, http://en.wikipedia.org/wiki/Alexander%27s_Ragtime_Band. Even more to the point, the story of Scott Joplin, whose "Maple Leaf Rag" of 1899 was the first instrumental piece to sell over a million copies of sheet music and the first composition for which a composer was paid a royalty, demonstrates, in all its complexity, how the copyright system simultaneously rewards and punishes those who fall within its purview. Joplin was paid $50 and the unprecedented one cent per copy royalty for his composition by the music publisher John Stark & Son. So, on a million sales, Joplin earned $50 plus $10,000. If John Stark & Son charged five cents a copy, they made $40,000. Plus, they owned dozens, even hundreds, of other songs, while Joplin had only his own music, which, soon enough, nobody wanted to publish. See "Maple Leaf Rag," *Wikipedia*, http://en.wikipedia.org/wiki/Maple_leaf_rag.

14 Steven Garabedian, "Reds, Whites, and the Blues: Lawrence Gellert, 'Negro Songs of Protest,' and the Left-Wing Folk-Song Revival of the 1930s and 1940s," *American Quarterly* 57, no. 1 (March 2005): 179–206; Richard Reuss and Joanne C. Reuss, *American Folk Music and Left-Wing Politics* (Lanham, MA: Scarecrow Press, 2000), 95–98.

15 Harry Smith, ed., *Anthology of American Folk Music* (Washington, DC: Smithsonian Folkways Recordings, 1997). It is noteworthy that a young generation began listening to the music of the Anthology because it was genuine, not fake; it was more authentically popular *because* it was noncommercial, unlike the pop music being sold to them by the music industry. This was so in spite of the fact that it had originally been recorded for commercial purposes. This is clearly ironic, but not in the sense that young folk revivalists were deluding themselves about the sources of their "bible." Rather, the irony lies in the music industry stumbling upon timeless music, priceless to those who loved it, and attempting to turn it into a fashionable consumer good, something that quickly becomes dated and of no further interest. As young people became increasingly aware, the music industry proved not to be their friend.

16   Alan Lomax, Woody Guthrie, and Pete Seeger, *Hard Hitting Songs for Hard-Hit People* (New York: Oak Publications, 1967).

17   Michael Denning, *The Cultural Front* (New York: Verso Books, 1997).

18   *The Peter Albin Story,* produced by Barry Flast (Artist Archives, 2007). I am grateful to Barry for sharing these unique documents.

19   Sam Hinton was a harmonica player well known both as a musician and as the founder of the San Diego Folk Song Society. Mike Seeger, Pete's brother, was a founder of the New Lost City Ramblers and a highly respected musician in his own right. Jean Ritchie was a dulcimer player, songwriter, and pioneer in the folk music revival, earning the moniker "The Mother of Folk."

20   Barbara Dane was a singer who established herself in both folk and jazz. She played a vital role in San Francisco, running a nightclub, Sugar Hill: Home of the Blues, and supporting political struggle. The Chambers Brothers (with whom Dane sometimes appeared) are discussed in Chapter 2 of this book. The Blues Project was closely aligned with the experimental flights usually associated with the better-known Grateful Dead. Members went on to form more widely known groups, including Blood, Sweat & Tears. Richard and Mimi Farina were a highly acclaimed folk duo, their promising career cut short by Richard's untimely death in 1966.

21   Interview with the author.

22   Interview with the author.

23   Interview with the author.

24   Jim McCarthy and Ron Sansoe, *Voices of Latin Rock: The People and Events That Created This Sound* (Milwaukee: Hal Leonard, 2004).

25   Barry Lewis, *The Hedds as I Remember It*, http://home.unet.nl/kesteloo/hedds.html.

26   Bendix, *In Search of Authenticity.*

27   Theodor Adorno, *The Jargon of Authenticity* (Evanston, IL: Northwestern University Press, 1973), 160.

28   Marshall Berman, *The Politics of Authenticity: Radical Individualism and the Emergence of Modern Society* (New York: Verso, 2009), 317.

29   Adorno, *The Jargon of Authenticity,* 162–63.

30   "Wrote a Song for Everyone" by John Fogerty was released on the Creedence Clearwater Revival album *Green River* (Columbia, 1969).

Chapter 5

1   This long phrase is the actual title of the song as it appeared on the vinyl record.

2   Dennis McNally, *A Long Strange Trip* (New York: Broadway Books, 2002), 204.

3   "The Hippies Are Coming," *Newsweek*, June 12, 1967, 28–29.

4   Marcia A. Eymann, *What's Going On? California and the Vietnam Era* (Oakland Museum and the University of California Press, 2004), 4.

5   Ibid., 4.

6   Jerry Stoll, *Sons and Daughters* (American Documentary Films, 1967).

7   See Chapter 7 of this book for more on the revolt in the armed services.

8   Find *The Movement* archived at "SNCC Movement Newspaper," *Farmworker Movement Archives*, https://libraries.ucsd.edu/farmworkermovement/ufwarchives/index.shtml#sncc.

9   Numerous issues of *The Movement* provided the details for this account. For specific articles dealing with the police in the Haight, see: "Hunters Point—Cops Shot Into Community Center Sheltering 200 Children, *The Movement*, October 1966, 1, https://libraries.ucsd.edu/farmworkermovement/ufwarchives/sncc/16B%20 -%20October%201966.pdf; "Haight Street Blues," and "Cannon's Tale . . . or How

They Beat My Ass," *The Movement*, September 1968, 3, https://libraries.ucsd.edu/farmworkermovement/ufwarchives/sncc/08_September%201968.pdf.

10 Abe Peck, *Uncovering the Sixties: The Life and Times of the Underground Press* (New York: Pantheon, 1985).

11 George Katsiaficas, *The Imagination of the New Left: A Global Analysis of 1968* (Boston: South End Press, 1987), 143. Original sources are *Washington Post*, July 6, 1970, and Howard Zinn, *A People's History of the United States* (New York: HarperCollins, 2003), 490.

12 See Appendix I for more details.

13 See the Chapter 1 of this book. See also Preservation Institute, "San Francisco, CA, Central Freeway," http://www.preservenet.com/freeways/FreewaysCentral.html.

14 For more details see: Charles Perry, *The Haight Ashbury: A History* (New York: Warner Books, 2005).

15 Ibid., 123. The SFPD conducted many military-style sweeps of the Haight-Ashbury district in the late 1960s, which turned into full-scale police riots on several occasions. One in particular occurred on Sunday, February 18, 1968. See *San Francisco Express Times* Vol. 1, no. 5 (February 22, 1968), 1.

16 Ralph J. Gleason, *The Jefferson Airplane and the San Francisco Sound* (New York: Ballantine Books, 1969), 37.

17 Eric Noble, "The Artists Liberation Front and the Formation of the Sixties Counterculture: The Early History of the Digger Movement," *The Digger Archives*, December 7, 1996, http://www.diggers.org/alf.htm.

18 Ibid.

19 An 8 PM curfew was established in these districts. The SFPD claimed the Haight was part of the "Greater Fillmore." There was a large demonstration against the curfew, which was attacked by the police. Dozens were arrested in the Haight. See "Hunters Point—Cops Shot Into Community Center Sheltering 200 Children, 1, https://libraries.ucsd.edu/farmworkermovement/ufwarchives/sncc/16B%20-%20 October%201966.pdf.

20 Gleason, *The Jefferson Airplane and the San Francisco Sound*, 37–38.

21 Two other components contributed to San Francisco's growing reputation. When the Paul Butterfield Blues Band performed at the newly opened Fillmore Auditorium in March 1966, they set in motion one of the most important musical developments in a period full of them. Not only did this group, which was composed of black and white musicians (a real novelty at the time), bring a hard-edged Chicago blues to a young, San Franciscan audience unfamiliar with such music, but they returned to Chicago and told their associates about the appreciative response the audience had given them. (Members of the Butterfield Band would migrate to San Francisco and base themselves there shortly thereafter, as would a growing number of musicians from elsewhere). They opened the door for a flood of great Chicago blues artists, including Muddy Waters, Buddy Guy, and James Cotton, who would all become mainstays on San Francisco stages in the years to come. The second component was connected to the first. The welcome Chicago blues musicians were receiving was not confined to them or their particular style of music; it led to an unprecedented mixing of musical styles. James Cotton found himself sharing the stage with Lothar and the Hand People, Otis Rush with the Mothers, Muddy Waters with the Grateful Dead, and so on. An exchange, therefore, went in many directions at once. Musical barriers were broken with astonishing speed, leading, for example, to previously undreamed of experiments like the Butterfield Band's second album *East-West*. Released in August 1966, the title track was a long exploration of a John Coltrane/Indian raga-inspired

jam. In fact, this album and this group were as responsible as any for fostering the rock jam, an innovation of the era, before it degenerated into self-indulgent noodling. The Dead would later become famous for their improvisational flights, but *East-West* and the Butterfield Band provided an initial inspiration. It should be added that the Butterfield Band and guitarist Michael Bloomfield were a major influence on Carlos Santana, who first took the Fillmore stage with a blues band. The "word of mouth" that connected touring musicians throughout the country spread the incredible news that San Francisco was a place where anything could happen, and often did. You could see it in the crazy posters that promoted the shows. You could see it in the crazy clothes people wore to these shows. And you could see it in the mind-boggling fact that these shows were open to everyone—no age limits, no alcohol. Wow!

22 "Love-Pageant-Rally Held to 'Celebrate' New LSD Law," *Sunday Ramparts*, October 23, 1966; cited in: David Farber and Beth Bailey, *The Columbia Guide to America in the 1960s* (New York: Columbia University Press 2001), 145.

23 George Metesky, "The Ideology of Failure," *Berkeley Barb*, November 18, 1966, 6, http://www.diggers.org/diggers/digart2.html#The Ideology of Failure.

24 Charles McCabe, "Remember the Love Circus?" *The Digger Archives* http://www.diggers.org/comco/ccpaps1b.html#cc002.

25 Noble, "The Artists Liberation Front and the Formation of the Sixties Counterculture."

26 "The Marty Balin Show," *Artist Archives with Barry Flast*, 2009.

27 Interview with the author. See also R.G. Davis, *The San Francisco Mime Troupe: The First Ten Years* (San Francisco: Ramparts Press, 1975), 101–6.

28 Jim McCarthy and Ron Sansoe, *Voices of Latin Rock: The People and Events That Created This Sound* (Milwaukee: Hal Leonard, 2004).

29 "Overview," The Digger Archives, http://www.diggers.org/overview.htm.

30 Interview with the author.

31 Interview with the author.

32 Interview with the author.

33 See Chapter 3 for more details.

34 Interview with the author.

35 Interview with the author.

36 See Chapter 7 for more on Wild West.

37 Michael Erlwine, "Interview with Chet Helms by Michael Erlewine," in *Classic Posters: The Interviews Book*, ed. Michael Erlwine (Big Rapids, MI: Heart Center Publications, 2011), 5–35, https://www.astrologysoftware.com/download/classic_posters_1.pdf.

38 Interview with the author; all Champlin quotes are from this interview.

39 Interview with the author.

40 See Chapter 10 of this book for more details.

41 See Chapters 7 and 8 of this book for more details.

42 Mime Trouper founder Ron Davis recalled: "I suggested we consider the problem of power in relation to teaching, directing toward change, and being an example of change. I had grown worried because, in the late sixties, we were moving in zippy political and consumer currents; instant revolutionaries, psychedelic visionaries, and rock millionaires impressed all of us and there was little time for reflection. The media became so ubiquitous that the difference between stage and street dissolved. Life-style acting, a slogan of the poetic crude communists, smogged all thoughts." Pointedly, Davis described what many people saw as the ultimate folly of the Yippies. "The Yippies have taken the life-style acting of the Diggers (ca. 1966) and the theatrics of the 1940s and used both for politics. They assume that media actions will make

changes: 'If it appears in the newspaper, it happened, Ronny,' Jerry Rubin told me in jest and belief." R.G. Davis, *The San Francisco Mime Troupe: The First Ten Years* (San Francisco: Ramparts Press, 1975), 170.

43   David Hilliard, *The Black Panther Party Service to the People Programs* (Albuquerque: University of New Mexico Press, 2008).

44   Interview with the author.

45   Jim McCarthy and Ron Sansoe, *Voices of Latin Rock: The People and Events That Created This Sound* (Milwaukee: Hal Leonard, 2004).

46   Ibid., 73

47   Interview with the author.

48   The author's personal experience.

49   Perry, *The Haight Ashbury*, 190.

50   Dennis McNally, *A Long Strange Trip* (New York: Broadway Books, 2002), 202–3.

51   John Glatt, *Rage & Roll: Bill Graham and the Selling of Rock* (New York: Birch Lane Press, 1993), 68–69.

52   Ralph J. Gleason, "Monterey Plans Shaping Up," *San Francisco Chronicle*, April 21, 1967.

53   Glatt, *Rage & Roll*, 68–71.

Chapter 6

1   There are numerous translations of Plato, differing in tone and emphasis. The translation used here is not the one used by Gleason. It is, however, the one referred to most often in the many published works, including song and album titles, that link Plato to music in the Sixties. The source for the translation used here is: Plato, "The Republic," Book IV, 424c, in *Complete Works*, ed. John M. Cooper (Indianapolis: Hackett Publishing Company, 1997), 1056.

2   Ralph J. Gleason, "Like a Rolling Stone," *American Scholar* 36, no. 4 (Autumn 1967): 555–63.

3   Ngugi wa Thiong'o, *Penpoints, Gunpoints, and Dreams* (Oxford: Oxford University Press, 1998).

4   Quoted in Michael Denning, *The Cultural Front* (New York: Verso Books, 1997), 332, citing Jerry Wexler and David Ritz, *Rhythm and Blues: A Life in American Music* (New York: Albert Knopf, 1993), 17, 33, 24, 37. See also Ronald Sklar, "The Man Behind Rhythm and Blues," http://www.popentertainment.com/wexler.htm. All Wexler quotes are from these sources.

5   Fred Goodman, *The Mansion on the Hill* (London: Jonathan Cape, 1997), xi.

6   Literature on these subjects is diverse, ranging from questions of censorship/repression to questions of racism and discrimination. See Eric Nuzum, *Parental Advisory, Music Censorship in America* (New York: HarperCollins, 2001) and Richard A. Reuss, *American Folk Music & Left-Wing Politics* (London: Scarecrow Press, 2000).

7   Denning, *The Cultural Front*. The Popular Front was the policy of the Comintern, implemented by the Communist Party USA and crucial to the mobilization of artists and musicians in opposition to fascism in the 1930s–40s. It was enormously successful rallying a broad cross-section including some of the most influential figures in American culture.

8   Plato, "Phaedrus," 244 b and c, in *Complete Works*, ed. John M. Cooper, 522–23.

9   Giambattista Vico, *The New Science* (Ithaca: Cornell University Press, 1988), 102.

10   Philosopher Ernst Bloch pioneered the exploration of utopia beginning with his earliest work, written in 1918, *The Spirit of Utopia*, Anthony A. Nassar, trans. (Stanford: Stanford University Press, 2000), and concluding with his magnum opus, written between 1938 and 1947, *The Principle of Hope*, trans. Neville Plaice, Stephen Plaice,

and Paul Knight (Cambridge, MA: MIT Press, 1995). Bloch's detailed study of fairy tales is also exemplary. See *The Utopian Function of Art and Literature* (Cambridge: Massachusetts Institute of Technology, 1988). Throughout the Sixties, Bloch was actively engaged in the student movement in Germany. See Peter-Erwin Jansen, "Student Movements in German, 1968–1984," trans., Geoffrey A. Hale, http://www.datawranglers.com/negations/issues/98w/jansen_01.html.

11   Plato, *Phaedrus*, 244 d, in *Complete Works*, ed. John M. Cooper (Indianapolis: Hackett Publishing, 1997), 523.

12   Alain Badiou, *Handbook of Inaesthetics* (Stanford: Stanford University Press, 2005).

13   Joel Selvin, "Don't Let the Tweed Jackets, Trench Coat and Pipe Fool You—Ralph J. Gleason Was an Apostle of Jazz and Rock with Few Peers," *SF Gate*, December 23, 2004, http://www.sfgate.com/entertainment/article/Don-t-let-the-tweed-jackets-trench-coat-and-pipe-2661831.php.

14   See Chapter 10 in this book for more details.

15   Ralph J. Gleason, "Perspectives: Pitfalls For the Critics," *Rolling Stone*, March 29, 1973.

16   Jann Wenner, "Ralph J. Gleason In Perspective," *Rolling Stone*, July 17, 1975, 39–49.

17   Ralph J. Gleason, "The Tragedy at the Greek Theatre," *San Francisco Chronicle*, December 9, 1964.

18   Herbert Marcuse, *One-Dimensional Man* (first published by Routledge & Kegan Paul, 1964; quotes are from Sphere Books edition, 1970), 29

19   Ibid., 52.

20   Ibid., 58.

21   Ibid., 58.

22   Ibid., 63.

23   See note 10 above.

24   Ngugi wa Thiong'o. *Penpoints, Gunpoints, and Dreams* (Oxford: Oxford University Press, 1998), 132.

Chapter 7

1   The exceptions were black radio stations.

2   Susan Krieger, *Hip Capitalism* (Beverly Hills: Sage Publications, 1979).

3   David Suisman, *Selling Sounds* (Cambridge, MA: Harvard University Press, 2009).

4   Payola scandals have been numerous, not limited to the one mentioned here, and overall they only confirm that the music industry is an arm of the state. See Chapter 1 of this book.

5   Krieger, *Hip Capitalism*, 34.

6   Ibid., 35.

7   *The Golden Age of Underground Radio Featuring Tom Donahue*, (Chatsworth, CA: DCC Compact Classics, 1989).

8   "Tom Donahue: A Man with a Unique Career," *Tam News*, May 1, 1970.

9   Krieger, *Hip Capitalism*, 151–56.

10   Quoted in ibid., 169–70.

11   *The Golden Age of Underground Radio Featuring Tom Donahue*.

12   "The Peter Albin Story," *Artist Archives With Barry Flast*, 2007.

13   Interview with the author; all Rubinson quotes are from this interview.

14   Interview with the author; all Stubblebine quotes are from this interview.

15   "The Jerry Slick Story," *Artist Archives with Barry Flast*, 2007.

16   Interview with the author.

17   John Glatt, *Rage & Roll: Bill Graham and the Selling of Rock* (New York: Birch Lane Press, 1993), 69.

18 Ralph J. Gleason, *The Jefferson Airplane and the San Francisco Sound* (New York: Ballantine Books, 1969), interview with Bill Graham.
19 Interview with the author.
20 Interview with the author; all Taj Mahal quotes are from this interview.
21 Glatt, *Rage & Roll*, 268.
22 Ludwig Feuerbach, *Preface to the second edition of The Essence of Christianity*, https://www.marxists.org/reference/archive/feuerbach/works/essence/ec00.htm.

Chapter 8

1 Theodore Roszak published *The Making of a Counter Culture* in 1969 but that book was based on articles written for *The Nation* in March–April 1968.
2 Peter Braunstein and Michael William Doyle, *Historicizing the American Counterculture of the 1960s and '70s* essay published in *Imagine Nation* (New York: Routledge, 2002), 7.
3 J. Milton Yinger, "Contraculture and Subculture," *The American Sociological Review* 25, no. 4 (October 1960): 625–35, quoted in Braunstein and Doyle, "Historicizing the American Counterculture of the 1960s and '70s," 7. Yinger cites Talcott Parsons as the first to use the term "counter-culture" in *The Social System* (New York: Free Press, 1951), 522.
4 Theodore Roszak, *The Making of a Counter Culture: Reflections on the Technocratic Society and Its Youthful Opposition* (New York: Anchor Books, 1969), xii–xiii.
5 Ibid., xiii.
6 Ibid., 66.
7 Ibid., 65–66.
8 The subtitle of *The Making of a Counter Culture* was *Reflections on the Technocratic Society and Its Youthful Opposition*. Roszak frequently refers to the "revolt against the Technocracy."
9 Joan Holden, "The Wild West Rock Show: Shooting Up a Rock Bonanza," *Ramparts* 8, no. 6 (December 1969): 70, http://www.unz.org/Pub/Ramparts-1969dec-00070.
10 Ibid.
11 The opposition also included San Francisco Newsreel, the Black Panthers, Chinatown's Red Guard, SDS, Canyon Cinema, the San Francisco State Black Students Union, Los Siete de la Raza, and the Mission Rebels. See, R.G. Davis, *The San Francisco Mime Troupe: The First Ten Years* (San Francisco: Ramparts Press, 1975), 115
12 Dennis McNally, *A Long Strange Trip* (New York: Broadway Books, 2002), 322. Frank Werber was the manager of the Kingston Trio and the owner of the Trident restaurant in Sausalito.
13 Holden, "The Wild West Rock Show," 70.
14 Ibid., 76.
15 Theodore Roszak, "When the Counterculture Counted," *SF Gate*, December 23, 2001, http://www.sfgate.com/books/article/When-the-counterculture-counted-2835958.php.
16 Jason Michael Ferreira, "All Power to the People: A Comparative History of Third World Radicalism in San Francisco, 1968–1974," PhD dissertation, University of California, Berkeley, Fall 2003, 6.
17 Ibid.
18 Max Elbaum, *Revolution in the Air* (London: Verso Books, 2002).
19 George Katsiaficas, *The Imagination of the New Left* (Boston: South End Press, 1987), 124.
20 Ibid., 117.

21   Ali made the statement when he refused induction into the armed services. See https://www.youtube.com/watch?v=vd9aIamXjQI. On accounts of Vietnamese appeals to black GIs, see: Richard Boyle, *GI REVOLTS, The Breakdown of the U.S. Army in Vietnam* (San Francisco: United Front Press, 1973).

22   David Cortright, *Soldiers in Revolt* (Chicago: Haymarket Books, 2005), 25.

23   Larry G. Waterhouse and Mariann G. Wizard, *Turning the Guns Around* (New York: Praeger Publishers, 1971), 59.

24   Col. Robert D. Heinl Jr., "The Collapse of the Armed Forces," *Armed Forces Journal*, June 7, 1971, https://msuweb.montclair.edu/~furrg/Vietnam/heinl.html.

25   See the outstanding film *Sir! No Sir!* for a more accurate assessment of actual GI resistance.

26   John Whiteclay Chambers II, *To Raise an Army: The Draft Comes to Modern America* (New York: Free Press, 1987), 218.

27   Ibid.

28   Ibid.

29   Until the 26th Amendment to the U.S. Constitution was enacted July 1, 1971, the voting age was twenty-one. Draft age was eighteen.

30   "Operation Dewey Canyon III" took place April 19–23, 1971.

31   Marvin Garson, *San Francisco Express Times*, March 1969.

32   This chronology appears so frequently in accounts of the Sixties that it has become legendary. Manson's crimes actually predated Woodstock (August 1969) and Altamont (December 1969), but his notorious trial only commenced in June 1970. In any case, the progression from dream to nightmare was allegorical, with Manson the demon of dystopia.

33   V.I. Lenin, "On Cooperation," *Pravda* no. 115–16, May 26–27, 1923, http://www.marxists.org/archive/lenin/works/1923/jan/06.htm

34   "Colonial domination, because it is total and tends to over-simplify, very soon manages to disrupt in spectacular fashion the cultural life of a conquered people. This cultural obliteration is made possible by the negation of national reality, by new legal relations introduced by the occupying power, by the banishment of the natives and their customs to outlying districts by colonial society, by expropriation, and by the systematic enslaving of men and women." "Speech by Frantz Fanon at the Congress of Black African Writers, 1959: Reciprocal Bases of National Culture and the Fight for Freedom," https://www.marxists.org/subject/africa/fanon/national-culture.htm.

35   "The pipe dream that socialism can be achieved with the help of the dull instruments left to us by capitalism (the commodity as the economic cell, profitability, individual material interest as a lever, etc.) can lead into a blind alley. When you wind up there after having traveled a long distance with many crossroads, it is hard to figure out just where you took the wrong turn. Meanwhile, the economic foundation that has been laid has done its work of undermining the development of consciousness. To build communism it is necessary, simultaneous with the new material foundations, to build the new man and woman." Che Guevara, "From Algiers, for *Marcha*," March 12, 1965, https://www.marxists.org/archive/guevara/1965/03/man-socialism.htm.

36   "At present, our objective is to struggle against and overthrow those persons in authority who are taking the capitalist road, to criticize and repudiate the reactionary bourgeois academic 'authorities' and the ideology of the bourgeoisie and all other exploiting classes and to transform education, literature and art and all other parts of the superstructure not in correspondence with the socialist economic base, so as to facilitate the consolidation and development of the socialist system." "Decision of the Central Committee of the Chinese Communist Party Concerning the Great

Proletarian Cultural Revolution," August 8, 1966, http://92644389.weebly.com/uploads/1/2/8/7/12875181/decision_of_the_central_committee_of_the_2.pdf.

Chapter 9

1   Terry Cannon, *All Power to the People: The Story of the Black Panther Party* (San Francisco: Peoples Press, 1970), 44.

2   "Joint Communique of the United States of America and the People's Republic of China (Shanghai Communique)," *China Through a Lens*, February 28, 1972, http://www.china.org.cn/english/china-us/26012.htm.

3   Oscar Brown Jr., "The Lone Ranger," *Brother Where Are You* (Atlantic Records, March 1974).

4   "War Newcastle City Hall June 1976," *Vintagerock's Weblog*, Originally found on War's website, currently available at: https://vintagerock.wordpress.com/category/war/.

5   Jim McCarthy and Ron Sansoe, *Voices of Latin Rock: The People and Events That Created This Sound* (Milwaukee: Hal Leonard, 2004).

6   Pat Thomas, *Listen, Whitey! The Sights and Sounds of Black Power 1965–1975* (Seattle: Fantagraphics Books, 2012).

7   Interview with the author.

8   Peter Doggett, *There's a Riot Going On* (Edinburgh: Canongate Books, 2007), 415.

9   W.E.B. Du Bois, *The Souls of Black Folk* (Chicago: McClurg, 1903), 13.

10   Ibid., 125.

11   "Proletariat," *Wikipedia*, https://en.wikipedia.org/wiki/Proletariat.

12   Karl Marx, *A Contribution to the Critique of Hegel's Philosophy of Right*, http://www.marxists.org/archive/marx/works/1843/critique-hpr/intro.htm; written in 1843.

13   Franz Fanon, *The Wretched of the Earth* (New York: Grove Press, 1963), 24; originally published in French in 1961.

14   "United States Census," *Wikipedia*, https://en.wikipedia.org/wiki/United_States_Census; "World Population Estimates," *Wikipedia*, https://en.wikipedia.org/wiki/World_population_estimates.

15   "Campus Commemorates 1968 Student-Led Strike," *SF State News*, http://www.sfsu.edu/news/2008/fall/8.html.

16   Joshua Bloom and Waldo E. Martin, *Black Against Empire* (Berkeley: University of California Press, 2013), 275; originally published in *Rolling Stone*, April 5, 1969, 14.

17   Kathleen Neal Cleaver, "Women, Power, and Revolution," in *Liberation, Imagination, and the Black Panther Party: A New Look at the Panthers and Their Legacy*, ed. Kathleen Cleaver and George Katsiaficas (New York: Routledge, 2001), 125.

18   George Katsiaficas, "Organization and Movement," in *Liberation, Imagination, and the Black Panther Party*, 142, 149.

19   Hoover wrote: "The Breakfast for Children Program (BCP) has been instituted by the BPP in several cities to provide a stable breakfast for ghetto children. . . . The program has met with some success and has resulted in considerable favorable publicity for the BPP. . . . The resulting publicity tends to portray the BPP in a favorable light and clouds the violent nature of the group and its ultimate aim of insurrection. The BCP promotes at least tacit support for the BPP among naive individuals . . . and, what is more distressing, provides the BPP with a ready audience composed of highly impressionable youths. . . . Consequently, the BCP represents the best and most influential activity going for the BPP and, as such, is potentially the greatest threat to efforts by authorities . . . to neutralize the BPP and destroy what it stands for." (FBI airtel from director to SACs in twenty-seven field offices. May 15, 1969); cited in Huey P. Newton,

War Against the Panthers: A Study of Repression in America (New York: Harlem River Press, 1996), 45, 46.

20 Eldridge Cleaver, "On Meeting the Needs of the People," *The Black Panther*, August 16, 1969; quoted in Philip S. Foner, ed., *The Black Panthers Speak* (Boston: Da Capo Press, 1995), 167.

21 Steve Yip, "Serve the People—Yesterday and Today: The Legacy of Wie Min She," in *Legacy to Liberation*, ed. Fred Ho (New York/Oakland: Big Red Media and AK Press, 2000), 17.

22 Ibid., 20.

23 Foner, *The Black Panthers Speak*, 227.

24 Yip, "Serve the People," 23–24.

25 Gil Scott-Heron, *Winter in America* (Strata-East Records, May, 1974).

26 Richard Nixon, "Annual Message to Congress on the State of the Union," January 22, 1971, in *Public Papers of the Presidents of the United States: Richard Nixon*, vol. 3 (Washington, DC: Government Printing Office, 1972), 58.

27 Michael Lydon, "Rock for Sale," *Ramparts*, December 1969, http://www.rocksbackpages.com/Library/Article/rock-for-sale.

Chapter 10

1 James Connolly, *The Reconquest of Ireland*, in *Collected Works* Vol. 1 (Dublin: New Books Publications 987), 239.

2 "Interview with Simone de Beauvoir 1976: The Second Sex 25 Years Later," http://www.marxists.org/reference/subject/ethics/de-beauvoir/1976/interview.htm; interview conducted by John Gerassi and originally published in *Society*, January-February 1976.

3 Simone de Beauvoir, *The Second Sex*, (New York, Vintage Books, 1974), xxxiv; originally published in French in 1949).

4 "Interview with Simone de Beauvoir 1976," http://www.marxists.org/reference/subject/ethics/de-beauvoir/1976/interview.htm.

5 Shulamith Firestone, "The Jeannette Rankin Brigade: Women Power?" in *Notes from the First Year*, ed. Kathie Amatniek et al. (New York: The New York Radical Women, 1968), 18, http://library.duke.edu/digitalcollections/wlmpc_wlmms01037/.

6 Mark Toney, "Revisiting the National Welfare Rights Organization," November 29, 2000, http://www.colorlines.com/archives/2000/11/revisiting_the_national_welfare_rights_organization.html.

7 Kathleen Neal Cleaver, "Women, Power and Revolution," in *Liberation, Imagination and the Black Panther Party: A New Look at the Panthers and Their Legacy*, ed. Kathleen Cleaver and George Katsiaficas (New York: Routledge, 2001), 126. Cleaver also notes: "according to a survey Bobby Seale did in 1969, two-thirds of the members of the Black Panther Party were women."

8 Todd Gitlin, *The Sixties: Years of Hope, Days of Rage* (New York: Bantam Books, 1989), 374–76.

9 Isaac Goldberg, *Tin Pan Alley: A Chronicle of the American Popular Music Racket* (New York: John Day, 1930), 95.

10 Ibid., 98.

11 David Suisman, *Selling Sounds* (Cambridge, MA: Harvard University Press, 2009), 46.

12 Convincing evidence of her talent is available, since Tharpe was recorded and filmed at the height of her popularity in the 1930s and 1940s. See "Sister Rosetta Tharpe—Down by the Riverside," https://www.youtube.com/watch?v=4xzr_GBa8qk; "Sister Rosetta Tharpe—Didn't It Rain," https://www.youtube.com/watch?v=SR2gR6SZC2M.

13 Alan Lomax, Woody Guthrie, and Pete Seeger, *Hard Hitting Songs for Hard-Hit People* (New York: Oak Publications 1967), 164.

14 Angela Y. Davis, *Blues Legacies and Black Feminism* (New York: Vintage Books, 1999), xii.

15 "Gullah," *Wikipedia*, https://en.wikipedia.org/wiki/Gullah; "Marquetta Goodwine," *Wikipedia*, https://en.wikipedia.org/wiki/Marquetta_Goodwine.

16 Aretha Franklin, "Think" (Atlantic Records, 1968); "Think (Aretha Franklin Song)," *Wikipedia*, https://en.wikipedia.org/wiki/Think_%28Aretha_Franklin_song%29. Aretha had previously released Otis Redding's "Respect," giving her version a feminist edge.

17 See Chapters 4, 6, and 10 for more on the subject of co-optation and repression.

18 Cases involving Creedence Clearwater Revival and Frank Zappa are just two famous but typical examples among countless others. See Chapters 7 and 10.

19 Abe Peck, *Uncovering the Sixties: The Life and Times of the Underground Press* (New York: Citadel Underground, 1991), 173–74.

20 "Reefer Madness," *Wikipedia*, https://en.wikipedia.org/wiki/Reefer_Madness.

21 "The Trip (1967 Film)." *Wikipedia*, https://en.wikipedia.org/wiki/The_Trip_%281967_film%29.

22 Beth Bailey, "Sex as a Weapon," in *Imagine Nation: The American Counterculture of the 1960s & 70s*, ed. Peter Braunstein and Michael William Doyle (New York: Routledge, 2002), 323.

Chapter 11

1 Noam Chomsky, "The Remaking of History," *Ramparts* 12 (August 1975): 30, available at http://www.unz.org/Pub/Ramparts-1975aug.

2 Herbert Marcuse, "The Failure of the New Left?" *New German Critique* 18 (Fall 1979): 3–11. This is an expanded version of a lecture given in April 1975 at the University of California, Irvine, http://www.marcuse.org/herbert/pubs.htm#1970s.

3 Ibid.

4 Betty Medsger, *The Burglary: The Discovery of J. Edgar Hoover's Secret FBI* (New York: Alfred A. Knopf, 2014).

5 On the Revolutionary Union, see: Aaron J. Leonard and Conor A. Gallagher, *Heavy Radicals: The FBI's Secret War on America's Maoists* (Alresford, UK: Zero Books, 2015).

6 Ibid.

7 Eric Nuzum, *Parental Advisory: Music Censorship in America* (New York: HarperCollins 2001), 168.

8 Richie Unterberger, *Turn! Turn! Turn!* (San Francisco: Backbeat Books, 2002), 263–64.

9 Ibid., 264.

10 The interview was conducted in 1999 by Brenda Norrell. Norrell explains: "The interview remained censored for seven years by Indian Country Today, where I served as a staff reporter. When Buffy's interview was finally published by ICT, one portion still remained censored. It was the portion about Anna Mae Aquash's death in relation to the fact that Pine Ridge was targeted for uranium mining at that time." Subsequently, in 2009, Norrell published the complete, uncensored interview online. See Brenda Norrell, "Buffy Sainte Marie: Uranium, an Interview and a Photograph," *The Atlantic Free Press*, September 3, 2009, http://www.atlanticfreepress.com/news/1/11369-buffy-sainte-marie-uranium-an-interview-and-a-photograph-.html.

11 Leonard Peltier, "From Lewisburg, Pennsylvania," *Nuclear Resister*, February 24, 2009, http://www.nukeresister.org/2010/04/01/from-lewisburg-pennsylvania-by-leonard-peltier/.

12   Daniel A. Simmons, "'Must Be the Season of the Witch': The Repression and Harassment of Rock and Folk Music during the Long Sixties," *Doctoral Dissertations* (Storrs, CT: University of Connecticut Digital Commons@UCon, 2013), http://digitalcommons.uconn.edu/dissertations/19/.

13   Martin A. Lee and Bruce Shlain, *Acid Dreams: The Complete Social History of LSD: The CIA, the Sixties, and Beyond* (New York: Grove Weidenfeld, 1992).

14   Simmons, "Must Be the Season of the Witch."

15   Ibid. See also David Cunningham, *There's Something Happening Here: The New Left, the Klan, and FBI Counterintelligence* (Berkeley: University of California Press, 2004); James Kirkpatrick Davis, *Assault on the Left: The FBI and the Sixties Anti-War Movement* (Westport, CT: Praeger Trade, 1997); David J. Garrow, *The FBI and Martin Luther King, Jr.* (New York: Norton, 1981); Ward Churchill and Jim Vander Wall, *Agents of Repression: The FBI's Secret War against the Black Panthers and the American Indian Movement* (Boston: South End Press, 1988).

16   George H. Lewis, ed., *Side-Saddle on the Golden Calf* (Pacific Palisades, CA: Goodyear Publishing Company, Inc. 1972).

17   Michael Lydon, "Rock for Sale," in ibid., 321.

18   Sol Stern, "Altamont: Pearl Harbor to the Woodstock Nation," in ibid., 336–37.

19   Fred Goodman, *The Mansion on the Hill: Dylan, Young, Geffen, and the Head-on Collision of Rock and Commerce* (London: Jonathan Cape, 1997).

20   Ibid., xii.

21   Ibid., xv.

22   "Children of the Future" was the title track of an album by San Francisco's Steve Miller Band (Capitol Records, June 1968).

23   Punk rock's deliberate attack on the music industry is particularly noteworthy. While tactics varied widely, the underlying premise was that means had to be devised to promote and protect the independence of music and musicians from the enemy, i.e., corporate and state control of music production and distribution. This led to the widespread and diverse practices gathered under the rubric of DIY ("do it yourself"). While the system would ultimately succeed in frustrating these efforts, they nonetheless served to foster a critical attitude toward the snares and delusions of the music business. Moreover, they exposed the fact that the music industry is an arm of the state.

24   Alain Badiou, *The Century* (Cambridge: Polity Press, 2007), 140.

25   Immanuel Wallerstein, "Antisystemic Movements, Yesterday and Today," *Journal of World-Systems Research* 20, no. 2 (Summer/Fall 2014): 158–72.

26   "There is an egalitarian presupposition at the basis of the aesthetic regime. On the one hand, that presupposition supports the capacity to see aesthetically in general, the possibility to perceive and appreciate objects and performances as artistic. On the other hand, there is an aesthetic utopia that has thrived on that presupposition, the program of a community of equals, where equality would be achieved in sensible life, in everyday life. In that case, the presupposition has been transformed into a telos. The enactment of equality always entails the risk of that transformation." Gavin Arnall, Laura Gandolfi, and Enea Zaramella, "Aesthetics and Politics Revisited: An Interview with Jacques Rancière," *Critical Inquiry* 38 (Winter 2012): 289–97, http://www.journals.uchicago.edu/doi/pdfplus/10.1086/662743.

27   André Breton, *Arcanum 17* (1944); quoted in Badiou, *The Century,* 140–41.

Appendix I

1   Even Joel Selvin's book *Summer of Love* opens with the sentence: "The Summer of Love never really happened." Joel Selvin, *Summer of Love: The Inside Story of LSD, Rock & Roll, Free Love, and High Times in the Wild West* (New York: Cooper Square Press, 1999).

2   Charles Perry, *The Haight-Ashbury: A History* (New York: Wenner Books, 2005) 89–90, 123, 162–63, 208–9, 273–74; each citation reports a different large-scale incident.

3   Ibid., 19–20.

4   The author attended Polytechnic High School at that time.

5   "California: End of the Dance," *Time*, August 18, 1967, http://content.time.com/time/magazine/article/0,9171,840956,00.html.

6   Ibid.

7   Theodore Roszak, *The Making of a Counter Culture: Reflections on the Technocratic Society and Its Youthful Opposition* (New York: Anchor Books 1969), 33.

8   Ibid., 34.

9   Hunter S. Thompson, *The Great Shark Hunt: Gonzo Papers Volume 1* (New York, Summit Books, 1979), 389.

10 Perry, *The Haight-Ashbury*, 159–60.

11 Ibid., 160.

12 Roszak, *The Making of a Counter Culture*, 41.

Appendix IV

1   When the author interviewed Mark Kitchell, director of award-winning documentary *Berkeley in the Sixties* (California Newsreel/First Run Features, 1990), Kitchell expressed surprise that he had not found *Revolution* while researching his film, and he was not alone.

2   Powell St. John, a member of Mother Earth, told the author that the band did not initially want to perform the song, a treacly pop tune provided by the film's LA producers. St. John went on to explain that Tracy Nelson, Mother Earth's soulful singer, insisted on giving the song an earthy edge and a musical twist, hence its R&B groove and its odd time signature.

3   Interview with the author.

About the author

Mat Callahan is a musician and author originally from San Francisco, where he founded Komotion International. He is the author of three books, *Sex, Death & the Angry Young Man*, *Testimony*, and *The Trouble with Music* as well as the editor of *Songs of Freedom: The James Connolly Songbook*. He currently resides in Bern, Switzerland.

Index

Page numbers in *italic* refer to illustrations. "Passim" (literally "scattered") indicates intermittent discussion of a topic over a cluster of pages.

Abrams, Jerry, 50, 263
A.B. Skhy, *150*
Ace of Cups, 263
Acid Dreams (Lee and Shlain), 231
Actor's Workshop, 10, 19
Adler, Lou, 78, 79, 101
Adorno, Theodor, 75, 76, 276n29
advertising, 79, 125, 219, 220
African Americans, xxv, xxviii, 19, 25–41 passim, 59; armed forces desegregation, 25; curfews, 86; Graham relations, 93; Great Migration, 11, 66; on "hippies" and "beatniks," 261–62; internal colonization, 29; school desegregation, 23, 25; urban rebellions, 27–28; Vietnam War, 180, 183; Wexler and, 105, 106. *See also* black music; Black Panther Party; civil rights movement; segregation; Soledad Brothers
age limitations, 46, 49, 72. *See also* all-ages shows
AIM. *See* American Indian Movement (AIM)
Albin, Peter, 67, 68, 83, 94, 127
Albin, Rodney, 67, 68, 83, 94
album art, 111
Alcatraz Island: Indian occupation (1964), 13–14; Indian occupation (1968–69), *152, 153,* 179, 192–93, 199, 200

alcohol, 49, 51, 72, 110, 264
"Alexander's Ragtime Band," 64–65
Ali, Muhammad, 180
all-ages shows, 283n21
All in the Family, 188
Altamont Speedway Free Festival, 96, 186
alternative press, 87, 105–6, 114, 176, 206, 224–25. *See also* underground press
alternative schools, 83, 99, 202
American Dream, 26, 30
American Indian Movement (AIM), 179, 200, 222, 228, 231
American Indians. *See* Native Americans
Angelou, Maya, *155*
Anna and the A-Train, *159*
Anthology of American Folk Music, 9, 65–66, 111, 280n15
anticommunism, xvii, 17, 20, 30–36 passim, 107, 119, 220, 228
antiwar movement, 183, 223, 227, 244, 250; benefit events, 53, 91, *137, 143;* demonstrations, 38, 81, 98, 124, 184, 198, 234; draft resistance, 183, 250; repression, 231. *See also* Vietnam Veterans Against the War
Aquash, Anna Mae, 290n10
Ark (Sausalito), *142*
Arnall, Gavin, 291n26
art, 9, 10, 85–90 passim, 117. *See also* album art; posters and poster art

Artists Liberation Front (ALF), 85–90 passim
arts policy, 85–88 passim, 233
Asian Americans, 80, 201, 203–5 passim
Atlantic (label), 107
auditoriums and ballrooms. See ballrooms and auditoriums
authenticity, 58–77 passim, 119, 245, 280n15, 279n1; personal, 178
Autumn Records, 72, 121, 122, 123
Avalon Ballroom, 46, 53, 187, 262
avant-garde music, 125–27
Azteca, 71, 129, 160, 161

Badiou, Alan, xxix, 112, 239
"bad" Sixties and "good" Sixties. See "good" Sixties and "bad" Sixties
Baez, Joan, xv, 33, 163, 279n22
Bailey, Beth, 222
Baldwin, James, 12, 36; The Fire Next Time, 26
Balin, Marty, 45–46, 67, 89, 159
ballrooms and auditoriums, 46, 53, 94, 158, 177, 187, 237, 262; Berkeley, 150; Richmond, 161; Santa Monica, 229; Stockton, 160. See also Fillmore Auditorium
Bardacke, Frank, 18–19
Barthol, Bruce, 164
Bay Area Revolutionary Union, 204, 228
Beals, Carol, 8
Beatles, xvi, xvii, 48, 72, 73, 101, 128; Ed Sullivan Show, xv, 13, 39; recording technology, 127; Sgt. Pepper, 123, 127
Beat movement, 9, 10, 18, 37, 38, 75; television, 277n14
Beau Brummels, 72
Beauvoir, Simon de, xxviii, 36; Second Sex, 210, 211–12, 223
be-ins, 48, 52, 84, 245, 253
Belafonte, Harry, 33, 164
benefit compositions, 126
benefit concerts, 47, 51, 52, 53, 92, 100; antiwar, 91; Black Panthers, 99, 100; posters, 90, 131, 136–44 passim, 155–56, 159–62
Berg, Peter, 90, 168
Berkeley: coffeehouses, 68, 162. See also Leopold Records, Berkeley; University of California, Berkeley

Berkeley Barb, 81, 83, 87, 113
Berkeley Community Theatre, 131, 155, 157
Berkeley Folk Festival, 176
Berkeley Strike Committee, 136
Berlin, Irving, 64
Berman, Marshall, 75
Bernays, Edward, 30
Bernstein, Leonard, 164; West Side Story, 106
Berry, Chuck, 31, 32, 72
Bessie, Alvah, 113–14
Bierce, Ambrose, 4
Big Brother and the Holding Company, 67, 94, 111, 127, 135, 137, 141
Billboard, 106–7
Bill Graham Presents, 92, 133, 136, 165
Billings, Warren, 7
Bin Hassan, Umar, 228
Bird, Bonnie, 8
birth control pill, 221, 252
black Americans. See African Americans
blacklisting, 33, 113, 114, 219, 229, 230
black music, xxv–xxviii passim, 31, 59–71 passim, 77, 130, 277n26; Black Panthers and, 99; "race music," 11, 31, 67, 106–7; radio airplay, xxvi, 31, 32, 41, 119; recording and production, 128; white imitators, 62–65 passim. See also blues music; gospel music; jazz music; rhythm and blues
Black Panther, 83, 149, 201–2
Black Panther Party, 29, 38, 52, 97–100, 163, 179, 197–203 passim; "Big Man" Howard, 195–96; Billy X Jennings, 69, 99, 100, 195; Brando support, 164; breakfast program, 99, 202–3, 288n19; David Hilliard, 124; demise, 205; Ericka Huggins, 190; Graham relations, 93, 165; Huey Newton trial, 82; Maoism, 20–22 passim; Marxism, 198; posters, 148, 154; "Power to the People," 190; repression of, 186, 228, 231; Santana benefit, 100, 234; Vietnam War view, 184; women, 213, 289n7
Black Power movement, 28, 38
Bloch, Ernst, 240
Bloody Thursday (1934), 8
Bloomfield, Mike, 158, 283n21

Blue Cheer, 95, *135*

Blues Legacies and Black Feminism (Davis), 216–17

blues music, 31, 46, 67, 68, 282n21

Blues Project, 68, 281n20

Blue Unicorn (coffeehouse), 83, 94, 246–48

Boar's Head, 67, 68

Bodacious, *159*

Booker T. and the MGs, 72

booking agencies, 101, 165, 167

Books Behind Bars, *162*

bookstores, 20–23, 67, 203, 204, 229

Both/And (nightclub), 83

Braunstein, Peter, 172–73

Bramlett, Delaney and Bonnie. *See* Delaney and Bonnie

Brando, Marlon, 164, 275n26

Breton, André, 241

bribery ("payola"), 120–21

Bridges, Harry, 8

Britain. *See* Great Britain

British invasion, xvi, 13, 73, 119, 277n23

Brown, H. Rap, 28, 60

Brown, James, 38, 69, 71, 99, 192, 202, 229, 280n3

Brown, Oscar, Jr., 192, 196

Brown, Willie, 88

Bruce, Lenny, 18, 36, 47, 87, 227

Bruhns, Dan, *137*, *141*

Buchla, Don, 126

Buckley, Lord, 36, 59–60

The Burglary: The Discovery of J. Edgar Hoover's Secret FBI (Medsger), 227, 228

Burns and Schreiber, 130

Butterfield Blues Band. *See* Paul Butterfield Blues Band

Caen, Herb, 20, 263

Cahill, Thomas, 252, 263

California Hall, 72, 84

California Institution for Women, *162*

Callahan, Mat, xv–xvii passim, *143*, 293

canonization, 195

Capitol Records, 129

Carmichael, Stokely, 28

Carousel Ballroom, 94, *177*

Carter, Jimmy, 236

Carter Family, 217

Casady, Jack, 46, *158*

Castell, Luria, 12, 48–50 passim, *132*, 278n7

Castro, Fidel, *151*

celebrity. *See* fame

censorship, 228, 290n10

Chambers Brothers, 40–41, 68, 130, 281n20

Champlin, Bill, 69, 91, 94, 95

charity, 167–68

charity concerts, 208, 236. *See also* benefit concerts

Charlatans, 111, *135*, *139*

Charles, Ray, xv, 37, 60, 69, 105, 106, 280n3

Chavez, Cesar, 89, *161*

Chess Records, 31

Chiarito, Gertrude, 68

Chicago, 31, 282n21

Chicago 8 (Chicago 7) trial, 124, *147*

El Chicano, *161*

Chicanos, 183, 201, 222

China, 8, 20–22 passim, 116, 197; Cultural Revolution, 21, 171, 172, 179, 189, 203, 287n35

China Books and Periodicals, 20–23

Chinatown, 3, 203–5

Chomsky, Noam, 206, 224–25, 265, 275n26

church music, 216, 217

City Lights Books, 9, 20, 72

civil rights movement, 11–17 passim, 26, 30, 37, 49; folk music and, 33, 40, 42, 55

Clash, 237

classicism, 112–13, 240

Cleaver, Eldridge, 32, 61, 202–3

Cleaver, Kathleen, 154, 201, 213, 289n7

Cleveland Wrecking Company, *144*

Close, Del, 45

Clover (band), *145*

coffeehouses, 49, 68, 83, 94, *162*, 246–48

CONTELPRO, 227–31 passim

Coit Tower murals, 9

Cold Blood, 41, 70

Cold War, 125–26, 58, 75, 115, 119

Cole, Natalie, 99

Coleman, Ornette, 62

colleges. *See* universities and colleges

colonization and decolonization, 188–89, 197–98

Coltrane, John, 195, 282n21

Columbia Records, 36, 41, 107, 129, 130, 163, 217

comedy recordings, 130

Commander Cody, 150

Committee (theater company), 44, 45, 143

communes and communalism, 174, 176, 177–78, 186

Communication Company, 87

communism, 116, 171, 185, 287n34. See also anticommunism

Communist Party, 18, 19, 20, 22, 171, 198, 284n7; China, 189, 287n35

Congress of Wonders (comedy team), 145

Connolly, James, 209–10

"consciousness expansion" (term), 243–44

contracts, 258–60

"coon songs," 64, 163

co-optation, 65, 100, 122, 187, 207, 224, 232–38 passim, 249; male supremacy and, 214; Phillips and Adler, 79; resistance to, 237; of "We Shall Overcome," 40

copyright, 64, 163, 280n13

"corporate rock," 234, 236, 237, 238

Cortright, David: Soldiers in Revolt, 181

Cotton, James, 282n21

counterculture/contraculture (concept), 81, 85, 172–74, 178, 184–89 passim, 248–49; Talcott Parsons, 286n3

counterrevolution, 168, 185, 188, 226–33 passim, 238, 239

country and western music, 31, 71, 194, 217

Country Joe and the Fish, 43, 95–96, 100, 105, 164, 175, 262; Barthol, 164; posters, 135, 137, 141, 144

court cases, 218. See also lawsuits; Supreme Court cases

Cowell, Henry, 126

Coyote, Peter, 90

The Cradle Will Rock (Blitzstein), 130

Creedence Clearwater Revival, 77, 96, 129, 153, 187, 188

Crosby, Leon, 122

Cross Country (band), 150

Crumb, Robert, 111, 222

Cuba, 50, 70, 71, 116, 126, 132, 179. See also Castro, Fidel

"cultural revolution" (term), 188

curfews, 86, 282n19

Czechoslovakia, 170, 171, 189, 210

Dakila, 157, 160

dance hall permits, 49, 93

dancing, 32–33, 42, 48, 53, 55–56, 71, 72; crazes, 48, 64, 67, 109, 220. See also modern dance

"Dancing in the Streets," 48

Dane, Barbara, 45, 68, 281n20

Davis, Angela, 19, 124, 148, 222, 275n26; Blues Legacies and Black Feminism, 216–17

Davis, Clive, 41

Davis, Miles, 62, 196

Davis, Ron, 10, 51, 88–92 passim, 130, 262–65 passim, 275n22, 283n42

Day on the Green, Oakland, 233, 234

Debord, Guy, 276n29

Decker, Barry, 263

decolonization. See colonization and decolonization

de Gouges, Olympe de. See Gouges, Olympe de

Delaney and Bonnie, 96

Dellums, Ron, 157

Democratic Party, 113, 208, 236

demonstrations, 52; anti-curfew, 282n19; anti-freeway, 16; anti-HUAC, xvii, 17, 18; antiwar, 38, 81, 98, 124, 184, 198, 234; civil rights, 15–16, 17. See also sit-ins

Denning, Michael, 11

Detroit, 205, 244; rebellion of 1967, 27. See also Motown

didacticism, 112

Diggers, 21, 52, 85–94 passim, 124, 165, 168, 246, 248; China Books, 20; influence on Yippies, 283n42; mirrored by Black Panthers, 99; Monterey Pop, 101, 102; in Revolution, 261–62; "Summer of Love," 245. See also free stores

Disney, Walt, 109

Dixon, Aaron, 99

Donahue, Tom, 45, 72, 120–23, 163, 176

Donovan, 264
Doobie Brothers, 129, 279n21
Doyle, Michael William, 172–73
draft, military. *See* military draft
dress codes, 49, 56, 165
"dropping out," 252–54
drugs, 35, 95, 110, 219–22 passim, 229,
    251–52, 262, 264; arrests, 218;
    psychotropic, 52, 102, 110, 221, 251.
    See also LSD; marijuana
drum machines, 126
Du Bois, W.E.B., xxviii, 63, 198; *The Souls
    of Black Folk*, 196, 223
Du Bois Club. *See* W.E.B. Du Bois Club
Duncan, Isadora, 4–8, 274n4
Dylan, Bob, xv, 17, 32, 33, 54, 106, 130, 222;
    Columbia signing, 36; radio airplay,
    122; "Times They Are a-Changin',"
    xv, 39

East Bay. *See* Berkeley; Oakland;
    Richmond
East Coast. *See* New York City;
    Philadelphia
East-West (Butterfield Blues Band),
    282n21
ecstatic experience, 110
Ed Sullivan Show, xv, 13, 39, 67
electric music and amplification, 33, 45,
    72, 127
electronic music, 126
Ellington, Duke, 35, 106
Eno, Brian, 126
Escovedo family, 70–71, 100
Everybody's Bookstore, 203, 204
existentialism, 36, 58, 73, 75

Fallon, Michael, 246–47
fame: desire for, 90; manufacture of, 59,
    217–18
Family Dog, 12, 19, 47–52 passim, 72,
    83, 94, 102, 177; strikes against, 177;
    "Summer of Love," 245
Fanon, Frantz, 188–89, 287n33; *The
    Wretched of the Earth*, 197
Farina, Mimi, 68, 281n20
Farina, Richard, 37, 68, 281n20
farmworkers' movement, 81, 89, *156–61
    passim*

FBI, 36, 202, 227–31 passim, 252, 288n19;
    Media office break-in, 227
Feather, Leonard, 114
feminism, 214, 219, 221, 222
Ferlinghetti, Lawrence, 9, 84, 88; *Poetry
    as Insurgent Art*, 24
Ferrandino, Joe, 277n26
Ferreira, Jason, 178–79
festivals, 48, 53, 83–86 passim, 91, 94, 96,
    114, 175–78 passim, 234; faux, 236;
    posters, *156*. *See also* folk music:
    festivals
Feuerbach, Ludwig, 168
Fiesta Campesina, 156
Fillmore Auditorium, 46, 49, 52, 53,
    69–70, 93, 125, 187; Butterfield Blues
    Band, 282n21; posters, *133, 136, 141,
    143, 144*; *Revolution*, 262
Fillmore District, 16, 29, 86, 100, 176, 253
Fillmore West, 94
films, 80, 185, 261–66, 292nn1–2 (appendix
    4); drugs in, 220; Graham in, 167;
    mockumentaries, 237; Monterey
    Pop, 102; Vietnam War in, 182
folklore studies, 63, 73–74
folk music, 17, 18, 56, 66–68 passim, 75,
    277n25, 281n19; attraction of, 74;
    authenticity and, 58; civil rights
    movement and, 33, 40, 42; festivals,
    33, 40–41, 68, 176; nexus with
    rock, 45, 46; revival, xxvi, 33, 40, 42,
    55–59 passim, 66, 281n19. See also
    Anthology of American Folk Music
Fortunate Eagle, Adam, 13, 14
Fourth Way, 129
France, 36, 74, 170, 184, 197, 209, 211, 239
Franklin, Aretha, 36, 60, 99, 105, 202, 218,
    290n16, 280n8
"freak" (word), 72, 247
free concerts, 85, 233. *See also* Altamont
    Speedway Free Festival
Freed, Alan, 32, 120
Freedom Highway (band), *135*
freedom of speech, 18. *See also* Free
    Speech Movement; obscenity
Freedom Singers, *131*
Free Fairs, 85–89 passim
free food distribution, 87, 90, 91, 99,
    202–3
free medical clinics, 91, 99, 167, 202, 263

Free Speech Movement, xvi–xvii, 13, 16, 49, 50, 114
free stores, 90, 261–62
Freeway Revolt (1964), 16, 84, 247, 248, 253
Freiberg, David, 67
Fugs, 228–29
fundraising concerts. *See* benefit concerts

Gandolfi, Laura, 291n26
gangs, 30, 186, 193, 201
Garcia, Jerry, 67, *157, 158. See also* Grateful Dead
Garden of Delights, *144*
Garson, Marvin, 185
Gasca, Luis, *156, 157*
Gaye, Marvin, 99
gay liberation, 179, 201, 238–39, 243
Geffen, David, 236
Gellert, Lawrence, 65, 66
gender, xxvii, xxviii, 213, 221, 249. *See also* feminism; male supremacy; women's liberation
General Strike of 1934, xvii, 8
general strikes, students'. *See* student strikes
Genet, Jean, 19
Gianquinto, Alberto, 99–100
Gillette, Charlie, 32, 61
Ginsberg, Allen, 10, 18, 84, 249; *The Fall of America*, 24; *Howl*, 9, 18, 20, 37, 75
Gleason, Ralph, 10, 47, 50–55 passim, 62, 88, 113–14; on Free Fairs, 85, 86; on Free Speech Movement, 114; Graham interview, 165; *The Jefferson Airplane and the San Francisco Sound*, 47, 244, 261; on Monterey Pop, 101–2; *Rolling Stone*, 113; Tom Donahue relations, 122; view of music and state, 104; Wild West festival, 176
Goldberg, Isaac, 62; *Tin Pan Alley*, 214–15, 216
Golden Gate Park, 1, 84, 176, 233–34; Polo Fields, 16, 85, 234; Speedway Meadow, 85, 91, 234, 263. *See also* Human Be-In (1967); Panhandle
Goldhaft, Judy, 90
Gold Rush, 2, 3
Goldwyn, Samuel, 58

Goodlett, Carlton, 11–12
Goodman, Fred: *Mansion on the Hill*, 236–37
"good" Sixties and "bad" Sixties, 179, 180, 186
Gordy, Berry, 244
gospel music, 33, 40, 68, 110, 278n1
Gottlieb, Lou, 174, 262
Gouges, Olympe de, 209
Graham, Bill, 49, 51, 88, 91–96 passim, 114, 164–68; charity concerts, 236; Day on the Green, 233, 234; Rubinson and, 130; Sex Pistols, 237; strikes against, 177; Wild West festival, 176; Woodstock, 175. *See also* Bill Graham Presents
Gramsci, Antonio, 276n29
grape boycott and strike, 81, 89, *159*
Grateful Dead, 51, 67, 80, 94, 282–83n21; Black Panther benefit, 100, *154*; Champlin on, 95; Lesh, 127; posters, *135, 137*
Great Britain, 238. *See also* British invasion
The Great Rock 'n' Roll Swindle, 237
Great Society (LBJ programs), 28, 173, 249
Great! Society (band), 45, 72, 111, 128, 278n3
"Green Onions," 72
Griffin, Susan, *162*
Grogan, Emmet, 87, 90
Grossman, Albert, 102, 164, 165, 166
groupies, 218, 219
Guevara, Che, 189, 287n34; "Song for Che," 195
gullibility, 109, 111
Gunning, Sarah Ogan, 66, 216, 217
Gurley, Jim, 127
Guthrie, Arlo, 236–37
Guthrie, Woody, 43, 54, 66, 236–37

Haight-Ashbury, 38, 71, 73, 81–87 passim, 245, 248; Black Panthers, 100; Free Fair, 86; free store, 261–62; GIs, 80; John Phillips, 101; living conditions, 253. *See also* Panhandle
Haight-Ashbury Free Medical Clinic, 91, 99, 167, 263
Haight-Ashbury Job Co-op, 263, 264

Haight Ashbury Neighborhood Association, 16, 248, 253
Haight Commune, 176, 177–78
Haight Independent Proprietors (HIP), 84, 253
Hallinan, Terence, 12
Hallinan, Vincent, 12–13
Halprin, Anna, 263
Ham, Bill, 50
Hammond, John (producer), 36, 105–6, 278n1
Hancock, Herbie, 155
"happenings," 48, 51, 84. See also Human Be-In (1967)
Hard Hitting Songs for Hard-Hit People, 66
Harlem riot of 1964, 27–28
Harlem Six, 126
Havens, Richie, 163, 175
Hearst, William Randolph, 2
Hearst newspaper empire, 7, 247
Hedds, 72, 133
Heinl, Robert D., 181
Hells Angels, 186
Helms, Chet, 12, 13, 94, 127
Hendricks, Jon, 80
Hendrix, Jimi, 41, 95, 99, 102, 175
Herbert, Herbie, 234
Herder, Johann Gottfried von, 74, 111
high schools, 23–24, 72, 83, 100. See also Polytechnic High School
Hill, Joe, 54, 65, 66, 112
"hillbilly music," 11, 31, 67, 217
Hilliard, David, 124, 148
Hinton, Sam, 68, 281n19
"hip" and hipness, 34–38 passim, 51, 60–61, 91, 111, 235, 246; Digger views, 90; marijuana, 251
Hip Capitalism (Krieger), 120, 121
"hippie" (word), 38, 246–47, 262
Hobsbawm, Eric, 31, 36, 277n23
Ho Chi Minh, 184
Hoffman, Abbie, 175, 205
Holden, Joan, 176, 177–78
Holiday, Billie, 36, 106, 277n26
Honkey Blues, 60
hootenannies, 67
Hoover, J. Edgar, 31, 202, 228, 232, 288n19
"Hound Dog," 33, 277n26
housing, 1, 11, 16, 202, 203; segregation, 23

Howard, Albert "Big Man," 195–96
Howl (Ginsberg), 9, 18, 20, 37, 75
HUAC hearings (1960), xvii, 17, 18
Huggins, Ericka, 154
Hughes, Langston, 25, 36; The Panther and the Lash, 25, 26
Human Be-In (1967), 52, 84, 245, 253
Human Beinz, 142
hungry i (nightclub), 18
Hunter, Robert, 67
Hunters Point, 2, 16, 250, 253; curfews, 86; Free Fair, 86; police killing and riot, 29, 86, 87, 134
Hurok, Sol, 166
Huxley, Aldous, 173; Doors of Perception, 110
"hysteria," 220–21

"I Hate the Capitalist System" (Gunning), 216
illusion, sacred (Feuerbach), 168
Impressions, 99
"In C" (Riley), 126
"Incident at Neshabur," 99
Indian Country Today, 230m 290n10
Indians. See Native Americans
Industrial Workers of the World, 65, 112
International Hotel, 203, 204, 238
International Longshoremen's and Warehousemen's Union (ILWU), xvii, 8, 11, 18, 31
internet, 107–8, 258, 260
interracial bands, 41, 62, 96, 187–88, 282n21
interracial marriage and sex, 28, 35, 198
Ireland, 209–10
irony, 110–11
Irwin Street Warehouse, 91, 138

Jackson, George, 19, 186, 275n26
Jackson, Jonathan, 275n26
Jackson State killings (1970), 180, 186
jam sessions, 52, 83, 85, 94
Jargon of Authority (Adorno), 76
jazz music, 17, 18, 33–37 passim, 43–49 passim, 70–75 passim, 194–96; authenticity, 75; Black Panthers and, 195–96; Both/And club, 83; Free Fairs, 85; Gleason, 10, 47, 114; Great Migration and, 66; jam sessions, 85;

marijuana, 251; North Beach, 10, 18, 72; radio, 122; revolutionary politics, 222; rock fusion, 193; Stoll photos, 275n12; Wexler, 105, 106
The Jazz Scene (Hobsbawm), 36
Jazzwomen (Placksin), 216
Jefferson Airplane, 46–47, 67–68, 89, 90, 101; cover of *Life*, 187; recording and production, 129; posters, *133, 136, 143*; "White Rabbit," 101, 110, 278n3
The Jefferson Airplane and the San Francisco Sound (Gleason), 47, 244, 261
Jennings, Billy X, 69, 99, 195–96
Jerry Hahn Brotherhood, 129
Johnson, James Weldon, 63
Johnson, Joy, 72
Johnson, Lyndon, 28, 40, 182, 229. *See also* Great Society (LBJ programs)
Johnson, Matthew, 29, 86, 87, *134*
Johnston, Tom, 279n21
Joplin, Janis, 68. *See also* Big Brother and the Holding Company
Joplin, Scott, 64–65, 280n13
Journey, 234
"Jump Jim Crow," 64
juvenile delinquent (film trope), 30

Kantner, Paul, 67
Kaukonen, Jorma, 46, 67, *158*
Kerner Report, 27
Kerouac, Jack, 10; *On the Road*, 9, 37, 58, 75
Kesey, Ken, 127
Kezar Stadium, 176, 234
Khan, Chaka, 99
King, Martin Luther, Jr., 2, 28; assassination, 27, 170
Kingston Trio, 33, 67
Kitt, Eartha, 229
KMPX, 119–20, 122, 124, 125
KPFA, 68, 119, 124
Krieger, Susan: *Hip Capitalism*, 120, 121
KSAN, 119, 120, 124, 125
KSOL, 71
KYA, 41, 121

labor movement, xvii, 8, 31, 65. *See also* strikes
Lafarge, Peter, 194

Landau, Saul, 92
Last Poets, 228
Latin music, 70–71, *156, 157, 160, 161,* 193–94. *See also* Mexican music
Latinos, 70–71, 89–90; political prisoners, *148, 150*
Laughlin, Chandler, 123
lawsuits, 129, 167
Leary, Timothy, 70, 84, 90
Lee Mah strike, 205
left press. *See* alternative press
Legal Aid benefit, *158*
Leighton, Elliot, 14
LEMAR (Legalization of Marijuana), 94, 247
Lenin, Vladimir, 188
Leopold Records, Berkeley, 125
Lesh, Phil, 127
Lewis, George, 37
"liberation" (word), 244
Liberation News Service, 83, 228
Liberty Hill Aristocrats, 67
Life, 187
light shows, 44, 45, 50, 51, 92, 102, 127; posters, *137, 141, 144*; *Revolution*, 262, 263; strikes, 177
Lipscomb, Mance, 45
Lipset, Seymour, 180
Lisch, Arthur, 86
Listen, Whitey! (Thomas), 60, 194
Little Richard, 32–33, 72
live performance fees, 260
Loading Zone, 70, *144*
Lock, Seymour, 50
Lomax, Alan, 65, 66
Lomax, John, 65
London, Jack, 4
Longshoremen's Hall, 83–84, 127, *137*
Lopez, Trini, 72
Los Angeles, 48, 79, 129
"love and peace" (phrase). *See* "peace and love" (phrase)
Love Pageant Rally (1966), 87
Loving v. Virginia, 28, 198
Lovin' Spoonful, 45, 46
LSD, 51, 70, 95, 231, 251, 263; criminalization, 86
Lydon, John. *See* Rotten, Johnny
Lydon, Michael, 235
lyrics. *See* song lyrics

Mad River, 70, 95, *138, 143*

Magee, Ruchell, *154*

Magenta Raindrop, *139*

Mailer, Norman, 58; "The White Negro," 34–35

male chauvinism. *See* sexism

male supremacy, 22, 214, 218, 238

Malcolm X, 22, 28

Mallarmé, Stéphane, 239

Malo, 90, 129, 130, *155, 156, 160,* 193–94

mania, 109. *See also* dance crazes

Mansion on the Hill (Goodman), 236–37

Manson, Charles, 186, 287n31

Mao Zedong, 202, 203; *Little Red Book,* 20–21, 69

Marcuse, Herbert, 225–26, 240, 241, 249; *One Dimensional Man,* 22, 114–15

marijuana, 35, 61, 94, 95, 123, 247, 251, 263

Marin County, 69, 275n26. *See also* Muir Beach Tavern

Marx, Karl, xxix, 78, 197; *Communist Manifesto,* 223; *Grundrisse,* 276

Marxists and Marxism, 22, 179, 196, 203, 226, 249; Black Panthers, 179, 198; means of production, 128; "middle class" and, 250; Rousseau and, 75. *See also* New Communist Movement

"the masses." *See* "the people" ("the masses")

Matrix (nightclub), 46, 47

McCarthyism. *See* anticommunism

McClure, Michael, 84

McDonald, Country Joe, 175. *See also* Country Joe and the Fish

MC5, *145*

McKay, Glenn, 50, 263

McKernan, Ron "Pigpen," 67

McQueen, Dave, 123, 124

Means, LaNada, 200

media: censorship, 290n10; corporate, 28, 79, 163, 175, 187, 227–28, 246–47, 251; Jerry Rubin view, 283–84n42; "Summer of Love," 245. *See also* alternative press; radio; *San Francisco Chronicle*

medical clinics, free. *See* free medical clinics

Meeropol, Abel, 36

Melvin, Milan, 123

Merritt College, 195

Merry Pranksters, 51

Methedrine, 95

Metromedia, 124

Mexican music, 70, 71, 77

Mexico City Olympics (1968), 170

middle-class nature of movement (myth), 249–51

Midnight Special (radio program), 68

migration, 74, 76, 79–80, 245, 252. *See also* Great Migration

military draft, 182–84

Milk, Harvey, 239

Miller, Larry, 122, 125

Miller Blues Band, *141. See also* Steve Miller Band

Mills, C. Wright: *Letter to the New Left,* 22

Mills College, 126, 127

Mime Troupe. *See* San Francisco Mime Troupe

Mingus, Charles, 36–37

minimalism, 126

minstrelsy, 62, 64, 65, 76, 163, 214

miscegenation. *See* interracial marriage and sex

Mission District, 16, 70, 71, 81, 86, 176, 193, 234

Mitchell, Bobby "Tripp," 45, 121

Moby Grape, 123, 130

modern dance, 4–8

Monterey Pop Festival (1967), 91, 95–96, 100–102, 114, 245–46, 263

Mooney, Tom, 7

Morning Glory (band), *138, 139*

Morning Star Ranch, 174

Morrison, Jim, 99

Mother Earth, 70, *135, 143,* 262, 263, 292n2 (appendix 4)

Mother's (nightclub), 45, 122

Mothers of Invention, 58, 78, 282n21. *See also* Zappa, Frank

Motown, 71, 190, 244

Mount Rushmore (band), *135, 144*

Movement (newspaper), 1–2, 81, *82, 134*

"the movement" (term), 243

Muir Beach Tavern, 91, *139*

murals and muralists, 9, 90

Murray, George Mason, 199–200

music festivals. *See* festivals

music industry, 62–66 passim, 76, 79, 89, 105–14 passim, 129, 163–68 passim, 175, 234–39 passim; contracts, 258–60; male supremacy in, 214; manufacturer of celebrity, 217–18; Monterey Pop, 102; Nashville, 194; racist exploitation, 277n26. *See also* booking agencies; Columbia Records; music recording and production; Tin Pan Alley
music publishing. *See* sheet music
music recording and production, 43, 63, 66, 127–29, 164; contracts, 258–60

Nancarrow, Conlon, 125
Nashville, 194
National Guard, 8, 27, 29
National Welfare Rights Organization, 212
Native Americans, 76, 229–30; Alcatraz occupations, 13–14, 123–14, *152*, 153, 179, 192–93, 199, 200; influence, 84; Johnny Cash and, 194; Pine Ridge, 230, 290n10; rock bands, 192–93; termination policy, 206; Vietnam War, 183. *See also* American Indian Movement (AIM)
Negro Songs of Protest, 65
neighborhood associations, 16, 87, 248, 253
Nelson, Tracy, 292n2 (appendix 4)
New Communist Movement, 22–23, 204
New Left, xxvii, 21, 22, 54, 117, 179, 185–86, 249; FBI repression, 228; Marcuse influence, 22, 114, 249; Marcuse on, 225, 226, 241; Roszak on, 173; student strike, 180; women's liberation, 212
New Lost City Ramblers, 67, 111, 281n19
New Masses, 105–6, 114
New Orleans music, 193, 244
Newport Folk Festival (1965), 33, 40–41
New Riders of the Purple Sage, *158*
New Salvation Army Band, *135*
Newton, Frankie, 36
Newton, Huey, 29, 98, 99, *154*, 195
New York City, 34, 36, 48, 105, 129, 215; Harlem, 26, 27–28, 36, 105, 126
New York Times, 207, 219
nightclubs, 18, 43, 45, 46, 49, 83

Ngugi wa Thiong'o, xxv, 55; *Penpoints, Gunpoints, and Dreams*, 105, 117
Nisker, Scoop, 123, 124
Nixon, Richard, 207, 225, 232
Norrell, Brenda, 290n10
North Beach, 2–3, 18, 45, 72
Noyes, Henry, 20
nuclear weapons, 108, 115
Nuzum, Eric: *Parental Advisory*, 228

Oakes, Richard, 200
Oakland, 70, 71, 81, 193; Black Panthers, 29, 97, 98, 246; Day on the Green, 233, 234
Oakland Army Base, 80
Oakland Coliseum, 96, 233
Oakland Induction Center, 183
obscenity, 18, 20, 121, 221–22
Ochs, Phil, 33, 163, 228
O'Connell, Jack: *Revolution*, 261–66
Old Left, xxvii, 19, 21, 34, 54, 112, 117, 249
Oliveros, Pauline, 126
One Dimensional Man (Marcuse), 22, 114–15
On the Road (Kerouac), 9, 37, 58, 75
Oracle. See San Francisco Oracle
Oyewole, Abiodun, 61

Palo Alto, 67, 68
Panhandle, 16, 85, 86, 87, 234, 246, 247
The Panther and the Lash (Hughes), 25, 26
Parental Advisory: Music Censorship in America (Nuzum), 228
parks, 51, 85, 92, 94; Berkeley, *146*. *See also* Golden Gate Park
Parks, Rosa, 26, 30
participatory singing, 55
patriarchy. *See* male supremacy
Paul Butterfield Blues Band, 282n21
Peace and Freedom Party, 98, *144*, 201
"peace and love" (phrase), 248
Penpoints, Gunpoints, and Dreams (Ngugi), 105, 117
"the people" ("the masses"), 74, 191, 225, 232, 241. *See also* polls; "Power to the People" (phrase)
People's Park, Berkeley, *146*
performance sites, 62, 91. *See also* ballrooms and auditoriums;

coffeehouses; dance hall permits; nightclubs; Straight Theater
Perry, Charles: *The Haight-Ashbury*, 247
Philadelphia, 121, *149*, 201
Phillips, John, 78, 79, 101, 102
philosophy, xxix–xxx, 168–69, 197, 276n29
Phoenix (band), *135*
"pig" (word), 166
Pigpen. *See* McKernan, Ron "Pigpen"
"the pill." *See* birth control pill
Pine Ridge Indian Reservation, 230, 290n10
Placksin, Sally: *Jazzwomen*, 216
Plato, 55, 104, 105, 116, 168
Pointer Sisters, 130, 193
police, 49, 81, 86, 93, 245–48 passim, 252; Berkeley, xvii, 114; Black Panthers and, 97, 166; Bloody Thursday, 8; drug busts, 218; Haight-Ashbury repression, 245, 282n15, 282n19; HUAC demo, xvii; Oakland, 97, 98; in *Revolution*, 263; shootings by, 29, 86, *134*; student strike repression, 199
political prisoners, 7, 98, *148*, *154*, 190
Pollar, Mary Ann, *131*
polls, 179
Polte, Ron, 70, 176
Polytechnic High School, 23, 100, 250
population data, 11, 38, 198, 255–57
posters and poster art, 19, 44, 50, 53, 90–92 passim, 102, *131–62*
Potlatch (Redbone), 192–93
"Power to the People" (phrase), 29, 98, 101, 120, 190–91, 196–200 passim, 204, 208
Prague Spring (1968), 170, 171, 189
Preparedness Day Bombing (1916), 7
Presley, Elvis, xv, 31, 33, 67, 277n26
Preston, Billy, 128
prisoners, 194, 222. *See also* Books Behind Bars; political prisoners
"proletariat" (word), 196–97
Proposition P (1967), *143*
Proposition 22 (1972), 157
protest songs, 42, 54, 65, 187
public opinion polls. *See* polls
Public Works of Art Project (PWAP), 9
Pullice, *139*
punk rock, 237–38, 292n23
Pyewacket, *138*

Quicksilver Messenger Service, 67–68, 262–63; posters, *135*, *136*, *137*, *141*

"race music" (label), 11, 31, 67, 106–7
racialization, 197; censuses, 198, 255
radio, 43, 67, 68, 119–25, 229; AM, 67, 69, 70, 119, 121; black airplay, xxvi, 31, 32, 41, 119; blacklisting, 229; black stations, 43, 71; public 119
ragtime, 64–65
Raisner, Christian, *132*
Ramparts, 87, 176, 206, 224–25, 236
RCA Victor, 89
Reagan, Ronald, xxvii, xxviii, 54, 56, 238, 249
rebellion, 38; Breton on, 241; cultural, 181, 218–22 passim; Eldridge Cleaver on, 61; in military, 180; redirection of, 55; Roszak on, 178; songs of, 65
rebellions, urban, 27–28
record contracts. *See* music recording and producing: contracts
recording and production. *See* music recording and production
Redbone: *Potlatch*, 192–93
Redding, Otis, 102
Red Guards (I Wor Kuen), 201, 204
Red Star Singers, 162
Reefer Madness, 220
reggae, 235, 238
Reich, Steve, 126, 127
resistance to freeway construction. *See* Freeway Revolt (1964)
Revolution (1968 film), 261–66, 292nn1–2 (appendix 4)
"revolution" (word), xxviii. *See also* "cultural revolution" (term)
Revolutionary People's Constitutional Convention (RPCC), *149*, 201–2
Revolutionary Union. *See* Bay Area Revolutionary Union
Rexroth, Kenneth, 9, 16, 85–86, 88
Reynolds, Malvina, 16
rhythm and blues, xxvi, 31–32, 59, 60, 66–72 passim, 107, 278n1; radio, 119; Sly Stone, 68, 128
Rhythmicon, 126
Rice, T.D. "Daddy," 64
Richmond Civic Auditorium, 161
Riley, Terry, 126, 245

riots, 27–28, 29, 86, 98, 239; by police, 282n15
Ritchie, Jean, 68, 281n19
Rivera, Diego, 9
Roach, Max, 36–37, 43, 196
Robeson, Paul, 8, 43, 66, 230
Rock Against Racism, 238
Rock and Roll Hall of Fame, 125, 236–37
"Rock Me," 278n1
Rolling Stone, xix, 113–14, 195, 207, 219, 235–36
Rolling Stones, 186, 222
romanticism, 109, 111, 112
Rosemont, Franklin, 6
Roszak, Theodor, 172, 173, 178, 184, 248–49, 252, 254, 277n14
Roth, Fred, 69–70
Rotten, Johnny, 237–38
Rousseau, Jean-Jacques, 74, 75, 111, 274n4
royalties, 259, 260, 280n13
Rubin, Jerry, 84, 283–84n42
Rubinson, David, 41, 52, 127, 128–29, 130, 176, 193, 258
runaways, 252–54 passim
Rush, Otis, 282n21
Russian Revolution, 6, 196, 210

Sahm, Doug, 60, 279–80n3
Sainte-Marie, Buffy, 33, 76, 219, 229–30, 290n10
Saint-John, Powell, 292n2 (appendix 4)
La Salamandra Coffee House, *162*
Salomon, Larry, 11, 12
Salvation. *See* New Salvation Army Band
Sanders, Ed, 229
San Diego Folk Song Society, 281n19
"San Francisco (Be Sure to Wear Flowers in Your Hair)," 78–79, 87, 91, 97, 100, 245–46, 254, 263
San Francisco Chronicle, 20, 46, 47, 94, 263
San Francisco Conservatory of Music, 126
San Francisco Examiner, 246–47
San Francisco Mime Troupe, 14, 19–21 passim, 44, 51, 83, 88–92 passim, 246; Graham, 92; Howard Street studios, 51, 84, 88, 92; Human Be-In, 52; Jefferson Airplane, 47; music composed for, 127; Ron Davis, 10,

51, 88, 92; Rubinson, 130; Wild West festival, 176
San Francisco Oracle, 81, 84, 90, 245, 251
San Francisco Public Health Department, 247, 253, 263
"San Francisco sound" (myth), 244–45
San Francisco State College, 44, 50, 83, 88, *129*, 174; student strike, 199, 202, 203
San Francisco Tape Music Center, 83, 126
San Jose, 68
San Jose State College, *156*
San Mateo City College, 68
Santa Monica Civic Auditorium, 229
Santana, 71, 90, 99–100, *129*, 187, 234
Santana, Carlos, 99, 193, 283n21
Santana, Jorge, 193
Sapo, *161*
Sartre, Jean-Paul, 197
Saunders, Merl, *157*, *158*
Sausalito, *142*
"Say It Loud, I'm Black and I'm Proud," 38
schools. *See* alternative schools; high schools; universities and colleges
Scott-Heron, Gil: *Winter in America*, 206–7
SDS. *See* Students for a Democratic Society (SDS)
Seale, Bobby, 29, 98, *154*, 204
Second Sex (Beauvoir), 210, 211–12, 223
Seeger, Mike, 68, 281n19
Seeger, Pete, 17, 40, 43, 54, 66, 72, 194, 275n26; blacklisting, 230
segregation, 43. *See also* desegregation
Selvin, Joel, 94, 113, 166
Sender, Ramon, 126, 127
Sgt. Pepper's Lonely Hearts Club Band (Beatles), 123, 127
Serrano, Nina, 10
"sex, drugs, and rock 'n' roll" (phrase), 219–22 passim
sexism, 6, 172, 212, 218, 221. *See also* male supremacy
Sex Pistols, 237–38
Sexual Freedom League, 247, 263
sexuality, 35, 61. *See also* gay liberation; interracial marriage and sex
Shankar, Ravi, 95, 122
sheet music, 63–64, 215, 258, 259, 280n13
Sheraton Palace Hotel, 15

Shrieve, Michael, 100
Side-Saddle on the Golden Calf, 235–36
Los Siete de la Raza, *148, 150*, 179
Simmons, Daniel A., 230–31
Simone, Nina, 60, 219
sing-alongs. *See* participatory singing
Sir Douglas Quintet: *Honkey Blues*, 60
sit-ins, xvii, 15, 16, 17, 26
ska, 238
slavery, 64, 65, 209, 259
Slick, Grace, 278n3
Slick, Jerry, 128
Sly and the Family Stone, 24, 96, 128, 129,
    187, 188, 235, 280n8; *Stand!*, 187. *See
    also* Stone, Sly
Smith, Harry: *Anthology of American
    Folk Music*, 9, 65–66, 111, 280n15
Smith, Mamie, 216
Smith, Trixie, 278n1
SNCC. *See* Student Nonviolent
    Coordinating Committee (SNCC)
Snyder, Gary, 70, 84
socialists and socialism, 4, 7, 8, 177,
    210, 226; Beauvoir, 210, 212; Black
    Panthers, 98–99, 198, 204; Che
    Guevara, 189, 287n34; China, 287n35;
    international, 21–22; Marcuse, 225–26
Socialist Workers Party (SWP), 198
Socrates, 108
Soldiers in Revolt (Cortright), 181
Soledad Brothers, 19, *148*, 222, 275n26
song lyrics, 42, 54
Sons and Daughters (Stoll), 80
Sons of Champlin, xviii, 91, 94, 129–30,
    139, 144, 159
Sopwith Camel, 86, *137*
soul music, xxvi, 59, 68, 71, 119, 181, 190.
    See also Motown
The Souls of Black Folk (Du Bois), 196, 223
Soviet Union, 8, 21–22, 115, 116, 171, 179,
    189
Sox, Ellis D., 253, 263
Speedway Meadow, 85, 91, 234, 263
Spock, Benjamin, 221, 275n26
Springsteen, Bruce, 36, 46
stadium concerts, 94, 96, 176, 234, 236
Stanford University, 3, 44, 69, 120
Stanley, Owsley, 51–52, 279n13
Stender, Fay, 275n26
Stern, Sol, 235–36

Steve Miller Band, 262
Stewart, Sylvester. *See* Stone, Sly
Stockton Civic Auditorium, *160*
Stoll, Jerry, 274–75n12; *I Am a Lover*, 10,
    274n12; *Sons and Daughters*, 80
Stone, Sly, 41, 62, 68–69, 71, 280n8; as
    producer, 72, 123, 128, 129, 278n3. *See
    also* Sly and the Family Stone
Storey, John, 279n18
Straight Theater, *135, 145*, 245
"Strange Fruit," 36
street theater, 90
strikes, 16; Chinatown, 205; farmworkers,
    89; France, 170; light show operators,
    177; radio, 124. *See also* General Strike
    of 1934; student strikes
Stubblebine, Paul, 52, 70, 128, 129–30
Stubbs, Bob, 247
Student Nonviolent Coordinating
    Committee (SNCC), 1–2, 50–51, 60,
    81, 83, *131*, 183
Students for a Democratic Society
    (SDS), 22, 231
student strikes, 180, 199, 202, 203
subculture, 3, 34, 61, 95, 172–73, 184
Subotnick, Morton, 126, 245
Sugar Hill (nightclub), 45, 281n20
Suisman, David: *Selling Sounds*, 215
"Summer of Love" (myth), 245–46, 292n1
    (appendix 1)
Superspade. *See* Thomas, William
    "Superspade"
Supreme Court cases, 25, 28, 64, 164, 198,
    206
synthesizers, 126
Syracuse, Russ, 121
"the system" (term), 55, 185, 243

Taj Mahal, 129, 130, *155, 156*, 165, 167, 229
Tape Music Center. *See* San Francisco
    Tape Music Center
tape recording, 125, 126, 127
Taylor, Derek, 101
Teatro Campesino, 44, 89–90, 112
Teatro los Topos, *156*
technology, 75–76, 109, 184; in avant-
    garde music, 43; Marcuse view,
    114–15; recording, 66, 125–26, 127, 128
teenagers: demographic, 48; invention of,
    30–34, 38; runaways, 252–54

Tenderloin, 86, 87, 246

Tharpe, Rosetta, 216, 278n1

Thatcher, Margaret, xxviii, 56

theater, 10, 14, 44, 81, 89–92 passim. *See also* Committee (theater company); San Francisco Mime Troupe; Teatro Campesino

Theremin, Leon, 126

Third World Liberation Front (TWLF), 199, 200

Thomas, Pat: *Listen, Whitey!*, 60, 194

Thomas, William "Superspade," 251

Thornton, Big Mama, 33, 277n26

Tillmon, Johnnie, 212

"Time Has Come Today" (Chambers Brothers), 40–41

"Times They Are a-Changin'" (Dylan), xv, 39

Tin Pan Alley, 64, 65, 112, 163, 215–18 passim; women, 215, 216

Tin Pan Alley (Goldberg), 214–15, 216

Toropov, Yuri, 86

Toussaint, Allen, 193

Tower of Power, 41, 96, 129, 130, 187; *What Is Hip?*, 235

Towle, Jack, 123, 278n7

Townshend, Pete, 126

Transatlantic Railroad, *138, 139*

Trans-Love Energies, *145*

The Trip (Corman film), 220

Tripp, Bobby. *See* Mitchell, Bobby "Tripp"

Trips Festival (1966), 83–84, 127

Truth, Sojourner, 209, 213

Tubman, Harriet, 209, 213

Turning the Guns Around (Waterhouse), 181

Twenty-Sixth Amendment, 206

underground press, 81, *82*, 83, 84, 87, 90, 113, 163. See also *San Francisco Oracle*

Underground Press Syndicate, 83

unions, 31, 190; farmworkers, 81, 89, 90, *156–61 passim*. *See also* strikes

universities and colleges, xvi–xvii, 4, 37, 44, 50, 68, 126, 127; ethnic studies, 203; music venues, *150, 156, 159*; Oakland, 195; student opinion, 179–80. *See also* San Francisco State College; Stanford University

University of California, Berkeley, xvi–xvii, 4, 50, *150*

University of California, Davis, *159*

Unterberger, Richie: *Turn! Turn! Turn!*, 229

urban rebellions. *See* rebellions, urban

USSR. *See* Soviet Union

U.S. Constitution. Twenty-Sixth Amendment. *See* Twenty-Sixth Amendment

U.S. Supreme Court cases. *See* Supreme Court cases

Valdez, Luis, 89

Vallejo, California, 68, 71

Valley Peace Center benefit concert (1967), *142*

Van Zandt, Steve, 32

venues, performance. *See* performance sites

Vico, Giambattista, 108, 115

Vietnam Summer Project (1967), 79, 91, *138, 139, 140*

Vietnam Veterans Against the War, 163, 184, 205

Vietnam War, 26–27, 53, 55, 59, 76, 79–81 passim, *151, 179*; Chomsky on, 224–25; conclusion, 206; country music industry, 194; GI and veterans' movements, 180–82; North Vietnam benefits, *141*; Tet Offensive, 170; Tom Donahue on, 121; women's movement, 212. *See also* antiwar movement

Vindication of the Rights of Woman (Wollstonecraft), 209

Voting Rights Act of 1965, 28

Wailers, 46, 235

Walker, Doris, 19

Walker, T-Bone, 45

Wallerstein, Immanuel, xxi, 170, 240–41

War (band), 96, 193

Warner Brothers Records, 102, 217

Waterhouse, Larry G.: *Turning the Guns Around*, 181

Waters, Muddy, 282n21

Weavers, 33, 277n25

W.E.B. Du Bois Club, 12, 50

Week of Angry Arts (1967), *137*

Wei Min She, 203, 204
Welfare Rights Organization. *See*
    National Welfare Rights
    Organization (NWRO)
Wenner, Jann, 113, 235–36
Werber, Frank, 176, 177
"We Shall Overcome," 40, 130
West Pole, 70
West Side Story, 106
Wexler, Jerry, 105, 165
What Is Hip? (Tower of Power), 235
white identity, 60
"The White Negro" (Mailer), 34–35
"White Rabbit," 101, 110, 278n3
white supremacy, 59, 61, 62, 64, 172
Wildflower (band), 135
Wild West Festival (planned), 94, 114,
    176–77
Wildwood Boys, 67
Williams, Cecil, 263
Williams, Robert F., 28
Wilson, Dick, 230
Winter in America (Scott-Heron), 206
Winterland Ballroom, *158*, 237
Wollstonecraft, Mary, 209
women's liberation, 172, 201, 205–23
    passim, 243; dance role, 5, 6
women's prison. *See* California
    Institution for Women
Woodstock festival (1969), 53, 96, 175–76,
    178, 186, 188
working class, xxvii, 11, 18, 71–73 passim,
    187–93 passim, 197, 250, 254; in armed
    forces, 182, 183; Bay Area population,
    4; Ireland, 210; Sarah Gunning, 216.
    See also "proletariat" (word)
Wounded Knee occupation (1975), 230
World War II, 10, 11, 28, 182, 183
The Wretched of the Earth (Fanon), 197

X, Malcolm. *See* Malcolm X

Yancey, Mama, 45
Yankelovich, Daniel, 179
Yinger, J. Milton, 172
Yip, Steve, 203–5 passim
Yippies, 283–84n42
Young, Roland, 124
Young Lords (YLP), *148*, 201, 228

Zappa, Frank, 187
Zaramella, Enea, 291n26
Zeitlin, Denny, 129

ABOUT PM PRESS

PM Press was founded at the end of 2007 by a small collection of folks with decades of publishing, media, and organizing experience. PM Press co-conspirators have published and distributed hundreds of books, pamphlets, CDs, and DVDs. Members of PM have founded enduring book fairs, spearheaded victorious tenant organizing campaigns, and worked closely with bookstores, academic conferences, and even rock bands to deliver political and challenging ideas to all walks of life. We're old enough to know what we're doing and young enough to know what's at stake.

We seek to create radical and stimulating fiction and non-fiction books, pamphlets, T-shirts, visual and audio materials to entertain, educate, and inspire you. We aim to distribute these through every available channel with every available technology—whether that means you are seeing anarchist classics at our bookfair stalls, reading our latest vegan cookbook at the café, downloading geeky fiction e-books, or digging new music and timely videos from our website.

PM Press is always on the lookout for talented and skilled volunteers, artists, activists, and writers to work with. If you have a great idea for a project or can contribute in some way, please get in touch.

PM Press
PO Box 23912
Oakland, CA 94623
www.pmpress.org

FRIENDS OF PM PRESS

These are indisputably momentous times—the financial system is melting down globally and the Empire is stumbling. Now more than ever there is a vital need for radical ideas.

In the years since its founding—and on a mere shoestring—PM Press has risen to the formidable challenge of publishing and distributing knowledge and entertainment for the struggles ahead. With over 300 releases to date, we have published an impressive and stimulating array of literature, art, music, politics, and culture. Using every available medium, we've succeeded in connecting those hungry for ideas and information to those putting them into practice.

Friends of PM allows you to directly help impact, amplify, and revitalize the discourse and actions of radical writers, filmmakers, and artists. It provides us with a stable foundation from which we can build upon our early successes and provides a much-needed subsidy for the materials that can't necessarily pay their own way. You can help make that happen—and receive every new title automatically delivered to your door once a month—by joining as a Friend of PM Press. And, we'll throw in a free T-shirt when you sign up.

Here are your options:

- **$30 a month** Get all books and pamphlets plus 50% discount on all webstore purchases

- **$40 a month** Get all PM Press releases (including CDs and DVDs) plus 50% discount on all webstore purchases

- **$100 a month** Superstar—Everything plus PM merchandise, free downloads, and 50% discount on all webstore purchases

For those who can't afford $30 or more a month, we have **Sustainer Rates** at $15, $10 and $5. Sustainers get a free PM Press T-shirt and a 50% discount on all purchases from our website.

Your Visa or Mastercard will be billed once a month, until you tell us to stop. Or until our efforts succeed in bringing the revolution around. Or the financial meltdown of Capital makes plastic redundant. Whichever comes first.

Songs of Freedom: The James Connolly Songbook

Edited by Mat Callahan
with a Preface by Theo Dorgan
and Foreword by James Connolly Heron

ISBN: 978-1-60486-826-5
$12.95   96 pages

Songs of Freedom is the name of the songbook edited by James Connolly and published in 1907. Connolly's introduction is better known than the collection for which it was written, containing his oft-quoted maxim: "Until the movement is marked by the joyous, defiant singing of revolutionary songs, it lacks one of the most distinctive marks of a popular revolutionary movement, it is the dogma of a few and not the faith of the multitude." Though most of the songs were of Irish derivation, the songbook itself was published in New York and directed to the American working class, explicitly internationalist in its aims.

"My grand aunt Nora Connolly, in her book We Shall Rise Again, *said of rebel songs: 'For more may be remembered of a country's history and treasured deep in the heart of a people through a song or a poem than through the pages of a history book'—how true. It was Nora who taught singers her father's songs. 'After 1916,' she said, 'I never did any more singing'—how sad. Now with this project and through the great talent and commitment of all involved we can hear Nora sing again."*
—James Connolly Heron, great-grandson of James Connolly and author of *The Words of James Connolly*

Songs of Freedom (CD)

The James Connolly
Songs of Freedom Band

ISBN: 978-1-60486-831-9 UPC: 760137574125
$14.95   53 mins

From the rollicking welcome of "A Festive Song" to the defiant battle cry of "Watchword of Labor," *Songs of Freedom* accomplishes the difficult task of making contemporary music out of old revolutionary songs. Far from the archival preservation of embalmed corpses, the inspired performance of a rocking band turns the timeless lyrics of James Connolly into timely manifestos for today's young rebels. As Connolly himself repeatedly urged, nothing can replace the power of music to raise the fighting spirit of the oppressed.

On the Ground: An Illustrated Anecdotal History of the Sixties Underground Press in the U.S.

Edited by Sean Stewart
with a preface by Paul Buhle

ISBN: 978-1-60486-455-7
$24.95   208 pages

In four short years (1965–1969), the underground press grew from five small newspapers in as many cities in the U.S. to over 500 newspapers—with millions of readers—all over the world. Completely circumventing (and subverting) establishment media by utilizing their own news service and freely sharing content amongst each other, the underground press, at its height, became the unifying institution for the counterculture of the 1960s. Frustrated with the lack of any mainstream media criticism of the Vietnam War, empowered by the victories of the Civil Rights era, emboldened by the anti-colonial movements in the third world and with heads full of acid, a generation set out to change the world. The underground press was there documenting, participating in, and providing the resources that would guarantee the growth of this emergent youth culture. Combining bold visuals, innovative layouts, and eschewing any pretense toward objectivity, the newspapers were wildly diverse and wonderfully vibrant.

Neither meant to be an official nor comprehensive history, *On the Ground* focuses on the anecdotal detail that brings the history alive. Comprised of stories told by the people involved with the production and distribution of the newspapers—John Sinclair, Art Kunkin, Paul Krassner, Emory Douglas, John Wilcock, Bill Ayers, Spain Rodriguez, Trina Robbins, Al Goldstein, Harvey Wasserman and more—and featuring over 50 full-color scans taken from a broad range of newspapers—*Basta Ya, Berkeley Barb, Berkeley Tribe, Chicago Seed, Helix, It Ain't Me Babe, Los Angeles Free Press, Osawatomie, Rat Subterranean News, San Francisco Express Times, San Francisco Oracle, Screw: The Sex Review, The Black Panther, The East Village Other, The Realist*, and many more—the book provides a true window into the spirit of the times, giving the reader a feeling for the energy on the ground.

"On the Ground *serves as a valuable contribution to countercultural history.*"
—Paul Krassner, author of *Confessions of a Raving, Unconfined Nut: Misadventures in the Counterculture*

"*One should not underestimate the significant value of this book. It gives you real insights into the underground press and its vast diversity of publications, which translated into a taste of real people's power.*"
—Emory Douglas, former Black Panther Party graphic artist and Minister of Culture

West of Eden: Communes and Utopia in Northern California

Edited by Iain Boal, Janferie Stone, Michael Watts, and Cal Winslow

ISBN: 978-1-60486-427-4
$24.95   304 pages

In the shadow of the Vietnam war, a significant part of an entire generation refused their assigned roles in the American century. Some took their revolutionary politics to the streets, others decided simply to turn away, seeking to build another world together, outside the state and the market. *West of Eden* charts the remarkable flowering of communalism in the '60s and '70s, fueled by a radical rejection of the Cold War corporate deal, utopian visions of a peaceful green planet, the new technologies of sound and light, and the ancient arts of ecstatic release. The book focuses on the San Francisco Bay Area and its hinterlands, which have long been creative spaces for social experiment. Haight-Ashbury's gift economy—its free clinic, concerts, and street theatre—and Berkeley's liberated zones—Sproul Plaza, Telegraph Avenue, and People's Park—were embedded in a wider network of producer and consumer co-ops, food conspiracies, and collective schemes.

Using memoir and flashbacks, oral history and archival sources, *West of Eden* explores the deep historical roots and the enduring, though often disavowed, legacies of the extraordinary pulse of radical energies that generated forms of collective life beyond the nuclear family and the world of private consumption, including the contradictions evident in such figures as the guru/predator or the hippie/entrepreneur. There are vivid portraits of life on the rural communes of Mendocino and Sonoma, and essays on the Black Panther communal households in Oakland, the latter-day Diggers of San Francisco, the Native American occupation of Alcatraz, the pioneers of live/work space for artists, and the Bucky dome as the iconic architectural form of the sixties.

Due to the prevailing amnesia—partly imposed by official narratives, partly self-imposed in the aftermath of defeat—*West of Eden* is not only a necessary act of reclamation, helping to record the unwritten stories of the motley generation of communards and antinomians now passing, but is also intended as an offering to the coming generation who will find here, in the rubble of the twentieth century, a past they can use—indeed one they will need—in the passage from the privations of commodity capitalism to an ample life in common.

"As a gray army of undertakers gather in Sacramento to bury California's great dreams of equality and justice, this wonderful book, with its faith in the continuity of our state's radical-communitarian ethic, replants the seedbeds of defiant imagination and hopeful resistance."
—Mike Davis, author of *City of Quartz* and *Magical Urbanism*

Other Avenues Are Possible: Legacy of the People's Food System of the San Francisco Bay Area

Shanta Nimbark Sacharoff

ISBN: 978-1-62963-232-2
$14.95   200 pages

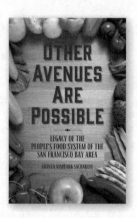

Other Avenues Are Possible offers a vivid account of the dramatic rise and fall of the San Francisco People's Food System of the 1970s.

Weaving new interviews, historical research, and the author's personal story as a longstanding co-op member, the book captures the excitement of a growing radical social movement along with the struggles, heartbreaking defeats, and eventual resurgence of today's thriving network of Bay Area cooperatives, the greatest concentration of co-ops anywhere in the country.

Integral to the early natural foods movement, with a radical vision of "Food for People, Not for Profit," the People's Food System challenged agribusiness and supermarkets, and quickly grew into a powerful local network with nationwide influence before flaming out, often in dramatic fashion. *Other Avenues Are Possible* documents how food co-ops sprouted from grassroots organizations with a growing political awareness of global environmental dilapidation and unequal distribution of healthy foods to proactively serve their local communities. The book explores both the surviving businesses and a new network of support organizations that is currently expanding.

"In this book, Shanta Nimbark Sacharoff inspires us all by recounting how cooperation created other avenues for workers and consumers by developing a food system that not only promoted healthy food but wove within it practices that respect workers and the environment."
—E. Kim Coontz, executive director, California Center for Cooperative Development

"I have been waiting more than twenty years for this book! Shanta Nimbark Sacharoff's Other Avenues Are Possible *details the history of the People's Food System, a grand experiment in combining good food and workplace democracy. Other Avenues answers many of my questions about how the food politics of the Bay Area developed and points the way towards a better—and more cooperative—future. A must-read for anyone who eats food."*
—Gordon Edgar, author of *Cheesemonger: A Life on the Wedge* and a worker owner of Rainbow Grocery Cooperative

Love and Struggle: My Life in SDS, the Weather Underground, and Beyond

David Gilbert
with an introduction by Boots Riley

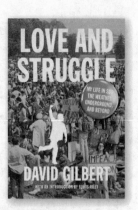

ISBN: 978-1-60486-319-2
$22.00   384 pages

A nice Jewish boy from suburban Boston—hell, an Eagle Scout!—David Gilbert arrived at Columbia University just in time for the explosive Sixties. From the early anti-Vietnam War protests to the founding of SDS, from the Columbia Strike to the tragedy of the Townhouse, Gilbert was on the scene: as organizer, theoretician, and above all, activist. He was among the first militants who went underground to build the clandestine resistance to war and racism known as "Weatherman." And he was among the last to emerge, in captivity, after the disaster of the 1981 Brinks robbery, an attempted expropriation that resulted in four deaths and long prison terms. In this extraordinary memoir, written from the maximum-security prison where he has lived for almost thirty years, David Gilbert tells the intensely personal story of his own Long March from liberal to radical to revolutionary.

Today a beloved and admired mentor to a new generation of activists, he assesses with rare humor, with an understanding stripped of illusions, and with uncommon candor the errors and advances, terrors and triumphs of the Sixties and beyond. It's a battle that was far from won, but is still not lost: the struggle to build a new world, and the love that drives that effort. A cautionary tale and a how-to as well, *Love and Struggle* is a book as candid, as uncompromising, and as humane as its author.

"David's is a unique and necessary voice forged in the growing American gulag, the underbelly of the 'land of the free,' offering a focused and unassailable critique as well as a vision of a world that could be but is not yet—a place of peace and love, joy and justice."
—Bill Ayers, author of *Fugitive Days* and *Teaching Toward Freedom*

"Like many of his contemporaries, David Gilbert gambled his life on a vision of a more just and generous world. His particular bet cost him the last three decades in prison, and whether or not you agree with his youthful decision, you can be the beneficiary of his years of deep thought, reflection, and analysis on the reality we all share. If there is any benefit to prison, what some refer to as 'the involuntary monastery,' it may well look like this book. I urge you to read it."
—Peter Coyote, actor, author of *Sleeping Where I Fall*

"This book should stimulate learning from our political prisoners, but more importantly it challenges us to work to free them, and in doing so take the best of our history forward."
—Susan Rosenberg, author of *An American Radical*

Creating a Movement with Teeth: A Documentary History of the George Jackson Brigade

Edited by Daniel Burton-Rose
with a preface by Ward Churchill

ISBN: 978-1-60486-223-2
$24.95   320 pages

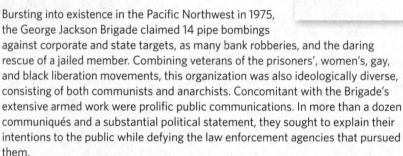

Bursting into existence in the Pacific Northwest in 1975, the George Jackson Brigade claimed 14 pipe bombings against corporate and state targets, as many bank robberies, and the daring rescue of a jailed member. Combining veterans of the prisoners', women's, gay, and black liberation movements, this organization was also ideologically diverse, consisting of both communists and anarchists. Concomitant with the Brigade's extensive armed work were prolific public communications. In more than a dozen communiqués and a substantial political statement, they sought to explain their intentions to the public while defying the law enforcement agencies that pursued them.

Collected in one volume for the first time, *Creating a Movement with Teeth* makes available this body of propaganda and mediations on praxis. In addition, the collection assembles corporate media profiles of the organization's members and alternative press articles in which partisans thrash out the heated debates sparked in the progressive community by the eruption of an armed group in their midst. *Creating a Movement with Teeth* illuminates a forgotten chapter of the radical social movements of the 1970s in which diverse interests combined forces in a potent rejection of business as usual in the United States.

"*Creating a Movement with Teeth is an important contribution to the growing body of literature on armed struggle in the 1970s. It gets us closer to knowing not only how pervasive militant challenges to the system were, but also the issues and contexts that shaped such strategies. Through documents by and about the George Jackson Brigade, as well as the introduction by Daniel Burton-Rose, this book sheds light on events that have until now been far too obscured.*"
—Dan Berger, author of *Outlaws of America: The Weather Underground and the Politics of Solidarity*; editor of *The Hidden 1970s: Histories of Radicalism*.

"*The popular image of the 70s urban guerrilla, even on the left, is that of the student radical or New Left youth activist kicking it up a couple of notches. Daniel Burton-Rose's documentary history of the George Jackson Brigade is an important corrective in this regard. The Brigade, rooted in prison work, white and black, straights, bisexuals and dykes, was as rich a mixture of the elements making up the left as one could perhaps hope for. We all have much to learn form the Brigade's rich and unique history.*"
—André Moncourt, coeditor of *The Red Army Faction: A Documentary History*.

The Angry Brigade: A History of Britain's First Urban Guerilla Group

Gordon Carr
with prefaces by John Barker
and Stuart Christie

ISBN: 978-1-60486-049-8
$24.95   280 pages

"You can't reform profit capitalism and inhumanity. Just kick it till it breaks." —*Angry Brigade, communiqué*

Between 1970 and 1972, the Angry Brigade used guns and bombs in a series of symbolic attacks against property. A series of communiqués accompanied the actions, explaining the choice of targets and the Angry Brigade philosophy: autonomous organization and attacks on property alongside other forms of militant working class action. This book covers the roots of the Angry Brigade in the revolutionary ferment of the 1960s, and follows their campaign and the police investigation to its culmination in the "Stoke Newington 8" conspiracy trial at the Old Bailey—the longest criminal trial in British legal history. Written after extensive research—among both the libertarian opposition and the police—it remains the essential study of Britain's first urban guerilla group. This expanded edition contains a comprehensive chronology of the "Angry Decade," extra illustrations and a police view of the Angry Brigade. Introductions by Stuart Christie and John Barker (two of the "Stoke Newington 8" defendants) discuss the Angry Brigade in the political and social context of its times—and its longer-term significance.

The Angry Brigade: The Spectacular Rise and Fall of Britain's First Urban Guerilla Group

$19.95   DVD (NTSC) 60 minutes

This documentary, produced by Gordon Carr for the BBC (and first shown in January 1973, shortly after the trial), covers the roots of the Angry Brigade.

Extra: The Persons Unknown (1980, 22 minutes) The so-called "Persons Unknown" case in which members of the Anarchist Black Cross were tried (and later acquitted) at the Old Bailey on charges of "conspiring with persons unknown, at places unknown, to cause explosions and to overthrow society." Featuring interviews and footage of Stuart Christie, Nicholas Walter, Crass and many other UK anarchist activists and propagandists of the time.

The Red Army Faction, A Documentary History
Volume 1: Projectiles For the People

Edited by J. Smith and André Moncourt
Forewords by Russell "Maroon" Shoats and Bill Dunne

ISBN: 978-1-60486-029-0
$34.95   736 pages

The first in a three-volume series, this is by far the most in-depth political history of the Red Army Faction ever made available in English. *Projectiles for the People* starts its story in the days following World War II, showing how American imperialism worked hand in glove with the old pro-Nazi ruling class, shaping West Germany into an authoritarian anti-communist bulwark and launching pad for its aggression against Third World nations. The volume also recounts the opposition that emerged from intellectuals, communists, independent leftists, and then—explosively—the radical student movement and countercultural revolt of the 1960s.

It was from this revolt that the Red Army Faction emerged, an underground organization devoted to carrying out armed attacks within the Federal Republic of Germany, in the view of establishing a tradition of illegal, guerilla resistance to imperialism and state repression. Through its bombs and manifestos the RAF confronted the state with opposition at a level many activists today might find difficult to imagine.

For the first time ever in English, this volume presents all of the manifestos and communiqués issued by the RAF between 1970 and 1977, from Andreas Baader's prison break, through the 1972 May Offensive and the 1975 hostage-taking in Stockholm, to the desperate, and tragic, events of the "German Autumn" of 1977. The RAF's three main manifestos—*The Urban Guerilla Concept*, *Serve the People*, and *Black September*—are included, as are important interviews with *Spiegel* and *le Monde Diplomatique*, and a number of communiqués and court statements explaining their actions. Providing the background information that readers will require to understand the context in which these events occurred, separate thematic sections deal with the 1976 murder of Ulrike Meinhof in prison, the 1977 Stammheim murders, the extensive use of psychological operations and false-flag attacks to discredit the guerilla, the state's use of sensory deprivation torture and isolation wings, and the prisoners' resistance to this, through which they inspired their own supporters and others on the left to take the plunge into revolutionary action.

Portugal: The Impossible Revolution?

Phil Mailer, with an afterword
by Maurice Brinton

ISBN: 978-1-60486-336-9
$24.95   288 pages

After the military coup in Portugal on April 25, 1974,
the overthrow of almost fifty years of Fascist rule, and
the end of three colonial wars, there followed eighteen
months of intense, democratic social transformation
which challenged every aspect of Portuguese society. What started as a military
coup turned into a profound attempt at social change from the bottom up and
became headlines on a daily basis in the world media. This was due to the intensity
of the struggle as well as the fact that in 1974–75 the moribund, right-wing
Francoist regime was still in power in neighboring Spain and there was huge
uncertainty as to how these struggles might affect Spain and Europe at large.

This is the story of what happened in Portugal between April 25, 1974, and
November 25, 1975, as seen and felt by a deeply committed participant. It
depicts the hopes, the tremendous enthusiasm, the boundless energy, the total
commitment, the released power, even the revolutionary innocence of thousands
of ordinary people taking a hand in the remolding of their lives. And it does so
against the background of an economic and social reality which placed limits on
what could be done.

"An evocative, bitterly partisan diary of the Portuguese revolution, written from a
radical-utopian perspective. The enemy is any type of organization or presumption of
leadership. The book affords a good view of the mood of the time, of the multiplicity of
leftist factions, and of the social problems that bedeviled the revolution."
—Fritz Stern, Foreign Affairs

"Mailer portrays history with the enthusiasm of a cheerleader, the 'home team' in
this case being libertarian communism. Official documents, position papers and
the pronouncements of the protagonists of this drama are mostly relegated to the
appendices. The text itself recounts the activities of a host of worker, tenant, soldier
and student committees as well as the author's personal experiences."
—Ian Wallace, Library Journal

"A thorough delight as it moves from first person accounts of street demonstrations
through intricate analyses of political movements. Mailer has handled masterfully the
enormous cast of politicians, officers of the military peasant and workers councils, and
a myriad of splinter parties, movements and caucuses."
—Choice

Asia's Unknown Uprisings
Volume 1: South Korean Social
Movements in the 20th Century

George Katsiaficas

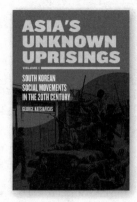

ISBN: 978-1-60486-457-1
$28.95   480 pages

Using social movements as a prism to illuminate the
oft-hidden history of 20th century Korea, this book
provides detailed analysis of major uprisings that have
patterned that country's politics and society. From the 1894 Tonghak Uprising
through the March 1, 1919, independence movement and anti-Japanese resistance,
a direct line is traced to the popular opposition to U.S. division of Korea after World
War Two. The overthrow of Syngman Rhee in 1960, resistance to Park Chung-hee,
the 1980 Gwangju Uprising, as well as student, labor, and feminist movements
are all recounted with attention to their economic and political contexts. South
Korean opposition to neoliberalism is portrayed in detail, as is an analysis of
neoliberalism's rise and effects. With a central focus on the Gwangju Uprising
(that ultimately proved decisive in South Korea's democratization), the author uses
Korean experiences as a baseboard to extrapolate into the possibilities of global
social movements in the 21st century.

Previous English language sources have emphasized leaders—whether Korean,
Japanese, or American. This book emphasizes grassroots crystallization of counter-
elite dynamics and notes how the intelligence of ordinary people surpasses that of
political and economic leaders holding the reins of power. It is the first volume in
a two-part study that concludes by analyzing in rich detail uprisings in nine other
places: the Philippines, Burma, Tibet, China, Taiwan, Bangladesh, Nepal, Thailand,
and Indonesia. Richly illustrated, with tables, charts, graphs, index, and footnotes.

*"George Katsiaficas has written a majestic account of political uprisings and social
movements in Asia—an important contribution to the literature on both Asian studies
and social change that is highly-recommended reading for anyone concerned with
these fields of interest. The work is well-researched, clearly-argued, and beautifully
written, accessible to both academic and general readers."*
—Prof. Carl Boggs, author of *The Crimes of Empire* and *Imperial Delusions*

*"This book makes a unique contribution to Korean Studies because of its social
movements' prism. It will resonate well in Korea and will also serve as a good
introduction to Korea for outsiders. By providing details on 20th century uprisings,
Katsiaficas provides insights into the trajectory of social movements in the future."*
—Na Kahn-chae, Director, May 18 Institute, Gwangju, South Korea

Asia's Unknown Uprisings Volume 2

People Power in the Philippines, Burma, Tibet, China, Taiwan, Bangladesh, Nepal, Thailand, and Indonesia, 1947–2009

George Katsiaficas

ISBN: 978-1-60486-488-5
$26.95   448 pages

Ten years in the making, this book provides a unique perspective on uprisings in nine places in East Asia in the 1980s and 1990s. While the 2011 Arab Spring is well known, the wave of uprisings that swept East Asia in the 1980s became hardly visible. This book begins with an overview of late 20th-century history—the context within which Asian uprisings arose. Through a critique of Samuel Huntington's notion of a "Third Wave" of democratization, the author relates Asian uprisings to predecessors in 1968 and shows their subsequent influence on the wave of uprisings that swept Eastern Europe at the end of the 1980s. By empirically reconstructing the specific history of each Asian uprising, significant insight into major constituencies of change and the trajectories of these societies becomes visible.

It is difficult to find comprehensive histories of any one of these uprisings, yet this book provides detailed histories of uprisings in nine places (the Philippines, Burma, Tibet, China, Taiwan, Bangladesh, Nepal, Thailand, and Indonesia) as well as introductory and concluding chapters that place them in a global context and analyze them in light of major sociological theories. Richly illustrated, with tables, charts, chronologies, graphs, index, and footnotes.

"George Katsiaficas has written a majestic account of political uprisings and social movements in Asia—an important contribution to the literature on both Asian studies and social change that is highly-recommended reading for anyone concerned with these fields of interest. The work is well-researched, clearly-argued, and beautifully written, accessible to both academic and general readers."
—Carl Boggs, author of *The Crimes of Empire and Imperial Delusions*

"George Katsiaficas is America's leading practitioner of the method of 'participant-observation,' acting with and observing the movements that he is studying. This study of People Power is a brilliant narrative of the present as history from below. It is a detailed account of the struggle for freedom and social justice, encompassing the different currents, both reformist and revolutionary, in a balanced study that combines objectivity and commitment. Above all, he presents the beauty of popular movements in the process of self-emancipation."
—James Petras, professor of sociology at Binghamton University

Dance the Eagle to Sleep

Marge Piercy

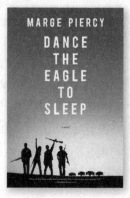

ISBN: 978-1-60486-456-4
$17.95   208 pages

Originally published in 1970, Marge Piercy's second novel follows the lives of four teenagers, in a near future society, as they rebel against a military draft and "the system." The occupation of Franklin High School begins, and with it, the open rebellion of America's youth against their channeled, unrewarding lives and the self-serving, plastic society that directs them. From the disillusionment and alienation of the young at the center of the revolt, to their attempts to build a visionary new society, the nationwide following they gain and the brutally complete repression that inevitably follows, this is a future fiction without a drop of fantasy. As driving, violent, and nuanced today as it was 40 years ago, this anniversary edition includes a new introduction by the author reflecting unapologetically on the novel and the times from which it emerged.

"Dance the Eagle to Sleep is a vision, not an argument… It is brilliant. Miss Piercy was a published poet before she resorted to the novel, exploiting its didactic aspect, and her prose crackles, depolarizes, sends shivers leaping across the synaptic cleft. The 'eagle' is America, bald and all but extinct. The 'dance' is performed by the tribal young, the self-designated 'Indians,' after their council meetings, to celebrate their bodies and their escape from the cannibalizing 'system.' The eagle isn't danced to sleep; it sends bombers to devastate the communes of the young… What a frightening, marvelous book!"
—New York Times

"It's so good I don't even know how to write a coherent blurb. It tore me apart. It's one of the first really honest books this country has ever produced. In lesser hands it would've been just another propaganda pamphlet, but in Marge Piercy's it's an all-out honest-to-God novel, humanity and love hollering from every sentence and the best set of characters since, shit I dunno, Moby Dick or something. At a time when nearly every other novelist is cashing in on masturbation fantasies, the superhip college bullshit stored up in their brains, even on the revolution itself, here is somebody with the guts to go into the deepest core of herself, her time, her history, and risk more than anybody else has so far, just out of a love for the truth and a need to tell it. It's about fucking time."
—Thomas Pynchon, author of Gravity's Rainbow